The Body Royal

Biblical Interpretation Series

EDITORS
R. ALAN CULPEPPER
ELLEN VAN WOLDE

ASSISTANT EDITORS
DAVID E. ORTON
ROLF RENDTORFF

EDITORIAL ADVISORY BOARD
JANICE CAPEL ANDERSON
MIEKE BAL
PHYLLIS A. BIRD
ERHARD BLUM
WERNER H. KELBER
EKKEHARD STEGEMANN
VINCENT L. WIMBUSH
JEAN ZUMSTEIN

VOLUME 78

THE BODY ROYAL

The Body Royal

The Social Poetics of Kingship in Ancient Israel

BY

Mark W. Hamilton

Society of Biblical Literature
Atlanta

Copyright © 2005 by Koninklijke Brill NV, Leiden,
The Netherlands

This edition published under license from Koninklijke Brill NV,
Leiden, The Netherlands by the Society of Biblical Literature.

All rights reserved. No part of this work may be reproduced or transmitted in any form or by any means, electronic or mechanical, including photocopying and recording, or by any means of any information storage or retrieval system, except as may be expressly permitted by the 1976 Copyright Act or in writing from the Publisher. Requests for permission should be addressed in writing to the Rights and Permissions Department, Koninklijke Brill NV, Leiden, The Netherlands.

Authorization to photocopy items for internal or personal use is granted by Brill provided that the appropriate fees are paid directly to The Copyright Clearance Center, 222 Rosewood Drive, Suite 910, Danvers, MA 01923, USA. Fees are subject to change.

Library of Congress Cataloging-in-Publication Data

Hamilton, Mark W.
   The body royal : the social poetics of kingship in ancient Israel / by Mark W. Hamilton.
     p. cm. – (Biblical interpretation series ; v. 78)
   Reprint. Originally published : Leiden: Brill, 2005.
   Includes bibliographical references and index.
   ISBN 978-1-58983-382-1 (paper binding : alk. paper)
   1. Kings and rulers–Biblical teaching. 2. Body, Human–Biblical teaching. 3. Jews–Kings and rulers. 4. Bible. O.T.–Criticism, interpretation, etc. I. Title.
   BS1199.K5H35   2005
   221.8'3216–dc22   2008040689

Printed in the United States of America
on acid-free paper

For Samjung, Nathan, and Hannah

וישגב אביון מעוני וישם כצאן משפחות

(Psalm 107:41)

CONTENTS

Acknowledgements	xi
Abbreviations	xiii

Chapter One   Introduction: The Undiscovered Territory
of the Body 1
   Why the Body? 9
   How Bodies? On Signification 15
   Whose Bodies? 21
   Conclusions and Prospects 29

Chapter Two   Creating the Body of the King in the
Royal Psalms 32
   Psalm 45 38
      The Text of a Ritual and the Ritual of a Text 39
         The Ritual Entrance 40
         The Body of the Ritual 42
         The Ritual Exit 45
      The Body of the King in Psalm 45 46
   A Related Text, Song of Songs 5:10–16 55
   Coronation Psalms: Psalms 2, 110, 72, and 101 60
      Psalm 2 61
      Psalm 110 65
      Psalm 72 75
      Psalm 101 79
   Preliminary Conclusions 82

Chapter Three   The Royal Body at Work 83
   The King as Builder: Psalm 132 84
   Psalms of Petition: Psalms 89, 144, and Isaiah 38 87
      Psalm 89 88
         The Promised Body 89
         The Body Unknit 92
         Summary 94
      Psalm 144 94
      Isaiah 38:9–20 97
         Summary 101

A Thanksgiving Psalm: Psalm 18 (= 2 Samuel 22) 102
Military Anthems: Psalms 20 and 21 105
    Psalm 20 106
    Psalm 21 107
A Royal Oracle: Isaiah 11:1–9 108
The Semiotics of the King's Body 111
Appendix A: The King's Body in Iron Age Levantine
    Inscriptions 117

Chapter Four   Stories of the Coronation of the King 118
The Crowning(s) of Saul 119
The Choice of David 128
The Coronation of Joash 135
Retrospects and Prospects 141

Chapter Five   While Horse and Hero Fell: Royal Death
and Sickness 145
The Death of the King 146
    The Death of Saul (1 Samuel 31–2 Samuel 1) 149
        David's קינה 153
        The Amalekite's Tale 159
        The Narrator's Version 160
        Summary 169
    The Death of the "King of Israel" (1 Kings 22) 170
    The Death of Joram, Jezebel, and the Family of
        Ahab 174
    Assassination: Joash of Judah (2 Kings 12:21–22) 175
    Assassination: Amaziah (2 Kings 14:17–20) 176
    Josiah (2 Kings 23:29–30) 178
    Summary of the Death of Kings in the DH 179
The King in Narrative 180

Chapter Six   The Body of the King in War and Peace 183
The Endangered and Dangerous King 183
    The Dangerous King 185
        Saul's Hunt for David 196
    The Endangered King 207
    The King as Medical Patient 213
    Summary 215

The King as Eulogist 216
The King as Builder 218
Conclusions 221

Chapter Seven   The Body of the Foreign King 223
   Kings in the Conquest Tradition 225
   Kings of Neighboring States 227
      The King(s) of Tyre 228
      The Kings of Aram/Damascus 237
      The Kings of Moab 241
      Summary 247
   The Superpowers: Egypt, Assyria, and Babylon 247
      Egypt and the Pharaoh 248
      The Kings of Assyria 255
      The King of Babylon 261
   Conclusion 263

Chapter Eight   Conclusions and Implications 266

Works Cited 275
Indices 301

ACKNOWLEDGEMENTS

Anyone writing a work as complex as this one depends upon the aid of many persons. Chief among them are the readers of the dissertation at Harvard University from which this work grew: Professors Peter Machinist, Jo Ann Hackett, and Sarah Coakley. Their generous advice, meticulous weighing of arguments, and unfailing enthusiasm for the project helped me keep going when entropy might well have taken its toll. In addition, others have listened patiently to my ideas, offering suggestions, corrections, and bibliographical leads. During student days, these included: Pamela Barmash, Catherine Beckerleg, Marianne Palmer Bonz, Shaun Casey, Cindy Chapman, Anne Custer, Mark Kurtz, Gregory Mobley, Irene Monroe, and Avi Winitzer. My colleagues at Abilene Christian University, especially Frederick Aquino, Timothy Sensing, James Thompson, and John T. Willis have been a constant source of encouragement, correction, and stimulation. My graduate assistants Philip Stambaugh, Harry Conner, and especially Kelly Shearon have pointed out places where the argument could be clearer; Ms. Shearon's extraordinary care for the manuscript and the arguments it contains deserve especial recognition. Audiences at regional and national SBL meetings and at the Southwest Biblical Studies Seminar led by Roy Melugin of Brite Divinity School have also helped me sift these ideas. My readers might have been better served if I had taken more of the advice of all these fine scholars and friends. Much of what is valuable here certainly owes its existence to these collaborators; much of what is objectionable stands in spite of them.

Most of all I thank my family, my wife and intellectual and emotional soul mate Samjung Kang-Hamilton and the children who grace our lives, Nathan and Hannah. They have lived with the body of the king for a long time, and have done so with the charmingly bemused sympathy everyone should receive from a family. To them this work is dedicated.

ABBREVIATIONS

ÄAT	Ägypten und Altes Testament
AB	Anchor Bible
ABD	*Anchor Bible Dictionary*
ABRL	Anchor Bible Reference Library
ADAIK	Abhandlungen des Deutschen Archäologischen Instituts Kairo, Ägyptologische Reihe
AHw	*Akkadisches Handwörterbuch*, ed., Wolfram von Soden
ALASP	Abhandlungen zur Literatur Alt-Syrien-Palästinas
AnBib	Analecta Biblica
ANRW	*Aufstieg und Niedergang der römischen Welt*
AOAT	Alter Orient und Altes Testament
ASAM	Association of Social Anthropologists Monograph Series
ATD	Altes Testament Deutsch
ATR	*Anglican Theological Review*
BA	*Biblical Archaeologist*
BAR	*Biblical Archaeology Review*
BASOR	*Bulletin of the American School of Oriental Research*
BBB	Bonner Biblische Beiträge
BBET	Beiträge zur biblischen Exegese und Theologie
BDB	*Hebrew and English Lexicon of the Old Testament*, ed., Francis Brown, S. R. Driver, and C. C. Briggs
Ber	*Berytus*
BF	Baghdader Forschungen
Bib	*Biblica*
BibInt	*Biblical Interpretation*
BibOr	Biblica et Orientalia
BIS	Biblical Interpretation Series
BJS	Brown Judaic Studies
BKAT	Biblischer Kommentar Altes Testament
BTS	Beiruter Texte und Studien
BWANT	Beiträge zur Wissenschaft vom Alten und Neuen Testament
BZAR	*Beihefte Zeitschrift für Altorientalische und Biblische Rechtsgeschichte*
BZAW	*Beihefte zur Zeitschrift für die alttestamentliche Wissenschaft*
CAD	*Chicago Assyrian Dictionary*
CANE	*Civilizations of the Ancient Near East*, ed., Jack M. Sasson et al.
CBOTS	Coniectanea Biblica, Old Testament Series
CBQ	*Catholic Biblical Quarterly*
CHA	*Cambridge History of Africa*
CWSSS	*Corpus of West Semitic Stamp Seals*, ed. Nahman Avigad and Benjamin Sass
DNWSI	*Dictionary of North-West Semitic Inscriptions*, ed. J. Hoftijzer and K. Jongeling
EI	*Eretz Israel*
EthL	*Ephemerides theologiae Lovanienses*
ExpTimes	*Expository Times*
FAT	Forschungen zum Alten Testament
FB	Forschung zur Bibel
FOTL	The Forms of Old Testament Literature

FRLANT   Forschungen zur Religion und Literatur des Alten und Neuen Testaments
FSÖT   Forschungen zur systematischen und ökumenischen Theologie
GKC   *Gesenius' Hebrew Grammar*, ed. E. Kautzsch, trans. A. E. Cowley
HÄB   Hildesheimer Ägyptologische Beiträge
HAT   Handbuch zum Alten Testament
HBS   Herders Biblische Studien/Herder's Biblical Studies
HDR   Harvard Dissertations in Religion
HistRel *History of Religions*
HKAT   Handkommentar zum Alten Testament
HO   Handbuch der Orientalistik
HSM   Harvard Semitic Monographs
HTR   *Harvard Theological Review*
HUCA   *Hebrew Union College Annual*
ICC   International Critical Commentary
IEJ   *Israel Exploration Journal*
Int   Interpretation
JANES *Journal of the Ancient Near Eastern Society of Columbia University*
JAOS   *Journal of the American Oriental Society*
Jastrow *A Dictionary of the Targumim, the Talmud Babli and Yerushalmi, and the Midrashic Literature*, ed., Marcus Jastrow
JBL   *Journal of Biblical Literature*
JFSR   *Journal of Feminist Studies in Religion*
JNES   *Journal of Near Eastern Studies*
JNWSL *Journal of Northwest Semitic Languages*
JPSTC   Jewish Publication Society Torah Commentary
JQR   *Jewish Quarterly Review*
JRS   *Journal of Ritual Studies*
JSOT   *Journal for the Study of the Old Testament*
JSOTSS   Journal for the Study of the Old Testament Supplement Series
JTS   *Journal of Theological Studies*
KAI   *Kanaanäische und Aramäische Inschriften*, ed., H. Donner and W. Röllig
KAT   Kommentar zum Alten Testament
KHKAT   Kürzer Handkommentar zum Alten Testament
KTU   *Keilalphabetischen Texte aus Ugarit*, ed., Manfried Dietrich, Oswald Loretz, and Joaquín Sanmartín, 2nd ed.
LCL   Loeb Classical Library
MAOG   Mitteilungen der Altorientalischen Gesellschaft
MAQ   *Medical Anthropology Quarterly*
OBO   Orbis Biblicus et Orientalis
OLA   Orientalia Lovaniensia Analecta
OLP   *Orientalia Lovaniensia Periodica*
Or   Orientalia
OTL   Old Testament Library
OTWSA *Die Ou Testamentiese Werkgemeenskap in Suid-Afrika*
OTS   Oudtestamentische Studiën
RÄRG   *Reallexikon der ägyptsichen Religionsgeschichte*, ed. Hans Bonnet
RB   *Revue Biblique*
RdM   Die Religionen der Menschheit
Rel   *Religion*
RIMA   Royal Inscriptions of Inscriptions of Mesopotamia, Assyrian Periods
RIMB   Royal Inscriptions of Mesopotamia, Babylonian Periods
RLA   *Reallexikon der Assyriologie*, ed. E. Ebeling, B. Meissner, and D. Edzard
SAA   State Archives of Assyria
SAAB   *State Archives of Assyria Bulletin*

SAAS	State Archives of Assyria Studies
SAOC	Studies in Ancient Oriental Civilization
SBLDissS	Society of Biblical Literature, Dissertation Series
SBLMS	Society of Biblical Literature Monograph Series
SBT	Studies in Biblical Theology
SBS	Stuttgarter Bibel-Studien
Sem	*Semeia*
SGV	Sammlung Gemeinverständlicher Vorträge
SHR	Studies in the History of Religions
SJOT	*Scandinavian Journal of the Old Testament*
StPh	Studia Phoenicia
StPohl	Studia Pohl, Series Maior
SVC	Supplements to Vigiliae Christianae
TCBAI	Transactions of the Casco Bay Assyriological Institute
TDOT	*Theological Dictionary of the Old Testament*
TWAT	*Theologisches Wörterbuch zum Alten Testament*
UBL	Ugaritisch-Biblische Literatur
UF	*Ugarit Forschungen*
VAT	Vorderasiatische Texten (in the Staatliche Museen, Berlin)
VT	*Vetus Testamentum*
VTSupp	Vetus Testamentum Supplements
WBC	Word Biblical Commentary
WMANT	Wissenschaftliche Monographien zum Alten und Neuen Testament
WdO	*Welt des Orients*
ZA	*Zeitschrift für Assyriologie*
ZAW	*Zeitschrift für die alttestamentliche Wissenschaft*
ZB	Zürcher Bibelkommentare
ZDPV	*Zeitschrift des Deutschen Palästina-Vereins*

CHAPTER ONE

INTRODUCTION:
THE UNDISCOVERED TERRITORY OF THE BODY

> [T]he current fascination with the body ... is only the most recent phase and direct consequence of a long cultivation of the body in the West. A fascination has, in a way, discovered itself.[1]

Whatever their current ties to the consumerist, self-absorbed cultures of the West, neither the cultivation of, nor the fascination with, the body is new. Rather, the body remains an abiding obsession of the human species as far back as we can trace it, not least for ancient Israel. What is new is the recognition that societies' understandings of the body are historically contingent and therefore open to study. Thus Israelite texts obsess about the origins, nature, and proper use of the human body, framing what we would call community life, politics, and religion in bodily terms. But these contemplations of the body have received too little attention.

For example, the famous biblical story of the choice of Israel's first king, Saul, recounts a surprising event: "As Saul turned his shoulder to go from Samuel, God turned over for him another heart (ויהפך־לו אלהים לב אחר; 1 Sam. 10:9). . . ." Once we reject an anachronistic psychological explanation for this verse, we must ask, what has the heart to do with the king's rule? Why does this transformation of Saul's body occur at just this point in the story?

---

[1] James I. Porter, "Introduction," in *Constructions of the Classical Body* (ed. idem; Ann Arbor: University of Michigan Press, 2002) 1. On the political and intellectual agendas behind some of the emphases on the body, see Terry Eagleton, *The Illusions of Postmodernism* (Oxford: Blackwell, 1996) 69–75; Sarah Coakley, "Introduction: Religion and the Body," in *Religion and the Body* (ed. eadem; Cambridge: Cambridge University Press, 1997) 6–7; also Mary Midgley, "The soul's successors: philosophy and the 'body'," in Coakley, *Religion and the Body*, 53–68. Despite the contradictions in the contemporary study of the body that Coakley and other contributors to her volume identify, it should be possible to examine notions of embodiedness without succumbing to a rigidly secularist, consumerist, and religiously reductionist point of view, which the present study attempts to do.

The Bible's descriptions of kings, Israelite and otherwise, often focus upon hearts, hands, eyes, heads, and other parts of the physical body. The proper physical training of the monarch, the culturally acceptable means of his self-display, even reflections on his anatomy all figure prominently in Israel's understanding of kingship. The biblical texts locate Israel's discourses about power, gender (here, maleness), and religion upon the king's body, or rather, as the medievalist Ernst Kantorowicz would have it,[2] his bodies. The physical body intersects with a political, transcendental one like that of Yahweh, whose viceroy and offspring the king was.

What notions did Israelites hold, then, concerning the appropriate display, use, understanding, training, and criticism of their kings' bodies? This problem demands attention because, although the biblical texts themselves raise it repeatedly, modern scholars have more or less neglected it. Some of the biblical scholars who have raised parallel questions have done so in the absence of real controls of the historical evidence, arguably in pursuit of a postmodern literary reading of the text that is ultimately ahistorical. The problem is important because it offers a window onto Israelite notions of gendered (in the present case, male) behavior and thus of one basic and indispensable part of the culture's view of the world. In short, we need to investigate how Israel "constructed" its view of the monarch in the non-trivial sense that its view of how he should behave was not biologically or economically inevitable but came to seem so to Israelites.[3] And we need to explore the problem in ways that do not merely serve some contemporary political or social agenda, however noble, but are historically focused.

For reasons that will become clear, understanding the problem requires a careful examination of a wide range of Israelite texts, notably the royal psalms, the narratives of the DH, various prophetic utterances, and the Song of Songs. Ancient Near Eastern iconography and texts provide apt comparisons and contrasts shedding light on the characteristics of the Israelite royal body moving among his subjects, peers, and enemies.

---

[2] Ernst Kantorowicz, *The King's Two Bodies: A Study in Mediaeval Political Theology* (Princeton: Princeton University Press, 1957).

[3] On this definition of "social construction," see Ian Hacking, *The Social Construction of What?* (Cambridge: Harvard University Press, 1999) 6–14.

Understanding the problem also requires intense reflection on what we mean by "the body." It is possible to study uses of Hebrew words such as פגר or נופה referring to the (dead) body, or simply to collect other terms relating to body parts, and such studies have their place. But such studies would not really get at the breadth of Israelite reflections on the body, and indeed would be question-begging exercises since they would assume that mere anatomy equaled social meaning. The body is a social entity and must be studied as such. It is necessary then to broaden our conception of the problem so that we can examine ways in which Israelites talked about the human body, its display and care, and rules for disciplining it so as to achieve the (changing, negotiable) goals of their society. Inevitably, this investigation risks misunderstanding of Israel's social conventions and tempts us toward the historian's cardinal sin, anachronism. But, as I hope will be clear, careful attention to the available evidence will reduce such risk to manageable proportions.

While the study of royal bodies has taken place for numerous premodern Mediterranean and Asian cultures, current study of Israelite kingship still focuses largely on recovering the history of events or interpretation rather than on reconstructing social ideas about kingship in general, and of the king's body in particular.[4] Shifting the focus to these larger issues of *histoire conjoncturelle* offers the possibility of new insight into old texts.

Among the few studies of the body by Hebrew Bible scholars are the essays collected by Timothy Beal and David Gunn, as well as the more comprehensive recent surveys of Jon Berquist and of Thomas Staubli and Silvia Schroer.[5] Several chapters in Beal and Gunn's collection are especially valuable, including those by Carol Newsom

---

[4] This is true of the histories of David by Baruch Halpern (*David's Secret Demons: Messiah, Murderer, Traitor, King* [Grand Rapids: Eerdmans, 2001]) and Steven McKenzie (*King David: A Biography* [Oxford: Oxford University Press, 2000]), and of Josiah by Marvin Sweeney (*King Josiah of Judah: The Lost Messiah of Israel* [Oxford: Oxford University Press, 2001]). A notable exception is Stuart Lasine's stimulating *Knowing Kings: Knowledge, Power, and Narcissism in the Hebrew Bible* (Atlanta: Scholars, 2001), with whose approach I ultimately have serious, though respectful disagreements.

[5] Timothy K. Beal and David M. Gunn, eds., *Reading Bibles, Writing Bodies: Identity and the Book* (London: Routledge, 1997); Jon L. Berquist, *Controlling Corporeality: The Body and the Household in Ancient Israel* (New Brunswick, NJ: Rutgers University Press, 2002); Thomas Staubli and Silvia Schroer, *Body Symbolism in the Bible* (Collegeville, MN: Liturgical Press, 2001).

and Mark George.⁶ George's contribution, in particular, is part of a larger body of work, whose theoretical basis rests on the work of Foucault, Derrida, and other so-called postmodernists, that includes his dissertation and a recent article on the Goliath story.⁷ The essays in Beal and Gunn's work, unfortunately, lack a common definition of "body" or even a shared orientation, and some seem to be using "body" as a receptacle for sundry dissatisfactions with the status quo of the biblical field while accepting uncritically theoretical work from outside the field.⁸

Further advancing the discussion is the work of Jon Berquist.⁹ Like his theoretical progenitor Foucault, Berquist underscores the fragility of a society's construction of the body, seeking its meaning at the boundaries where coercion and resistance meet. He examines: (1) Israelite perceptions of the whole body; (2) sexuality and fertility; (3) sexuality outside the household; (4) the aging process; (5) reactions against the stranger; (6) priests and the religious regulations of the body; and (7) Hellenism and its influence on Judaism. The introduction lays out the work's approaches and assumptions. The first is that bodily experiences, though individually variable on the one

---

⁶ Carol A. Newsom, "Woman and the Discourse of Patriarchal Wisdom," in Beal and Gunn, *Reading Bibles, Writing Bodies*, 116–31; and Mark K. George, "Assuming the Body of the Heir Apparent," in Beal and Gunn, *Reading Bibles, Writing Bodies*, 164–74.

⁷ Mark K. George, "Body Works: Power, the Construction of Identity, and Gender in the Discourse on Kingship" (Ph.D. diss., Princeton Theological Seminary, 1995); and idem, "Constructing Identity in 1 Samuel 17," *BibInt* 7 (1999) 389–412. His work will play a role in the discussion in Chapters 3–4 below.

⁸ A good example of the confusion appears in the essay by Howard Eilberg-Schwartz ("The Problem of the Body for the People of the Book," in Beal and Gunn, *Reading Bibles, Writing Bodies*, 34–55). Eilberg-Schwartz argues that early Judaism (which he, confusingly, apparently equates with ancient Israel, at least sometimes) found the body "problematic," because the priests (exemplified in P) and later the rest of the society tried to regulate it through purity rules. The problematics of the body resulted also in difficulties in conceiving the male deity, whose body must be like that of human males: "If God has the physical likeness of a male, the female body is by definition problematic. But...a monotheistic, male God also leaves males in conflict with their own bodies. If males are to be like God, then their penises are only for show; they should not be used for reproduction" (48). This chain of conflicts arises, however, more from (post)modern discontent than the texts themselves. For example, does governance of the body, present in all human groups, imply discomfort with it, or perhaps a sense that the body can be trained for something more?

⁹ Jon Berquist, *Controlling Corporeality*.

hand and biologically conditioned on the other, are still culturally conditioned. Each society envisions an ideal body and commits resources, both physical and ideological, to achieve that body in any given individual. The second assumption is that the lives of non-elite Israelites, particularly at the household level, changed little from the Late Bronze Age to the Persian period, and thus texts of widely varying dates can illuminate a single cultural reality (13). (This despite the recognition that "Rituals of the body and rituals of the state are closely intertwined. . . ." [11]). Third, the body exists in a reciprocal relationship with the household, each defining the other. Fourth, Berquist, unlike Foucault, the most influential thinker in studies of the body, seeks (ultimately unsuccessfully) to understand discourses about the body as more than attempts to regulate sexuality.

Although Berquist's book raises important questions, three areas are significant concerns. First, although he occasionally demurs from the tradition of body studies that originates with Foucault and focuses primarily on restriction and the formation and transgression of boundaries (jargon that Berquist does not always use precisely), most of his work reflects precisely and almost exclusively these concerns. This is a significant problem, already considered by some classicists (listed in the book's bibliography but not seriously discussed in the book). Boundaries are not everything.

Second, quite apart from quibbles over various historical decisions Berquist makes or his assumption (which I believe to be demonstrably wrong) that notions of the body remained static over the first millennium of Israelite history, is the ultimate ahistoricality of this work. Issues of rank or class do not enter into this discussion significantly, as though the household of the king and that of a peasant were indistinguishable in their regulation (training, discipline, display) of the body. That is, this study is not historically or literarily sensitive enough to pick up subtle differences that might and do exist.

Third, the legitimate (if ultimately excessive) focus on sexuality has all but crowded out other topics relevant to the Israelite body, such as food laws, bodily adornment, use of economic resources for the cultivation of the body, prayer as an act of the body. In part the choices Berquist makes reflect the Western (postmodern) cultural history of body studies in the Foucauldian tradition. I would not depreciate what he has examined but invite a wider range of topics.

These significant beginnings in the study of the Israelite body reflect larger intellectual trends. Scholars in many disciplines have recognized that every conception of the body has a history, and crucially that the Western, medicalized understanding of the body, which dominates much of our scholarship, dates back no more than two or three centuries.[10] Other cultures, ancient and modern, large- and small-scale, had different notions, which need examination. As Lawrence Sullivan has observed, "the body is so often demonstrated to be a primary instrument of knowledge, and... the understanding of the body can vary markedly from one culture and epoch to another...."[11] As I understand it, Sullivan's statement means both that we know through our body as we display it, treat it medically, and learn how to move it in socially appropriate ways, as well as that we know about other bodies as they do similar things around us. Such uses of the body take on importance in the complex interactions of meaning and activity within a culture. Bodily knowledge thus varies to some (though not an infinite) degree from culture to culture. Studying this variety provides a window onto fundamental characteristics of a society.

Such study also raises serious epistemological and axiological problems, which we cannot solve here but which nevertheless continue to challenge our historical reconstruction. Passing behind the Cartesian revolution (falsely) dichotomizing mind (or soul) and body, we find the Israelite texts positing thought as the function of a bodily organ, the heart. For Israelites, the shape and condition of the heart determined how one thought. The currently much-discussed "mind/body" problem would be impossible in their intellectual categories.[12] Perforce we must speak of the body in terms we understand post-

---

[10] On which see Barbara Duden, *The Woman Beneath the Skin: A Doctor's Patients in Eighteenth-Century Germany* (Cambridge: Harvard University Press, 1991); eadem, *Disembodying Women: Perspectives on Pregnancy and the Unborn* (Cambridge: Harvard University Press, 1993). On the convergence of medical and aesthetic interest in what he calls the "somatic body," see Sander L. Gilman, *Making the Body Beautiful: A Cultural History of Aesthetic Surgery* (Princeton: Princeton University Press, 1999); and (with an interest in body and "race"), idem, *The Jew's Body* (New York: Routledge, 1991).

[11] Lawrence E. Sullivan, "Body Works: Knowledge of the Body in the Study of Religion," *HistRel* 30 (1990) 86–99.

[12] For a history of the problem and its religious implications, see Owen Flanagan, *The Problem of the Soul: Two Visions of Mind and How to Reconcile Them* (New York: Basic Books, 2002); Gregory Peterson, *Minding God: Theology and the Cognitive Sciences* (Minneapolis: Fortress, 2003).

Descartes while simultaneously recognizing that our categories differ from those of the Israelites we are studying. The terminological slippage can beget categorical slippage, which one must work hard to avoid through meticulous examination of the relevant ancient evidence and vigilance toward the theoretical issues involved.

Investigating the problem of the Israelite royal body, then, first of all demands the critical reading of texts, often in a multilinear way that moves behind the text's surface to a hypothesized world of codes of knowledge that allowed the text to make sense to its earliest audiences, and then back to the text that fits into that re-created world. The research is always circular, with the goal being greater and greater refinement of the reading of the texts. The historian using ancient texts must also try to understand why they persuaded people in the past, or failed to do so, and this discovery requires examining the social setting of texts and the preexisting conventions informing them. Sometimes, we may check our readings against artifacts—inscriptions, architecture, art, and other human creations that involve sophisticated manipulation of symbols. We may also test our work against similar research in other cultures, although here the test is even less direct.

To put this another way, the goal of this study is the discernment among the textual and nontextual facts of a code of signs relating to kings, male bodies, and royal bodies, that is, a set of ideas and behaviors that existed in ancient Israel and, in different ways, in its neighbors. Such an inquiry demands that we both explicate the workings of texts and their relationships to ancient users of them (and modern ones, in different ways) and simultaneously respect the surface meaning of the texts (and pictures, limitedly) without believing such communicative devices to correspond to reality in a one-to-one way.[13] Reality creates interpretive limits for the users of a text ("Napoleon was emperor of France" cannot describe the career of the author of the present work), but in complicated ways.[14] As Thomas Sebeok

---

[13] Note that I am not proposing here a hermeneutic of suspicion, but rather a pragmatic style of reading that does not judge a text by its conformity to preconceived notions of how the universe does or should work (on fallibilistic reading, see the remarks of Peter Ochs, *Peirce, pragmatism and the logic of scripture* [Cambridge: Cambridge University Press, 1998] 26). At the same time, I affirm that texts do refer to something beyond themselves, the universe and specifically human experiences, which impose some limits on the possible meanings a text can have.

[14] See the discussion in Umberto Eco, *Kant and the Platypus: Essays on Language and Cognition* (New York: Harcourt, 2000) esp. 280–336.

(following C. S. Peirce) puts it, "the meaning of a message is the behavior it induces."[15] Conversely, the meaning of a behavior is the message it induces. Texts, regardless of their genre or surface "intention," contain arguments about, or representations of, reality, not reality itself, whatever that might be (except insofar as they themselves are real). These arguments provoke behaviors, including the writing of texts, in those who use them.

The almost exclusively literary nature of our sources for the ideas of ancient Israel also prompts caution. Studies of the Egyptian, Assyrian, or Babylonian states, could examine a sizable corpus of sculpture and texts (often on the same piece of stone).[16] For Israel, however, no graphic representation of the king exists, with the difficult (and for the Israelites, undesirable) exception of the picture of Jehu kneeling to Shalmaneser III on the so-called Black Obelisk. For Israelite views of the royal body, texts, primarily the Bible, but also letters, inscriptions, and seals remain the main sources revealing Israel's social (and not merely literary) conventions about the nature and proper treatment of the royal body. Still, in many texts, from different times and reflecting divergent perspectives, the royal body explicitly or implicitly figures.

The remainder of this chapter aims to do three things. First, it explores possible meanings of the phrase "the body," giving some account of current research trends on this subject (including in biblical studies) and then arguing for a working definition that can inform further investigation. Second, it identifies features of the theoretical work, mostly from outside the world of biblical studies, useful for the student of ancient Israel. Third, it situates this study of the king's body in the context of past and present research on Israelite

---

[15] Thomas A. Sebeok, *Semiotics in the United States* (Bloomington: Indiana University Press, 1991) 65.

[16] See, for example, Ursula Magen, *Assyrische Königsdarstellungen: Aspekte der Herrschaft* (Mainz: von Zabern, 1986); Irene J. Winter, "The Body of the Able Ruler: Toward an Understanding of the Statues of Gudea," in *DUMU-E$_2$-DUB-BA-A: Studies in Honor of Åke Sjöberg* (ed. Hermann Behrens, Darlene Loding, and Martha T. Roth; Philadelphia: Kramer Fund, 1989) 573–83; eadem, "Idols of the King: Royal Images as Recipients of Ritual Action in Ancient Mesopotamia," *Journal of Ritual Studies* 6 (1992) 13–42; and eadem, "Sex, Rhetoric, and the Public Monument: The Alluring Body of Naram-Sin of Agade," in *Sexuality in Ancient Art: Near East, Egypt, Greece, and Italy* (ed. Natalie Boymel Kampen; Cambridge: Cambridge University Press, 1996) 11–26; see also John Malcolm Russell, *The Writing on the Wall: Studies in the Architectural Context of Late Assyrian Palace Inscriptions* (Winona Lake, IN: Eisenbrauns, 1999).

monarchy. On this point, I have not sought exhaustiveness but have aimed for what the late church historian George Hunston Williams often publicly called "luminous particularity," the presentation of the telling detail that illuminates the whole.[17]

Why the Body?

As an essay at luminous particularity, one should point to a few key landmarks in recent research on the social meaning of the royal body, as well as set up warning beacons in areas that may sidetrack us. Critical interlocution with several different trends and thinkers is the only way to situate this study in the current debates.

The conversation might begin with the brilliant 1957 book by Ernst Kantorowicz, in which he studied the development of the late medieval notion of the king's two bodies, alerting historians to the myriad ways in which cultures have understood kingship in bodily terms, and the lengths to which they have gone to justify, reinforce, and extend those notions.[18] Medieval theologies of the royal body, taking their cue from earlier christological discussions, understood the king to have two bodies, just as did Christ, whose earthly representative and simulacrum the king was. Kantorowicz quotes the sixteenth-century jurist Plowden:

> For the King has in him two Bodies, viz., a Body natural, and a Body politic. His Body natural ... is a Body mortal, subject to all Infirmities that come by Nature or Accident. ... But his Body politic is a Body that cannot be seen or handled, consisting of Policy and Government ... and this Body is utterly void of Infancy, and old Age, and other natural Defects and Imbecilities.[19]

This medieval theology of kingship broke down in the sixteenth and seventeenth centuries with the advent of the modern state,[20] but not before creating a complex set of speculations about the royal body,

---

[17] Oral conversation with the author, Fall 1996.
[18] Kantorowicz, *King's Two Bodies*. See also Janet L. Nelson, "The Lord's anointed and the people's choice: Carolingian royal ritual," in *Rituals of Royalty: Power and Ceremonial in Traditional Societies* (ed. David Cannadine and Simon Price; Cambridge: Cambridge University Press, 1987) 137–80.
[19] Kantorowicz, *King's Two Bodies*, 7.
[20] On the breakdown of this idea, see Paul Kléber Monod, *The Power of Kings: Monarchy and Religion in Europe, 1589–1715* (New Haven: Yale University Press, 1999).

which large groups of people accepted, or if not, resisted consciously and at a cost. The maleness, wholeness, and physical fitness of his body guaranteed his fitness for rule. Defects in his body, whether the frailty resulting from old age or, more profoundly, some sexual dysfunction caused by defective genitalia, could unsuit him for rule. Conversely, anointing at the coronation conferred the indwelling of the Holy Spirit, superhuman competencies, and immortality. The king, according to medievals, died, but the King never did.

Whatever the adequacy or otherwise of Kantorowicz's presentation of the details of medieval political theology, his recognition that governance takes place through bodies, not merely through disincarnated institutions, provides an important launching point for this discussion. Kantorowicz alerted historians to the important fact that governance in past societies did not always, or even primarily, center upon the allegedly rational arts of bureaucratic administration.[21] A fundamental misunderstanding of ancient politics arises from failing to see that the royal body was a "natural symbol"—in Mary Douglas's first sense as "an organ of communication" essential to the well ordering of society,[22] the ramifications of which shape every aspect of social relations in a traditional monarchy.[23]

In the meantime, a profound ambiguity lies at the base of his, or any, analysis of the body: to what does the term apply? As Kantorowicz himself noted, even the medievals and their early modern commentators acknowledged the problem.[24] One need not be a philosopher to recognize the epistemological complexities that arise from claiming, as Sullivan does, that "the body is an instrument of knowledge" or of talking about the body as somehow separate from the self (as the phrase "the king and his body" implies). I have struggled with

---

[21] A point already lavishly explored in Max Weber, *Economy and Society: An Outline of Interpretive Sociology* (1920; ed. Guenther Roth and Claus Wittich; 2 vols.; Berkeley: University of California Press, 1978) 2.901–1211; see also the studies in Porter, *Constructions*.

[22] Mary Douglas, *Natural Symbols: Explorations in Cosmology* (1973; London: Routledge, 1996) xxxvi.

[23] But see the claim of Judith Butler (*Bodies That Matter: On the Discursive Limits of "Sex"* [New York: Routledge, 1993] 30): "The body posited as prior to the sign, is always posited or signified as prior. This signification produces as an effect of its own procedure the very body that it . . . claims to discover. . . ." One may discount this extremely counterexperiential claim as a bit of rhetorical pyrotechnics, but Butler's influential questioning of the givenness, the "naturalness," of gender deserves attention.

[24] Kantorowicz, *King's Two Bodies*, 4.

this problem throughout this work. To claim that human bodies impinge on actions is to state the obvious. However, to call the body an actor emphasizes how it is displayed or hidden, adorned or disfigured (a kind of adornment after all), as well as how persons and groups teach and learn bodily skills.[25] No agreement on the precise topic of the study of the body has yet been reached, and profound disagreements over the methods and operating assumptions of the line of inquiry remain. Broadly speaking, scholars disagree over whether one studies "the body" for what it "does" or what it "signifies," even if, as I will argue, this is ultimately a false dichotomy. Nevertheless, let me sketch out some ideas that offer orientation for my own understanding of the subject.

Perhaps the earliest, and still one of the most suggestive, studies of "the body" as a focus of human behavior appeared in an essay by Marcel Mauss.[26] Mauss, who is usually taken to be on the "does" side of the question (though this is too simple a reading of him), began by observing the contrasts between English and French techniques of marching, digging, walking, sitting at a dinner table, and so on. He concluded that such actions (or basic uses) of the body were learned behaviors, and that they varied by sex and age (107). None of them is "natural," by which he means purely biologically determined. Mauss does not explain these differences in terms of different significations that societies might attach to them; he is content to point out that the movement and resting of the body result from education. The body is thus a social, cultural phenomenon, as well as a biological one.

Yet, important as Mauss's insight is, analysis can hardly be content with it, for, to take one of his examples, the placement or nonplacement of one's elbow on a table varies because such a use of the body signifies something to someone. To an American, this behavior appears moderately uncouth. That is, this use of the body marks a person in specific ways, locating him or her in a whole range of relationships and bestowing (lack of) status. Bodily actions signify something else; they are parts of sign systems. When the problem is

---

[25] See the discussion in Caroline Bynum, "Why All the Fuss About the Body? A Medievalist's Perspective," *Critical Inquiry* 22 (Autumn 1995) 1–33; and Peter Brown, *The Body and Society: Men, Women, and Sexual Renunciation in Early Christianity* (New York: Columbia University Press, 1987).

[26] Marcel Mauss, "Body Techniques," in idem, *Sociology and Psychology: Essays* (London: Routledge, 1979) 97–123. The essay first appeared in 1935.

not elbows on tables, but adornment, or training for warfare, the problem of signification becomes greater. For this reason, I cannot agree with Talal Asad's proposal, based on his exegesis of Mauss, that the sole subject of an anthropology (or any other mode of scholarly inquiry) of the body is "a bodily competence at something,"[27] that is, the culturally-taught (rather than innate) bodily skills of human beings. (Mauss himself offers such examples as the then recent practice of teaching French sailors to swim, something that had not occurred before, or the Anzac soldiers' practice of sitting on their haunches in World War I trenches.) Asad rejects the assumption that talk about the body is about something else, that the study of the body primarily involves sign systems ("symbolization" in his nomenclature). However, this position fails to account for many data in the field: reactions to elbows on tables surely indicate more than judgment on the offender's competence in a learned habit.

Competence implies judgment, which implies culture and therefore "symbolization." Admittedly, as Asad cautions, lurking in this search for the signification of the body is the danger that a student of a culture, past or present, will misunderstand how it uses the body.[28] Yet, this risk always faces us, and the reductionist view that Asad offers does not limit it.

This detour on Asad's exegesis of Mauss serves to raise important points. Not surprisingly the manifold ways in which humans signify the body and use it to signify other things (as a "symbol," but see below) have been a major preoccupation of social scientists and humanists. Merely listing the studies responding to this concern would

---

[27] Talal Asad, "Remarks on the Anthropology of the Body," in Coakley *Religion and the Body*, 47; see also Douglas, *Natural Symbols*, 69–72.

[28] For more on this problem, see James L. Hevia, "Sovereignty and Subject: Constituting Relations of Power in Qing Guest Ritual," in *Body, Subject & Power in China* (ed. Angela Zito and Tami E. Barlow; Chicago: University of Chicago Press, 1994) 181–200. Hevia demonstrates that Western studies of the Qing (Manchu) *kowtow* ritual profoundly misconstrued the ritual as the embodiment of "oriental despotism" because Westerners imposed their own conceptions of the significations of ritual actions upon the Chinese practices. He is thus quite skeptical of studies of the body that focus on its "symbolic" aspects, believing that the experiences and cultural assumptions of the scholar inevitably and fatally color his or her understanding of the foreign culture's understanding of the significations of bodily actions and decorations. His concern is legitimate, but his solution may not be helpful. The proper remedy for bias is more careful examination of intellectual, i.e., "symbolic" systems.

require a large volume, and so I can only sample a few central themes that have emerged.[29] The most obvious is sexuality, and both feminist and nonfeminist[30] writers have spilled oceans of ink on the "social construction of gender," so that nowadays no one can ignore the fact that cultures shape gender roles, using biological raw material to be sure, but always in an alterable, non-inevitable way.[31] (In biblical studies, some research has examined the shaping of gender roles, notably those of women, though more work on both men and women remains a desideratum.)[32] Closely related are studies that emphasize the governance and discipline of the body, the emphasis resting on notions of power, coercion, and subjection. Feminists have pointed the way here,[33] but perhaps the most influential thinker on this set of issues has been Michel Foucault.

Many readers of the present work will be surprised to see his name appearing so rarely in it, particularly since he has influenced some students of the Bible's views of the body.[34] Foucault examines

---

[29] See the typologies worked out by Alison M. Jaggar, *Feminist Politics and Human Nature* (Sussex: Harvester, 1983); see also the bibliography in Natalie Zemon Davis and Arlette Farge, eds., *A History of Women: Renaissance and Enlightenment Paradoxes* (Cambridge: Harvard University Press, 1993) 543–69; and in the same volume, Sara F. Matthews Grieco, "The Body, Appearance, and Sexuality," 46–84.

[30] Of whom the most prominent is Michel Foucault; see his *Discipline and Punish* (New York: Pantheon, 1977); and *The History of Sexuality* (3 vols.; New York: Vintage, 1988–90). For a trenchant critique of Foucault's gynephobia, see Lin Foxhall, "Pandora Unbound: A Feminist Critique of Foucault's *History of Sexuality*," in *Rethinking Sexuality: Foucault and Classical Antiquity* (ed. David H. J. Larmour, Paul Allen Miller, and Charles Platter; Princeton: Princeton University Press, 1998) 122–37; and Amy Richlin, "Foucault's *History of Sexuality*: A Useful Theory for Women?" in Larmour, Miller, and Platter, *Rethinking Sexuality*, 138–70; Giulia Sissa, "Sexual Bodybuilding: Aeschines against Timarchus," in *Constructions of the Classical Body* (ed. James I. Porter; Ann Arbor: University of Michigan Press, 2002) 147–68; more broadly, the essays in Catherine Gallagher and Thomas Laqueur, eds., *The Making of the Modern Body: Sexuality and Society in the Nineteenth Century* (Berkeley: University of California Press, 1987). For a different view, see Donald G. MacRae, "The Body and Social Metaphor," in *The Body as a Medium of Expression* (ed. Jonathan Benthall and Ted Polhemus; London: Lane, 1975) 59–73.

[31] See Hacking, *Social Construction*, 1–59.

[32] For example, the provocative essays of: Newsom, "Woman and the Discourse of Patriarchal Wisdom," 116–31; Jo Ann Hackett, "Can a Sexist Model Liberate Us? Ancient Near Eastern 'Fertility' Goddesses," *JFSR* 5 (1989) 65–76; and eadem, "In the Days of Jael: Reclaiming the History of Women in Ancient Israel," in *Immaculate and Powerful* (ed. Clarissa Atkinson, Constance Buchanan, and Margaret Miles; Boston: Beacon, 1985) 15–38; and the volumes of *The Feminist Companion to the Bible*, edited by Athalya Brenner.

[33] See n. 17 above.

[34] See Berquist, *Controlling Corporeality*.

both what the body signifies and what it does, or rather, what is done to it. Yet, despite his frequently one-sided attention, especially in his early work, to power as coercion and the body as the (threatened, decomposing) object of said coercion misses too much of the complexity of real life.³⁵ Contrary to vulgar appropriations of Foucault, in actual life, coercion comes to seem natural and becomes unquestioned (hence non-coercive), and the process by which this occurs (legitimation) demands the historian's attention. Foucault's interest in the body in prison or insane asylums led to an excessive emphasis on it as an object of discipline (negatively conceived) and manipulation. Or, as Lois McNay puts it, "Foucault's work finishes in an unresolved contradiction between a view of social relations as fragmented and contestable and a vision of a totally administered society."³⁶ To be fair, Foucault later moved toward a more balanced position in which he saw that "relations of power are interwoven with other kinds of relations (production, kinship, family, sexuality) for which they play at once a conditioning and a conditioned role," and that "there are no relations of power without resistances...."³⁷ I share this understanding of power and the body as an instrument of power; but Foucault's major body of work must be used with great caution.

On the other hand, Foucault, among many others, has raised awareness of key features of the social meaning of bodies, notably of what is ponderously called the social construction of gender. How does a culture decide which gestures, actions, adornments, or even notions about anatomy are appropriate or inappropriate, competent or incompetent for males and females respectively? What do these choices say about other aspects of the culture, notably about its distribution of power? For example, at funerals, post-battle celebrations, and other occasions in which a culture ritually celebrates male vigor or condemns male failure, women play a prominent role as singers or storytellers who bring male success or failure to symbolic expres-

---

[35] Most obviously in Michel Foucault, *Discipline and Punish* (New York: Pantheon, 1977).

[36] Lois McNay, *Foucault: A Critical Introduction* (Cambridge: Polity, 1994) 111 (and 85–132 for a critique of his notions of power in general); see also Jürgen Habermas, "Some Questions Concerning the Theory of Power: Foucault Again," in *Critique and Power: Recasting the Foucault/Habermas Debate* (ed. Michael Kelly; Cambridge: MIT Press, 1994) 79–107; and see n. 21 above.

[37] Michel Foucault, *Power/Knowledge: Selected Interviews and Other Writings 1972–1977* (New York: Pantheon, 1980) 142.

sion. Who has the power here? What does power mean after all?

If by power we mean the ability to get someone to do something whether or not he or she wishes to do so, then of course a king is powerful. This can be a revelation to no one. The question is, in what ways is he powerful? Since the greatest power remains hidden, cloaked as right or convention, how does the king gain and use power?[38] That is, how does he persuade other men, and women, to do his will? What are the limits of this power? To pick up the concerns of the late Foucault, in what ways and to what extent do lower-status persons exert power upon the king, limiting (or enhancing) his power? And, how does the discipline, display, or exercise of the body play a role?

In part in order to begin to answer this long list of questions, and to propose related ones, in the following section, I will attempt to describe theoretical "borrowings"—the term is significant—that help shape this study. I have tried to weave out of many threads a skein of questions and approaches that allow an adequate answer to the problem at hand, rather than foisting upon the evidence a unilinear line of questioning.

To repeat, then, we are studying both learned behaviors and the symbolization surrounding them. The body both does and signifies. One can profitably pursue both dimensions, and combining them offers greater insight still. The question is how to conduct the pursuit.

How Bodies? On Signification

If the foregoing recitation of a few recent trends in the anthropology and history of the body seems too cursory, nevertheless my purpose is not to rehearse every detail of this vast literature. It is instead to borrow from it a few central orientations that will help the study of how various groups within Israel (the king, the court, the people) and beyond understood the body of the king as a locus of power, model of maleness, and site for religious reflection, among other "uses."

---

[38] Frederick Ahl's description of the Julio-Claudian principate is apt here: "... the best way to retain power once it is acquired might well be to induce people to forget not just how you came by it, but that you really had it—or even still existed..." (Frederick M. Ahl, "The Rider and the Horse: Politics and Power in Roman Poetry from Horace to Statius," *ANRW* II.32.1 [1984] 47).

The following chapters will cite, along with biblical scholars, several influential anthropologists and semioticians. These scholars teach that human behaviors often signify, and emerge out of, networks of ideas, that humans perform roles that others judge on the basis of those ideas, that through analyzing behavior it is possible to understand the underlying ideas, and that this effort is indispensable if we would understand people. Since the modus operandi of this study is not to impose a theory snatched from another discipline on the Israelite texts, it is sufficient to borrow from these scholars orientations and insights and to place them in dialogue them with a close literary-critical, historical-comparativist reading of the relevant textual and non-textual data. This study seeks to be historical-critical, but modulated into a new key.

Already, then, the previous pages have tossed about terms such as "sign," "semiotics," "sign system," "ritual," "gender," and the like. Since some of these words mean different things to different people, now is the time to explain how I use them and to justify their use.

Let us begin with the first three locutions: sign, semiotics, and sign system. A sign is *"everything* that, on the grounds of a previously established social convention, can be taken as *something standing for something else."*[39] Semiotics is the study of signs and the social conventions, or codes, that generate them. The scope of this field is very wide, embracing kinesics and proxemics, paralinguistics, musical codes, formalized languages (such as in mathematics), written languages, visual communication, and so on (9–14). A sign system or code is "a system of signification, insofar as it couples present entities with absent units" (8). Codes may include not only the signs themselves, but the rules for interpreting them. Different codes may coexist, sometimes uneasily, within a given communicative transaction (such as a text).[40] To take an example from the stories of Israel's kings, consider the famous tale of Michal's criticism of David's dance before the Ark (2 Sam. 6:20–23). She condemns him for dancing lewdly (?) before maidens, while he boasts of dancing piously before Yahweh. More

---

[39] Umberto Eco, *A Theory of Semiotics* (Bloomington: University of Indiana Press, 1976) 16; emphasis in the original.
[40] In this work, I use "text" in its commonsensical meaning as the (printed, but possibly oral) words of a literary work. Behaviors, pictures, and other signification systems are not texts in this discussion, although many scholars reasonably use the word to refer to such. If my working definition is arbitrary or even old-fashioned, it has the merit of clarity.

than personal prejudices are at stake. Michal misconstrues or ignores or repudiates a code that understands David's movements and undress as display before God; for her the display is before her rivals, the maidens. David and Michal fail to understand each other because they understand the same action, dancing, radically differently in terms of two different codes, his religio-political, hers sexual-political. Again, more it stake than individual feeling or marital strife.[41]

Rather than adducing more Israelite examples,[42] let me offer a brief history of this terminology and then a test case of it. Semiotics (or semeiotic or semiology)[43] has roots in the work of Ferdinand de Saussure and especially Charles Sanders Peirce.[44] Peirce, in particular, developed an elaborate schema of signs (or sign functions, since signs are not static entities but relationships). All sign relationships, he argued, have three components: representamen, object, and interpretant. The representamen is the sign itself, the object the sign that it generates in a person, and the interpretant that person with all the competency at reading signs that he or she brings to bear.[45] To take a simple example, a red octagon posted alongside a road (a representamen, not under its aspect as a physical object, but because it can signify something to someone) signifies "stop" (an object) to a driver who knows the traffic laws (together, an interpretant; the sign would still mean "stop" in the absence of any given driver). Since octagons do not intrinsically, that is, "naturally," mean "stop," this signification makes sense in the context of a cultural code. An individual cannot declare that purple pentagons mean "stop," since the cultural code has not allowed this possibility. Signs are not completely arbitrary. A different case obtains when, say, smoke signifies "fire" to someone who knows it should. Smoke has a natural, intrinsic

---

[41] See the discussion in C. L. Seow, *Myth, drama, and the Politics of David's Dance* (HSM; Atlanta, Ga.: Scholars Press, 1989).

[42] An early piece of biblical scholarship influenced by semiotics appears in Antti Laato, *History and Ideology in the Old Testament Prophetic Literature: A Semiotic Approach to the Reconstruction of the Proclamation of the Historical Prophets* (CBOTS 41; Stockholm: Almqvist & Wiksell, 1996). Interest in the approach is spreading, though many of its practitioners seem more interested in current uses of the biblical text than in its ancient significations.

[43] On the terminological distinctions, see Eco, *Theory of Semiotics*, 30 n. 1.

[44] Ibid., 14–15; Sebeok, *Semiotics*, 127–28.

[45] All of Peirce's notebooks were published posthumously. For a convenient summary of these ideas, see Charles S. Peirce, "Logic as Semiotic: The Theory of Signs," in *Introducing Semiotics: An Anthology of Readings* (ed. Marcel Danesi and Donato Santeramo; Toronto: Canadian Scholars' Press, 1992) 11–28, esp. 11–12.

relationship to fire. But, in either case, signification works by means of this triadic relationship. Moreover, since a sign always implies other signs to the interpretant, semiosis is unlimited in principle:[46] analysis of signs could never end except arbitrarily. In the following pages, "sign" always implies a triadic relationship, at least in principle. A red octagon signifies "stop" to someone on the basis of a preexistent code (of sign relationships). Likewise, a part of the royal body signifies something to an Israelite on the basis of previous significations. One of the historian's task is to excavate the Israelite sign system.

Many scholars have further developed Peirce's original insights, the most influential of whom for my own work has been Umberto Eco. Eco sought to systematize semiotics as a rigorous outlook on all human experience, insisting that signs are not purely mental constructs (he is not a nominalist), but correspond to real relationships in the material-intellectual world.[47] The task of the semiotician is to recover the code that produced any given sign, since "codes provide the rules which *generate* signs as concrete occurrences in communicative intercourse."[48] The task of the present study, inspired by Eco, is to recover how ancient Israelites related signs such as /royal body/ to /power/, /piety/, /male/, /brave male/, and so on.

Again, this way of thinking about human thought and thus action—not merely about communication—has also proven valuable to a number of anthropologists who seek to circumvent the impasse between those who emphasize symbols and those who focus on reified structures. Semiotics is interested in all the ways humans (and possibly other species) use signs. This is not to say that everything in the world is a sign, but that everything can be understood as a sign. The use of signs by humans implies the existence of society and concomitantly, the social dimensions of signs. Understanding the use of signs requires a cultural competence, which a historian, like an anthropologist, must acquire. Semiotics is not merely a game that literary critics play when they are pretending to be mathematicians.

---

[46] Eco, *Theory of Semiotics*, 68.

[47] Notably, Eco, *Theory of Semiotics*; and idem, *The Role of the Reader: Explorations in the Semiotics of Texts* (Bloomington, IN: Indiana University Press, 1979). For his critique of deconstructionism, see Umberto Eco, et al., *Interpretation and Overinterpretation* (Cambridge: Cambridge University Press, 1992).

[48] Eco, *Theory of Semiotics*, 49.

Among the anthropological studies that have semiotic concerns, those of Michael Herzfeld have especially influenced my work. Herzfeld is interested in the social performances, especially of males (especially in Greece), that is, in all the ways in which these persons work out their maleness by words and deeds.[49] Gender has a genetic basis, but this is only part of the story. Successful performances of manhood depend on skillful use of codes of appropriate behavior and speech. Words like "successful" and "skillful" imply the judgment of others, hence society and a social dimension of signs.

Herzfeld makes an important contribution when he recognizes that sign systems—and ideologies, sign systems having the sanction of power—are not static and do not control the mindless users of them, as some analysts would have us believe. In regard to ideologies, cultures experience disemia in regard to ideologies: "the formal or coded tension between official self-representation and what goes on in the privacy of collective introspection."[50] Indeed, matters are still more complicated than this, and official ideas about rulers and ruled are very malleable, though not infinitely so. We shall have occasion to return to this insight many times in later chapters.

In the meantime, it is worth noting that Herzfeld himself drew on several sources, including the performativist anthropology of Stanley Tambiah, who drew in turn on the classic work of J. L. Austin. Austin sought to move past the analytical philosophers of mid-century (from Russell to Wittgenstein) by studying the workings of ordinary language, where he discovered locutions that were not analytical or descriptive, but performative.[51] Tambiah built on Austin's work,

---

[49] See, notably, Michael Herzfeld, *The Poetics of Manhood: Contest and Identity in a Cretan Mountain Village* (Princeton: Princeton University Press, 1985); idem, "On some Rhetorical Uses of Iconicity in Cultural Ideologies," in *Iconicity: Essays on the Nature of Culture* (ed. Paul Bouissac, Michael Herzfeld, and Roland Posner; Tübingen: Stauffenberg, 1986) 401–19; idem, *Anthropology through the looking-glass: Critical ethnography in the margins of Europe* (Cambridge: Cambridge University Press, 1987); idem, "The Poeticity of the Commonplace," in *Semiotic Theory and Practice* (ed. Michael Herzfeld and Lucio Melazzo; 2 vols.; Berlin and New York: Mouton/de Gruyter, 1988) 1. 383–91; idem, *Cultural Intimacy: Social Poetics of the Nation-State* (New York/London: Routledge, 1997).

[50] Herzfeld, *Cultural Intimacy*, 14; cf. Terry Eagleton, *Marxism and Literary Criticism* (Berkeley: University of California Press, 1976) 6–7: ". . . an ideology is never a simple reflection of a ruling class's ideas: on the contrary, it is always a complex phenomenon, which may incorporate conflicting, even contradictory, views of the world."

[51] J. L. Austin, *How to do Things with Words* (2d ed.; Cambridge: Harvard University Press, 1975).

recognizing that actions as well as words have a performative dimension: persons say or do them in order to make things happen, they point to other things, and they can be felicitous or infelicitous, successful or unsuccessful.[52] For example, just as "I pronounce you man and wife," when said by a minister to persons eligible to marry, makes them married, so too can a ritual action bring a new cosmic reality to pass: the elevation of the Host creates the body of Christ under two aspects, as both the transubstantiated bread and as the community of believers.

This performativist approach, again, offers a set of orientations helpful for exploring the language of the texts about Israelite kings and the actions they depict and often judge. Beyond the positivist question "what happened?" we can ask, "why is a given ritual action felicitous or otherwise?" Recognizing the performative nature of language and other sign systems allows one to avoid positivistic readings of these texts, to understand that they contain arguments and beliefs, not merely reportage of facts. These recognitions also allow a careful, rigorous reconstruction of those arguments and beliefs without undue influence of preconceived notions.

To summarize this section, then, I bring to bear an array of thinkers outside biblical studies whose work has influenced my own. To be specific, the semioticians help us recognize that behaviors described in texts, and the descriptions themselves, fit into arguments that groups and persons in the texts' earliest settings had about the limits of appropriate behavior and thoughts. A semiotic sensibility, without a monotonous larding of the discussion with semiotic jargon, allows us to put together texts that seem at first unrelated.

Similarly, the students of ritual orient us to the importance that ritual plays in the life of the king, where it is a central concern and a primary means of communicating ideas and shaping behaviors of the king and his subjects and enemies. These scholars also provide a language for discussing what we see in the Israelite texts about kings as ritualizers. Meanwhile, anthropologists such as Herzfeld alert us to the poetics of the everyday, that is, the ways in which all behavior is at some level performative. Accordingly, in the following chapters, the word "performance" and its cognates will denote both

---

[52] Stanley Tambiah, "A Performative Approach to Ritual," *Proceedings of the British Academy* 45 (1979) 113–69.

what happens in a temple or palace (coronations, funerals, sacrifices)—ritual in the narrow sense—and other behaviors calculated to enhance the king's power, status, or wealth.

This study, then, assimilates these various thinkers and approaches into a basically historical-critical reading of the biblical and non-biblical texts and other artifacts in order to elucidate a hitherto mostly neglected problem: how did Israelites understand the royal body and, by extension, their king as the model male?

Whose Bodies?

The preceding pages have delineated the problems under consideration and the assumptions and methods that will help tackle them. Before we can examine the evidence in detail, plotting a course for research also necessitates retracing the steps of prior explorers. Many milestones of past generations will appear throughout this work, but a comprehensive history of this scholarship would require another volume, for biblical interpreters never lost interest in the kings of Israel and Judah.[53] Countless books and articles in the past two centuries have addressed some aspects of Israelite monarchy, and recounting the details of this research would serve little purpose.[54] Here it is sufficient to sketch the main outlines of research and indicate what remains to be done.

The consolidation of "the history of Israel" as a historiographical genre in the early nineteenth century inevitably led to research on that nation's monarchy. While the outlines of nineteenth- and early-twentieth-century histories of the dual Israelite kingdoms mainly followed that of the Deuteronomistic History, with a few evaluations of the probable facticity of the narrative thrown in, it paid little attention to the rhetoric of the relevant texts.[55] This research concentrated

---

[53] See, for example, the essays in Raymond-Jean Frontain and Jan Wojcik, eds., *The David Myth in Western Literature* (West Lafayette, IN: Purdue University Press, 1980); or the idiosyncratic work of James W. Flanagan, *David's Social Drama: A Hologram of Israel's Early Iron Age* (Sheffield: Almond, 1988).

[54] For surveys of the literature, see Karl-Heinz Bernhardt, *Das Problem der altorientalischen Königs-Ideologie im Alten Testament* (VTSupp 8; Leiden: Brill, 1961); Scott R. A. Starbuck, *Court Oracles in the Psalms: The So-Called Royal Psalms in their Ancient Near Eastern Context* (SBLDissS 172; Atlanta: Society of Biblical Literature, 1999) 1–66.

[55] See the works of Heinrich Ewald, *Geschichte des Volkes Israel* (3d ed.; 7 vols; Göttingen: Dieterisch, 1864–68) esp. vols. 3–4; Bernhard Stade, *Geschichte des Volkes*

upon the religious and political dimensions of kingship, though with little interest in theories of religion that might raise interesting questions, treating the biblical narratives as basically accurate depictions of the actions of the rulers named in them. These scholars' literary analysis paid little attention to the possible ideological underpinnings of the text under consideration, seeking instead to discover "what really happened."

When, in the 1870s and 1880s, first Eberhard Schrader and then Bernhard Stade (among others) introduced the new Assyriological evidence to the discussion, this at first did little to change the basic picture of Israelite kingship that had emerged.[56] Interest in theology and surface political structures dominated the discussion. Little work was done on the basic cultural conceptions underlying surface behaviors, and most relevantly for the current discussion, the Israelite notions of the royal body attracted little attention. (An interesting exception to this was the depiction of Solomon as the very model of the so-called oriental despot, who ultimately failed to consolidate his father's gains.)[57] What is more, everyone in the nineteenth century agreed (following the Deuteronomistic history's view of things) that the so-called United Monarchy introduced foreign (mainly Canaanite) elements into Israelite systems of belief, including governance: monarchy itself was a foreign intrusion. I can find little evidence that scholars of the period asked how such putatively foreign elements fitted into Israelite views of the world and behaviors deriving from those views.

Many features of this consensus have persisted until today, despite the rapid increase of available archaeological and (extra-Israelite) tex-

---

Israel (2 vols.; Berlin: Grote'sche Verlagsbuchhandlung, 1887); Rudolf Kittel, *Geschichte des Volkes Israel*, vol. 2: *Das Volk in Kanaan: Quellenkunde und Geschichte der Zeit bis zum babylonischen Exil* (3d ed.; Gotha: Perthe, 1917); and Julius Wellhausen, *Israelitische und jüdische Geschichte* (2d ed.; Berlin: Reimer, 1895; reprint ed. Berlin: de Gruyter, 1958).

[56] Stade, *Geschichte*, esp. vol. 2 passim; see also Eberhard Schrader, *Die Keilinschriften und das Alte Testament* (Giessen: Ricker, 1872; 3d ed.; Berlin: Reuther, 1903).

[57] See, for example, the colorful portrayal of Solomon by Kittel (*Volk in Kanaan*, 246–47): "Er [Solomon] hat mehr Sinn für die Rechte des Königtums und seine Annehmlichkeit als für seine hohen Pflichten und Aufgaben. Die despotischen Neigungen des Vaters, dort nur zuweilen durchblickend und immer wieder gezügelt oder gehoben, werden beim Sohne zu einem Grundzug des Charakters." For a more nuanced view of "Salomos Persönlichkeit," Eduard Meyer, *Geschichte des Altertums*, vol. 2: *Der Orient vom zwölften bis zur Mitte des achten Jahrhunderts* (2d ed.; Stuttgart: Cotta, 1931) 262–64.

tual evidence. New ideas have gained currency—consider Albrecht Alt's distinction between charismatic kingship in Israel and dynastic kingship in Judah, which will be discussed in passing later[58]—yet much of the nineteenth-century presentation of the subject remains intact. The DH still provides the basic outline of the history of the monarchy, and therefore of Israelite views of kingship, in many of the standard histories. Kingship still seems to many a foreign intrusion (following a literal-minded reading of 1 Sam. 8–10), though better explanations do exist.[59]

Early in this century, however, a new set of concerns, based in part on reevaluation of old evidence, came to the fore. First, Hermann Gunkel convincingly argued that the royal psalms dated to the Iron Age, not the Hellenistic period.[60] These texts thus furnished evidence for royal rhetorics of kingship. Second, the widespread interest in the history of religions led to a reconceptualization of Israelite kingship. The problem for many scholars, especially between the World Wars, was not to decide upon the accuracy of the biblical history of events, but to work out a typology of Israelite kingship in general. The goal was not the discovery of the actions of a given monarch, but the ideas and affects shaping the entire culture's view of kings. The royal psalms, since they seemed to reflect royal ritual, hence royal religion, hence underlying conceptions of kingship, provided some of the evidence.[61] For example, in a classic work on the evolution of Israelite/Jewish messianic ideals, Hugo Gressmann identified the royal psalms as exemplars of a Levantine *Hofstil*, which served as the deep background for later messianism, but originally served the royal courts of Israel, Judah, and their neighbors.[62] With some modifications, this hypothesis has endured well and informs much of my own thinking about these texts.

---

[58] Albrecht Alt, "Das Königtum in den Reichen Israel und Juda," in *Kleine Schriften zur Geschichte des Volkes Israel* (ed. idem; 2 vols.; Munich: Beck, 1953) 2. 116–34; for a critique, see T. C. G. Thornton, "Charismatic Kingship in Israel and Judah," *JTS* 14 (1963) 1–11.

[59] E.g., Norman Gottwald, *The Politics of Ancient Israel* (Louisville: Westminster John Knox, 2001) esp. 172–76.

[60] Hermann Gunkel, "Die Königspsalmen," *Preussische Jahrbücher* 158 (October-December 1914) 42–68; idem, *Einleitung in die Psalmen* (1933; ed. Joachim Begrich; 2d ed.; Göttingen: Vandenhoeck & Ruprecht, 1966) 140–71.

[61] For a review of the literature, see Subhasito S. Patro, "Royal Psalms in Modern Scholarship" (Ph.D. diss., University of Kiel, 1976).

[62] Hugo Gressmann, *Der Messias* (FRLANT 43; Göttingen: Vandenhoeck & Ruprecht, 1929).

Gressmann's work did not stand alone. Including the royal psalms in the mix also led to a reevaluation of the narrative texts about kingship. Johannes Pedersen[63] spent seventy-four pages of his monumental psychosocial profile of Israelite culture treating the evolution of kingship out of chieftainship, dealing with such topics as election to the throne, charisma, sacral kingship, and so on. Pedersen focused most closely on the king in the cult, who, he felt, possessed the divine spirit at all times "because he was Yahweh's anointed and Yahweh's son, and this power of the king's could only be upheld by constant renewal in the cult. Hence... the whole position of the king demands a cult which serves especially to strengthen him."[64]

This concern with king and cult, with anointing and sacrifice, informed many studies, but curiously did not result in a systematic exploration of the dimensions of the royal body itself. At some level, my own investigation stands in the tradition of these scholars, though I hope to avoid their mistakes and to ask anew their questions (and others) with new theoretical dispositions (and at times new evidence). There is no need to rehearse here the theories of "divine" or sacral kingship, and their connection to notions about the enthronement festival of Yahweh, that consumed much print at mid-century, since the more extreme hypotheses are mere curiosities.[65] The interest in the religious dimensions of kingly rule remains compelling, however, especially as a corrective of a sharp distinction between "secular" and "religious" aspects of governance.[66] Also valuable is the hypothesis that the biblical stories about kings concern individuals less than the monarchy in general (Pedersen, for example, recognizes this). Like the history of religions school, I seek to understand how kings

---

[63] Johannes Pedersen, *Israel: Its Life and Culture* (2 vols.; Oxford: Oxford University Press, 1940; reprint ed. Atlanta: Scholars, 1991) 32–106.
[64] Ibid., 86.
[65] See, for example, Aubrey R. Johnson, *Sacral Kingship in Ancient Israel* (Cardiff: University of Wales Press, 1955); idem, "Hebrew Conceptions of Kingship," in *Myth, Ritual, and Kingship* (ed. S. H. Hooke; Oxford: Clarendon, 1958) 204–35; Sigmund Mowinckel, *Psalmenstudien 2: Das Thronbesteigungsfest Jahwäs und der Ursprung der Eschatologie* (Kristiania: Dybwad, 1922); idem, *He That Cometh* (New York: Abingdon, 1955); J. de Fraine, *L'aspect religieux de la Royauté Israélite* (Rome: Pontifical Biblical Institute, 1954); cf. Hans Schmidt, *Die Thronfahrt Jahwes* (Tübingen: Mohr/Siebeck, 1927); and the literary review in Bernhardt, *Problem der altorientalischen Königs-Ideologie*.
[66] As in, for example, Martin Noth, *The History of Israel* (London: Black, 1958): "though charismatic leadership was compatible with the traditions of a tribal society subject to a divine law, a 'secular' monarchy was not..." (175); or unlike David's rule, Ishbaal's "was entirely without religious foundation..." (178).

were ritualizers, but also seek to recast the problem in wider terms by paying meticulous attention to each piece of evidence on its own terms without rushing toward a procrustean phenomenology of Israelite kingship.

Since about 1960, then, the investigation of the ritualized, affective features of kingship (in history of religions perspective) has been less active than formerly. With some important exceptions,[67] the major histories of Israel have accepted the sounder conclusions of the two previous waves of research on kingship (one literary-critical, the other *religionsgeschichtlich*) but have not pushed the inquiry further.

An important exception to this is Tryggve Mettinger's work *King and Messiah*, whose influence exerts itself throughout the present work.[68] While one may disagree with some of his conclusions—for example that נגיד is the crown prince rather than the king[69]—his basic approach of reading narratives and psalms in light of each other, and all with a view toward developing a picture of kingship in general and then its outworkings in specific situations, remains unexcelled. The structure of the present study borrows this method of correlating narrative and psalmic texts but extends Mettinger's work to show that the king's constellated bodies exist on a sliding scale, with ordinary humans (especially males) on one end, and Yahweh on the other.

On somewhat different lines are two recent collections of essays, edited by Norman Gottwald and John Day, respectively. In *Semeia* 37, Gottwald collects the studies of several scholars who try to break away from the literary sources and rely on sociological models of state formation and governance. The volume has been influential in biblical studies, for the good reason that it breathed into the field a new set of questions and theoretical orientations. So, for example, Coote and Whitelam attribute the rise of monarchy to the machinations of the landed gentry interested in enriching themselves, and Gottwald underscores the ways in which the tenth-century Israelite

---

[67] Notably Roland de Vaux, *Ancient Israel: Its Life and Institutions* (1961; reprint ed.; Grand Rapids: Eerdmans, 1997) 100–38, possibly the best contemporary discussion of "the person of the king."

[68] Tryggve N. D. Mettinger, *King and Messiah: The Civil and Sacral Legitimation of the Israelite King* (CBOTS 8; Lund: Gleerup, 1976).

[69] Ibid., esp. 151–84; for a critique, see Tomoo Ishida, *History and Historical Writing in Ancient Israel* (Leiden: Brill, 1999) 62–63; Gerhard Hasel, "נגיד nāgîd," *TDOT* 9 (1998) 187–202.

state transformed free agrarians into peasants.[70] All of the contributors to the volume, though in different ways, seek a material-cultural explanation of kingship that deliberately avoids the biblical texts "in order that they [the contributors] might break free from the agenda-setting mandates inherent in the interpreting traditions surrounding those texts."[71]

All the same, I find the approach(es) of the contributors to *Semeia* 37 less than satisfying, for various reasons. True, the attempt to relativize the biblical texts merits pursuing, not least because of the latent theological special pleading, based on these texts, which is present in many histories of Israel. But this approach risks reducing the biblical texts to mere "propaganda," a dubious genre of literature implying deceit, false consciousness, and other finally unanalyzable phenomena. One must ask, for example, why depictions of the king as a near-divine figure (which will emerge in the following chapters) convinced at least some Israelites, who were presumably neither universally stupid nor venally self-interested. All of the essays in *Semeia* 37 deepen our understanding of Israelite kingship and, not incidentally, force us to recognize the theological or idealist assumptions that easily influence our view of the relevant evidence. On the other hand, the emphasis on origins and material cultural explanations thereof risks neglecting an important part of our evidence, namely the biblical texts, by dismissing their own self-understanding. This is particularly true when scholars assume, without proof or even argument, that the religious claims of the text merely mask power interests of elites. Can we be sure of that? Even if we are, it is worth knowing why elites said what they did, and why they believed that such claims would convince others (and themselves). That is, the question of legitimacy remains in play. Since the argument that religion is epiphenomenal itself has a social history (and is therefore not a given that one can assume while pretending to objectivity), the

---

[70] Robert B. Coote and Keith W. Whitelam, "The Emergence of Israel: Social Transformation and State Formation Following the Decline in Late Bronze Age Trade," *Sem* 37 (1986) 107–47; cf. Norman K. Gottwald, "Introduction," *Sem* 37 (1986) 1–8; and idem, "The Participation of Free Agrarians in the Introduction of Monarchy to Ancient Israel: An Application of H. A. Landsberger's Framework for the Analysis of Peasant Movements," *Sem* 37 (1986) 77–106.

[71] Gottwald, "Introduction," 5; he is describing the article by Coote and Whitelam, but the description fits all of the volume's essays. See also Gottwald, *Politics of Ancient Israel*.

contributors to Gottwald's collection, despite their many positive contributions, involve themselves in a contradiction when they propose a material-cultural reading of the Bible as a way of escaping bias. Without pushing this discussion too far, I seek to register my own discontent with the approach to Israelite kingship that the contributors to *Semeia* 37 represent and my belief that a different approach, that outlined in this chapter and developed in those that follow, offers a better way of understanding the evidence.

Still more recently, Day has published a volume of twenty essays ranging over many subjects related to kingship in ancient Israel, Egypt, and Mesopotamia. Topics include Canaanite influence on Israelite monarchy, queenship, the king in various literary genres in the Bible, and the afterlife of Israelite kingship in Christian and Jewish messianism.[72] Without exception, the essays in this volume are competent historical-critical and literary-critical pieces, and some of them have offered direct help on particular points in the texts under consideration here. They clear away some of the uninformed conclusions that we have inherited from older scholarship. I single out the excellent article by Alison Salvesen on "The Trappings of Royalty in Ancient Hebrew," which examines the clothing and furniture that kings used.[73] In short, the collection offers a good sample of the current state of the question regarding Israelite kingship. Yet, Day's contributors (intentionally?) offer little reflection on the methods of research that the topic requires and so do not advance the overall discussion significantly.

Still more recently, the publication of studies of David by Halpern and McKenzie and of Josiah by Sweeney[74] have helped our understanding of these kings and ancient portrayals of them. I will consider them in detail later in the book. I am not persuaded with Halpern that the David stories, for example, date to the tenth century, but he has shown them to be rather early, justifying fully my treatment of them as texts predating the seventh century. Sweeney's recognizes that DtrH reached its final form in mid-sixth century (318–20)

---

[72] John Day, ed., *King and Messiah in Israel and the Ancient Near East: Proceedings of the Oxford Old Testament Seminar* (JSOTSS 270; Sheffield: Sheffield Academic Press, 1998).

[73] Alison Salvesen, "The Trappings of Royalty in Ancient Hebrew," in Day, *King and Messiah*, 119–41.

[74] See n. 4 above.

though incorporating large amounts of earlier material from which the ideology of Josiah's reign (and presumably earlier reigns) can be reconstructed. Again this supports my basic approach to the material in the DH. I will consider these works in detail in later chapters.

Considering kingship more generally, Stuart Lasine emphasizes the "narcissism" of the monarchy, offering a postmodern reading with which I will interact but ultimately find dissatisfying.[75] Lasine's interpretation tends to ignore that question of why monarchy worked, that is, of why a society accepts monarchy as normal, right, or divinely sanctioned. I believe that, though extremely stimulating, his work fails to address serious historical questions such as how surveillance would work in an ancient society.

A more compelling work is that of Dale Launderville, who compares Israelite ideas of proper kingship with those of Homeric Greece and second-millennium Babylonia.[76]

In 2003 Oswald Loretz sought to explore the royal psalms' portrayal of the king's body, drawing explicitly on Kantorowicz.[77] My own research goes back to the late 1990s, and as this volume will show, the concern with the royal body is much more extensive than Loretz recognizes, spanning many Israelite texts and from varying points of view. Still, his contribution and his larger discussion of the king as "gerechte Richter" makes a good contribution to the study of Israelite monarchy.

To summarize, it is necessary to penetrate behind the text to the ideas and beliefs that inform it, and then to move back to the text to understand how those ideas and beliefs can play themselves out. This double movement offers a richer understanding. It allows us to recognize that the Israelite texts make arguments about proper royal behavior, and that those arguments are themselves part of the historical record. Through the texts, it is possible to understand, at least in part, the beliefs and attitudes, the local knowledge of Israel and Judah. As historians, we need not necessarily accept the ancients'

---

[75] Lasine, *Knowing Kings*.

[76] Dale Launderville, *Piety and Politics: The Dynamics of Royal Authority in Homeric Greece, Biblical Israel, and Old Babylonian Mesopotamia* (Grand Rapids: Eerdmans, 2003).

[77] Oswald Loretz, *Götter—Ahnen—Könige als gerechte Richter: Der "Rechtsfall" des Menschen vor Gott nach altorientalischen und biblischen Texten* (AOAT 290; Münster: Ugarit, 2003) 691–714.

views as true, but we do need to understand them. I hope that the current study will contribute to this understanding.

Conclusions and Prospects

To conclude, the present study seeks connections—connections between theory and evidence, among various theories, and among different types of evidence. There is nothing new about a study of Israelite kingship. There is much new in one that tries to understand Israelite conceptions of the different anatomy, and then appropriate display, discipline, purification, and training of, and care for, the royal body. As will become clear, the Israelites themselves understand what we would call politics and governance (and, of course, religion) at least partly in terms of bodily practices. Here I seek to show how they did this, to make new connections and rethink old ones. Rather than either following slavishly the biblical narratives or constructing a rigid etic (material-cultural or otherwise) model of kingship, this work identifies crucial moments in the life of kings and tries to understand how the available evidence bears upon them.

I seek, finally, to rethink the social (and, derivatively, literary) conventions informing Israelite kingship. The following chapters achieve this by considering: the royal psalms (Chapters 2–3), the (mostly) Deuteronomistic narratives about kings (Chapters 4–6), and Israelite descriptions of foreign kings (Chapter 7). Chapter 9 summarizes results of the work and identifies items for future research. The aim is to build a cumulative argument, to show that the proper understanding and treatment of the royal body underlay much thinking (and therefore text production) in Israel throughout the Iron Age. It will become clear that, while the royal psalms present a fairly consistent "official" view of the royal body, this view did not convince everyone equally or in the same way, and that, therefore, many narratives and prophetic texts explore the limits of the official view. The narratives embedded in the DH do not, for example, understand the king's body to be inviolable, though they remain aware of that viewpoint. Nowhere do they understand him to be אלהים, which indicates that his "divine" status was situational and an argument, not a common assumption about a fixed "reality." The narratives also portray the royal body in danger, which the royal psalms are reluctant to do. Moreover, the discussion of foreign kings will show that Israelites knew about other cultures' views of rulers but read these views through the lenses of their own experiences creating a newly complex view of kingship in general, and the royal body in particular. The Song of Songs will show, too, that the royal imagery could take on new significations of surprising plasticity. This sweeping combination of evidence allows for a fairly comprehensive grasp of the problem at hand and reveals missed connections, as we shall see.

All of this is to say that the study of the royal body sheds new light on what we might call "normative maleness" in Israel, that is, on what Israelites took to be admirable in a king and by extension all males who aspired to high status as well as rank. The successful kings, most notably David, can display their bodies in ways that serve higher purposes, ultimately divine ones, and these displays deserve the emulation of Israelites. The royal body offers, in short, a window on some of the central conceptions (and their related behaviors) in ancient Israel. With apologies to Kantorowicz and his muse Plowden, the Israelite royal body is manifold, but the visible, imbecilic body of the king reveals the invisible, pristine body (politic) of the King.

A final point: as will become clear, this connection between the biosocial royal body and Israel's salient assumptions about the structure of the cosmos derives from the close resemblance between the embodied behavior of the king and that of his notional father and teacher, Yahweh. It matters little which character came first—whether kingship served as a model for the deity or vice versa.[78] (Indeed, it seems clear that the depictions of the two mutually influenced each other.) What matters is that in Israel's symbolic universe, the king was "son of Yahweh," an Elohim who was responsible for insuring that Israel and the international political system at large ran in accordance with what Rappaport calls "Ultimate Sacred Postulates," i.e., those ideas that simply cannot be doubted without the demolition of an entire social order (such as the Shema in Judaism or the Nicene Creed in Christianity).[79] Kingship, far from being an alien intrusion

---

[78] On the relationship of characterizations of the two figures, see Marc Zvi Brettler, *God is King: Understanding an Israelite Metaphor* (JSOTSS 76; Sheffield: Sheffield Academic Press, 1989).

[79] See the discussion in Roy Rappaport, *Ritual and Religion in the Making of Humanity* (Cambridge: Cambridge University Press, 1999) 236–76.

on Israelite life, became a bundle of signs quintessentially representing its notions of human and divine power and nurturance. Yet, because society's do not construct unilinear sign systems but elaborate networks embedding significant tensions and contradictions, the "meaning" of the social body of the king hardly escaped contestation.

CHAPTER TWO

CREATING THE BODY OF THE KING
IN THE ROYAL PSALMS

Any description of the Israelite king's body's signification always implies a study of the signifier. What does the body mean and to whom does it mean it? To ask how ancient Israel described its king displaying, training, governing, hiding, or working with, his body in order to perform his kingly role properly, is to inquire sequentially into the valuations the king, his subjects, and their enemies place on these doings. Let us begin with the royal court, whose views survive in the royal psalms in the Psalter and a few other poems outside it. These poems, undoubtedly originating within the liturgies of the court sanctuaries of Jerusalem and perhaps northern sites (Dan, Bethel, or even Samaria) reveal how the elites believed the proper king's body to impinge upon governance, piety, and, in short, successful rule in a successful society. These psalms date to the Iron Age and reflect the ideas of the Israelite courts and cults. Unlike the Israelite narratives that we will consider later, the psalms do not deliberately ambiguate their characterizations of the monarch. Rather, they are state pronouncements, liturgies of political ritual. They praise the king unstintingly and describe his body in the most florid terms as a near divine entity. Their composers apparently assumed that their claims about the monarch, created and displayed ritually, were shared by their audience, however disputatious the objections to these views on the part of various Israelites might have been.

At the same time, as parts of political ritual, the royal psalms do not attempt to foist improbable beliefs on an unsuspecting public (no vulgar Marxist explanation can suffice). Rather, as texts of political ritual, as Catherine Bell would put it, they "orchestrate a cosmic framework within which the social hierarchy headed by the king is perceived as natural and right."[1] Through "symbols and symbolic action" they "depict a group of people as a coherent and ordered

---

[1] Catherine Bell, *Ritual: Perspectives and Dimensions* (Oxford: Oxford University Press, 1997) 129.

community based on shared values and goals," and they also demonstrate the legitimacy of these values and goals by establishing their iconicity with the perceived values and order of the cosmos."[2] While other Israelites outside the court contested the vision of the cosmos adumbrated by the royal psalms, it is precisely this vision that formed the basis for the contestation.

Although nineteenth-century scholars often located these psalms in the theological speculations of the Second Temple period,[3] ironically recapitulating the premodern view of these texts as messianic, eschatological hymns,[4] most research in the past century has taken for granted Gunkel's arguments for an Iron Age dating for the royal psalms in particular.[5] As Roberts has argued, reasons exist for dating some of these psalms to as early as the tenth century,[6] though I think that in general the psalms may be a bit later. I see no reason to follow Gerstenberger and some other German scholars in dating, for example, Ps. 2 "sometime between the sixth and third centuries," and indeed he offers no explanation.[7] Although later datings for some

---

[2] Ibid.

[3] See, e.g., Bernhard Duhm, *Die Psalmen* (2d ed.; KHKAT; Tübingen: Mohr/Siebeck, 1922), who, e.g., attributes Ps. 45 to the reign of Aristobulus I (p. 190)! Similarly Charles and Emilie Grace Briggs (*The Book of Psalms* [ICC; 2 vols.; Edinburgh: Clark, 1906]) understand Ps. 2 messianically (1. 11–13), but locate Ps. 45 in Jehu's marriage (!) (1. 383) and Ps. 72 to the accession of Josiah (2.132). It is difficult to discern a set of methodological criteria for these judgments, however. Interestingly, the later dating of the royal psalms has been revived in some cases, e.g., by Michael Goulder (*The Psalms of the Return [Book V, Psalms 107–150]* [JSOTSS 258; Sheffield: Sheffield Academic Press, 1998] esp. 90–101); but see below. On Ps. 8 as a possible royal psalm, see Thomas Podella, *Das Lichtkleid JHWHs: Untersuchungen zur Gestalthaftigkeit Gottes im Alten Testament und seiner altorientalischen Umwelt* (Tübingen: Mohr/Siebeck, 1996) 259–63.

[4] On premodern Psalms scholarship and the biography of David, see for example Yair Zakovitch, "David's Birth and Childhood in the Bible and in the Midrashim on Psalms," in Erich Zenger, ed., *Der Psalter in Judentum und Christentum* (HBS 18; Freiburg: Herder, 1998) 185–98; Gerhard Bodendorfer, "Zur Historisierung des Psalters in der rabbinischen Literatur," in Zenger, *Psalter in Judentum*, 215–34.

[5] See recently Eckart Otto, "Psalm 2 in neuassyrischer Zeit: Assyrische Motive in der judäischen Königsideologie," in Klaus Kiesow and Thomas Meurer, eds., *Textarbeit: Studien zu Texten und ihrer Rezeption aus dem Alten Testament und der Umwelt Israels* (FS Peter Weimar; AOAT 294; Münster: Ugarit-Verlag, 2003) 335–49.

[6] J. J. M. Roberts, "Zion in the Theology of the Davidic-Solomonic Empire," in Tomoo Ishida, ed., *Studies in the Period of David and Solomon and Other Essays* (Winona Lake, Ind.: Eisenbrauns, 1982) 93–108.

[7] Erhard Gerstenberger, *Psalms, Part 1 With an Introduction to Cultic Poetry* (FOTL 14; Grand Rapids: Eerdmans, 1988) 48; of course, Gerstenberger's analysis of individual psalms is often very insightful.

psalms continue to be proposed, particularly by European scholars, in most cases such a dating seems much less convincing than one in the monarchic period. In some cases, it is possible to identify close parallels between a biblical psalm and Assyrian material, for example.[8] The precise dating, which in any case remains unrecoverable, is not essential to my analysis, but a location of these texts during the period of the Israelite monarchy is important. Gunkel argued that Pss. 2, 18, 20, 21, 45, 72, 89, 101, 110, and 132 (later adding 144) were *Königspsalmen* from the period of the Israelite monarchies.[9] His interpretation avoided many intellectual contortions and so, with modifications, it remains the regnant hypothesis.

It soon became clear that the attribution of these psalms to the royal court(s) and attendant temple(s) opened the door to using them to reconstruct the religious and political ideas behind Israelite kingship as well as the language used to express those ideas. Accordingly, Hugo Gressmann spoke of a *Hofstil* in Pss. 2, 72, and 110 (especially), connecting the rhetoric of those texts to court language in other parts of the ancient Near East.[10] The Davidides, he believed, borrowed Egyptian and "Amorite" (meaning Canaanite, especially as revealed in the Amarna letters) courtly language and ideas, including the notion of the king as a near-divine figure. Gressmann, unfortunately, did not pay attention to the king's body as a focal point for the depictions of the king, even though such a consideration would have strengthened his overall program.

The other early-twentieth-century figure whose work continues to shape research on the Psalter is Sigmund Mowinckel, whose importance can hardly be overestimated, even if his thesis that the king enacted the coronation of Yahweh at Rosh Hashanah, and that many psalms reflect this occasion remains doubtful.[11] Although his understanding of the alleged background of this ritual kingship, the

---

[8] E.g., see Martin Arneth, *"Sonne der Gerechtigkeit": Studien zur Solarisierung der Jahwe-Religion im Lichte von Psalm 72* (BZAR 1; Wiesbaden: Harrassowitz, 2000).

[9] Hermann Gunkel, "Die Königspsalmen," *Preussische Jahrbücher* 158 (October-December 1914) 42–68; idem, *Einleitung in den Psalmen* (ed. Joachim Begrich; Göttingen: Vandenhoeck & Ruprecht, 1933) 140–71.

[10] Hugo Gressmann, *Der Messias* (FRLANT 43; Göttingen: Vandenhoeck & Ruprecht, 1929) 1–64, esp. 50–53.

[11] First adumbrated in Sigmund Mowinckel, *Psalmenstudien II: Die Thronbesteigungfest Jahwäs und der Ursprung der Eschatologie* (Kristiania: Dybwad, 1922) 6–8; cf. Aubrey Johnson, *Sacral Kingship in Ancient Israel* (Cardiff: University of Wales Press, 1955) 103–5, 118–25.

Babylonian Akitu festival,[12] is questionable, his instinct for a ritual background of monarchy was on the right track. He correctly observed, for example, that military imagery in these psalms does not concern merely earthly politics by other means,[13] but the mythic combat between God and the forces of chaos. Or rather, the texts interpret human combat through a mythological grid. Since the 1920s and especially since the eclipse of the History of Religions approach to biblical and Near Eastern studies during the heyday of the so-called Biblical Theology movement,[14] Mowinckel's hypothesis has come under fire from various directions, but it remains influential, even among its detractors.[15] His insight that temple ritual is the background of many of the royal psalms is surely correct and of far-reaching importance, because he thus can account for their use in the Second Temple[16] and, more importantly, for the many allusions to the cult in the psalms themselves.[17] For the purposes of the present analysis, it matters little whether Mowinckel is correct in assuming a royal basis for the popular cult or Gerstenberger is right in arguing for the opposite,[18] for in fact all aspects of the Israelite cult must have operated within the complex network of sign relationships existing in the culture.

Since the middle of the twentieth century, in any case, the works of Gunkel and Mowinckel have become a fixed point in the landscape of biblical studies. In contemporary scholarship, the assignment

---

[12] For current understandings of the king's roles in the Babylonian and Assyrian Akitu festivals, see Beate Pongratz-Leisten, *Ina Šulmi Īrub: Die kulttopographische und ideologische Programmatik der akītu-Prozession in Babylonien und Assyrien im 1. Jahrtausend v. Chr.* (BF 16; Mainz: von Zabern, 1994) esp. 106–11.

[13] To paraphrase Carl von Clausewitz (*On War* [New York: Penguin, 1968] I.1.24 [p. 119]): "We see, therefore, that War is not merely a political act, but also a real political instrument, a continuation of political commerce, a carrying out of the same by other means."

[14] See Patrick Miller, "Israelite Religion," in Douglas A. Knight and Gene M. Tucker, eds., *The Hebrew Bible and Its Modern Interpreters* (Chico: Scholars, 1985) 201–37, esp. 201–5. On the theological concerns of the *Religionsgeschichtliche Schule*, see Karsten Lehmküller, *Kultus und Theologie: Dogmatik und Exegese in der religionsgeschichtliche Schule* (FSÖT; Göttingen: Vandenhoeck & Ruprecht, 1996).

[15] See, e.g., John H. Eaton, *Kingship and the Psalms* (2d ed.; Sheffield: JSOT Press, 1986).

[16] Sigmund Mowinckel, *The Psalms in Israel's Worship* (2 vols.; Oxford: Blackwell, 1962) 1. 2–5; for post-Second Temple usage and evidence for usage in the Second Temple itself, see Günter Stemberger, "Psalmen in Liturgie und Predigt der rabbinischen Zeit," in Zenger, *Psalter in Judentum*, 199–213.

[17] Mowinckel, *Psalms in Israel's Worship*, 1. 5–12; 2. 85–103.

[18] Gerstenberger, *Psalms Part 1*, 19.

of the royal psalms to the Iron Age is secure, even if a few scholars have sought to date some of these psalms later.[19] Very much in dispute, though, is the number of these psalms. John H. Eaton proposes to add about fifty psalms to Gunkel's corpus.[20] He correctly notes the spread of royal terminology into many psalms, but, of course, use of royal terminology or ideas need not necessarily make a psalm royal. To fit this category, the human king must be the subject of the poem as a whole. To illustrate this point, consider how Ps. 22 became a kind of royal psalm when early Christians used it to shape the telling of the passion narrative.[21]

Steven Croft, similarly, has rethought the nature of the royal psalms, reopening the issue of the identity of the individual in the psalms,[22] which Mowinckel and his student Birkeland had adumbrated in the mid-twentieth century.[23] Agreeing with them that "I"

---

[19] A recent challenge of this identification of the Sitz im Leben of the royal psalms appears in Scott R. A. Starbuck, *Court Oracles in the Psalms: The So-Called Royal Psalms in their Ancient Near Eastern Context* (SBLDissS 172; Atlanta: Society of Biblical Literature, 1999). Starbuck argues that since ancient Near Eastern kings did not typically reuse hymns and prayers, there is no reason to assume that the Israelite royal psalms were reused (208); they may therefore have originally included the names of their royal users (210). And many of them exhibit a tendency toward a democratization of royal imagery, a process that accelerated in the Second Temple period. Starbuck's arguments are powerful, but not, I think ultimately convincing. Ancient Near Eastern kings could recycle *incantations*, which are not so different from prayers; this is clear from ritual texts such as that for the *bît rimki* ritual purifying the Assyrian kings; for the texts see Jørgen Laessøe, *Studies on the Assyrian Ritual and Series* bît rimki (Copenhagen: Munksgaard, 1955). On another point, Starbuck's distinction between the royal psalms as "merely ideological trappings of the royal court" (which he deems a bad view) and as reflections of "Israel's continued faith upon [sic], wrestling with, and reinterpretation of promises made by Yahweh that Israel would be a secure royal nation" (212) creates a false dichotomy. Loaded words such as "propaganda" and "faith" both denote systems of significations, and avoiding the invidious connotations of such terminology is sounder historiographical method. Though Starbuck argues his case intelligently, his false dichotomies trip him up here.

[20] John H. Eaton, *Kingship and the Psalms*. Eaton's certain royal psalms are, in addition to Gunkel's, Pss. 3, 4, 7, 9–10, 17, 22, 23, 27, 28, 35, 40, 41, 57, 59, 61, 62, 63, 66, 69, 70, 71, 75, 89, 91, 92, 94, 108, 118, 138, 140, and 145 (cf. 44, 60, 74, 80, 83, and 84). Less clear ones are 5, 11, 16, 31, 36, 42–43, 51, 52, 54, 55, 56, 73, 77, 86, 102, 109, 116, 120, 121, 139, 141, and 142.

[21] See Matt. 27:46 and Mark 15:34 on Ps. 22:2; Matt. 27:35; Mark 15:24; Luke 23:24; John 19:24; and *Gospel of Peter* 4:3.

[22] Steven J. L. Croft, *The Identity of the Individual in the Psalms* (JSOTSS 44; Sheffield: Sheffield Academic Press, 1987).

[23] Harris Birkeland, *Die Feinde des Individuums in der israelitischen Psalmenliteratur* (Oslo: Grøndahl, 1933); Mowinckel, *Psalms in Israel's Worship*, 1. 42–80, 193–246. Mowinckel admits, though, that the "I" in some psalms may be a courtier or high priest (76).

equals the king, Croft thinks that the indisputable royal individual psalms are Pss. 3, 18, 22, 27, 28, 44, 59, 61, 63, 89, 91, 94, 118, and 144, with Pss. 4, 5, 7, 13, 16, 23, 25, 30, 40, 42–43, 51, 54, 62, 70, 71, 73, 86, 92, 109, 140, 142, and 143 being probably royal.[24] Like Eaton's, however, Croft's arguments for making a psalm royal often appear unconvincing,[25] and his entire project is tied up in the unproven idea of an autumn festival in which the king was a major player.[26] Like Eaton, Croft fails to allow for the spread of royal metaphors to non-royal settings.

The most economical approach is to examine those psalms that were beyond reasonable doubt royal in their original settings. The psalm in question must explicitly feature the king as its hero, either by referring to one of his royal titles or by depicting him in actions that only the king could do. One may start with Gunkel's list of royal psalms, and then consider others on a case-by-case basis. Gunkel's list has been widely, perhaps universally, accepted because each psalm in it casts the king as an important actor in the poetic drama.

In addition, one should note that not all relevant psalms are in the Psalter. This and the following chapter will, accordingly, examine Isa. 11 and 38 as well as Psalms 2, 18, 20, 21, 45, 72, 89, 101, 110, 132, and 144. These texts fall into the following literary categories: an epithalamium (Ps. 45; cf. Song of Songs 5:10–16), coronation hymns (Pss. 2, 72, 101, and 110), a hymn commemorating the founding of the Jerusalem temple (Ps. 132), petitionary psalms (Pss. 89, 144, and Isa. 38), thanksgiving hymns (Ps. 18 [= 2 Sam. 22]), military anthems (Pss. 20 and 21), and a birth oracle (Isa. 11). The procedure here is to examine each poem in detail, paying attention to the mentions of parts of the king's body, its display, care, adornment, and movement in ritual. After laying out the pieces of evidence, this and the following chapters move toward a synthesis

---

In his *Psalmenstudien I: Āwän und die individuellen Klagepsalmen* (Kristiania: Dybwad, 1921) esp. 76–133, he argued that the enemies were sorcerers and that the "I" could be any Israelite.

[24] Croft, *Identity of the Individual*, 73–132.

[25] As, for example, when he claims that a psalm's being "far too general in content" to be a prayer of any innocent person must indicate that it is a royal psalm (90, for Ps. 26).

[26] For a critique of Mowinckel's *Psalmenstudien II*, see e.g., M. R. Hauge, "Sigmund Mowinckel and the Psalms: A Query into His Concern," *SJOT* 2 (1988) 56–71.

of the semiotic code(s) relating to the human body of the king as that code appears in these psalms. Since the focus here is upon the role of these texts before they became part of a canon (or even individual books), any order of their presentation is arbitrary. Ps. 45, because it introduces many themes that echo through the other texts, offers an excellent entry point.

Psalm 45

Typically labeled an epithalamium primarily because of its reference to the presentation of the queen to her apparently new husband and lord,[27] Ps. 45 views the king as warrior, as well as progenitor. The psalm also echoes the royal coronation, indicating that Israelites understood the marriage and accession rites as two species in the same genus.[28] The king ritually relates himself to his wife, his subjects, his foreign neighbors (at least in the imagination of the participants of this ritual), and the deity. This occurs through the display of the royal body. Several aspects of the king's body as a sign come into play. Prior to considering these aspects, however, it is first necessary to explicate the text's ritual shape and function.

In a now classic essay, Stanley Tambiah defines ritual as

> a culturally constructed system of symbolic communication. It is constituted of patterned and ordered sequences of words and acts, often expressed in multiple media, whose content and arrangement are char-

---

[27] Briggs and Briggs, *Book of Psalms*, 1. 383 (who think it a song from the marriage of Jehu, a view shared by Samuel Terrien, *The Psalms: Strophic Structure and Theological Commentary* [Eerdmans Critical Commentary; Grand Rapids: Eerdmans, 2003] 367–68); Hermann Gunkel, *Die Psalmen* (Göttingen: Vandenhoeck & Ruprecht, 1929) 189; Artur Weiser, *Die Psalmen* (ATD; Göttingen: Vandenhoeck & Ruprecht, 1955) 243; Johannes S. M. Mulder, *Studies on Psalm 45* (Nijmegen: Witsiers, 1972); Hans-Joachim Kraus, *Psalmen* (BKAT; Neukirchen-Vluyn: Neukirchener, 1960) 330; Mitchell Dahood, *Psalms 1–50* (AB 16; Garden City, NY: Doubleday, 1965) 271; Peter C. Craigie, *Psalms 1–50* (WBC 19; Waco, TX: Word, 1983) 337; Klaus Seybold, *Die Psalmen* (HAT 1.15; Tübingen: Mohr/Siebeck, 1996) 185. For a history of scholarship on the psalm, see Philip J. King, *A Study of Psalm 45 (44)* (Rome: Lateran Pontifical University, 1959). On the use of the psalm in early Christian theology, where it was thought to refer to the groom Jesus and was accordingly a centerpiece of christological exegesis, see Elisabeth Grünbeck, *Christologische Schriftargumentation und Bildersprache* (SVC 26; Leiden: Brill, 1994).

[28] One might conceivably argue that Ps. 45 stems from the coronation, but this seems unlikely since any given king could be a minor or unmarried, hence lacking the wife who figures so prominently in the psalm.

acterized in varying degree by formality (conventionality), stereotypy (rigidity), condensation (fusion), and redundancy (repetition).[29]

He goes on to argue that ritual is performative in at least three senses: (1) in the "Austinian sense wherein saying something is also doing something"; (2) in the sense that it is a staged performance; and (3) in the "sense of indexical values ... being attached to and inferred by actors during the performance" (or, in other words, words, actions, costumes, smells, and other features of a ritual may signify something other than their surface meaning; so, for example, the elevation of a piece of bread in the Catholic mass points toward the crucifixion of Jesus, the offering of him as a sacrifice, and the transformation of bread into the *corpus Christi* that nourishes souls, among other levels of signification).[30] The following pages examine the royal body within the unfolding structure of the Israelite royal nuptials, though with the abiding awareness of the issues that Tambiah has raised, which allow analysis to escape a rigidly structural understanding of the layers of ritual.

The Text of a Ritual and the Ritual of a Text

Since no full description of a royal wedding (or any other kind, for that matter) survives from ancient Israel, gaps must remain in our understanding of this song. Nevertheless, certain features of the ritual are discernible, including the entrance of the king (vv. 3–6), the entrance of the queen and her retinue (vv. 10–13), the presentation of gifts by notables (v. 13), as well as addresses to the various wedding participants. The royal participants wore their extravagant clothing, and the king was armed. The entrance of attendants with the queen must have impressed all observers with the might and splendor of the Israelite court and the king who led it. Reinforcing this impression is the psalm's allusion to the coronation ritual, which may have been recapitulated (see below). Each feature will be considered below.

---

[29] Stanley Tambiah, "A Performative Approach to Ritual," *Proceedings of the British Academy* 45 (1979) 119; reprinted in idem, *Culture, Thought, and Social Action: An Anthropological Perspective* (Cambridge: Harvard University Press, 1985) 128.
[30] Ibid.

The Ritual Entrance (v. 2)

The psalm opens with a self-introduction by the person performing it (v. 2). Often, the speaker here has been identified as a cult prophet,[31] although this claim founders in the absence of any prophetic formulae (such as כה אמר יהוה or דבר יהוה). While he may be the speedy scribe (סופר מהיר) of v. 2, it is impossible to decide whether the speaker is a courtier, a prophet, or a priest. A more useful point to observe is that the self-predication of the singer in v. 2 is an effort at self-affirmation, a boast that indicates his worthiness to sing the song, to preside at the ritual, to declaim the king's and queen's merits. Note that the singer states his or her worthiness in bodily terms: "A good word stirs my *heart*; I intone my compositions concerning the king; my *tongue* is the pen of a speedy scribe!" (רחש לבי דבר טוב אמר אני מעשי למלך לשוני עט סופר מהיר).

The expression "good word" (דבר טוב) in the Bible does not denote simply well chosen words by an ordinary person, but rather a technical term referring to divine promises (often of victory over enemies).[32] דבר טוב denotes a range of appropriate utterances[33] or even appropriate actions by someone. Thus, to take another biblical example, the seasoned courtiers around Rehoboam urge him to speak דברים טובים (here "conciliatory words") to his subjects in order to keep them so (1 Kings 12:7 = 2 Chron. 10:7). These good words presage good deeds that make a king seem good to good subjects. Rehoboam must persuade his discontented subjects to throw in with him. He must be a good king who speaks well. Admittedly, the phrase there is in the plural, and singular in Ps. 45, but the singular and plural can appear side-by-side without any change of meaning being indicated (see Josh. 23:14–15). Hence, the phrase דברים טובים can also refer to appropriate, "kingly" words that the king speaks, or the actions that his words cause to occur. (This would, by the way, explain the curious claim in 2 Chron. 12:12 that Rehoboam's

---

[31] Kraus, *Psalmen*, 332. But see Craigie, *Psalms 1–50*, 338; and Weiser, *Psalmen*, 243, who calls this a "profaner Lyrik." Craigie's distinction between art and liturgy is difficult to defend, but not crucial to his refutation.

[32] For this usage, see Josh. 21:45, 23:14–15; 1 Kings 8:56, 14:13; Jer. 29:10, 33:14; Zech. 1:13 (pl.); cf. also Ps. 119:65 (where the word pair is split); the phrase denotes divine promises of salvation. See also the discussion of דבר in W. H. Schmidt, "דבר dābhār," *TDOT* 3 (1978) 84–125.

[33] See Prov. 12:25, where it is the opposite of דאגה ("anxiety"); on usages of the Akkadian equivalents, see Benno Landsberger, "Das 'gute Wort'," in *Altorientalische Studien* (Bruno Meissner Festschrift; Leipzig: Harrassowitz, 1928–29) 294–321.

performance of penitential rites led to "good words" being in Judah. Although later, this text offers evidence that the monarch's words, like those of God or God's prophet, could be called טוב, and that when the king correctly performed rituals, positive results accrued.)[34] Words uttered and rituals performed can create conditions under which "good words" exist. Or, to put it another way, the reference to "good words" describes a condition of society generated by the actions of its leader, the king.

The meaning of this phrase is important to the present discussion, then, because the speaker in Ps. 45:2 asserts the right to speak by referring to something preexisting, here, the beneficent conditions of the king's rule. The "good word" bubbling up in the singer[35] is identical to the following utterance "about"[36] the king, which in turn encapsulates and prefigures the rest of the psalm. Since the following verses describe the characteristics of the king (admittedly in an ideal form), the subject of the speaker's song is the *res gestae* of the king, especially as these relate to his wedding. Again the picture is idealized, not dependent on an individual's king's actions or biography, but in some ways a summary of what the court believed kingship to entail.[37] The singer asserts his or her right to speak by referring to this set of cultural ideals about the king.

The last part of the verse alludes to the singer's tongue, which is said to be the "pen of a speedy scribe." The metonym tongue → pen depends on the underlying sign /instrument of communication/

---

[34] Sara Japhet (*I & II Chronicles* [OTL; Louisville: Westminster/John Knox, 1993] 679) understands the last part of 2 Chron. 12:12 to introduce a new subject: the moral excellence of the Judahites, parallel to that of Rehoboam. The simpler explanation, however, seems to be that it is Rehoboam's actions that produce דברים טובים ("good words").

[35] On the hapax רחש, see Dahood, *Psalms 1–50*, 270. Dahood understands this as a metathesized form of חרש, which might explain the reference to the pen of the scribe later in the verse; but the explanation remains conjectural. It is also possible that the pun רחש/חרש suggested the "pen of a quick scribe" simile.

[36] למלך could also be direct address, with ל being a vocative particle (hence, "I intone my compositions, O king"; see Dahood, *Psalms 1–50*, 271). This is grammatically possible, but not necessary.

[37] These beliefs come from the court because they are unstintingly laudatory; the reference to "the richest of the people" (עשירי עם) also points to this setting. For remarks on the social location of "official" religious texts in Israel (though without a mention of Ps. 45), see Jacques Berlinerblau, "Preliminary Remarks for the Sociological Study of Israelite 'Official Religion'," in Robert Chazan, William W. Hallo, and Lawrence H. Schiffman, eds., *Ki Baruch Hu: Ancient Near Eastern, Biblical, and Judaic Studies in Honor of Baruch A. Levine* (Winona Lake, IN: Eisenbrauns, 1999) 153–70.

or some such. The tongue is the instrument of oral communication, the pen or stylus of written communication. Ancient Near Eastern kings recounted their deeds in both oral and written (inscriptional or chronistic) narrative. The psalmist alludes to this practice and defines writing and speaking about the king as identical activities. This connection between oral and written praise of the king leads one to cite an observation that H. L. Ginsberg made several decades ago, when he noted that many of the psalms had the same communicative function in Israel as inscriptions had in neighboring cultures.[38] Ginsberg focused primarily on petition and thanksgiving texts, but his insight also applies to this psalm, despite its different genre. The psalmist's comparison of his tongue to a scribe's pen implies the further comparison of the orally delivered psalm to a written text (tongue:psalm::pen:text/inscription). Just as written texts, especially inscriptions, commemorating a king's deeds and celebrating his majesty build or confirm his status among his subjects (or even succeeding generations), so too does this psalm. That is, the singer evokes the written word for this description of a ritual, or more precisely, for the set of interlocking signs relating to kingship which this ritual explicates.[39] His psalm is the functional equivalent of a royal inscription, in that each commemorates the king's deeds and legitimates his rule, thus inviting the audience's assent to the royal claims.

The Body of the Ritual (vv. 3–16)
After the singer's self-introduction, the text next turns to direct address to the king and queen. The verses in the body of the psalm describe a series of movements by the principles in the wedding: the entrance of the king (vv. 3–10), and that of the queen (vv. 10–16). V. 10 marks the transition, and v. 16 brings the two parts together, with the queen and her ladies entering her new husband's palace. The psalm skillfully and unobtrusively marks out these movements of the dramatis personae.

---

[38] H. L. Ginsberg, "Psalms and Inscriptions of Petition and Acknowledgement," in *Louis Ginzberg Jubilee Volume* (New York: American Academy for Jewish Research, 1945) 159–71; also Patrick D. Miller ("Psalms and Inscriptions," in J. A. Emerton, ed., *Congress Volume: Vienna 1980* [VTSupp 32; Leiden: Brill, 1981] 311–32) further develops this point.

[39] For a discussion of the similarities between biblical and Levantine inscriptional narrative, see Simon B. Parker, *Stories in Scripture and Inscriptions: Comparative Studies on Narratives in Northwest Semitic Inscriptions and the Hebrew Bible* (Oxford: Oxford University Press, 1997).

The addresses to the monarchs are carefully structured with numerous corresponding elements, to be discussed presently. For now, though, the relevant question is what the psalm reveals about royal ritual. Commentators commonly explain the shifting images as reflections of the ritual behind the psalm.[40] If this hypothesis is correct, it means that the wedding involved the presentation of the king in military attire (vv. 5–6) and the queen in elaborate robes (v. 14), along with the offering of gifts (v. 13). The decisive gesture seems to be the queen's bowing before her husband (v. 12). The question is how far to press the imagery: for example, does the king sit on the throne; is he anointed again as at his coronation; does he ride into the area of the ritual? Even if not, the audience must nevertheless imagine their ruler doing these things.

Let us return here to Tambiah's definition of ritual, which, emphasizes that it is (1) culturally (= socially) constructed, (2) communicative, (3) patterned, (4) enacted in multiple media, and (5) performative in several ways. Psalm 45 evinces all these elements.

First, it is socially constructed. At the most obvious level, it reflects the political realities of Levantine states. Leaving aside for the moment the question of whether this poem comes from Israel or Judah,[41] it is worth noting that the text presupposes the social system of nested hierarchies that operated in these ancient societies. The monarchs sit atop a pyramid of free and unfree servitors, who nevertheless negotiate a place in society through their skill in role performance. So, various subjects bring gifts to the newlyweds (v. 13), and the "people" become subject to the king in the person of the queen.

The wedding ritual creates and reinforces a set of relationships in which rulers and subjects give (and rulers receive) gifts in order to mark out their roles. Likewise, the queen is her husband's subordinate, a relationship she enacts by bowing before him. Whatever may have been the realities of their day-to-day interactions,[42] the two now married partners are ideally unequal, though inseparable and interdependent. At the same time, only she has the right to bow to him

---

[40] E.g., Weiser, *Psalmen*, 243; Craigie, *Psalms 1–50*, 340.

[41] Many commentators attribute the psalm to the court of Samaria, based primarily on the mention of the "daughter of Tyre" in v. 13. For a thoroughgoing critique of this position, see Kraus, *Psalmen*, 333; we do not know enough about the origins of the Israelite and Judahite queens to decide the question.

[42] Note the role of Bathsheba in 1 Kings 1–2, for example. The psalm expresses a complex ideal, not necessarily the equally complex reality of royal families.

in this way at this time, which means that her subordination simultaneously marks her lofty status (much as the right to kowtow to the Chinese emperor was reserved for the high nobility and representatives of foreign rulers).[43] In other words, a simplistic understanding of this gesture as an indicator of one-way power relationships (male versus female) misses the complexity of the social reality that the gesture embodies. Here, the queen's body becomes the Queen's body in contradistinction to both her husband and her new subjects, as well as her erstwhile fellow-foreigners.

Second, following Tambiah, the ritual communicates information; it does not merely evoke feeling. Structure and imagery intertwine to transmit information about the ritual's participants and the political and religious realms to which they relate. The king's body lies at the center of this network of signification, for he is the well-trained warrior who conquers enemies and protects his subject, the fertile male whose impregnation of his wife leads to the success of his kingdom, and the near-divine figure who reigns "forever." I will develop this point when considering the language of the ritual.

Third, this communication arises through pattern. Note that the various elements of the description of the king find parallels in that of the queen. This meticulous structuring, which is more intricate than can easily be graphed, in itself indicates the order which the poem is trying to create. The text has the following elements:

- a. Address to the king (3)
- b. His attractiveness (4–5)
- c. The submission of the enemies (6)
- d. The reenacted coronation (7–8)
- e. His adornment (9a)
- f. His presentation (9b–10)
- a'. Address to the queen (11a)
- b'. Her attractiveness (12a)

---

[43] See James L. Hevia, "Sovereignty and Subject: Constituting Relations of Power in Qing Guest Ritual," in Angela Zito and Tani E. Barlow, *Body, Subject & Power in China* (Chicago: University of Chicago Press, 1994) 181–200. In Israel, too, "obeisance or deferential greeting... are employed to affirm or reaffirm relationships of direct subservience, not to affirm relationships which logically derive from these" (Mayer I. Gruber, *Aspects of Nonverbal Communication in the Ancient Near East* (StPohl 12; 2 vols.; Rome: Biblical Institute Press, 1980) 1. 195. The parade example of this appears in 2 Sam. 18:21–28, where the Cushite messenger bows to Joab, but not to David, while Joab and Ahimaaz, another high status male, bow to the king. The Cushite is not high-ranking enough to bow to David.

c'. The submission of the queen (11b, 12b–c)
d'. The offering of gifts (13)
e'. The queen's adornment (14)
f'. Her presentation (15–16)

While this pattern operates at the level of surface meaning (with vocabulary linkages being still more elaborate), outlining it illustrates the care with which the psalm and, presumably, the ritual behind it are structured. The pattern exhibits a movement from the king's body to the queen's and finally back again to them as a pair that will produce a never-ending line of rulers who will continue to celebrate the ritual.

Fourth, the ritual works in various media. These include not only language, but also gesture (bowing, offering gifts, perhaps sitting on a throne), the wearing of clothing, and the use of space (the ritual takes place in the royal palace; v. 16).

Fifth, the ritual is performed, and this performance creates a new reality for the king, his queen, and their kingdom. This performance operates at many levels, not only in the Austinian sense in which the words make the king and queen they describe, but also in Tambiah's other two senses. That is, the psalm presupposes the presence of an audience of courtiers and household servants and perhaps foreign emissaries escorting the queen. The ritual also embeds multiple layers of signification, as both the preceding and the follow detailed exegeses show.

The Ritual Exit (vv. 17–18)

The psalm concludes with another invocation of the king, for whom the singer wishes successful reproduction, which is crucial to the stability and prosperity of the state. The preservation of the dynasty will lead to the perpetual praising of the king's name: that is, his ability to produce heirs will be one of his principal achievements. The purpose of the locution, however, is to indicate the immortality of the king, at least in the restricted sense of the continuity of his dynasty. This limited sort of immortality is, as is well known, a commonplace idea in royal ideology of the ancient Levantine kingdoms,[44] and elsewhere in the Near East. In this sense, then, the

---

[44] See Levantine mentions of dynastic continuity and the preservation of the memories of past rulers in, e.g., KAI 1.1 from Byblos; 214.1 from Zençirli; 224.24–25; cf. KAI 35.2.

song's ending is not very different from the rituals for safe childbearing that are common throughout the ancient Near East but are surprisingly lacking in the Bible (though they must have existed in Israel), in that both seek to protect mother and child (and thus the family and its father) from danger.[45] This text focuses on male fecundity, to be sure, but also assumes the female's role. The exit from the ritual lays out the central theme of the psalm, and in some sense the coronation as a whole. In view is not merely the present king, but the immortal King, whose body the ritual helps create.

The Body of the King in Psalm 45

This reflection on the quasi-immortal body of the king leads now to a fuller consideration of the psalm's portrayal of it. V. 3 begins with a direct address to the king, claiming that he is more beautiful than all other humans. The "proof" of this statement comes in the following verses describing his lips, arms, attire, and stance. At the same time, one should note that these statements need not refer to any particular king's actual physical appearance. That is, the physiognomy of the king in the psalm reflects an ideal, not necessarily a picture drawn from life. Not merely "factual," these statements fill performative roles; that is, they make the "real" king celebrating the ritual into the "ideal" king depicted by the ritual. He apparently enters the locale of the ritual—or at least its audience imagines him doing so—armed and prepared for battle, the successful conclusion of which the queen enacts when she submits to him as the representative of foreign lands (Section c'). The entire ritual makes the king into the warrior he seeks to be. To be such, he must master the skills of the warrior (riding, fighting) and must look the part. Now, claiming that the psalm presents an ideal body prompts a question: in the absence of Israelite graphic representations of the king, how can we be sure of this? Partial confirmation comes from the fact that, as will emerge soon, the king's body resembles that of

---

[45] For a survey of the literature, see Walter Farber, "Lamashtu," *RLA* 6 (1980–83) 439–42. Cf. idem, *Schlaf, Kindchen, Schlaf: Mesopotamische Baby-Beschwörungen und Rituale* (Winona Lake: Eisenbrauns, 1989); idem, "Magic at the Cradle: Babylonian and Assyrian Lullabies," *Anthropos* 85 (1990) 139–48; for a tantalizing Iron Age Palestinian equivalent, see Mordechai Cogan, "A Lamashtu Plaque from the Judaean Shephelah," *IEJ* 45 (1995) 155–61. A possible Israelite allusion to such a rite may be the enigmatic text Exod 4:24–26.

Yahweh's, not surprisingly since the deity creates the king to serve him.[46]

At this point, however, it seems useful to consider which parts of the king's body come under consideration and how they do so. Obviously, any part of his physiognomy was potentially available for the poem. Yet the text focuses upon those that underscore his role as speaker (hence, giver of laws, commander) and warrior.

To begin, v. 3 speaks of the king's lips (שפתותיך), upon which "graciousness is poured." "Lips" may bear words of truth or falsity (Ps. 17:1; 59:13). For the king, they are instruments of repentance (Ps. 89:35) and justice (Isa. 11:4). In Ps. 45, however, the most immediate connections of v. 3 are with v. 2: just as the psalmist's tongue (לשון) can record the king's deeds, so can the latter's lips make that deed.[47] "Graciousness" (חן) apparently means here "eloquence," as in Prov. 22:11.[48] The very condensed style of the psalm does not allow one to move much beyond the dictionary definition of the words here toward the "encyclopedia" of the terminology of Israelite eloquence, in the parlance of semiotics.[49] That is, the text does not spell out which aspects of kingly eloquence are under consideration, whether his ability to frame a prayer (as in 1 Kings 8), his ability to give prebattle speeches (as David does at various times), his astute

---

[46] On the relevance of Mesopotamian myth to this issue, see John Van Seters, "The Creation of Man and the Creation of the King," ZAW 101 (1989) 333–342; for a similar idea in Neo-Assyria, see Eva Cancik-Kirschbaum, "Konzeption und Legitimation von Herrschaft in neuassyrischer Zeit," WdO 26 (1995) 5–20 (on VS 24.92, which describes the formation and investment of the king). See also A. Wendell Bowes, "The Basilomorphic Conception of Deity in Israel and Mesopotamia," in K. Lawson Younger, William W. Hallo, and Bernard F. Batto, eds., *The Biblical Canon in Comparative Perspective* (Scripture in Context 4; Lewiston: Mellen, 1991) 235–75.

[47] On the pair lašānu/šaptu in Ugaritic, see KTU 1.103.31–32, an omen text. The absence of the tongue and lower lip on an offering indicate disaster. I cite this text only to indicate that the word pair did exist in Northwest Semitic literature and that it had a variety of meanings.

[48] See BDB, 336. The best discussion is in Mulder (*Studies on Psalm 45*, 102), who cites Prov. 22:11, חן שפתיו רעהו מלך ("Whoever has graciousness on his lips, has the king as a friend"). The only other appearance of חן/לשון (+ שפה), where, however, the word pair (now a triad) is broken up by the content of the text.

[49] On "encyclopedic" meanings, see Umberto Eco, *A Theory of Semiotics* (Indianapolis: Indiana University Press, 1976) 98–100; and idem, *Kant and the Platypus* (New York: Harcourt Brace, 2000) 224–79. Words as signs relate to many other words as signs, always in ways not easily captured by brief denotative definitions. Yet the psalm at hand does not allow a full description of this.

handling of court cases (1 Kings 3), or his skill on some other occasion demanding appropriate words in view. Choosing among these options remains impossible, and the ambiguity of the mention of royal eloquence allows for all possible occasions for his speaking. More to the point, though, the psalmist points toward the king's reputation for gracious speech of all kinds. While any given king might be a poor speaker, the ideal King, which the real king becomes in this ritual (as Austin would have it), plays the role of orator skillfully.[50] Since reputation is the result of the successful acting out of roles, performed according to the rules of culturally-determined and accepted good behavior,[51] including speaking, the mention of the king's eloquence builds his prestige and thus underscores his right to rule (and, here, to marry).

Ps. 45:4, meanwhile, moves from the king's lip to his thigh/waist (ירך; where he wears a sword, presumably on his left side, as in the Assyrian and Levantine statuary of the first millennium)[52] and then in v. 5 his right hand (ימינך). The emphasis falls upon the king's skill at chariotry and archery. What is difficult to explain here is not that a king's military prowess should be celebrated in this idealized way (regardless of the achievements of the actual king),[53] but rather (1) that it should be so in a wedding context, and (2) that the language used should be so clearly evocative of portrayals of Yahweh.

The first point has led Mulder to describe vv. 4–9 as speaking "of the king himself, without a reference to his wedding...."[54] This distinction is unnecessary, for the text argues for, or rather insists upon, the king's suitability to marry, hence to reproduce, to sire the dynasty, to rule. The king, because he is a skilled warrior, deserves to marry the queen and to excite her desire. Since she is part of

---

[50] See also the discussion in Dale Launderville, *Piety and Politics: The Dynamics of Royal Authority in Homeric Greece, Biblical Israel, and Old Babylonian Mesopotamia* (Grand Rapids: Eerdmans, 2003) 60–69.

[51] See Michael Herzfeld, *The Poetics of Manhood: Contest and Identity in a Cretan Mountain Village* (Princeton: Princeton University Press, 1985); idem, "The Poeticity of the Commonplace," in Michael Herzfeld and Lucio Melazzo, eds., *Semiotic Theory and Practice* (2 vols.; Berlin and New York: Mouton/de Gruyter, 1988) 1. 383–91.

[52] See the plates in T. A. Madhloom, *The Chronology of Neo-Assyrian Art* (London: Athlone, 1970) esp. pls. i, ii, vii, xxxiv, xxxv, xxxvi, xxxviii, xxxix. A right-handed warrior would naturally wear his weapon on the left to allow easy drawing.

[53] Again, this assumes that the psalms reflect more than one temporal setting, but see n. 19 above.

[54] Mulder, *Psalm 45*, 23; similarly, Gerstenberger, *Psalms Part I*, 188.

the song's audience, the portrayal of her husband as a great warrior serves to entice her to his side.

More provocatively, the text describes the king's body in terms otherwise appropriate to the body of Yahweh.⁵⁵ For example, the stock phrase הוד והדר refers to Yahweh in Pss. 96:6, 104:1, 111:3, 145:5, and 1 Chron. 16:27, and to the king in Ps. 21:6 (where God is said to confer הוד והדר upon him). The reference in v. 6 to the king's arrows is reminiscent of numerous poetic references to God as an archer.⁵⁶ The choice of language otherwise characteristic of the deity indicates that the king is no mere mortal, but a being approaching deity. This will become clearer later in the psalm, and in other psalms. A central feature of the royal propaganda is thus the extraordinary, godlike status of the king.⁵⁷

V. 5 is the most problematic, for the textual traditions vary widely. The MT must be incorrect, at least in part. The first two words (הֲתָעוּף עֵינֶיךָ) as pointed are grammatically impossible (the first also being a dittograph from v. 4). The LXX's καὶ ἔντεινον καὶ κατευοδοῦ ("both move forward and succeed!") reflects the same consonantal text as MT, but reads both words as imperative verbs, the first as the Hiphil imperative of דרך (*wahadrîk*), and the second as the Qal of צלח.⁵⁸ This is probably correct, and it means that the MT's apparent reference to bodily display vanishes.

The next clause is more complex and bears directly on the topic at hand. MT's רכב על דבר אמת ("ride upon a word of truth") is not

---

⁵⁵ On the resemblances between the king's and the deity's bodies, see Podella, *Lichtkleid JHWHs*; and William P. Brown, *Seeing the Psalms: A Theology of Metaphor* (Louisville: Westminster/John Knox, 2002) 167–95, esp. 187–93.

⁵⁶ See Num. 24:8; Job 6:4; Pss. 7:14, 18:15 (= 2 Sam. 22:15), 38:3, 58:8, 64:8, 144:6; Ezek. 5:16 (equals famine); and Zech. 9:14. See also Dahood, *Psalms 1–50*, 115, 272, who refers to Aqhat's possession of the magic bow. On God as the warrior in the Psalter, see Martin Klingbeil, *Yahweh Fighting from Heaven: God as Warrior and as God of Heaven in the Hebrew Psalter and Ancient Near Eastern Iconography* (OBO 169: Göttingen: Vandenhoeck & Ruprecht, 1999).

⁵⁷ How to formulate the king's place? He is more than a man, even a powerful man. The application to him of deific language must be more than "flattery," as one reads in the handbooks. The king is a liminal being; but even "betweenness" (with Yahweh on one end of a continuum, ordinary mortals on the other, and the king somewhere in the middle) does not quite get at the Israelite idea. See further below.

⁵⁸ But see C. F. Whitley, "Textual and Exegetical Observations on Ps 45, 4–7," *ZAW* 98 (1986) 278, who (incorrectly) understands this as a noun. See also RSV, "In your majesty ride forth victoriously," which apparently takes צלח and רכב as a hendiadys and inserts a sentence initial preposition ב.

the equivalent of LXX's βασίλευε ἕνεκεν ἀληθείας ("act as a king on the basis of truth"; = מלך על אמת [Qal]).[59] It is difficult to explain either reading as the result of a simple copyist's mistake for the other. It may be that the two versions reflect different performance traditions and that both variants are equally old. To be sure, both agree in emphasizing the centrality of language to the king's successful rule. Probably, however, the jarring, extravagant metaphor of riding upon a word of truth (rather than upon a horse, or a cloud,[60] as Yahweh does) seemed too contrived to the tradents behind the Hebrew texts used by the LXX translators. The MT reading seems preferable, if one must choose, precisely because it is less prosaic.[61]

If this is correct, the poet has daringly returned to the theme of v. 3, the king's extraordinary facility with speech, making this skill also into a sign of military prowess, and no ordinary prowess, but one like Yahweh's. Any mortal can ride a horse, but the king mounts a nobler steed. Concomitantly, his speaking (hence an allusion to his vocal organs) signifies his rule.

Nowhere is the king's status more elevated than in the direct address of vv. 7–8: כסאך אלהים עולם ועד ("Your throne, Elohim, endures forever and ever"). The MT/LXX text, though grammatically unproblematic, has provoked a variety of emendations and/or

---

[59] The key problem is LXX βασίλευε instead of MT רכב: βασιλεύειν usually translated the Qal, Hiphil, or Hophal of מלך, or a construction with the noun מֶלֶךְ. It may also render ישׁב ("to sit, reside"), as in 2 Kings 15:5.

[60] On which see Moshe Weinfeld, "'Rider of the Clouds' and 'Gatherer of the Clouds'," *JANES* 5 (1973) 421–26; Frank Moore Cross, *Canaanite Myth and Hebrew Epic* (Cambridge: Harvard University Press, 1973) 156–63.

[61] It is also possible that the clause could be repointed and rendered "mount the temple cella (בביר) of truth." In Ugaritic (though apparently not in Hebrew), the root R-K-B refers to the scaling of a building (by a king, incidentally) in the *Kirta Epic* (KTU 1.14.2.74 and 1.14.4.166; *la ṣuri magdāli rkub*). The celebration of rituals atop buildings was, of course, commonplace in the Levant. Note, for example, Sennacherib's depictions of the siege of Lachish (see David Ussishkin, *The Conquest of Lachish by Sennacherib* [Tel Aviv: Tel Aviv University, Institute of Archaeology, 1982]) or the story of Kirta (already cited). Another option, again repointing the consonants, which I regard as still less likely but nevertheless grammatically possible, would be to translate the clause as "mount (sexually) the steppe of the maidservant." R-K-B can refer to sexual intercouse in Akkadian (*Šumma Izbu* 194.33; BWL 218.16; see *AHw* 3. 944). Having intercouse in the steppe is a theme not only in the "Cow of Sin," but in KTU 1.5.5.18 and 1.6.2.20 (the word for steppe is *dubru* = Hebrew *dōber*; cf. Isa. 5:17 and Mic. 2:12). אמה would be an old spelling for *amat*, "handmaid" (later אמה). Again, while I regard this reading as possible and attractive in a wedding setting, it would destroy the parallelism with the other military metaphors in the verse and therefore seems a poorer reading.

repointings, primarily because of the "difficulty of the sense in context," as Craigie puts it.[62] King, after noting the apologetic nature of many of these interpretations, cites various instances of אלהים denoting beings other than (and subordinate to) the chief god of Israel.[63] However, in view of the influence of Egyptian models on the court language of Judah,[64] it should not be surprising that an Egyptianizing motif of a "divine" king[65] might find a place in the marriage liturgy of a king there or in the northern kingdom. On the other hand, this elevated view of the monarch may be indigenous to Israel/Judah. In either case, avoiding the simplest translation of the verse could only be a response to apologetic needs. Granting that the king is Elohim—a title that could denote a range of ontic possibilities—we should ask which of these is in view. What would such an epithet mean?

To address that question, one should note that the psalm does not offer any speculation on the superhuman nature of the royal body. Rather, it speaks of the king as a skilled soldier and now one sitting on a throne wielding a scepter of uprightness (שבט מישר; cf. Akkadian *ḫattu išartu* and *ḫattu mišarim*),[66] that is, a royal scepter (שבט מלכותך). The emphasis of this ritual language is on the king's display, particularly during the coronation ceremony, which the psalmist here recalls. Note the parallel actions of the king in Ps. 45 and 1 Kings 1:44–46:

---

[62] Craigie, *Psalms 1–50*, 337; he follows Dahood (*Psalms 1–50*, 273) in repointing כסא as a verb. Weiser (*Psalmen*, 243) "solves" the problem by translating אלהים as "Göttlicher."

[63] King, *Psalm 45(44)*, 75–83.

[64] See J. J. M. Roberts, "Whose Child Is This? Reflections on the Speaking Voice in Isaiah 9:5," *HTR* 90 (1997) 115–30. But see Siegfried Morenz, "Ägyptische und davidische Königstitulatur," in idem, *Religion und Geschichte des Alten Ägyptens* (Cologne: Böhlau, 1975) 401–3.

[65] The current consensus among Egyptologists appears to be that the Pharaoh was "divine" only provisionally, i.e., primarily after death. He could be called a "god" (*nṯr*) "in verschiedenen Aspekten (z.B. in der Ähnlichkeit der Handlungen)...." (Mechthild Schade-Busch, *Zur Königsideologie Amenophis' III.: Analyse der Phraseologie historischer Texte der Voramarnazeit* [Hildesheimer Ägyptologische Beiträge; Hildesheim: Gerstenberg, 1992] 75). Admittedly Schade-Busch's evidence predates this psalm by several centuries, but, on the other hand, it is unclear just when the courtly language of Egypt was borrowed by the Hebrew monarchies.

[66] For an ample discussion of the scepter and terminology for it in Neo-Assyria, see J. P. J. Olivier, "The Scepter of Justice and Ps. 45:7b," *JNWSL* 7 (1979) 45–54; see also *CAD* 10/2 (1977) 118.

Ps. 45
Riding (v. 5)
Sitting on the throne (v. 7)[67]
Being anointed (v. 8)
Public rejoicing (שׂמח; v. 9)

Blessing of the dynasty (vv. 17–18)

1 Kings 1:44–47
Riding (the royal mule) (v. 44)
Being anointed (v. 45)
Public rejoicing (שׂמח; v. 45)
Sitting on the throne (v. 46)
Blessing of the dynasty (v. 47)

While the two texts do not position the elements in exactly the same order, the psalmist clearly has in mind the royal coronation. This reference back to another ritual moment in the king's life makes sense, because the coronation marks and constitutes the progression of kingship to a new generation, just as the marriage leads to the conception of a legitimate heir. The element missing from the psalmist's recounting of it is the mention of the Davidic dynasty.

The extraordinarily detailed mention of the coronation ritual must point toward the intimate connection between royal marriage and the preservation of the dynasty and state. (The same consideration also explains the mention of the martial features of the monarchy.) Concomitantly, the notice of the king's status as Elohim places his sexual behavior above the realm of ordinary intercourse, if not in the realm of the gods (as a so-called sacred marriage), then at least in a realm of its own.

Picking up, then, the connection between rule and sexuality (and thus the royal body), the psalmist points toward the coronation ritual at precisely the point when he calls the king Elohim. This would suggest that the king becomes Elohim at this point during the coronation, that his being such is a situational condition, not a permanent one. In a polygamous society, where several princes are potential heirs, the delay of divinization to the time of coronation avoids obvious intellectual and even political complications. The psalm's diviniza-

---

[67] The mention of the throne implies the king's sitting on it, but the verse does not spell this out explicitly, nor does it need to do so.

tion of the king is not mere "flattery," but neither is it a case of ontological speculation. Rather, it is a statement about a relationship between king and God, on one side, and the king and his subjects, on the other. He is אלהים when he displays himself on the throne, bearing the insignia of power. Evoking this status of Elohimhood, so to speak, during his wedding moves the king into such a state again. But, again, the psalmist does not engage in ontological speculation, but rather emphasizes the king's position before his subjects, to whom he is (not, "is like") Elohim.

This status appears to vanish in v. 9, where the focus tightens onto the sex act of the king and his bride (although it is not impossible that, since divine figures can copulate in many Near Eastern mythologies, the connection between superhuman status and sexuality seems incongruous only to modern readers).[68] Here the emphasis is on the king's odor, or rather, that of his clothes. Adorned with the spices myrrh, cardamum (or aloes?),[69] and cassia (מר ואהלות קציעות), the king displays himself before his wife to be and presumably his own retinue. The pair of spices אהלות/ים and מר could be aphrodisiacs. Note Song 4:14 and especially Prov. 7:17, where the seductress is said to "bedeck my bed with myrrh, aloes (אהלים), and cinnamon." While the third member of the trio of spices differs in these two passages, it appears clear enough that many Israelites thought that the spreading of spices enhanced the sexual experience. The use of spices in the wedding ritual thus serves to stimulate sexual desire, or at least to signify its importance to the king and queen (and those who know that the spices are present, hence, the audience of the psalm).

To be sure, in Ps. 45:9 not the marriage bed (and eventually a naked body reclining on it) but the clothed royal body itself smells of various spices. Among other uses, including as medicine or

---

[68] One might duly note, of course, that there is nothing incongruous about a Near Eastern אל/אלוהים engaging in intercourse. Finding Israelite evidence for this is more difficult, however—hence the present reading of the verse.

[69] The LXX reading שתחכאתס seems to reflect a reading לם ("cardamum"; cf. Gen 37:25, 43:11), probably a corruption of the MT reading. Note the transliteration of אהלות as קולא in Song 4:14 LXX, which would indicate the elision of ה in the Hebrew dialect known to the translators (cf. אהרון → Ααρων). This could have led to confusion with לם (with a prothetic aleph?). This also indicates that the meaning of אהלות was lost among at least some of the translators whose work became the LXX.

embalming chemicals,⁷⁰ these spices may serve to enhance lovemaking, as the Song of Songs and Proverbs passages show. Speaking of spices in this context alerts the poem's audience to what will shortly take place in the royal bedchambers. Odors could be a sign to an Israelite audience of the role of the king as procreator and ruler. This depiction is thus a way of simultaneously displaying and hiding the king's body. Interestingly, it also underscores the necessity of the king's enticing the queen into his bed: the text seems to assume that she will be attractive to him, but not vice versa (she needs no spices!). His attractiveness arises from the recitation of his (idealized) deeds and the display and now adornment of his body. The hearers of the poem, the celebrants of the marriage, know that their monarch will soon engage in various sexual activities, presumably that he will be nude, that he will (obviously) no longer carry about the godlike trappings of power (scepter, sword), and yet that his activities in bed will decide the political stability of the kingdom as a whole.⁷¹ The ritual that the king performs presages and defines a later sexual "performance" that will allow the propagation of the dynasty, the stability of the kingdom, and ultimately the begettal of a new king who will become, in turn, Elohim. The queen, meanwhile, enters the royal harem.⁷² Yet, the psalm makes none of this explicit, engaging in a kind of regal fan dance that simultaneously reveals and hides the king's sexuality.

To summarize, then, the king of Israel was a godlike figure who became such at his coronation. He was a mighty warrior who claimed far-flung sovereignty by virtue of his superior warriorly skills. He thus establishes himself as a powerful male by winning battles and marrying foreign princesses, who serve as booty at one level, but at another also become the progenetrices of the dynasty. The foreign becomes the sine qua non of the native: without the foreign queen there is no Israelite king. The female is simultaneously the counterpoising opposite and the necessary precondition of the male.

---

⁷⁰ See Federico de Romanis, *Cassia, Cinnamomo, Ossidiana: Uomini e merci tra Oceano Indiano et Mediterraneo* (Rome: Bretschneider, 1996) 43 n. 40 and passim.

⁷¹ Interestingly, the psalm does not make much of the possible association of the sex of the king as אלהים with the *hieros gamos*.

⁷² On פבימה as "harem" in v. 14, see Abraham Malamat, "Is There a Word for the Royal Harem in the Bible? The *Inside* Story," in David P. Wright, David Noel Freedman, and Avi Hurvitz, eds., *Pomegranates and Golden Bells: Studies in Biblical, Jewish, and Near Eastern Ritual, Law, and Literature in Honor of Jacob Milgrom* (Winona Lake, IN: Eisenbrauns, 1995) 785–87.

A Related Text, Song of Songs 5:10-16

If Ps. 45 evokes a set of signs related to human love, procreation, fecundity, and thus social stability, the same is true of the pericope I wish to consider next, Song of Songs 5:10-16, a *wasf* for the book's male lover. Although the Song as a whole probably dates later than the Iron Age,[73] units within it plausibly date earlier. This is particularly true of 5:10-16, a description of the male lover's body as a statue, a text with its closest parallels coming from Neo-Assyrian love songs for deities. It seems highly unlikely that such a unit could have originated during the post-exilic era, when Israelites took aniconism for granted. The fact that a later editor could use the image as part of an elaborate network of images of a male body indicates only that the unit had gained some status and that its background could be overlooked.

Before analyzing the text in detail, we should note that Song of Songs does draw on ancient Near Eastern conventions of love poetry dating to the second millennium or earlier.[74] It uses these images to construct an elaborate set of relationships among the male lover, the female lover, and Solomon (who may or may not be the same as the male lover).[75] In particular, 3:6-11 portrays Solomon riding a litter to gather in the beautiful female lover; this text explicitly evokes the royal marriage. (However, the word אפריון in 3:9 may be a loan-word from Greek φορεῖον).[76]

A more direct pointer to the royal identity of the lover appears in the *wasf* for the male in 5:10-16. The text reads:

---

[73] But see the arguments in Marvin Pope, *Song of Songs* (AB 7C; Garden City, NY: Doubleday, 1977) 22-33.

[74] See Michael V. Fox, *The Song of Songs and the Ancient Egyptian Love Songs* (Madison, WI: University of Wisconsin Press, 1985) esp. 191-93; idem, "The Cairo Love Songs," *JAOS* 100 (1980) 101-9; but cf. Virginia Lee Davis, "Remarks on Michael V. Fox's 'The Cairo Love Songs'," *JAOS* 100 (1980) 111-14.

[75] Against identifying the two characters, see Roland Murphy, *Song of Songs* (Hermeneia; Minneapolis: Fortress, 1990) 83-85; but Iain Provan, "The Terrors of the Night: Love, Sex, and Power in Song of Songs 3," in J. I. Packer and Sven Soderlund, eds., *The Way of Wisdom* (Waltke FS; Grand Rapids: Zondervan, 2000) 150-67, esp. 157-58.

[76] So most commentaries; but see Ernest Klein, *A Comprehensive Etymological Dictionary of the Hebrew Language for Readers of English* (Jerusalem: Carta/University of Haifa, 1987) 49; not all his arguments are probative, however. Also see J. Cheryl Exum, "Seeing Solomon's Palanquin (Song of Songs 3:6-11)," *BibInt* 11 (2003) 301-16, esp. 311.

¹⁰My lover is dazzling and ruddy,
outstanding among a myriad.
¹¹His head is gold, pure gold
his hair palm fronds,
black as a raven.
¹²His eyes are like doves on watercourses,
washed⁷⁷ in milk, set in place.
¹³His cheeks are like beds of spice
putting forth perfumes,
his lips (like) lotuses,
dripping flowing myrrh.
¹⁴His hands are rods of gold,
encrusted with Tarshish stones.
His belly is ivory work,
studded with sapphires.
¹⁵His haunches are pillars of alabaster,
resting on gold sockets.
His appearance is like Lebanon's,
choice like cedars.
¹⁶His palate is sweetness,
and his entirety is delight.
This is my lover, this is my friend,
O daughters of Jerusalem!

דודי צח ואדום
דגול מרבבה
ראשו כתם פז
קוצותיו תלתלים
שחרות כעורב
עיניו כיונים על אפיקי מים
רחצות בחלב ישבות על מלאת
לחיו כערוגת הבשם
⁷⁸מגדלות מרקחים
שפתותיו שושנים
נטפות מור עבר
ידיו גלילי זהב
ממלאים בתרשיש
מעיו עשת שן
מעלפת ספירים
שוקיו עמודי שש
מיסדים על אדני פז
מראהו כלבנון
בחור כארזים
חכו ממתקים
וכלו מחמדים
זה דודי וזה רעי
בנות ירושלם

4:1–5:1 includes the male's praise of the female lover, and 5:2–9 the expression of the separation of the two lovers. The juxtaposition of these two pericopes creates an atmosphere of frustrated bodily connection, which mirrors the delay in consummation that gives the Song as a whole much of its dramatic power. Surrounding 4:1–5:9, then, with the descriptions of Solomon's litter in 3:6–11 and the body of the male lover here in 5:10–16 highlights the desirability and impressiveness of the male body for which the female lover—and her audience, the "daughters of Jerusalem" and all subsequent readers—longs.

5:10–16 form a unit understandable in its own terms, but 5:9 places the depiction of male beauty in the *wasf* in a larger context by having the Jerusalemite women ask about his superiority: "How

---

[77] Murphy (*Song of Songs*, 166) adds שניו ("his teeth") here, on the assumption that the "teeth" are white and set in a row (cf. Song 4:2, 6:6). This is possible but unnecessary.

[78] Read the Piel of גדל here (see Murphy, *Song of Songs*, 166; Pope, *Song of Songs*, 540); MT means "towers."

does your lover differ from (another) lover, most beautiful of women" (מה דודך מדוד היפה בנשים)? As in many cases in biblical narrative, women here certify the male as truly such.

Turning to the *wasf* itself, I make two observations: first, as scholars have long recognized, 5:10–16 portray the male lover as a statue;[79] and second, the *wasf* echoes both the form and content of similar Mesopotamian texts that refer to deities.[80] What is the purpose of this imagery, then?

The Song's sudden transformation of the male lover into a statue is surprising. Since the few surviving Iron Age Levantine statues depict deities or rulers—and this would be especially true of one covered with gold, as here—it seems unlikely that any statue of a commoner would be in view here.[81] Either we are dealing with a real statue of a king or deity, or else the poet has transferred regal or divine imagery to a commoner in love. The first option fits better with the evidence already cited, and the second would call for much more elaborate explanation.

In a recent essay, Martti Nissinen has argued for a close parallel between the Song of Songs and an Akkadian love poem regarding the deities Nabû and Tašmetu, which is attested in a Neo-Assyrian copy.[82] In addition to the interplay of references to Nabû and "the king" (*šarru*), who must be the same person, this hymn resembles the Song of Songs in mentioning gardens, the elusiveness of love, the incomparability of the female lover; there are even a chariot (*narkabtu eššetu*) and other martial imagery (r. 4). Again, the fact that the lovers here are deities spoken of at times in royal terms confirms

---

[79] Murphy, *Song of Songs*, 172; Pope, *Song of Songs*, 539; Helmer Ringgren and Otto Kaiser, *Das Hohe Lied-Klagelieder-Das Buch Esther* (3d ed.; ATD 16.2; Göttingen: Vandenhoeck & Ruprecht, 1981) 278; Oswald Loretz, *Studien zur althebräischen Poesie 1: Das althebräische Liebeslied* (AOAT; Neukirchen-Vluyn: Neukirchener, 1971) 36.

[80] Although sometimes divine imagery describes Mesopotamian kings. A signal example is from the Epic of Tukulti-ninurta 1 (thirteenth century BCE); see the translation in Benjamin R. Foster, *Before the Muses: An Anthology of Akkadian Literature* (2 vols.; Bethesda: CDL, 1996) 1. 212–30; and the unpublished critical edition of Peter Machinist.

[81] See e.g., Ora Negbi, *Canaanite Gods in Metal: An Archaeological Study of Ancient Syro-Palestinian Figurines* (Tel Aviv: Tel Aviv University Institute of Archaeology, 1976).

[82] The text is TIM 9.54 = SAA 3.14. See Martti Nissinen, "Love Lyrics of Nabû and Tašmetu: An Assyrian Song of Songs?" in Manfried Dietrich and Ingo Kottsieper, eds., *"Und Mose schrieb dieses Lied auf"* (Loretz Festschrift; AOAT 250; Münster: Ugarit, 1998) 585–634; idem, "Akkadian Rituals and Poetry of Divine Love," in R. M. Whiting, ed., *Mythology and Mythologies* (Melammu Symposia 2; Helsinki: Neo-Assyrian Text Corpus Project, 2001) 93–136.

the notion that a sliding scale between the royal and divine bodies exists for Mespotamia. So, the Song of Song's depiction of the male lover as a statue makes sense in an environment in which human males (specifically, kings) and gods share the same kind of body.

Why, then, does the poet of the Song employ this imagery, and how does he or she do so? Notice that Mesopotamian *wasf*s generally refer to male deities. For example, KAR 307[83] describes a male deity beginning, as in Song of Songs 5, from the head and moving downward to his groin. This text, and a similar one describing Dumuzi in SAA 3.38 (r. 9–17), differ in detail from the Song of Songs text, and they depart more freely from the statues that ground them in physical reality. Like the *wasf* in Song of Songs 5, these texts create a body of gold, silver, precious stones, palm fronds, and aromatics. Unlike the Song of Songs, the Mesopotamian texts also include internal organs and bodily fluids. A significant contrast appears in the Mesopotamian texts' mention of the golden semen (*riḫûtu*) and boxthorn pubic hair of the god, elements that conspicuously lack an explicit parallel in the biblical text (although the יד ["hand"] of Song of Songs 5:14 may be a euphemism for penis[84] or at least a double entendre).[85] These Mesopotamian texts also make elaborate astrological and cosmological associations between the divine body parts and observable natural phenomena, as one might expect of speculation on divine bodies. This element is absent from the Song of Songs. That is, the song picks up the divine imagery, applies it to the human lover, all without making the final leap of deifying the human being. The lover is not a god, but his body and bodily actions resemble those of a god.

Before asking what significance the Song's use of the *wasf* has, we should also note that another aspect of divine statuary in Mesopotamia is its placement and then ritual vivification in a garden (*kīru*) located

---

[83] = SAA 3.37 (in Alasdair Livingstone, *Court Poetry and Literary Miscellanea* [SAA 3; Helsinki: Helsinki University Press, 1989] 99–100).

[84] Cf. Isa. 57:8–10; KTU 1.23.33–34 illustrating that *yad* can equal "penis" in Northwest Semitic texts.

[85] One should not, by the way, attribute this absence of explicitly sexual imagery in the Song to any squeamishness about genitalia, but rather to the book's brilliantly coy technique about depicting sex acts, bodily fluids, and whatnot as other things. On this practice, see for example, Abraham Mariaselvam, *The Song of Songs and Ancient Tamil Love Poems: Poetry and Symbolism* (Rome: Pontifical Biblical Institute, 1988) 222–27 and the commentaries. See also André LaCocque, *Romance She Wrote: A Hermeneutical Essay on Song of Songs* (Harrisburg, PA: TPI, 1998) 123 n. 26.

in the temple precincts. The garden became a model of the cosmos itself,[86] and the placement of the statue there signifies the location of the deity in the universe.[87] Song 6:2 retains this idea when it claims that the lover, that is, the statue, "has gone down to his garden" (דודי ירד לגנו). Here again, however, the biblical text has transferred divine imagery to a human being.

Thus, when the Song of Songs employs the basic idea of a description of a male body beginning with the head and proceeding downward, it adopts imagery suitable for a deity, though it must make certain accommodations. Such accomodations would fit what we have seen elsewhere in the Bible about Israelite conceptions of a king, though hardly of any other human being. We saw already in the royal psalms that the bodies of the king and Yahweh resemble each other closely, that the two are moving points on a continuum. Like the deity, whose son he is, the king trains for war, strikes his enemies, extends his reach over the sea, and so on. The Psalms feel free to employ divine imagery for the human king in a way inappropriate for other mortals.[88] This means that the burden of proof lies with anyone who would argue that the statue of Song 5:10–16 portrays a commoner. We are left with two choices, then: either the statue in this section of the Song is of a god, or it is of a king. The prohibition of divine images in Israel might pose a problem for the former interpretation, though not necessarily so if the text dates from the Iron Age II.[89] A more serious problem with designating this a divine statue is that nothing else in the Song seems to depict the male lover as a deity, myth and ritual interpretations of the text notwithstanding.[90] This leaves the king as the figure whom the statue

---

[86] See Lawrence Stager, "Jerusalem and the Garden of Eden," *EI* 26 (1999) 183*–94*.

[87] On the Mesopotamian manufacture of images and the rituals attendant upon their installation, see the articles in Michael B. Dick, ed., *Born in Heaven, Made on Earth: The Making of the Cult Image in the Ancient Near East* (Winona Lake, IN: Eisenbrauns, 1999). I owe this reference to Ms. Catherine Beckerleg.

[88] For a good discussion of this, see Thomas Podella, *Das Lichtkleid JHWHs: Untersuchungen zur Gestalthaftigkeit Gottes im Alten Testament und seiner altorientalischen Umwelt* (FAT 15; Tübingen: Mohr/Siebeck, 1996) 252–64.

[89] See the essays in Karel van der Toorn, ed., *The Image and the Book: Iconic Cults, Aniconism, and the Rise of Book Religion in Israel and the Ancient Near East* (Leuven: Peeters, 1997), esp. Herbert Niehr, "In Search of YHWH's Cult Statue in the First Temple," 73–95; and Dick, *Born in Heaven, Made on Earth*.

[90] See Pope, *Song of Songs*, 145–53.

represents, and the sliding scale we see in the psalms between the divine and royal bodies explains how the *wasf* in Song 5 can use imagery that in Mesopotamia is especially appropriate for a divine image to describe the body of the king (that is, the male lover) precisely because the king and the deity are so closely related. The sliding scale between king and god can be documented to some degree for Mesopotamia,[91] and so one should not be surprised to find it in Israel as well, just as in Ps. 45.

Coronation Psalms: Psalms 2, 110, 72, and 101

If Ps. 45 reflects the importance of conceptions of the king's body impinging on his marriage and procreative activities and Song 5 evokes divine love songs for a human, kinglike figure, then it should not be surprising that the body also attracts attention in the psalms related to the royal coronation (also in the background of Ps. 45), another major rite of passage in the king's life, and one closely related to marriage. Two psalms—2 and 110—are generally treated as coronation psalms; Pss. 72 and 101 probably fit this category as well. Pss. 2 and 110 are undoubtedly from the coronation of the Judahite king, since they both mention Zion.[92] Both also mention the royal birth (via ritual) to divine sonship (at the coronation), and so they can stand together as evidence for views of his body during the period of the monarchy. They bear so many close resemblances that it seems most economical to assume that they are songs from the same ritual cycle. The less economical alternative would be to suppose that one was used for one coronation, the other for another, while both were somehow nevertheless preserved for future generations. If this is correct, moreover, Ps. 2 apparently comes later in the ritual than Ps. 110, since the latter seems to indicate the moment at which the king becomes "son of God," whereas the former presumes that status and calls upon the participants to offer obeisance ("kiss the son"). Both psalms, in any case, understand the coronation to be the moment at which God begets the king, bestowing on him a body fit to rule.

---

[91] See n. 45 above.
[92] But see the reservations on Psalm 110 of Starbuck, *Court Oracles*, 152. Whether the psalm emanates from a coronation ceremony or recalls it *in extenso* matters little ultimately.

Ps. 72 is more problematic. Although most scholars who offer an opinion think this also to be a Judahite coronation psalm,[93] this ritual location remains uncertain, as does its precise connection to the other coronation psalms. Finally, the identification of Ps. 101 as a coronation text is also not certain, although positing this *Sitz im Leben* is more parsimonious than other possibilities offered.

These coronation hymns simultaneously reveal the king as warrior and ritually create the body such a person requires. He is an offspring of Yahweh, begotten from the dawn, displaying himself at Yahweh's right hand (a location that identifies the human ruler as a copy and associate of the divine one). This warrior king also engages in contest with other males, whose bodies fail them at the critical moment, when they must confront the king and his divine father and patron. Now to fill in the details.

Psalm 2

Ps. 2, well known for its later messianic interpretations,[94] is generally described in modern scholarship as a coronation hymn.[95] This attribution depends primarily upon vv. 6–8, which depict Yahweh "setting" his king (מלך equals the משיח ["anointed one"] of v. 2) "on Zion," announcing his birth,[96] and promising him whatever he wishes, including universal rule.

The psalm opens, however, in a taunt of foreign rulers, who posture as conquerors.[97] The text names no specific rulers or states and

---

[93] E.g., Briggs and Briggs, *Book of Psalms*, 2. 132; Weiser, *Psalmen*, 342; Dahood, *Psalms 51–100* (AB 17; Garden City, NY: Doubleday, 1968) 502; Klaus Seybold, *Die Psalmen* (HAT I/15; Tübingen: Mohr/Siebeck, 1996) 277.

[94] For a convenient summary, see John T. Willis, "A Cry of Defiance—Psalm 2," *JSOT* 47 (1990) 33–50.

[95] *Inter alios* Gressmann, *Messias*, 9; Mowinckel, *Psalms in Israel's Worship*, 1. 62–63; Craigie, *Psalms 1–50*, 62; Frank-Lothar Hossfeld and Erich Zenger, *Die Psalmen I* (Würzburg: Echter, 1993) 50.

[96] The prevalent interpretation of the line "today I have given you birth" (אני היום ילדתיך) is that it refers to an adoption of the king by God (see, e.g., Aage Bentzen, *Messias, Moses redivivus, Menschensohn* [Zurich: Zwingli, 1948] 14). Roberts ("Whose Child Is This?"; for an earlier argument along similar lines, see Sigmund Mowinckel, *He That Cometh* [trans. G. W. Anderson; Nashville: Abingdon, 1955] esp. 67) has shown convincingly, however, that: (1) there is no evidence for legal adoption procedures in Israel; (2) Egyptian parallels suggest that the king was "born" to the god at the former's coronation; and (3) therefore, one should read this psalm literally to mean that the king is thought of as the legitimate offspring of God. I will discuss this more when examining Psalm 110.

[97] See the comments of Gerstenberger, *Psalms Part 1*, 46–47; he dates the Psalm much too late, but his comments on its literary shape are useful.

views them all—improbably—as vassals of Judah. The lack of a precise geopolitical reference means that one should not seek a specific revolt or war as the background of the psalm: foreign kings always potentially threaten the Davidides in Jerusalem.[98] The crucial features of the text from the point of view of this study are the various ways in which the king of Judah is portrayed as a male in competition with other males, the foreign kings. For, however appropriate it is to employ the modern category "statehood" to describe the south Levantine political entities,[99] the biblical texts themselves speak of contests between their kings, not between abstractions called "states." For the author of Ps. 2, all politics derives from the interactions of notables, especially monarchs. All successful politics derives from the ruler's ability to act vigorously when appropriate, to speak eloquently, and to display oneself in culturally sanctioned ways. In short, all politics derives from the body, and different actors can manipulate boundaries of "statehood," both physical and semiotic to serve their own agendas.[100] This point is significant because it reminds us of the importance of understanding Israelite political theory (to reintroduce the modern terminology to our discussion) on its own terms. The focus should be on three points: (1) rivalry as male contestation, especially insofar as it is a performance (that is, it involves actions that others can judge good or ill); (2) the use of the body as an icon in this rivalry; and (3) the ideational or even moral implications of rivalry.

---

[98] The proposal of Dahood (*Psalms 1–50*, 8), that the psalm was composed in the tenth century BCE and reflects the historical chaos of several centuries earlier (the Amarna Age), seems gratuitous. Political intrigue was common enough throughout the history of Palestine, and it is difficult to see what import the Late Bronze Palestinian mayors and their struggles could have had for the larger Iron Age kingdoms.

[99] On which issue, see, e.g., Robert B. Coote and Keith W. Whitelam, "The Emergence of Israel: Social Transformation and State Formation Following the Decline in Late Bronze Age Trade," *Sem* 37 (1986) 107–47; Norman K. Gottwald, "The Participation of Free Agrarians in the Introduction of Monarchy to Ancient Israel: An Application of H. A. Landsberger's Framework for the Analysis of Peasant Movements," *Sem* 37 (1986) 77–106.

[100] See Michael Herzfeld, *Cultural Intimacy: Social Poetics of the Nation-State* (New York/London: Routledge, 1997). He notes that "The nation-state is ideologically committed to ontological self-perpetuation for all eternity" (p. 21). Yet subjects of the state may use its ideologies for their own ends, even rejecting them altogether. How much more is this the case in antiquity, when structures for control of the population by the center were less elaborate than is often true today.

First, the poet avoids painting the rivalry among the kings primarily in terms of military activities (even if יחצבו in v. 2 may mean, "they assemble") or warlike skills (as in Ps. 45). Rather, the emphasis is on boasting (by the enemies) and laughing (by God). The foreign kings' words are a performative act (in Austin's sense): when they say, "Let us rip away their fetters, let us throw their cords away from us" (ננתקה את־מוסרותימו ונשליכה ממנו עבתימו),[101] they intend these words to effect the changes they describe. The words are infelicitous (ineffective) because the "kings" do not have the "right" or power to realize their plans.[102] This is because Yahweh also engages in a series of illocutionary performative acts:

> I set my king on Zion, my holy mount. . . .
> My son you are; today I have given you birth (אני היום ילדתיך).
> Ask (anything) from me,[103] and I will make the nations your patrimony (נחלך), the ends of the earth your heritage (ואחזתך)!
> You will shepherd them with an iron rod;
> You will shatter them like a potter's vessel!

Yahweh, that is to say, fashions a proper body for the king (through "birth") and then displays it before all so that no one can mistake the source and extent of the power of the ruler of Judah. This address to the Judahite king by God (or, rather, by a priest, prophet, or courtier speaking in God's behalf) during the coronation ritual creates for the audience of the ritual a sense that the king is a mighty ruler under divine protection. Opposition to him is opposition to God. This identification of the king with God is depicted in terms of both the king's birth to Yahweh and his own self-display (he wields an iron rod as a weapon, and implicitly [cf. v. 3] the rebellious vassal kings are unable to extract themselves from his cords as they seek to do).[104]

---

[101] The stock phrase נתק את מוסרות appears in Jer. 2:20, 5:5, 30:8; Nah. 1:13; and Ps. 107:14.

[102] On this type of infelicity, see J. L. Austin, *How to Do Things with Words* (2d ed.; Cambridge: Harvard University Press, 1975) 34–35.

[103] But see Dahood (*Psalms 1–50*, 12), who points ממנו as *māmōnī* = "wealth from me." This is possible, but awkward in positing an unusual construction and an Aramaic loanword.

[104] The imagery here is like that in some Neo-Assyrian inscriptions. Cf., for example, Esarhaddon's victory stele at Zençirli, depicting the victorious Assyrian holding the ends of cords to which the necks of his defeated enemies were leashed; Jutta Börker-Klähn, *Altvorderasiatische Bildstelen und Vergleichbare Felsreliefs* (2 vols.; BF 4; Mainz: von Zabern, 1982) 213 (no. 219).

The former point is especially important. V. 7 is spoken by the king himself, quoting God. The citation of the divine appointment by the king himself rather than by the speaker of vv. 1–6 (and 10–12, if the speaker is the same) serves to portray the king in an attitude of self-acclamation before all the world, including his enemies. He thus proclaims his legitimacy and agrees to act accordingly. The claim to have been sired by God is simultaneously self-effacing and self-aggrandizing. The king promotes himself without appearing to do so.

I will return to the question of the king's birth when discussing Ps. 110. Not an act of adoption,[105] but also not explicated even mythologically, this trope here in Ps. 2 becomes a claim to be the offspring of Yahweh, and whatever its mythological background, this claim serves here not only as an illocutionary performative act (the king's claim makes him the offspring; see below), but as a specimen of royal bravado in the face of opposition.

This brings us to the second issue. The psalm does not expatiate upon the king's body, but does portray the proper way in which it is to be displayed vis-à-vis various subjects. Most notable is the command in v. 12a, "Kiss the son" (נשקו בר).[106] While there is some evidence from the versions for a reading $b\bar{o}r$ ("pure"),[107] and the "purity" (*burru*) of the king is a major concern in Levantine (specifically Ugaritic) ritual,[108] the mention of the "birth" of the king (at his coronation) in v. 7b makes the traditional rendering "kiss the son" more probable.[109] Indeed, the use of בר ("son") in the Phoenician inscription of the Anatolian king Kilamuwa (KAI 24.1, 4, 9) indicates that scholarly concern with the Aramaism in Ps. 2 is misplaced. The salient point is, then, that Ps. 2 focuses upon the divine sonship of the king. What this says about Jerusalemite conceptions of the king's body will become clearer when we consider Ps. 110.

---

[105] See n. 70, above.
[106] The addition of ברגליו "on his feet" in one MS. (see BHS apparatus) is not well supported and seems to smooth out a harder reading; hence it is unlikely to be original, but it does captures the intent of the verse accurately. The addition does, however, reflect the notion of submission seen also in Ps. 110:1 (הדם לרגליך).
[107] See Craigie, *Psalms 1–50*, 64.
[108] See, e.g., KTU 1.41.24, 32, 37, 38, 55 1.46.16; 1.105.2, 19, 22; 1.109.11, 31, 33; 1.112.5; 1.119.5; 1.124.8, 9; 1.127.22 etc. Often the verb *barara* parallels *yirtaḥḥiṣ* ("he washed himself").
[109] This argument goes back at least as far as Qimhi, who probably knew the alternative vocalization and interpretation. He writes ובר כמו בן ("*bar* equals *ben*" ["son"]) and then cites v. 7 as justification.

Third, what does the psalm's moral vision of rivalry mean? The expectation of the psalm is that Judahite rule of many foreign lands is the normal, expected state of affairs. While it is difficult to imagine a real historical occasion that would have given rise to such a notion (except the possible existence of the so-called Davidic-Solomonic empire),[110] it may be that a historical condition was unneeded. Judahite dominance is the ideational norm of the psalm, the ritual of which it is part, and by extension the entire Judahite royal self-conception (or propaganda, if we may use the word). The king in Jerusalem is a successful male who can successfully dominate foreign kings without his own subjects questioning the legitimacy of such a state of affairs. The royal ritual indexes, not contemporary geopolitical realities, but a code of royal language with its own interior logic. The conflict between reality and ideals will, in part, inform our discussion of the narratives of kingship in the DH.

Psalm 110

Like Ps. 2, Ps. 110 has a long interpretive history, having been a crucial text in the formation of the Christian passion narrative.[111] Most modern commentators have understood this as a coronation hymn,[112] although Johnson speculates that it is part of a recurring ritual commemorating the coronation,[113] Dahood thinks it a celebration of a military victory,[114] and Gerstenberger has dated it (implausibly in my view) to a later period.[115] Given the importance of military imagery in both Pss. 2 and 45, Dahood's proposal seems unnecessary, while Johnson's depends upon the unproven hypothesis of an autumnal festival of divine and human kingship. Recently, J. Doré has argued, based especially on v. 4, that the psalm is part of a festival celebrating David's transfer of the Ark to Jerusalem, but the

---

[110] On which seen the astute comments of Baruch Halpern, *David's Secret Demons: Messiah, Murderer, Traitor, King* (Grand Rapids: Eerdmans, 2001) 208-59, 427-78.

[111] See Matt. 22:41, 26:64; cf. 1 Cor. 15:25ff.; 1 Pet. 3:22 etc.

[112] Gunkel, *Einleitung*, 141; Gressmann, *Messias*, 22; Mowinckel, *Psalms in Israel's Worship*, 2. 153; Weiser, *Psalmen*, 459; Leslie C. Allen, *Psalms 101-150* (WBC 21; Waco, TX: Word, 1983) 83.

[113] Aubrey R. Johnson, *The Cultic Prophet and Israel's Psalmody* (Cardiff: University of Wales Press, 1979) 81-82.

[114] Mitchell Dahood, *Psalms 101-150* (AB 17A; Garden City, NY: Doubleday, 1970) 112.

[115] Erhard Gerstenberger, *Psalms Part 2 and Lamentations* (FOTL 15; Grand Rapids: Eerdmans, 2001) 266.

psalm never mentions the Ark and so this view is also speculative.[116] To explain the psalm's references to the king as triumphant warrior (vv. 1b–2), priest (v. 4b), and judge of the nations (v. 6), and then the reference to dynastic succession in v. 7, one must posit a ritual setting in which all of these were items of concern. The most economical explanation, then, remains that the psalm comes from the coronations of the Judahite king, not annual commemorations thereof. (Some corroboration of this may come from the Neo-Assyrian "Coronation Hymn" of Assurbanipal, which seeks divine guarantees of his military, priestly, and economic success, though not in precisely the language of Ps. 110.)[117]

The incipit נאם יהוה, a technical term, indicates that the speaker of the psalm is a prophet and the psalm an oracle to the king, who is thus spoken to and spoken about. He is both the psalm's audience and the spectacle to which it alludes. Whether this poem stems from the earliest period of the monarchy, as, e.g., Mowinckel[118] argued, is unclear, but the mention of Melchizedeq harks back to second-millennium BCE traditions or at least first-millennium beliefs about the earlier, pre-Israelite period, and this serves to anchor the coronation ritual in antiquity.

Like Ps. 2, Ps. 110 emphasizes the king's triumph over (unnamed and unlocated) enemies, his placement on a throne, and his extraordinary "birth." The repetition of these themes in the coronation ritual is important, for it is an example of what Tambiah calls redundancy.[119] That is, the coronation ritual as a whole overloads communication channels with mentions of the king's military prowess and his astonishing birth. It is possible, though unfortunately not subject to proof, that the repetition of these themes was an act of intensification, a common feature of rituals in which the second performance of words, signs, gestures, etc. is stronger and more effective than the first.[120] Minimally, this repetition singles out the military and priestly features of kingship, as well as the special birth that makes them possible, for special attention.

---

[116] J. Doré, "L'évocation de Melchisédech et le problèm de l'origine du *Psaume* 110," *Transeuphratène* 15 (1998) 19–53.

[117] VAT 13831 = SAA 3.11 (in Alasdair Livingstone, ed., *Court Poetry and Literary Miscellanea* [Helsinki: Helsinki University Press, 1989] 26–27).

[118] Mowinckel, *Psalms in Israel's Worship*, 1. 125, 2. 153.

[119] Tambiah, "Performative Approach to Ritual," 119.

[120] Ibid., 140.

In addition to all this, we hear of the king's priesthood and a possible ritual involving drinking. Let us examine each feature in turn.

First, the triumph over enemies mirrors the notions of Ps. 2. The king's foes remain anonymous males, their hostility unexplained and treated as a given. The king may vanquish them because of his military prowess (עזך מטה; רדה בקרב איביך), but their chief conqueror is Yahweh, who makes them into the king's footstool (הדם).[121] Whether this means that they become a footstool on which he rests his feet or that they merely kneel at his footstool is unclear. Perhaps the psalmist avoids specificity in order to allow for either possibility. Either way, the kneeling of the king's foes before him signifies his prowess, as does his sitting beside Yahweh.

Second, scholars have long recognized the Egyptianizing origin of the posture of sitting beside a deity.[122] Given the longstanding Egyptian cultural and political dominance in Palestine, the adoption and then domestication of features of the larger state's ceremony of power by the smaller Levantine states is hardly surprising. Indeed, Phoenician art often depicts the monarch sitting, as does the Assyrianizing Judahite ostracon painting from Ramat Rahel.[123]

Less obvious is what v. 1 might mean ritually to Israelites themselves. The prophet here invites the king to sit on Yahweh's right side (שב לימיני). Assuming that this is not an empty metaphor, one asks what the king must do, what ritual he must perform. If there were an image of Yahweh in the Jerusalem temple, this request could be a performative utterance: the king's throne was placed beside the image, and the king sat down on the throne. The existence of such a divine image, though probable, remains a conjecture, however.[124]

---

[121] On footstools in the Bible, see Isa. 66:1; Ps. 99:5, 132:7; Lam. 2:1; and 1 Chron. 28:2 (where it is the Ark!); and T. C. Mitchell, "Furniture in the West Semitic Texts," in Georgina Herrmann, ed., *The Furniture of Western Asia, Ancient and Traditional* (Mainz: von Zabern, 1996) 55–56; on Assyrian footstools, see John Curtis, "Assyrian Furniture: The Archaeological Evidence," in Herrmann, *Furniture of Western Asia*, 173–75.

[122] See Gressmann, *Messias*, 21. This is especially true for the 19th and 20th Dynasties (see Klaus Koch, *Geschichte der ägyptischen Religion: Von den Pyramiden bis zu den Mysterien der Isis* [Stuttgart: Kohlhammer, 1993] 370; see Starbuck, *Court Oracles*, 152–53.

[123] Rüdiger Schmitt, *Bildhafte Herrschaftsrepräsentation im eisenzeitlichen Israel* (AOAT 283; Münster: Ugarit-Verlag, 2001) 95–99, 160–65; Yohanan Aharoni, *Excavations at Ramat Rahel: Seasons 1961 and 1962* (Rome: Centro di Studi Semitici, 1964) 85–94.

[124] For a discussion of the issues and data, see Herbert Niehr, "In Search of YHWH's Cult Statue in the First Temple," in Karel van der Toorn, ed., *The Image*

Alternatively, the throne might have been placed near the Ark, although the darkness of the chamber in which the latter resided might have posed a problem for those viewing the coronation. Unless the image were paraded from the temple to the palace, which is possible, this part of the ritual must have taken place in the temple precincts, presumably in or near the דביר. Either way, the placement of the royal throne near an icon of Yahweh, and more likely in the temple itself signifies the new monarch's close association with Yahweh.

Third, the text alludes in v. 3 to the royal birth (ילדתיך ... רחם). As in Ps. 2, this "birth" occurred, ritually speaking, during the coronation itself. That is, when the prophet proclaims the king's birth, this is again a performative utterance, making the supernatural nascence a reality. Now, the specifics of this verse have elicited a large amount of discussion. One must read the text on multiple levels in order to do justice to it, and a reading that insists on only one meaning for each phrase will fail to do justice to the whole. Moreover, doubts arise about the textual integrity of the verse.

A recent, and very helpful, discussion of the verse is that of William P. Brown, who offers a text for 3aγ–b:[125]

> In holy splendor, out of the womb, towards the dawn go forth!
> Like the dew, I have begotten you.
>
> בהדרי קדש מרחם משחר לך כטל ילדתיך

This reconstruction is commendable because it requires changing only one letter from the consonantal text of MT (an additional כ, lost, Brown assumes, owing to haplography) and repointing in reliance on LXX. The principal problem lies with the repointing מִשַּׁחַר (שַׁחַר + מִן), which Brown renders "toward the dawn." This translation posits a directional meaning for מִן that is attested, though rare.[126]

A simpler rendering would be "from the dawn." Then the questions becomes, what does the phrase mean: "from the east," or "at dawn" ("with the dawning sun behind the king entering the temple precinct")? It may well mean both: the ritual takes place at dawn when the king enters the temple precinct from the east. We cannot

---

and the Book: Iconic Cults, Aniconism, and the Rise of Book Religion in Israel and the Ancient Near East (Leuven: Peeters, 1997) 73–95.

[125] William P. Brown, "A Royal Performance: Critical Notes on Psalm 110:3aγ–b," *JBL* 117 (1998) 93–96.

[126] Ibid., 94; but cf. GKC §119v–z.

be sure of this, but since rituals occurring at dawn following overnight preparations are widely attested in the ancient Near East,[127] the hypothesis deserves consideration. In this context, "from the dawn" implies "toward the temple," indicating movement from the perimeter of the temple precinct toward the sanctuary itself. Again, this interpretation is not completely demonstrable, but it at least allows a plausible reconstruction of the movement of the ritual of coronation.

Lying behind this suggestion of mine is a larger-scale understanding of the verse. V. 3, though obscure, may be understood as being full of terminology applicable to the king. To begin, the phrase ביום חילך, usually translated "in the day of your power,"[128] could be repointed בְּיוֹם הִלְּךָ "in the day of your desacralization," the equivalent of the Ugaritic ritual technical term ḥillu malki ("[de] sanctification of the king"), which typically denotes a ritual act performed near dusk or shortly afterwards.[129] In short, the phrase in Ps. 110:3aβ refers to a purification rite performed at evening preceding the king's "birth" at dawn of the following day.

The next phase of the ritual is indicated in the phrase בהדרי קדש,[130] which seems to be an infinitive construct plus object: "at my visiting the holy [place]." The noun הדרה refers to a theophany in Ps. 29:2 and in KTU 14 III 50–51. There, Kirta has asked for a wife, and in a dream Ilu promises him one of extraordinary beauty. Lines 50–51 read

> Kirta yaḥiṭ waḥalāmu
> 'abdu ili wahadartu
> Kirta awoke and it was a dream;
>   the servant of Ilu and it was a visitation.

This indicates that the background of h-d-r is in ritual. In Ps. 110, then, בהדרי קדש refers to a divine appearance to the king, either in the form of a dream or following a purification rite at night.[131]

---

[127] Most obviously in the Babylonian New Year's festival itself (see F. Thureau-Dangin, *Rituels Accadiens* [reprint ed.; Osnabruck: Zeller, 1975] 128–54 for the text), but more relevantly in the Ugaritic coronation ritual (see KTU 1.132.25).

[128] The MT and LXX read חילך "your power," a sensible reading, except that the phrase "day of power" appears nowhere else in the Bible. This fact, though not fatal to the MT's understanding of the phrase, should give one pause.

[129] Follows 'arb šapši in KTU 1.41.48; 1.46.9; 1.87.52?, 57; 1.112.9; 1.119.4, 23–24; 1.132.27–28.

[130] The MT הדרי is preferable to Vulgate and Symmachus, הררי, on the principle of *lectio difficilior potior*.

[131] This interpretation is similar in some ways to that of Dahood (*Psalms 101–150*, 116), who, however, thinks of the entire psalm as a prebattle hymn.

Interestingly, Kirta's next action is ritual ablution: "he washed himself and reddled himself." The verb *yirtaḥḥiṣ* ("he washed himself") is a technical term in Ugaritic ritual, applied especially to the king who becomes "pure" (*burru*) upon washing, again confirming the reading of the previous clause as "in the day of your desacralization."[132] Ugaritic royal ritual emphasized the movement of the king from a state of sanctity to one of non-sanctity and back again, a movement usually requiring more than one day and the use of both sacred and profane space.[133] Perhaps the Judahite king has done much the same thing.

Next comes the royal birth, which comes "from the dawn." Again, there is no reason to decide between spatial and temporal meanings of the phrase. If, in the first half of the verse, the king has already purified himself, this would imply that he must have left the temple. Then he must reenter it to resume the ritual cycle. He does this at dawn, coming from the east. The power of the symbolism would have been inescapable for the viewers of the triumphal entrance. In any case, Roberts[134] has argued convincingly that Egyptian notions of the royal birth at the time of coronation underlie such texts as Isa. 9 and Ps. 2. The same background informs this text, and שׁחר here may refer to a goddess (even if Šaharu is male at Ugarit) paralleled to טל ("dew").[135] The king is "born" at dawn after a night of incubation. Yahweh appropriates the features of goddess to become

---

[132] KTU 1.41.3; 1.46.10; 1.87.3; 1.105.5–6; 1.106.26; 1.109.2; 1.112.10, 16; 1.119.5. On the terminology and its place in the Ugaritic sacrificial system, see also Gregorio del Olmo Lete, *Canaanite Religion According to the Liturgical Texts of Ugarit* (Bethesda, MD: CDL, 1999) esp. 37–39; and Paolo Xella, *I Testi Rituali di Ugarit I* (Rome: CNDR, 1981) 28–29.

[133] See Dennis Pardee, *Ritual and Cult at Ugarit* (Atlanta: Society of Biblical Literature, 2002) 57, 238–39; Olmo Lete, *Canaanite Religion*, 296–97.

[134] Roberts, "Whose Child Is This?"; cf. Otto, "Psalm 2."

[135] See KTU 1.23.52, the climax of the myth of Šaharu's birth. On the problem of this deity's gender, see Samuel A. Meier, "Shahar," *ABD* 5 (1992) 1150–51; B. Otzen, "טל," *TDOT* 5 (1986) 329; on the use of the name in Isa. 14:12, see Hartmut Gese, "Die Religionen Altsyriens," in Hartmut Gese, Maria Höfner, and Kurt Rudolph, *Die Religionen Altsyriens, Altarabiens und der Mandäer* (RdM 10.2; Stuttgart: Kohlhammer, 1970) 81; Luis I. J. Stadelmann, *The Hebrew Conception of the World* (AnBib 39; Rome: Biblical Institute Press, 1970) 89–91. Whatever the mythological background of Isa. 14:12, its portrayal of a ruler, this time of Babylon, as a son of Šaḥar confirms Israelite familiarity with this version of an idea of royal descent from deity, even if Isa. 14 dismisses such a royal claim as absurd (at least for a Babylonian ruler!). See R. Mark Shipp, *Of Dead Kings and Dirges: Myth and Meaning in Isaiah 14:4b–21* (Academia Biblica 11; Atlanta: SBL, 2002).

the parent of the king. V. 3b can thus be translated as "indeed, like Dew I have given you birth" (ל כטל ילדתיך [asseverative *la*]).[136] (This rendering merely redivides and repoints the MT consonants).

V. 3aβ–b thus reads: "In the day of your purification, when I 'visited' the holy [precinct], from the womb, from the east, I, like Dew, gave birth to you."[137] Admittedly, this is difficult Hebrew (though no more difficult than most of the dozens of other proposed renderings of the verse), and it may be that the text has lost one or more words. Still, it is possible to make sense of the verse. It envisions a ritual beginning at sundown (the commencement of a day) and continuing through the night. At dawn, the climax is reached when the king is "born."

If this is correct, then Ps. 110 demonstrates that the king is not "son of God" from the time of his physical birth, but he "becomes" such at a fixed point in time, marked by ritual. The shape and content of the ritual are mostly lost, although one can be sure that it took place in the temple and probably in different areas of the precinct. The king must have undergone some kind of ritual purification (as at Ugarit, our closest parallel, despite the temporal and geographical remove), although the nature of this is not explicated. The crucial point is, again however, that his divine sonship commences at this point.

V. 4 next adds still another royal title, that of priest (כהן). The sacerdotal aspects of kingship are downplayed in the Hebrew Bible, although they do appear occasionally, as when Ahaz alters the temple furnishings (2 Kings 16:10–20), David's "sons" serve as priests (2 Sam. 8:18), or Solomon offers sacrifices and prayers (1 Kings 8). These traces of royal priesthood only partially illuminate Ps. 110:4, however, for the king here is said to be a priest in the manner of Melchizedeq. Casting about for parallels, one notes that Phoenician kings may occasionally be called priests,[138] and that this is a major

---

[136] On asseverative *la* in Hebrew, see Robert Althann, *Studies in Northwest Semitic* (BibOr 45; Rome: Pontifical Biblical Institute, 1997) 108–12 (and his bibliography); admittedly, his incomplete list of examples does not include a case in which asseverative *la* precedes a preposition, as it must here, but this is not a serious difficulty.

[137] This ritualizing reading of the verse may gain even more force from the first two words, עמך נדבת. The MT understands the clause to mean "your people (will be) volunteer-minded" or some such. Also possible is the pointing עִמְּךָ נְדָבָת, "with you is a freewill offering" (reading נדבת as an archaic form of נדבה).

[138] KAI 11 (from Byblos, ca. 350 BCE; the father of king Paltiba 1 is Aziba 1, "priest of Ashtart," one assumes, though not without room for doubt, that the king's

aspect of the royal titularies in Assyria, in particular.[139] Presumably the king of Judah, like his opposite numbers elsewhere, had the right of entering the temple and celebrating sacrifices at certain times.[140] The specific occasions for this are lost, probably because the surviving form of the temple regulations reflects a period after the disappearance of the monarchy (or else, as in D, are critical of the monarchy).

The questions that remain are why did the psalm emphasize Melchizedeq, and what does the king's priesthood say about his body and genderedness? Taking the first query first, one should note that an earlier generation of scholars seized upon Gen. 14:18–20 and the unquestionably second-millennium date of Jerusalemite royal names with compounds of צדק[141] to argue that David himself felt a need to appropriate features of the Jebusite cult in order to legitimate his own kingship and Jerusalem as the capital.[142] This reconstruction, however, probably overemphasizes the discontinuity between Canaanites and Israelites (making kingship "alien" to Israel) and assumes a level of "national consciousness" among Israelites that may be hard to document for the tenth century. In some forms, the Jebusite hypothesis assumes the basic historicity of the biblical Melchizedeq tradition (which, admittedly, was probably far more extensive than the surviving fragments might lead one to think), a position from which one may reasonably dissent.

---

father was himself king); and 13.1, 2 (from Sidon, ca. 500 BCE; both Tabnit and his father Eshmunazor were simultaneously kings of Sidon and priests of Ashtart).

[139] See, for an ample list, M.-J. Seux, *Épithètes royales akkadiennes et sumériennes* (Paris: Letouzey, 1967) 21; and more recently, Barbara Cifola, *Analysis of Variants in the Assyrian Royal Titulary from the Origins to Tiglath-pileser III* (Naples: Istituto Universitario Orientale, 1995) 158.

[140] A trace of this may appear in 2 Chron. 26:16ff., the story of Uzziah's illegitimate (to the Chronicler) attempt to offer sacrifices. This story may be a midrashic addition to explain a gap in 2 Kings 15:5, which does not otherwise justify Yahweh's smiting the king with leprosy, but it is equally possible that the Chronicler knew of an ancient practice, which, in any case, parallels that of neighboring cultures (on literary issues, see Sara Japhet, *I & II Chronicles* [OTL; Louisville: Westminster/John Knox, 1993] 876, 884–85).

[141] On the onomasticon, see Ran Zadok, *The Pre-Hellenistic Israelite Anthroponymy and Prosopography* (OLA 28; Leuven: Peeters, 1988) 37; cf. F. Gröndahl, *Die Personennamen der Texte aus Ugarit* (StPohl 1; Rome: Gregorian Pontifical University, 1967) 187–88.

[142] See the criticism of this position by J. J. M. Roberts, "In Defense of the Monarchy: The Contribution of Israelite Kingship to Biblical Theology," in Patrick Miller, Paul Hanson, and S. Dean McBride, eds., *Ancient Israelite Religion* (Philadelphia: Fortress, 1987) 377–96.

However, the most relevant point is that the psalm draws on a tradition, of whatever historical validity, about a second-millennium king/priest.[143] Whether Abraham was already associated with Melchizedeq in the tradition is impossible to know, and Gen. 14:18–20 may be a false lead in our attempt to understand Ps. 110. Note that the god of Ps. 110 is Yahweh, who may or may not have been fused with El Elyon (who appears in Gen. 14) at the time of the psalm's composition. We simply do not know. What we can be sure of is that the king of Judah was not placed within the time-honored (Levitical?) priestly families (Aaronite or Mushite), but within another category. The precise reason for this placement is unclear, although one can assume that the psalm's appeal to the past was an attempt to use traditions about it (whatever they were) to add an air of sanctity to the king's role, in short, to place him in a line of royal priests from Jerusalem. Legitimating his position in the face of opposition is not the only possibility. Here—remembering Ginsberg's notion that some psalms in Israel function much like inscriptions elsewhere[144]—we recall the common Levantine inscriptional practice of listing the predecessors of the royal sponsors, occasionally as far back as four generations (KAI 24 and the "Ekron Inscription").[145] The purpose behind this practice is to link the king with the hallowed dead, that is, to emphasize the continuity of the monarchy: "The king is dead; long live the king!" Now, Ps. 110 does not offer a list of kings; at most it implies such a list by synecdoche, taking the first and last king (Melchizedeq and the reigning one) in the series. The inscriptional practice demonstrates that the need for "legitimation" is not the only reason to use the past as exemplum.

What, then, does this say about the king's body? First, being a priest means fulfilling ritual purification requirements. At Ugarit, the only Levantine state where it is possible to trace out the specifics of this, this meant ablutions and sacrifices and apparently an incubation

---

[143] S. David Sperling (*The Original Torah: The Political Intent of the Bible's Writers* [New York: NYU Press, 1998] 85–86) has argued that the story "served the needs of the Davidic monarchy to legitimate Jerusalem." This is plausible, of course, but equally plausible is that the need for justification came later in the monarchic period, and that the problem was a literary one: how to link Abraham with Jerusalem. This need would explain the Aqedah's being at Moriah.

[144] Ginsberg, "Psalms and Inscriptions."

[145] S. Gitin, T. Dothan, and J. Naveh, "A Royal Dedicatory Inscription from Ekron," *IEJ* 47 (1997) 1–16.

period.¹⁴⁶ The same seems to have true for Judah, even if the exact details of this purification are unknown. Second, this priesthood is לעלם ("forever"). Obviously, this is a kind of fiction, since everyone knows that the king will die. Yet his perdurance was an important feature of royal predication, both in Israel and in Phoenicia, as well as elsewhere.¹⁴⁷ To borrow the medieval phraseology, this is a case in which the king's two bodies are in play: the body of the king (the present incumbent on the throne) and that of the King (considered ideally).¹⁴⁸ Or, better yet, three royal bodies come under consideration: that of the male now being made king in the coronation ceremony, that body that results from the coronation, and that of the enduring King who does not die. This notion may, in turn, be rooted in the idea of Yahweh's (or any deity's for that matter) survival לעלם.¹⁴⁹

To conclude the discussion of Ps. 110, one notes that, after mixing metaphors in v. 5 by citing the common Near Eastern motif of a god striding¹⁵⁰ beside a king going into battle, v. 7 refers to the king taking a drink and then having his head raised.¹⁵¹ This taking a drink is often thought to refer to a ceremony at the Gihon Spring,¹⁵² but the relevant text in 1 Kings 1:38 does not mention the king

---

¹⁴⁶ See Olmo Lete, *Canaanite Religion*, 207–12.
¹⁴⁷ See 1 Kings 1:31; Neh. 2:3; cf. Ps. 21:5 and (mutatis mutandis) 45:7 (on the expression "eternal throne" [כסא עלם] see also KTU 1.106.28 and the comments in Paolo Xella, *Testi Rituali di Ugarit*, 85). At Karatepe, Azatiwada sought to have his reputation be "eternal like the reputation of the sun and moon (שם אזחוד יכן לעלם כם שם שמש וירח; KAI 26 A IV.2–3, C V.6–7).
¹⁴⁸ On medieval notions of royal nonmortality see the chapter "The King Never Dies" in Kantorowicz, *King's Two Bodies*, 314–450. For an application of the notion of three bodies to Assyrian kingship, see Irene J. Winter, "Art *in* Empire: The Royal Image and the Visual Dimensions of Assyrian Ideology," in Simo Parpola and R. M. Whiting, eds., *Assyria 1995* (Helsinki: Neo-Assyrian Text Corpus Project, 1997) 374.
¹⁴⁹ E.g., Exod. 3:15; Ps. 72:19; 89:53; 135:13.
¹⁵⁰ Presumably, the image of Yahweh in view here is that of a smiting god, a figure common in Palestine in the Late Bronze Age down to Iron I (see Ora Negbi, *Canaanite Gods in Metal: An Archaeological Study of Ancient Syro-Palestinian Figurines* [Tel Aviv: Tel Aviv University Institute of Archaeology, 1976) 30–41). For the reuse of such a figurine in Israelite Jerusalem, see Yigal Shiloh, *Excavations at the City of David: 1978–1982* (Qedem 19; Jerusalem: Hebrew University Institute of Archaeology, 1984) pl. 29. But see Dick, *Born in Heaven, Made on Earth*, 4–7.
¹⁵¹ Dahood (*Psalm 101–150*, 119) translated the verse "The Bestower of Succession set him on his throne," taking מנחל to be a Hiphil participle used substantivally, repointing ישתה as *yᵉšītēhū* ("he set him"), and taking דרם to mean "throne." However, the Ugaritic evidence he cites is of a feminine noun, and the traditional translation makes Hebrew sense, even if it is obscure.
¹⁵² For the bibliography, see Allen, *Psalms 101–150*, 82.

drinking. It is at least possible that he bathed—we simply do not know, and so reading Ps. 110:8 in this way is simply speculation, especially since the source of the water here is the נחל.[153] Since the previous clauses concern royal military prowess, it seems probable that the point of the verse is that the king on campaign can drink water (not wine) along the road. He bears the hardship of his troops without complaint. Accordingly, Yahweh raises his head.[154] The phrase רום in the Hiphil plus ראש appears only here and in Ps. 3:4 in the Bible. It may be an expression of joy comparable to the common נשא ראש, but this is not obvious in the context.[155] In any case, Yahweh approves of the king's successful playing of his role as a conquering male and signifies that by "raising his head."

To summarize, then, Ps. 110 is the libretto for the phase of the coronation ritual in which the king assumes a body that is לעלם and thus becomes able to wage war, execute judgment, and, in short, serve as Yahweh's viceroy. The king is "born" at this stage of the ritual.

Psalm 72

Like Pss. 2 and 110, Ps. 72 is almost certainly part of a coronation ritual, being specifically a prayer for the king's success and domination over foreign rulers (vv. 8ff.). As Kselman has demonstrated, in its extant form it is a carefully structured poem of five units ("strophes"), the sections being vv. 1–4, 5–8, 9–11, 12–15, and 16–17.[156] Moreover, although I cannot agree with Dahood in counting the heading לשלמה ("about Solomon") as evidence for dating the poem to the tenth century,[157] since the superscription could easily derive from a Second Temple era exegesis of the psalm, a location in Judah during the seventh century makes sense of the available evidence.

Turning now to the question of the king's body and gender-construction, one may begin with the first line. There is no convincing

---

[153] In 2 Chron. 33:14 נחון is בנחל ("in the wadi"), not equivalent to it. This formulation is late, however, and relevant only if one assumes that it is from נחון that the king of Ps. 110 drinks.
[154] Though note that some MSS. read ירום ("he [the king] raises [his own] head").
[155] See Gruber, *Aspects of Nonverbal Communication*, 2. 598–601.
[156] John S. Kselman, "Psalm 72: Some Observations on Structure," *BASOR* 220 (1975) 77–81; the structure proposed by Arneth (*"Sonne der Gerechtigkeit"*, 21–23) depends on his redaction-critical conclusions, not on final-form analysis.
[157] Dahood, *Psalms 51–100*, 179–80.

reason to interpret the paralleled מלך and בן־מלך in v. 1 as referring to two different persons. The present king is also the previous king's son (whether he literally is or not).[158] But the choice of the word pair emphasizes the reality of succession. The office of kingship, so to say, outlives any of its incumbents. As before in Ps. 110, it is not entirely clear here what connection the funeral of the dead king would have had to the coronation of his successor, whether there was a waiting period between the two and so on. It would not be surprising, however, if some mention were made in the demise of the previous king or perhaps some rite of removal were carried out to mark the transition of the dead king to the netherworld.[159] Unfortunately, no trace of such rituals exists in this psalm—only an allusion.

What is important here is the emphasis on the king's longevity. Vv. 5 and 17 form a kind of envelope construction framing the various references to the king's self-display:

> May he remain (וייראוך)[160] like the sun, and like the moon—for all generations (דור דורים)! (v. 5)
> May his name be eternal, like the sun, may his name bear fruit![161] (v. 17)

This envelope encloses various expectations of the king's reign, which the psalmist hopes to perpetuate and to replicate in succeeding generations. That is, the perdurance of the king's reputation directly

---

[158] On rules of succession, see Zafrira Ben-Barak, "Succession to the Throne in Israel and in Assyria," *OLP* 17 (1986) 85–100.

[159] Cf. KTU 1.161. Closer to the period of this psalm, note KAI 215, an inscription on a monumental statue that Bir-rakib of Samal erected in honor of his father Panamuwa II. KAI 1 indicates that Byblian kings sometimes dedicated sarcophagi for their fathers, although the later practice was to mention only the deceased father. The precise nature of rituals accompanying such burials is unknown.

[160] Following LXX καὶ συμπαραμένει; MT reads "may they fear you" (וייראוך), an unlikely reading. On the translation, see Shalom Paul, "Psalm 72:5—A Traditional Blessing for the Long Life of the King," *JNES* 31 (1972) 351–54.

[161] This points the consonants of MT as *y^enayyēn* ("may it bear fruit" < the root *nwn* (cf. Dahood, *Psalms 51–100*, 184). Most commentators prefers the LXX reading יכון (ἐπιμένει). The Hebrew verb posited by MT Qere and followed here is a *hapax*, and the LXX reading has the advantage of reflecting a well-known idiom (see Paul, "Psalm 72:5," 354–55). However, this very commonness is an explanation of how an easier reading arose. Moreover, the LXX reflects a later reworked Hebrew recension of the text; note that the expression ἔστω εὐλογημένον ("let it be praised") reflects a Late Biblical Hebrew construction of finite verb plus participle. This indicates that MT is an older reading, a recasting of a familiar stock phrase and hence to be preferred as more original.

relates to his fruitfulness, which must mean his ability to produce a legitimate heir. Now, let us note those features that impinge on the display of his body and, therefore, the conceptions behind such display.

The three themes of foreign conquest, fertility, and care of the poor intertwine.[162] Since the king was both judge and warlord, the presence of the first and last is not surprising. However, the subjugation of foreign enemies is a precondition of political stability, which in turn is a prerequisite of equitable economic relationships (the poor suffering most during war), the combination of the two themes may indicate that the psalmist recognized a causal link between foreign domination and the care for the poor at home. The foreign enemies and the domestic oppressors of the poor are linked metonymically as groups the king must defeat (hence the unusual expression וידכא עושק ["he will crush the oppressor"] in v. 4.[163] (One may, incidentally, observe this same connection between defeat of the foreign enemy and economic relief in Kilamuwa's inscription [KAI 24], indicating that the idea was widespread in the Iron Age Near East.)[164] The king's military prowess makes it possible for him to aid his weaker subjects, at least according to this psalm.[165]

The display of the royal body centers around his military bearing and the resultant offer of tribute by the trading powers of the region.[166] Vv. 9–11 form a chiasm focusing upon the presentation of tribute to the enthroned Israelite king. Note, for example, that

---

[162] On the geographical terminology in v. 8, see Magne Sæbø, "Vom Grossreich zum Weltreich: Erwägungen zu Pss. lxxii 8, lxxxix 26; Sach. ix 10b," *VT* 28 (1978) 83–91.

[163] But see Kselman, "Psalm 72," 77. This clause makes the verse a tricolon, but deleting it (with Kselman following Skehan) seems arbitrary.

[164] For a thorough discussion of which, see Mark W. Hamilton, "The Past as Destiny: Visions of the Past as Guide for the Future in Sam'al and Judah Under Assyrian Hegemony," *HTR* 91 (1998) 315–50.

[165] That this ideal was not always realized is obvious. Texts such as Deut. 17:14–20 depend upon just such disconnection between reality and propaganda.

[166] The merism "desert:sea" equals "Saba/Sheba:Tarshish." It is striking that nearer powers are not mentioned. The merisms denote political entities at the edge of Israel's world, as well as major trading powers. Indeed, they form part of the extended periphery of the Assyrian empire (see Seymour Gitin, "The Neo-Assyrian Empire and its Western Periphery: The Levant, with a Focus on Philistine Ekron," in *Assyria 1995* (ed. S. Parpola and R. M. Whiting; Helsinki: Neo-Assyrian Text Corpus Project, 1997) 77–103. Given the psalm's multilayered references to late preexilic life, it is difficult to agree with Martin Arneth that vv. 8–11 are a later addition (*"Sonne der Gerechtigkeit"*, 29–39).

אשכר in v. 10 (parallels מנחה) must be אשכר (with a *sin* not a *shin*), a noun with an aleph preformative based on the root שכר, "to hire," a technical term (or euphemism?) for paying tribute in Levantine texts from the ninth and eighth centuries BCE (KAI 24.7; Isa. 7:20). The psalm envisions these distant states paying tribute to the Israelite king, apparently after he has defeated them in battle and they have "licked the dust" (עפר ילחכו; v. 9).[167] The abased bodies of the foreigners become an index of the prowess of the Israelite king's warrior-like body.

In a provocative study of landscape as a focal point for power conceptions in Neo-Assyrian inscriptional art, Michelle Marcus has noted that scenery can "serve as a vehicle for ideological concepts... it can represent the way certain people see themselves."[168] Whatever the accuracy of her analysis of Assyrian visual propaganda, she makes an important observation when noting that graphic art (for example, on the Balawat Gate) often portrays scenes of foreign women enslaved or even raped by their conquerors (who also, incidentally, celebrate dominance over foreign males). In Ps. 72, by contrast, the female is essentially absent, and the conquered are males. Male contestation is in view. Even the references to the king's fertility in vv. 6–7 and 17 do not mention women explicitly. And since the specific powers cited could have fought against the Israelite kingdoms only with expeditionary forces (for which, of course, no evidence exists; but, then, the psalm is dealing with mythology, not real history), the foreign female does not come into view. Without placing too much emphasis on this point of contrast with Neo-Assyrian uses of geography—the geography of Ps. 72 is sketched only in the briefest terms—I observe that the king's maleness is not defined in contrast to women but to other men. Unlike, say, Assyrian inscriptions, which portray women as booty and even sexual trophies, the Israelite hymns simply ignore the women. Is this the first step in the long Western tradition of distinguishing between combatants and noncombatants?

---

[167] This is another case of dust being "figurative for what is low, defeated, contemptible..." (added to other examples in Delbert Hillers, "Dust: Some Aspects of Old Testament Imagery," in John H. Marks and Robert M. Good, eds. *Love & Death in the Ancient Near East* (Guilford, CT: Four Quarters, 1987) 106.

[168] Michelle Marcus, "Geography as Visual Ideology: Landscape, Knowledge, and Power in Neo-Assyrian Art," in Mario Liverani, ed., *Neo-Assyrian Geography* (Rome: CNR, 1995) 194–95.

Or is it (less probably) another example of the Bible's obscuration of the female?

This absence of the female does not, in any case, prevent the psalmist from emphasizing the fertility of the land and its human and animal inhabitants (vv. 6–7, 16) resulting from the king's successful rule and connected to his own fertility (v. 17). With its wish for the persistence of the king's reputation (שׁם) forever (לעולם), v. 17 offers a twist on the hope for dynastic survival.[169]

Martin Arneth has identified significant thematic connections between Psalm 72 and the coronation hymn of Assurbanipal (SAA 3.11), again indicating that the psalm originated in the orbit of the Assyrian empire and perhaps that its claim to universal sovereignty for the Judahite king explicitly makes a counterclaim to Assyrian propaganda.[170] In both texts, divinity provides the monarch the icons of kingship (crown, throne, weapon, "luminous splendor" (šalummatu), and a court for Assurbanipal; bowing subjects and delivered poor subjects for the ruler of Israel or Judah). While the Israelite text does not explicitly mention the investment of the king with icons of his power, it hints at such items by describing the results of royal rule under the aegis of Yahweh.

Psalm 101

In addition to the psalms that undoubtedly come from a coronation ceremony, Ps. 101 also appears to be a royal oath, almost an ancient *Fürstenspiegel*, plausibly uttered during the coronation.[171] Kselman has

---

[169] לעולם describes the king's "days" (ימים; Ps. 21:5), his throne (Ps. 45:7), and his seed (זרע; Ps. 18:51; 89:5, 37; cf. KAI 26A IV.2; 224.25), and his priesthood (Ps. 110:4).

[170] Arneth, *"Sonne der Gerechtigkeit"*, 54–108. Most of the parallels are also attested in earlier Assyrian texts (as Arneth notes) and in texts from Assyrian subject states (e.g., KAI 24). Indeed, the themes of royal prosperity connected to that of the land, the investment of the king with icons of power by deities date back to the third millennium and the coronation of Shulgi (see Jacob Klein, "The Coronation and Consecration of Šulgi in the Ekur [Šulgi G]," in *Ah Assyria . . .: Studies in Assyrian History and Ancient Near Eastern Historiography Presented to Hayim Tadmor* [ed. Mordechai Cogan and Israel Eph'al; Jerusalem: Magnes, 1991] 292–313.

[171] Gunkel, *Einleitung*, 145; Weiser, *Psalmen*, 428. Dahood (*Psalms 101–150*, 2–3) contests this, identifying the psalm as a lament, based on v. 2b, "when will you come to me?" (מתי תבוא אלי). He consequently understands the prefix conjugation verbs of the psalm as *yaqtul* preterites. While this proposal has much to commend it and must be taken seriously, it fails, I believe, because even following Dahood

proposed that vv. 6–7 and possibly 8 are the divine response to the king, and implicitly the answer to the query in v. 2aβ.[172] This hypothesis is plausible, but it rests on the assumption that the psalm is a lament (since laments often contain divine oracles responding to the supplicant). There are no clear internal clues to a switch in speakers, and everything in vv. 6–8 makes sense coming from the king. Accordingly, the psalm as a whole is best understood as the oath of the monarch.

Gerstenberger has questioned the more basic assumption that Ps. 101 is a royal psalm.[173] He assigns the text to "the theological anthropology of early Jewish communities."[174] I disagree for two reasons: first, the parallels from Mesopotamia are earlier and do reflect the moral commitments of the monarch; and second, what Gerstenberger calls "the violent language against the evildoers in vv. 7–8"[175] is difficult to attribute to commoners. To do so is to envision a society in which anarchy prevails, since the monarch (and thus the state) no longer enjoys a monopoly on violence. Such a condition seems quite out of place in ancient Israel. Even if we assume that the language is hyperbolical, it must nevertheless find some realization in the world of action.

Mirrors of princes not unlike Ps. 101 do survive from Mesopotamia. For example, DT 1 lists rules for a king of Babylonian who must variously heed his nobles and advisers, respect the prerogatives of the key cities of Babylonia, avoid bribery, and otherwise rule well.[176]

---

in taking the verbs as preterites (which he does not do in v. 2b, ironically!) leaves one not with an entire lament, but at most the protestation of innocence that makes up part of one. It may be that the psalm borrows the question from the lament form, but uses it for a different purpose. If, as Mowinckel suggested and I have argued above, the coronation took place in the Jerusalem Temple, one might expect a theophany to follow. Ps. 110 implies as much when it has the king sitting beside Yahweh. It may be that Ps. 101 comes prior to the "birth" of the king in the morning of the coronation ritual. This is speculative, I admit, but it offers a plausible solution of the problem that Dahood has raised. On the use of *qinah* meter here, see Oswald Loretz, *Die Königspsalmen: Die altorientalisch-kanaanäische Königstradition in jüdischer Sicht* (UBL 6; Münster: Ugarit-Verlag, 1988) 145–46.

[172] John S. Kselman, "Psalm 101: Royal Confession and Divine Oracle," *JSOT* 33 (1985) 45–62.

[173] Gerstenberger, *Psalms Part 2*, 206–9.

[174] Ibid., 209.

[175] Ibid., 208.

[176] See Tablet 53 of *Šumma ālu* in W. G. Lambert, ed., *Babylonian Wisdom Literature* (Winona Lake, IN: Eisenbrauns, 1996) 112–15, 316–17; and the commentary thereon in Erica Reiner and Miguel Civil, "The Babylonian Fürstenspiegel in Practice," in

Unlike Ps. 101, this text lists specific practices the king must avoid and the punishments that will befall him if he does not. Ps. 101, by contrast, is more vague, perhaps because it does not have in mind specific royal usurpations of power. Therefore, the analogy between the two texts is imperfect, but not irrelevant.

Ps. 101 also, significantly, yields a much higher quantity of body language. The "heart" (לבב; v. 2) and "eyes" (עינים; vv. 3, 5, 7) of the king are singled out and contrasted with the heart and eyes of various evildoers (v. 5b). The psalm plays upon the mentions of the body parts very artistically. Notice v. 2: "I will go in the perfection of my heart (לבב), in the midst of my house (בקרב ביתי)." The heart is pure, blameless within the royal palace. Both phrases indicate interiority, a space where the king is secluded. Yet the palace sits atop Jerusalem's acropolis (if below the Temple), is the city's largest and most lavish building, and symbolizes through its sheer scale and its iconography (if similar Levantine palaces are any indication) the king's prominence.[177] Likewise, the singing of the hymn makes the interiority of the heart exterior, public, available for the inspection of Yahweh, first, and the song's human audience (the court, the inhabitants of Jerusalem), second. Again, the royal body hides and reveals.

The demonstration of the perfection of the king's heart comes from his commitment in the following lines to avoid contact with, or even to persecute, various religious and economic criminals. Just as the crimes are couched in bodily images (לבב עקש, גבה־עינים ורחב מלושני בסתר, לבב), so also is the king's rectitude framed in terms of his use of his eyes. His gaze, or rather the absence of it, signifies his governance; he will avoid seeing evildoers.[178] Or rather, he would see them only insofar as this was necessary to regulate them, and concomitantly insofar as this was adequate to attract Yahweh's favorable gaze and that of the people. Yet, at the same time, the king's promise not to see evil, while he does in fact do so and thus eliminates

---

Societies and Languages of the Ancient Near East (Diakonoff Festschrift; Warminster: Aris & Phillips, 1982) 320–26.

[177] On Iron Age Palestinian (Israelite) palaces, see Ronny Reich, "Palaces and Residencies in the Iron Age," in Aharon Kempinski and Ronny Reich, eds., *The Architecture of Ancient Israel: From the Prehistoric to the Persian Periods* (Jerusalem: Israel Exploration Society, 1992) 202–22.

[178] On the gaze as a figure for the regulation of the body, see Michel Foucault, *Discipline and Punish* (New York: Pantheon, 1977) esp. 195–230.

its practitioners, mirrors his own visibility to his subjects and Yahweh. By promising not to see, the king allows himself to be seen, judged, by these human and divine spectators of his reign. They may see his now disciplined body that is fit to rule.

How does this impinge on the king's use of power? It is noteworthy that this psalm is unembarrassed by the use of royal power to create hardship in the lives of subjects deemed wicked. Unlike Pss. 2 and 72, which mark evil as "foreign," this psalm raises the specter of evil being inside the palace itself, although the psalmist is quick to eliminate that location as a real possibility. Still, the king here is a performer, literally as he intones the psalm (אשירה, אזמרה; v. 1), and metaphorically as he promises to rid the land of evil. His body itself is the proof of his piety and the sign of his successful performance of kingship.

Preliminary Conclusions

So far, the discussion of the royal body in the Psalter has argued that these lyrics from the official court sanctuary and the coronation and marriage rites that were performed there focus upon the creation of the king as a successful warrior and dominator of the foreign. Offering a direct challenge to the pretensions of outside rulers, these psalms envision a monarch who because of his connection to, indeed likeness to, the divine sovereign, never loses and never fails to execute justice for his subjects. Just as Assyrian court texts (state propaganda) and those of their vassals connect royal victory to the prosperity of the land, all insured by the divinely created body of the king as it exercises legitimate domination, so too do Israelite texts from the court and official cult. Also like the deity, the human king experiences (a kind of) immortality, though in this case this is notional. Wedding and coronation reflect multiple layers of the significations of the royal body, which in its genderedness, in turn reflects what society itself is to be, a body politic sound and whole.

CHAPTER THREE

THE ROYAL BODY AT WORK

The ritual creation ("birth") of the king allows him to build, to petition God, to go to war, and to receive oracles. The royal psalms reflect upon multiple significations of his body as he does these things. Once the king's body has come into being through ritual, it must act and be seen acting, and various royal psalms reveal such action as kings and their retainers wished them to be seen. That is, they assume the rules of royal bodily display that the Israelite monarchy believed its subjects would find most appropriate.

The Israelite court and its priesthood ritualized not only the coronation and marriage of the king, but also his work as builder and warrior. All such events were performances in the Austinian sense that they made the king and the dynasty did so publicly. In doing so, they could draw on already ancient Near Eastern practices. To return to Tambiah's point on ritual as performance, the texts stemming from these rituals embed multiple layers of signification and point to values that the ritualizers (or their royal sponsors) sought to produce (or assumed to be present) in their audience, namely, both the king's subjects and the deity.[1] Or, as Catherine Bell puts it, the goals of such political ritual are: (1) "to depict a group of people as a coherent and ordered community based on shared values and goals" and (2) to "demonstrate the legitimacy of these values and goals by establishing their iconicity with the perceived values and order of the cosmos."[2] The king, precisely as ruler of his loyal subjects, builds in imitation of Yahweh the builder of the cosmos; the king fights alongside the warrior deity.

---

[1] Extrapolating from Stanley Tambiah, "A Performative Approach to Ritual," *Proceedings of the British Academy* 45 (1979) 119; reprinted in idem, *Culture, Thought, and Social Action: An Anthropological Perspective* (Cambridge: Harvard University Press, 1985) 128.

[2] Catherine Bell, *Ritual: Perspectives and Dimensions* (New York: Oxford University Press, 1999) 129.

The King as Builder: Psalm 132

Among the major roles of a Near Eastern monarch was the sponsorship of monumental construction.[3] This sponsorship demanded ritualization and commemoration in texts, of which Ps. 132 is an example. In its present location in the Psalter, Ps. 132 is part of the so-called Psalms of Ascent, which seem to be the liturgy of a procession into Jerusalem.[4] The series of psalms in the Ascent complex (120–134) may not all date to the Iron Age,[5] but the fact that Ps. 132 does not reflect the Deuteronomistic view of the Solomonic origins of the Temple, indicates a preexilic date of the psalm.[6] Ps. 132 deserves study on its own, its ritual setting being postulated on the basis of internal and comparative evidence, without assuming that it originally functioned as part of a procession toward the temple.[7] Indeed, if we had only this psalm, we would conclude that David himself built the temple. Hence the request of vv. 10–11 that David's actions be the basis of divine blessing for his progeny. So one must reckon here with a different tradition of the origins of the temple. At a minimum, the focus is upon David as the model for later builders.

---

[3] For a study of the practical and ritual dimensions of royal building, see Sylvie Lackenbacher, *Le Roi Bâtisseur: Les recits de construction assyriens des origines à Teglatphalasar III* (Paris: ERC, 1982).

[4] On which see, e.g., Klaus Seybold, *Die Wallfahrtspsalmen: Studien zur Entstehungsgeschichte von Psalm 120–134* (Biblisch-theologische Studien 3; Neukirchen-Vluyn: Neukirchener Verlag, 1978).

[5] E.g., Ps. 126 longs for the return of the captives to Jerusalem, and Ps. 129 employs normally late (for Judahite Hebrew) grammatical features such as ש for אשר. On the Achaemenid period date of the complex, see Michael Goulder, *The Psalms of the Return (Book V, Psalms 107–150)* (JSOTSS 258; Sheffield: Sheffield Academic Press, 1998) esp. 20–115.

[6] See Scott R. A. Starbuck, *Court Oracles in the Psalms: The So-Called Royal Psalms in their Ancient Near Eastern Context* (SBLDS 172; Atlanta: Society of Biblical Literature, 1999)126; *contra* Erhard Gerstenberger, *Psalms, Part 2 and Lamentations* (FOTL 15; Grand Rapids: Eerdmans, 2001) 368. On archaic word formations in the psalm, see Frank Cross, *Canaanite Myth and Hebrew Epic* (Cambridge: Harvard University Press, 1973) 97 n. 24; for ideological reasons for an early date for the psalm, see ibid., 233; but cf. T. N. D. Mettinger, *King and Messiah: The Civil and Sacral Legitimation of the Israelite Kings* (CBOTS 8; Lund: Gleerup, 1976) 256–57 (who argues for the psalm's dependence on the DH, though not convincingly because his parallels are too general).

[7] See the cautions of Delbert Hillers, "Ritual Procession of the Ark and Ps 132," *CBQ* 30 (1968) 48–55.

Significantly, Mowinckel argued that the psalm dates to the monarchic period and was part of a festival commemorating the procession of the ark into Jerusalem (cf. 2 Sam. 6); the psalm is the script of a drama of reenactment.[8] Whatever its problems, this hypothesis has the merit of linking a ritual text with a cult legend.[9] Ps. 132:5 has David searching, not for the Ark, but for the residence of Yahweh, namely, the Temple.[10] This is a quest for the right place to build the Temple itself.

Mowinckel may be correct as regards the procession itself. On the other hand, Delbert Hillers argued that v. 8 actually does not mention the procession of the Ark, and that the Psalm is better understood in connection with acts of piety related to royal sponsorship of temple construction.[11] It is possible to extend Hillers's basic insight, emphasizing, however, the aspects of the psalm that impinge on the construction of the king's body and therefore his status as a powerful male. Notice that this is a poem celebrating the building ("finding") of the Temple, apparently by David (contrary to other traditions embedded in the Bible). The royal sponsorship of temple building and renovation is a major theme of state propaganda throughout the ancient Near East.[12] Concern for future reconstruction is sometimes provided

---

[8] Sigmund Mowinckel, *The Psalms in Israel's Worship* (Oxford: Blackwell, 1962) 1. 174–77. Gary Rendsburg (*Linguistic Evidence for the Northern Origin of Selected Psalms* [SBLMS 43; Atlanta: Scholars, 1990] 87–90) has argued for a northern origin of the psalm on the basis of supposedly Israelian grammatical features. Some of them, however, are simply archaisms, shared retentions from proto-Northwest Semitic (*-at* as the feminine singular ending, *zû* as the relative pronoun), and thus are not probative (on these two forms, see W. Randall Garr, *Dialect Geography of Syria-Palestine* [Philadelphia: University of Pennsylvania Press, 1985] 59–60 and 85–87 respectively). Accordingly, in view of this problem and the psalms's mention of David, Zion, and the Ark, Rendsburg's hypothesis cannot be taken seriously.

[9] Goulder (*Psalms of the Return*, 92–97), noting the speculative nature of Mowinckel's "divine drama" hypothesis, argues that v. 17a implies the restoration of a lost Davidic dynasty and thus a postexilic date for the psalm. His connection of the search for the *Temple* here to Nehemiah's legendary search for the lost *Ark and fire* in 2 Macc. 1:18–36 and 2:4–8 (and thus again a postexilic date for the psalm) is more speculative still.

[10] For this reason, I understand אביר יעקב in v. 3 as a divine epithet, not another name for the Ark (*contra* Terence Fretheim, "Psalm 132: A Form-Critical Study," *JBL* 86 [1967] 289–300, esp. 290).

[11] Hillers, "Ritual Procession of the Ark and Ps 132," 48–55.

[12] On Assyria, e.g., see Lackenbacher, *Le Roi Bâtisseur*; for Israel and the Near East, see Victor (Avigdor) Hurowitz, *I Have Built You an Exalted House* (JSOTSS 115; Sheffield: JSOT Press, 1992). For the Levant, see KAI 4.1; 14.15–17; 15; and 202 B 9–10; and the new Ekron Inscription.

for in inscriptions: future readers of the text are encouraged to rebuild as needed. A typical example appears in an inscription of Esarhaddon:

> If at any time in the future (*ina aḥrat ūmē*) during the days of the reign of some future prince (*ina ūmē palê [BALA]-šu*),[13] this work falls into disrepair, may (that prince) repair its dilapidated state! May he write my name with his own name! May he look at my royal inscription, anoint it with oil (*lipšuš*),[14] offer a sacrifice, (and) set (it) back in its place! The god Marduk will (then) hearken (*išemme*) to his prayers.[15]

The crucial features of this address to future readers include: (1) recognition of the achievements of the past king (the author of the inscription); (2) repair or construction of the temple; and (3) blessing of the future king. The first and last elements appear obviously in Ps. 132. The second is more elusive.

However, we do hear of renovations of the Jerusalem Temple under Joash (2 Kings 12), Ahaz (2 Kings 16), Josiah (2 Kings 23), and probably Hezekiah (see 2 Chron. 29), nor is there reason to think that DH (or Chronicles) provides an exhaustive list. Such renovations would have called for ritual, including ritual texts. These texts, in turn, would have mentioned the past king's achievements and linked him to his successors, just as Ps. 132 does. At some point in the ritual, the present king's piety in rebuilding the temple would doubtless have been mentioned. It does not appear explicitly in Ps. 132, although this need not be a deterrent to my hypothesis. As Hector Avalos has shown in connection with Dan. 9:24, the temple-rebuilding theme was well known in Israel and could be modified to fit the needs of a given author.[16] Mowinckel is correct, then, to link this psalm to some festival commemorating the building of the temple. He was, however, unable to produce parallels of such anniversary celebrations, whereas celebrations of rebuilding were common.

How, then, does this relate to the topic of this study? First, it is noteworthy that the Davidic dynasty bears Yahweh's promises to

---

[13] On the passage of eras, see Peter Machinist, "The Transfer of Kingship: A Divine Turning," in Astrid B. Beck, et al., *Fortunate the Eyes that See* (Grand Rapids: Eerdmans, 1995) 105–20.

[14] On the care of royal images, see Irene J. Winter, "Idols of the King: Royal Images as Recipients of Ritual Action in Ancient Mesopotamia," *Journal of Ritual Studies* 6 (1992) 13–42.

[15] RIMB 6.32.6.26–27.

[16] Hector Avalos, "Daniel 9:24–25 and Mesopotamian Temple Rededications," *JBL* 117 (1998) 507–11.

David, since his successors are the "fruit of [his] belly" (מפרי בטנך) [v. 11]; not "fruit of your loins," interestingly). Whatever is true of David is true of his descendants. The king must reproduce, and he will if he, like David, maintains the temple. Second, vv. 3–5 highlight David's bravura in searching for the correct place for the Temple: "I will not go into the tent of my house (באהל ביתי), I will not climb into my bed, I will not allow my eyes sleep, or my eyelids slumber, until I have found a place for Yahweh, dwellings for the Strong One of Jacob (אביר יעקב)." Self-imposed sleeplessness is a mark of the fearsome Assyrian warrior in Isa. 5:27, and here in Ps. 132, the reference to sleeplessness (expressed in bodily terms of eyes and eyelids), picking up a theme in Mesopotamian temple-building texts,[17] similarly positions the king as a male worthy of esteem. The unsleeping eye is a sign of his male vigor.

Ps. 132, then, uses body imagery sparingly but effectively to indicate the king's estimability before God and other males. Like David, the current ruler must be tireless in his piety. Building God's house also allows God to build David's house. Yahweh insures the fertility of each successive king and thus the perserverance of the dynasty. What is more, since the Jerusalem temple adjoined the royal palace, the deity becomes the audience and neighbor, so to speak, of the king.

Psalms of Petition: Psalms 89, 144, and Isaiah 38

Psalms of petition are the most common *Gattung* in the Psalter. Accordingly, it is not surprising that some of them apply to the king. Since they deal with sickness, political threat, or both—sickness could be the result of spells cast by political enemies, as in the Assyrian and Babylonian *bīt rimki* series[18]—they reveal the king's body constructed and deconstructed. The king appears as both a human subject to illness, danger, and death, and a superhuman whose very

---

[17] See Hurowitz, *Exalted House*, 324–25; Dale Launderville, *Piety and Politics: The Dynamics of Royal Authority in Homeric Greece, Biblical Israel, and Old Babylonian Mesopotamia* (Grand Rapids: Eerdmans, 2003) 325–31.

[18] See Jørgen Laessøe, *Studies on the Assyrian Ritual and Series* bīt rimki (Copenhagen: Munksgaard, 1955); on its putative Assyrian origins, see Walter Farber, "*Bīt rimki*—ein assyrisches Ritual?" in Hartmut Waetzoldt and Harald Hauptmann, eds., *Assyrien im Wandel der Zeiten* (29th Rencontre Assyriologique Internationale, 1992; Heidelberg: Heidelberger Orientverlag, 1997) 41–46.

body is the locus of the hopes of the nation and the blessings of the divine.

Psalm 89

One of the most discussed poems in the Psalter, Ps. 89 gives evidence of careful articulation that impinges on its conception of the king's body and therefore his maleness. In its current dress, the psalm is a petition (lament) for a Davidide in distress, perhaps reflecting the end of Judah in the sixth century or an earlier crisis.[19] Yet it also contains older material, including a version of the Davidide dynastic oracle.[20] Bernard Renaud has recently attempted to situate the psalm in the period of turmoil following Nebuchadnezzar's sack of Jerusalem in 587.[21] This makes intelligible sense of the text, although it is also possible that the crisis of 701 or an even earlier anxiety over foreign imperialism (as in Isa. 10:10–11) is in view, in which case the crisis in the Davidic dynasty would not be its disappearance, but its failure to defend the nation from Assyrian expansion. Whichever date one chooses, the psalm's usefulness as a window

---

[19] I leave to one side the proposal of Gösta Ahlström (*Psalm 89: Eine Liturgie aus dem Ritual des leidenden Königs* [Lund: Gleerup, 1959]), to wit, that the psalm began as a liturgy for the dying and rising god Dwd: "Der 89. Psalm hat also zu den Dwd-Zeremonien gehört und ist ein Beleg dafür, daß Vegetationsriten eine Grosse Rolle in der israelitischen Religion gespielt haben" (172). This hypothesis is a classical example of how the History of Religions school could allow an alleged ritual pattern to explain a text in defiance of all evidence to the contrary. This is not to neglect, however, the real insights that Ahlström also provides in his careful analysis of the text.

[20] For an *Überlieferungsgeschichtliche* analysis of the text, see Eduard Lipinski, *Le poème royal du Psaume LXXXIX 1–5, 20–38* (Paris: Gabalda, 1967) esp. 87–90. He argues that 1–5 and 20–38 were a pre-eighth-century text reworked after the Babylonian conquest. Gerstenberger (*Psalms, Part 2*, 154) claims a postexilic date, though without argumentation. See also Bernard Renaud's proposal ("Un oracle prophétique [2 S 7] invalidé? Une approche du Psaume 89," in Jean-Georges Heintz, ed., *Oracles et Prophéties dans l'antiquité* [Paris: Boccard, 1997] 223) that a separate hymn appears in vv. 2–3 and 6–19. The two agree that vv. 20–38 have a history prior to their incorporation into this psalm. These proposals remain unverifiable and unnecessary, however. For the purposes of this study, the crucial point here is to indicate the connections among the various sections of Ps. 89, even if these connections may finally be the creation of a poet working with older material. Yet even this poet must, as will become clear presently, have been familiar with the courtly language of Judah, because he or she lived during the time of the monarchy.

[21] Renaud, "Oracle prophétique," 215–29. See also Timo Veijola, *Verheissung in der Krise: Studien zur Literatur und Theologie der Exilszeit anhand des 89. Psalms* (Helsinki: Suomalainen Tiedeakatemia, 1982).

THE ROYAL BODY AT WORK 89

into Iron Age Judahite conceptions of kingship remains untarnished, as the presence of Iron Age royal terminology (e.g., צדקה, when referring to relationships between deities and kings)[22] and the strong connection between vv. 20–38 and 2 Sam. 7[23] indicate.

The Promised Body
Turning then to Ps. 89 itself, one should begin by examining vv. 20–38, which depict the king's body in a state of health and glory, and then vv. 39–52, where the body experiences sickness and ignominy.[24] V. 20 appeals to the past, offering a visionary experience as evidence of the truthfulness of what follows. Yahweh's *ḥasid* receives this vision.[25] Is this a prophet (Nathan as in 2 Sam. 7) or, as Ahlström has argued,[26] David himself? The latter may be more likely in the context, since we cannot be sure that the psalmist knew the story surrounding the dynastic oracle in the version contained in the DH.[27] If this is correct, then it means that a king can receive an oracle without the mediation of a prophet. Yet, either way, vv. 20–38 describe the king in health as the one fit to receive communication from God, while the one in danger must seek divine guidance.

One can be more confident that vv. 20–21 imagine (or recollect) a series of actions, a performance, by both Yahweh and the king. Anointing enables the king to rule well and outfight his enemies. It marks a transition from one bodily state to another. This seems clear from the chiasmus in 20aγ–21:

The difficult word here is עזר, which is often related to Ugaritic *ǵizru* ("hero"). Thus Dahood argues that v. 20aγ refers to David's

---

[22] E.g., צדק ("loyalty") appears in KAI 215.1 (restored), 11, 19; 216.4–5; 219.4.
[23] See Renaud, "Oracle prophétique," 217–21; Mettinger, *King and Messiah*, 254–56.
[24] Gerstenberger (*Psalms, Part 2*, 149) nicely labels vv. 6–19 an "inset hymn." Far from being a mere digression, however, these verses construct a vision of Yahweh as a mighty warrior who can protect his notional son, the king of Judah.
[25] Unlike other MSS., L reads the plural ("loyal ones"), but this makes little sense in context.
[26] Ahlström, *Psalm 89*, 99–100.
[27] For the evolution of 2 Sam. 7, see the survey in Eckhard von Nordheim, *Die Selbstbehauptung Israels in der Welt des Alten Orients* (OBO 115; Göttingen: Vandenhoeck & Ruprecht, 1992) 110–13.

supplanting of Saul in Yahweh's favor, and translates the clause "I have set [installed as king here] a youth instead of a warrior."[28] Yet, the fact that ğizrūma is a synonym of ṣabiūma ("soldiers") in KTU 1.3.ii.20 weakens Dahood's contrast between "youth" and "warrior," and thus his finding here a cognate of ğizru may be a case of over-reading.

Another solution proposed is that of BDB,[29] BHS[app], and RSV, namely to emend עזר to נזר ("crown"; cf. v. 40). This reading is intelligible in the context, but has no textual support.

Accordingly, I propose to read MT here and to translate the clause "I have placed help upon the hero." This is admittedly an odd locution, but it reflects the common Hebrew poetic practice of substitution. Just as a priest can be clothed with "righteousness" (Ps. 132:9), so can "help" be placed on a warrior (the king). This is a way of saying that Yahweh helps the king.[30] The chiasmus of vv. 20aγ-21 thus indicates a moment at which the king became a warrior by means of his anointing. Curiously, this is coupled with the notion of "finding" the king, which might be literally appropriate for David, but not his successors. As in Ps. 45:8, where the king is chosen "instead of your peers" (מחברים), as if the choice were not a foregone conclusion, here the search for the king ends in his anointing. The anointing, in turn, makes him king and validates the search process that led to his election.

This ritual of anointing with oil betokens the following promises of Yahweh, who swears (נשבע) to uphold (ידי תכון) and strengthen (תאמצנו זרעי) the king and not support his enemies (vv. 22–24; cf. vv. 4–5). Yahweh promises also to "lift up his horn" (תרום קרנו; v. 25). This seems odd until one remembers that Yahweh also has a horn, one of salvation (קרן־ישע; Ps. 18:3 = 2 Sam. 22:3), and that Late Bronze and Iron Age Levantine iconography portray striding gods wearing a helmet from which two horns protruded.[31] The horn is a synecdoche for the entire soldierly paraphernalia of God, and in Ps. 89 of the king.

---

[28] Dahood, *Psalms 51–100*, 316.
[29] BDB 740b; BHS[app] appeals to v. 40, however.
[30] On abstract nouns as "clothing," cf. the use of הוד and הדר in Isa. 63:1–6 and the discussion in Baruch Halpern, *The Constitution of the Monarchy in Israel* (HSM 25; Chico: Scholars, 1981) 133.
[31] See Ora Negbi, *Canaanite Gods in Metal: An Archaeological Study of Ancient Syro-Palestinian Figurines* (Tel Aviv: Tel Aviv University Institute of Archaeology, 1976) pl. 21–22 (items 1137 and 1319); Hab. 3:4.

This close linking of the divine and royal self-display continues in v. 26: "And I will put his hand (יד) in the sea (בים), his right hand (ימין) in the rivers (נהרות)." The pair "sea/river" is obviously well known from the Ugaritic "Baʻlu Epic," where Yammu/Naharu is the foe of Baʻlu, and so a mythic conception of struggle against forces of chaos may be in the background here.[32] Just as Yahweh can vanquish the chthonic forces of Nahar and Yam (Hab. 3:8), so too can the scion of the Davidic line. In the foreground, however, is the king's military prowess against his peers: in order for the king to take hold of rivers and sea, he must travel, must campaign against foreign powers, defeat them, and receive their submission. The psalmist suggests an ideal also common to many Assyrian inscriptions, which claim that the army washed its weapons in the sea (*kakkīya ina tâmti ullil*).[33] This practice was both a token of male derring-do, and a sign that conquests had been made. The psalmist expands even this imagery by having the king reach over the waters themselves. His body, like Yahweh's, is enormously powerful and outsized.[34]

The upshot of this military success is that the king may now claim divine paternity. V. 27 adds little to what one finds in Pss. 2 and 110 (see above),[35] but v. 28 ("Indeed, I will make him the firstborn, עליון to the kings of the earth") takes the notion of godly begettal to a new level. Most translations render the second phrase "highest among the kings of the earth," or some such. But this is surely a weak, apologetically motivated translation, since עליון is often the name of a god,[36] and the royal psalms make the king out to be a

---

[32] See Ahlström, *Psalm 89*, 108–11; Mowinckel (*Psalms in Israel's Worship*, 1. 155) thinks the verse to be a reference to the Mediterranean and the Euphrates, the supposed limits of the Davidic empire. See the discussion in Baruch Halpern, *David's Secret Demons: Messiah, Murderer, Traitor, King* (Grand Rapids: Eerdmans, 2001) 243–59.

[33] See, e.g., RIMA 0.102.10.25 and 1.102.28.20 (Shalmaneser III). Many occurrences of the practice are dated to the monarch's first regnal year, presumably as a way of claiming universal rule; on this literary device, see Hayim Tadmor, "History and Ideology in the Assyrian Royal Inscriptions," in F. Mario Fales, ed., *Assyrian Royal Inscriptions: New Horizons in Literary, Ideological, and Historical Analysis* (Rome: Istituto per l'oriente, 1981) 13–33.

[34] See also Marc Zvi Brettler, *God Is King: Understanding an Israelite Metaphor* (JSOTSS 76; Sheffield: Sheffield Academic Press, 1989) 57–68.

[35] Lipinski (*Psaume LXXXIX*, 66) argues that אבי אתה is treaty language, the "father" being the overlord. In view of the notion of divine sonship in Pss. 2 and 110, there is no reason, however, to decide between a "mythic" and a treaty meaning here. The psalm's audience could have tracked both levels of meaning.

[36] See recently, John Day, *Yahweh and the Gods and Goddesses of Canaan* (JSOTSS 265; Sheffield: Sheffield Academic Press, 2000) 20–21.

superhuman, almost divine figure. Ahlström is correct to say that, "Wie El Eljon ein Grosskönig über alle Götter ist, so ist auch sein Sohn und Erstgeborener Eljon über alle Könige der Erde."[37] Yet even this may not go far enough. Without stating baldly that the king *is* a god Elyon (any more than Moses *is* Elohim [Exod. 4:16]), it should be clear that the king receives resources from the foreign kings much as a god would (gods receive sacrifices, kings tribute, but the presentations of both are similar, which is why tribute can go to temples, temple treasuries can yield tribute in emergencies, and even why kings can receive sacrifices after their death).[38] Moreover the postures of obeisance to a king and to a god are similar. Ps. 89:28 explicitly claims that the king is a superhuman, even divine, figure with a superhuman body.

This godlikeness of the king expresses itself in a perpetual life, that is, in a body that endures through the dynastic succession. The divine progenitor begets both divinities (v. 7) and the king (vv. 27–28). As before, any given king may die, but the King and thus his body endure (vv. 29–38), just as one would expect of the offspring of Yahweh.

The Body Unknit
This citation in vv. 29–38 of the dynastic treaty with Yahweh serves in the psalm as a whole as a prelude to the accusation against the deity beginning in v. 39. In the strongest possible language, the psalmist charges Yahweh with reneging on his promises. The indictment begins where the recitation of the promise began, i.e., with a reference to the anointed king. Since it is at this point that the king is born as son of Yahweh, the reference to the anointing implies that Yahweh has abandoned his own offspring and has therefore in some way unknit the royal body he fashioned at the coronation. Next follows the undoing of all the successes promised in vv. 20–38.

The chief references to the king's undone body come in vv. 44–46. V. 44 speaks of the king's failure to wield his weapons effectively: his skills as a warrior, taught by Yahweh and now betrayed by the

---

[37] Ahlström, *Psalm 89*, 113.
[38] On the last point, witness the offering tables set before kings on an orthostat of Bir-rakib of Sam'al or on the Ahiram sarcophagus, to name a few examples (see also Edith Porada, "Notes on the Sarcophagus of Ahiram," in *The Gaster Festschrift* [*JANES* 5 (1973)] 355–72).

deity, are inadequate. V. 45 reads שבת מטהרו ("you turned away from his purity"),[39] which appears at first problematic since concern for the "purity" of the king is virtually absent from the royal psalms (but see the discussion of Ps. 18 below). On the other hand, "purity" (Akkadian *ellūtu*, adj. *ellu*) is an important feature of the self-predication of the Assyrian emperors who dominated the Near East in the period just before the final crises of the Davidic dynasty, as well as in Ugaritic royal texts.[40] The Neo-Assyrian rulers underwent extensive purification ceremonies allowing them to purify the armies[41] and otherwise engage in their kingly duties. A pure king is a fit warrior and general. If the parallel is probative, then Yahweh's refusal to acknowledge the Davidide king's purity serves as part of the divine refusal to aid his fighting. Yahweh has not carried out his end of the bargain, despite the purity of the king, and has allowed him to fail as a soldier. Again, the deity has ignored the true state of the royal body—pure, anointed, warriorly—and has aided the king's enemies. I shall return to this point when considering Ps. 18.

V. 46 brings to a climax—though it seems anticlimactic at first—this subversion of the royal body. Yahweh has cut short the king's youthfulness (עלומים), has "made him enwrap himself with sterility."[42] The verb עטה ("to enwrap") often takes clothing as its object.[43] The psalmist chooses the verb ironically: since engendering children requires nudity, the exposure of the body, the king's curse here is to be "covered," to be precluded from reproductive sex. When compared to the prospect of death in battle, to be sure, sterility seems a minor handicap. But the point of the verse is that the king's body is unable to produce offspring; and thus the dynasty is not long for power.

---

[39] Dahood (*Psalms 51–100*, 319) reads the consonants as *miṭhar*, a hapax that he connects to Ugaritic *ṭuhuru* ("gem"; but usually just "purity" like Hebrew טהרה [adj. טהור]). This seems unnecessary, however, since reading a privative מ plus a טהר makes sense. On the equation *ellu* = טהר, see E. Jan Wilson, *"Holiness" and "Purity" in Mesopotamia* (AOAT 237; Neukirchen-Vluyn: Neukirchener, 1994) 95.

[40] On the epithet, see Cifola, *Analysis of Variants*; Paul Garelli, "La Conception de la royauté en Assyrie," in F. Mario Fales, ed., *Assyrian Royal Inscriptions: New Horizons in Literary, Ideological, and Historical Analysis* (Rome: Istituto per l'Oriente, 1981) 1–11; for Ugarit, see Gregorio del Olmo Lete, *Canaanite Religion According to the Liturgical Texts of Ugarit* (Winona Lake, IN: Eisenbrauns, 2004) 144–60.

[41] See the full references in Ursula Magen, *Assyrische Königsdarstellungen: Aspekte der Herrschaft* (Mainz: von Zabern, 1986) esp. 69–91.

[42] On the ingenious translation of בושה (biform of ינש) as "dryness, sterility," see Dahood, *Psalms 51–100*, 319.

[43] Gen. 38:14; 1 Sam. 28:14; Isa. 61:10; Mic. 3:7 (?); Pss. 104:2; 109:19 (= לבש).

Summary

Ps. 89, then, frames the calamities befalling the nation (at the death of Josiah?) in terms of harm to the king's body, and specifically the subversion of the divine promises of health, fecundity, and skill in combat. In a general way, this demolition of the body is reminiscent of the treaty curses common in the seventh century (in Esarhaddon's vassal treaties or the Sefire treaties, for example), although the specifics are different in each case. In such treaties, the bodies of the treaty violator and his family suffer such fates as starvation, cannibalism, and disease.[44] In all these texts, the violent decomposition of the human body functions iconically to signify the loss of power and status by the monarch, who in turn is an index of the people he rules and whom his deity, the erstwhile guarantor of bodily integrity, also rules. As it stands, Psalm 89 functions performatively to evoke the possibility of such an inversion of the signs of royal power and by naming them, to reverse them. It is thus the liturgy of an apotropaic rite. Moreover, by invoking two distinct sets of sign relationships, /King as divine offspring/ and /king as defeated warrior/, the psalmist allows us to witness an intracultural debate as to the meaning of kingship. Kingship always exists one defeat removed from its undoing, both symbolically and literally.

Psalm 144

Like Ps. 89, Ps. 144 poses a number of problems even before one gets to its picture of the royal body. The date and unity of this psalm are in question. Following Gunkel, older scholars argued that vv. 12–15 were a later addition to a royal psalm,[45] itself actually a pastiche of quotations from other psalms.[46] This characterization has come under fire from several directions: Dahood argued convincingly for a high degree of originality for the poem,[47] while Kraus,

---

[44] See, e.g., Esarhaddon's "Vassal Treaty," lines 414–663 (in Kazuko Watanabe, *Die* adê *Vereidigung anlässlich der Thronfolgeregelung Asarhaddons* (Baghdader Mitteilungen 3; Berlin: Mann, 1987]; for the influence of Esarhaddon's treaties on Deuteronomy [and thus indirectly other biblical texts], see Hans Ulrich Steymans, *Deuteronomium 28 and die* adê *zur Thronfolgeregelung Asarhaddons: Segen und Fluch im Alten Orient und in Israel* [OBO 145; Göttingen: Vandenhoeck & Ruprecht, 1995]).

[45] Gunkel, *Einleitung*, 140. Cf. the remarks of Marc Brettler, "Images of YHWH the Warrior in Psalms," *Sem* 61 (1993) 135–65.

[46] Mowinckel, *Psalms in Israel's Worship*, 2. 158.

[47] Dahood, *Psalms 101–150*, 328–32.

Terrien, Gerstenberger and others have argued for its basic unity in spite of form critically disparate elements.[48] Goulder accepts the unity of the psalm but argues for its postexilic origins, based primarily on the presence of (usually) late grammatical features such as שׁ as a relative pronoun in v. 15 and the Aramaism זן in v. 13.[49] However, שׁ serves in Phoenician as a relative pronoun in the ninth-century (?) Nora Inscription (KAI 46.1, 2, 7) and is Proto-Semitic, even if it usually is late in Classical Hebrew (but see Judg. 5:7). זן is a demonstrative pronoun in the Ahiram Inscription from Byblos (KAI 1.1) already in the ninth century, and so is hardly an "Aramaism," as Goulder thinks. His relatively late date thus has little to support it, and the psalm's overall interest in what seems to be a living monarchy suggests a date in the Iron Age, perhaps toward the end of the monarchy like Ps. 89. Note, too, that the transition between vv. 11 and 12 is one between a plea for help and a notice of prosperity. Just such a transition is envisioned in the ninth-century inscription of Kilamuwa (KAI 24), again an indication that one is not dealing here with a postmonarchic Israelite hymn, but one very much at home in the Iron Age.

Turning, then, to analysis of the psalm, let us consider two aspects of the king's self-presentation. First, as in Ps. 101, he is the singer of the psalm, and calls attention to that fact (vv. 1 and 9). The cohortative אשׁירה in v. 9 presents the king as a worthy singer. His is a performative utterance in two senses: (1) in the obvious sense that the king sings the word as part of his larger song (illocution); and (2) in the more important that he is simultaneously persuading Yahweh of the desirability of intervening on his behalf and the

---

[48] Weiser, *Psalmen*, 550–51; Samuel Terrien, *The Psalms: Strophic Structure and Theological Commentary* (Eerdmans Critical Commentary; Grand Rapids: Eerdmans, 2003) 898; Gerstenberger, *Psalms, Part 2*, 431; see John Eaton, *Kingship and the Psalms* (2d ed.; Sheffield: JSOT Press, 1986) 127–28.

[49] See Goulder, *Psalms of the Return*, 271–72. Goulder argues for a late date for the entire psalm, based primarily on alleged borrowings from Pss. 18 and 33. This criterion is questionable, however, since these are first of all oral texts that use stock phrases in performances. On formulas in performance, see Albert Lord, *The Singer of Tales* (New York: Atheneum, 1968); Yitzhaq Avishur, *Stylistic Studies of Word Pairs in Biblical and Ancient Literatures* (AOAT 210; Neukirchen-Vluyn: Neukirchener Verlag, 1984); idem, *Studies in Hebrew and Ugaritic Psalms* (Jerusalem: Magnes, 1994); Susan Niditch, *Oral World and Written Word* (Louisville: Westminster/John Knox, 1996); Gregory Nagy, *Poetry as Performance: Homer and beyond* (Cambridge: Cambridge University Press, 1996).

psalm's human audience of the reality of such intervention (perlocution). To sing so, the king must have trained his body musically and have learned the words of the song.

Second, the king demonstrates his worthiness for divine rescue by citing Yahweh's previous (ongoing?) instruction of him in the art of warmaking (v. 1):

ברך יהוה צורי המלמד ידי לקרב אצבעותי ⁵⁰למלחמה

Blessed be Yahweh, my rock, who teaches my hands fighting, my fingers warfare!

On a literal level, this claim is a fiction: the king must have learned martial skills from other warriors, if at all, and everyone in the audience would have known that. The regimen necessary to acquire soldierly skills would have been available to other notables, as well. So, then, what is gained by the claim that Yahweh is the king's instructor? Just that when Yahweh is portrayed as a warrior, his hands and arms are emphasized, just as they are here, even though, obviously, other body parts (lungs, feet) are required for skillful fighting (see v. 7).[51] The king is like Yahweh, just as in Pss. 2 and 110. Yahweh gives the king the bodily strength and know-how to survive the attacks of enemies, to overcome the vaporous transience of human existence. In other words, according to v. 4 humankind (אדם) is like "wind" (הבל), but the king can survive.

Now, what does Yahweh teach the king? Presumably the lessons include archery, the use of a sword and spear, self-defense with a shield, and probably fighting from a chariot. Yahweh is often portrayed in the Psalms and elsewhere (Hab. 3; Exod. 15) wielding a bow or spear (lightning) and riding a chariot.[52] The king also appears in these roles, both in texts[53] and in glyptic art.[54] Yahweh does not

---

[50] The pair קרב/מלחמה appears elsewhere in the Bible in Job 38:23, where it also connected to divine use of natural forces (snow and lightning), just as in Ps. 144.

[51] On royal imagery in descriptions of the divine, see Thomas Podella, *Das Lichtkleid JHWHs: Untersuchungen zur Gestalthaftigkeit Gottes im Alten Testament und seiner altorientalischen Umwelt* (Tübingen: Mohr/Siebeck, 1996) 186–263; Silvia Schroer and Thomas Staubli, *Body Symbolism in the Bible* (Collegeville, MN: Liturgical Press, 2001) 150–80.

[52] For some of the references, see Marc Brettler, "Images of YHWH the Warrior in Psalms," *Semeia* 61 (1993) 135–65.

[53] See the narratives discussed in Chapters 4–5 below.

[54] See Rüdiger Schmitt, *Bildhafte Herrschaftsrepräsentation im eisenzeitlichen Israel* (AOAT 283; Münster: Ugarit-Verlag, 2001) 111–16.

need a shield, but he serves as one for the king (Ps. 144:2): the designation of Yahweh as מָגִנִּי ("my shield") is an intricate metonym related to the previous line (another sign of the poem's artistry). That is, the weaponry that the deity teaches the king to use is the deity himself! Yahweh also teaches the king the proper uses of strategic retreat and advance. Note that v. 2 calls Yahweh the king's refuge as well as the "one who makes peoples supine before me" (הָרוֹדֵד עַמִּי תַחְתָּי),[55] which implies a charge in battle. Yahweh thus instructs the king in all aspects of warfare.

It should be clear that behind the psalm's claim of divine training of the royal body lies a set of notions of corporeal discipline that are only partially recoverable. The king's training was not merely a matter of royal power, but a prerequisite of social stability. Since Judah was a tiny and weak kingdom for most of its history, the king's conquests were limited, and many of his wars defensive. His slaughter of enemies protects his subjects from death. Power and protection, enmity and community inextricably intertwine. The king's bodily regimen marks him as an adult, a male, a high-status male, and finally a superhuman. That is, we may speak of the king's *habitus* in Marcel Mauss's terms.[56] A set of learned bodily movements and the muscular development required for them come into play in this text. The king who learns them marks out his fitness to rule through martial training. Still it is possible to go beyond Mauss here, for the king's training signifies a larger, religiously imagined, world in which the king dominates all his foes, thanks to his divine trainer. The royal body sits at the center of this imagined world of domination. Around it kneel those who cannot stand up to the king's superior warriorly abilities. The weapons of the king are icons of his power to vanquish evil, but since this power derives from Yahweh, they are symbols of the divine itself, mediated by the divine encounter with the king and, through him, the rest of humanity.

Isaiah 38:9–20

If notions of the hale body inform Ps. 144, the sick one lies behind the text we now consider. Isa. 38:9–20 is part of a series of legends

---

[55] On the translation of v. 2b, see Dahood, *Psalms 101–150*, 329–30. רדד literally means "to hammer (out), to pound, to flatten."

[56] Marcel Mauss, "Body Techniques," in idem, *Sociology and Psychology: Essays* (London: Routledge, 1979) 101.

(chaps. 36–38[39]) associated with the prophet Isaiah and linking the first and second parts of the canonical book bearing his name.[57] The psalm attributed to Hezekiah has no equivalent in the parallel passage in 2 Kings 20, a fact that poses the question of what historical kernel gave rise to this story, but I leave that question to one side.[58] The crucial issue here is whether the psalm represents Iron Age conceptions of specifically royal sickness (as opposed to illnesses of non-royals), and if so what those conceptions are. This is doubly important because the poems in the Psalter that I have already considered avoid the subject of the king's illness, even though this was undoubtedly a serious intellectual and ritual problem.

To address the first issue, one may point to the work of Seitz, who, following Smelik in part,[59] has challenged the consensus that understands Isa. 36–39 as a unit dependent on 2 Kings 18–20 and thus dating to the sixth century or later.[60] Seitz has shown that the synopticism of the Kings and Isaiah passages is better explained when viewing Isa. 36–38 as prior—since the corresponding material in Kings does not easily fit the agenda of Dtr¹—and Isa. 39 as a later addendum derived from Dtr². This reconstruction explains the disjuncture between the hopeful dynastic promise in chap. 38 and the prophecy of Babylonian exile in chap. 39,[61] and accordingly would push Isa. 38:9–20 (as well as surrounding material) back into the seventh century or earlier. Even if the psalm has a (now unrecoverable) prior history, the Iron Age tradents of this narrative complex

---

[57] For a discussion of the redactional history of Isa. 36–39, see Christopher Seitz, *Zion's Final Destiny: The Development of the book of Isaiah, A Reassessment of Isaiah 36–39* (Minneapolis: Fortress, 1991); but cf. Otto Kaiser, *Isaiah 13–39* (OTL; London: SCM, 1974) 383–84; Brevard Childs, *Isaiah* (OTL; Louisville: Westminster/John Knox, 2001) 260–66. The place of chapter 38 within the complex remains controversial, though it has become clear that the chapter functions to concretize major themes in the rest of the complex, even if it was added at a later time; see Willem A. M. Beuken, *Isaiah, Part II*, vol. 2: *Isaiah Chapters 28–39* (Historical Commentary on the Old Testament; Leuven: Peeters, 2000) 382–86.

[58] See Seitz, *Zion's Final Destiny*, 173–91.

[59] K. A. D. Smelik, "Distortion of Old Testament Prophecy: The Purpose of Isaiah xxxvi and xxxvii," *OTS* 24 (1986) 70–93. From a different direction, Blenkinsopp appears to date the Isaianic version of Hezekiah's deeds to the late seventh century, still a date supporting the basic approach to this pericope as an Iron Age text (Joseph Blenkinsopp, *Isaiah 1–39* [AB 19; New York: Doubleday, 2000] 483).

[60] On this consensus, see Hans Wildberger, *Isaiah 28–39* (Continental Commentary; Minneapolis: Fortress, 2002) 452–53; Blenkinsopp, *Isaiah 1–39*, 482; but Childs, *Isaiah*, 281.

[61] Ibid., 149–91, esp. 189–90.

found it reasonable that the psalm in Isaiah could serve as a lament[62] for a king and thus a depiction of the sick royal body.

Curiously, however, this illness is described only in the most opaque ways, using imagery comparing the supplicant's impending demise to the rolling up of a rug or the folding of a tent. Nothing in the psalm sounds unique to a king's illness.[63] The obfuscation of royal suffering was intended to preserve, as far as possible, the illusion of the intactness of the king's body as an icon of royal power and a symbol of divine protection. Reticence about the details of illness, in sharp contrast to the celebration of the decomposition of the royal body in Esarhaddon's vassal treaty, for example, preserves the nation's sense of the integrity of the cosmos as a whole.

Consider the following propositions: (1) sickness requires a health care system, that is, a set of healing practitioners who transmit, manipulate, and supplement a body of knowledge;[64] but (2) sickness is nevertheless not simply a "given" of "nature" upon which healers work. Rather, it is an also an opportunity for persons to interact with others in society, oftentimes to their own benefit. The sick body is not a passive object upon which healers "operate." Illness allows self-display; how one deals with illness is perceived as an indication

---

[62] On the basis of the genre designation of this psalm as a מכתב (or is it מכתם?) in 38:9 of the phrase בחלתו ויחי מחליו ("when he [Hezekiah] was sick but survived his sickness") in v. 9, Begrich argued that the narrative foregrounds Hezekiah's healing, placing the psalm in the story (though not in the narrative) after the ministrations of Isaiah. Therefore, this is a psalm of thanksgiving. (See Joachim Begrich, *Der Psalm des Hiskia: Ein Beitrag zum Verständnis von Jesaja 38, 10–20* [FRLANT 25; Göttingen: Vandenhoeck & Ruprecht, 1926] 53, on the superscription; the idea is borrowed by Mowinckel, *Psalms in Israel's Worship*, 2. 8, 42, 88); see also Hans Wildberger, *Jesaja* (BKAT 10.1–3; 3 vols.; Neukirchen-Vluyn: Neukirchener, 1972–82) 3. 1458–59. Kaiser (*Isaiah 13–39*, 404) argues that the psalm is a thanksgiving hymn because it departs from standard lament format, but then must explain its deviations from the standard thanksgiving format by hypothesizing that it is either late or composed specially for its present context. But why would not the same explanation apply if the poem were a petition? Then one could avoid taking the verbs of the first two-thirds of the psalm as preterites and take 17ff. as an expression of hope for the future. Taken on its own, the psalm appears to be a petition (*Bittgebet*) or lament.

[63] This lack of specificity differs from the practice of the Mesopotamian parallels cited in William W. Hallo, "The Royal Correspondence of Larsa: 1. A Sumerian Prototype for the Prayer of Hezekiah," in Barry L. Eichler, ed., *Kramer Anniversary Volume* (AOAT 25; Neukirchen-Vluyn: Neukirchener, 1976) 209–24.

[64] On the Israelite health care system, and this passage in particular, see Hector Avalos, *Illness and Health Care in the Ancient Near East: The Role of the Temple in Greece, Mesopotamia, and Israel* (HSM 54; Atlanta: Scholars Press, 1995) esp. 270–73.

of one's character. Or, to put it in familiar terms, sickness is also a performance, a ritual even, in the sense that the sick and witnesses to his or her illness judge the appropriateness of behaviors against a preexisting code of felicitous or infelicitous behavior.[65] As the medical anthropologist Paul Brodwin puts it, "By talking about painful symptoms and by deciding to reveal them to certain audiences, the person does more than report something about her or his relationship. The person can actually bring about a change in a given relationship."[66] Hezekiah's acceptance of illness and his subsequent recovery convince his subjects of his special relationship to Yahweh (dare we say, sonship?).

The petition attributed to Hezekiah self-consciously speaks of speaking. The implied author acknowledges that he ("Hezekiah") "speaks" (אמרתי; v. 11) about his sickness, and that he "cries" (שועתי;[67] v. 13), "chirps" (אצפצ;[68] v. 14), and "groans, moans, caterwauls" (אהגה;[69] v. 14). The stereotyped reminder that no dead person can praise Yahweh (vv. 18–19), and the call (performative in the Austinian sense of a statement that makes something happen) for music by the healed king (v. 20) both indicate the performative nature of the psalm and indeed the illness itself. But performance for whose benefit? Surely royal illness is a matter of state, and as the story in 2 Kings 20:12ff. indicates, as we shall see, it could come to the attention of foreign powers (through their spy networks).[70] Yet, the king would hardly wish to advertise his illness. A more likely audience is thus the royal court, including the priesthood and prophets, and of course primarily Yahweh himself. The king's handling of illness before this audience

---

[65] The third sense of Tambiah ("Performative Approach to Ritual," 119).

[66] Paul Brodwin, "Symptoms and Social Performances: The Case of Diane Reden," in Mary-Jo Delvecchio Good, et al., eds., *Pain as Human Experience* (Berkeley: University of California Press, 1992) 93.

[67] MT's שויתי ("I place") makes little sense in context. The LXX omits the verb altogether. See Wildberger, *Jesaja*, 3. 1443.

[68] The verb presents a double entendre; birds chirp, making this clause parallel to the succeeding one ("I moan like a dove" [אהגה כיונה]). But so do necromancers (and/or the ghosts they call from the grave) in Isa. 8:19 and 29:4. Thus the psalm makes the king a virtual ghost.

[69] Cf. Ps. 2:1, "why do the peoples muse vainly" (ולאמים יהגו ריק). This verbal connection hardly seems accidental, since the foreign powers in Ps. 2 are complaining about their vassalage to Judah, and subjection to foreign powers can be expressed in bodily terms.

[70] See the broader discussion of royal surveillance in Stuart Lasine, *Knowing Kings: Knowledge, Power, and Narcissism in the Hebrew Bible* (Atlanta: SBL, 2000) 51–71.

is of capital importance. Required of him is not stoic silence in the face of suffering, but a certain amount of complaining, albeit complaining framed by ritual texts such as this one and calculated to elicit divine intervention and create among the king's subjects a respect for his piety.[71]

Now, the bodily imagery in the text carefully avoids the body parts (hands, arms) featured in depictions of the king as warrior (and therefore husband, as in Ps. 45). The poem mentions the petitioner's "eyes" (עיני; v. 14); נפשי (v. 15) could mean "my throat," a bodily reference, as well as "my spirit." The bones (עצמות; v. 13) are being broken as if by a lion, and the eyes languish (דלו עיני; v. 14b). The bones are obviously interior, invisible when the body is healthy. They also often serve as a synecdoche for the entire (dead) body.[72] To speak of them, and thereby to display them, is to open up the body for observation. The eyes, on the other hand, are always visible. The pair bones/eyes thus creates a merismus for the entire body, but one foregrounding those parts not emphasized in warfare.

Summary

The extant Israelite petitions of the king emphasize the reversal of the divine promises of the body. Danger to him may come in the form of exposure in battle or sickness (as is also true in Israelite narratives, as Chapter 4 will show), and in both cases rescue comes from Yahweh. The threat to the royal body implies the reversal of the right cosmic order, in which the properly trained royal body is equal to any military task and always healthy. And, so, these laments allow the king to announce the inappropriateness of his circumstances before an audience of his subjects and, most importantly, the deity, thus allowing the monarch to regain what he has lost. The body in distress thus becomes the locus of divine salvation and the centerpiece of Israelite society's understanding of itself in an orderly created world.

---

[71] See also 2 Sam. 12:15–24; and the discussion in Gary Anderson, *A Time to Mourn, a Time to Dance* (University Park, PA: Pennsylvania State University Press, 1991) 82–84.
[72] For example, Gen. 50:25; Exod. 13:19; Josh. 24:32; 2 Sam. 21:12–13; Amos 6:10; and KAI 9A5; 191B2.

A Thanksgiving Psalm: Psalm 18 (= 2 Samuel 22)

The complements of petitions are psalms of thanksgiving or praise.[73] Ps. 18 (= 2 Sam. 22)[74] offers thanksgiving for an unspecified act of divine deliverance (in battle?). V. 51 refers to the מלך/משיח ("anointed one/king"), the hero of the psalm as a whole. The style of the poem is "grandiose,"[75] and its lack of specificity suggests that it could have been reused on various ritual occasions. Dates suggested for the psalm vary from the beginning of the tenth century[76] to the early sixth[77] to the era of "early Jewish congregations."[78] The mention of the king in v. 51 and the clear echoes of the language of Iron Age inscriptions make a postexilic date unlikely. While Weiser argued that 2 Sam. 22 is a reworking of the older Ps. 18 text,[79] it seems more likely that each derives from a separate oral performance tradition because the various minor discrepancies between the two do not obviously fall into a pattern attributable to deliberate revision in one direction or the other or even to simple textual corruption.[80] In this discussion, I will focus upon vv. 25–40. This division does not correspond, of course, to the flow of the argument of the psalm, which shifts in v. 32 from consideration of Yahweh's prowess back to that of the king (already evident in vv. 28–29).[81] Yet the interest in the king's body exists on both sides of the psalm's major transition point.

V. 25 attributes Yahweh's intervention to the king's loyalty (צדק) and the purity (בר) of his hands. The first part of this theological

---

[73] See Claus Westermann, *Praise and Lament in the Psalms* (Louisville: John Knox, 1981); Walter Brueggemann, *The Psalms and the Life of Faith* (ed. Patrick Miller; Minneapolis: Fortress, 1995) 3–32.

[74] Versification is identical in the two chapters. For convenience, I have used Ps. 18 as the base text; whenever a citation such as "verse X" appears, the reference is to Ps. 18, and variants from 2 Sam. 22 are indicated as such.

[75] As Mowinckel (*Psalms in Israel's Worship*, 1. 71) puts it.

[76] Dahood, *Psalms 1–50*, 104; Craigie, *Psalms 1–50*, 172.

[77] Hossfeld and Zenger, *Psalmen*, 119; for a summary of various positions, see David Noel Freedman, "Divine Names and Titles in Early Hebrew Poetry," in Frank M. Cross et al., eds., *Magnalia Dei: The Mighty Acts of God* (New York: Doubleday, 1976) 55–102, esp. 75–77.

[78] Gerstenberger, *Psalms, Part 1*, 99. Gerstenberger offers no real arguments for this claim, however.

[79] Weiser, *Psalmen*, 122.

[80] Georg Schuttermayr, *Psalm 18 und 2 Samuel 22, Studien zu einem Doppeltext: Probleme der Textkritik und Übersetzung und das Psalterium Pianum* (Munich: Kösel, 1971) esp. 17–30.

[81] See Weiser, *Psalmen*, 122; Craigie, *Psalms 1–50*, 172.

claim was part of Levantine royal rhetoric: thus Yehawmilk of Byblos could appeal to the "Mistress of Byblos" for aid because he was a מלך צדק (KAI 10.9), and his predecessor Yehimilk four centuries earlier emphasized the same epithet (KAI 4.6). Moreover, Bir-rakib of Samal in the eighth century could cite his צדקה as the reason for Tiglath-pileser III's appointment of him as king (KAI 216.4, 5). In the Israelite psalm, the "righteousness/loyalty" of the king, understood largely in bodily terms, leads to the pleasant conditions that the following verses envision.

Vv. 26–27 consist of four aphorisms regarding God's reciprocal treatment of the חסיד, גבר,[82] נבר, and עקש. Since v. 28 addresses Yahweh in the second person, the addressee in the second person in vv. 26–27 must also be the deity. The list of moral attitudes in these verses reminds the king of his behavioral options before God. Fortunately, he has chosen the first three and not the fourth.

Of particular interest is the third aphorism (v. 27a): עם נבר תתברר ("with the pure, you act purely"). Uniquely in the royal psalms, the king is (implicitly) said to be "pure." As noted in the discussion of Ps. 2, √B-R-R expresses a major concern in second-millennium Ugaritic ritual texts (involving the king), but the root is largely absent from first-millennium Levantine texts, and so may be a vestigial element.

This lack of emphasis on royal purity is surprising, though understandable once one considers that most of the royal psalms concentrate upon the king as warrior. When shedding human blood, he can hardly be "pure." At this point in the "narrative" of Ps. 18, on the other hand, he has not yet taken a life.

In any case, the focus on the king's body sharpens in vv. 34ff., where the imagery concentrates on the king's military training by Yahweh (cf. Ps. 144). The psalm elaborates this theme extensively, mentioning the monarch's feet (רגלים v. 34), hands and arms (ידים, זרועה; v. 35), and ankles (קרסלים; v. 37). Here again, the king appears as a skilled warrior whose body is aided in battle by Yahweh.

In the following verses, the king pursues his enemies; his invigorated body allows this pursuit. But the key to the psalm's portrayal of the king's body appears in vv 35–37. Here, the king appears "pressing down" ([ה]נחת) a bronze bow,[83] which could mean that he

---

[82] 2 Sam. 22:26 reads נבור, with an internal *mater lectionis*.
[83] V. 35. On the bow as a sign, see Udo Rütersworden, "Der Bogen in Genesis 9:

is shooting it, or, as in various Neo-Assyrian reliefs, receiving tribute from already conquered enemies.[84] He is also standing on treacherous ground (hence the need for ankles that do not slip), and taking long strides—again, rather like the Canaanite striding gods—all in order to defeat the enemies.[85] The strength of the state is literally embodied in his hands and feet.

Part of the way the psalm works out the significance of the king's body is in contrast to the bodies of his enemies (vv. 38–49). He pursues (רדף) them; by contrast, in the royal psalms, the king is never "pursued," even when in distress, since he cannot be depicted fleeing. They fall "beneath my feet" (תחת רגלי; v. 39), where they give the king their necks (נתתה לי ערף)[86] and submit to execution. Nevertheless, it is they, and not he, who are called "men of violence" (איש חמס; v. 49). That is, the moral ambiguity of warfare and international relations vanishes in the face of the triumph of the king of Judah. Violence to bodies other than his is the act of Yahweh and his instrument, the king. The enemies' bodies are legitimately abased, killed, and dismembered. The king steps on their necks (v. 41) and then executes them. The upshot of this is to make the Davidide king the "head of the nations" (ראש גוים; v. 44).[87] This imagery is grotesque

---

Militärhistorische und traditionsgeschichtliche Erwägungen zu einem biblischen Symbol," *UF* 20 (1988) 249–63. "Bronze" must refer to fittings on the bow, not the entire weapon. On fittings for bows (though not specifically bronze fittings), see T. A. Madhloom, *The Chronology of Neo-Assyrian Art* (London: Athlone, 1970) 58–60.

[84] The king stands in right profile facing his foes and guards escorting them to him. In his hand is a bow. He also holds a bow when making sacrifices, though that may be less relevant here. So, the psalmist may have picked up this imagery for his king. For illustrations of this use of the bow, see Magen, *Assyrische Königsdarstellungen*, pl. 12.

[85] See n. 30.

[86] Cf. Gen. 49:8, ידך בערף איביך ("your hand is upon the neck of your enemies"). This *vaticinium ex eventu* oracle about Judah (meaning obviously the Davidic dynasty) indicates that the posture of the king grasping (or standing upon; see Dahood, *Psalms 1–50*, 116, for references) the neck of the enemy is part of the Judahite imagery of the monarch.

[87] Cf. Jer. 31:7, the only other biblical appearance of this phrase, where, however, it denotes all Israel ("Jacob") rather than the monarch. For ראש as a leader, see Exod. 18:25; Judg. 10:18, 11: 8–11; Num. 1:16; etc. Dahood (*Psalms 1–50*, 117) proposes to read (with 2 Sam. 22:44 and the Targum) תשמרני ("you have kept me") and to understand ל to mean "from" and ראש to be ראש II, "poison." He thus reads v. 44b "[you] protected me from the venom of nations." This is obviously not impossible, although the Targum reading is clearly a harmonization and thus indirect evidence for the relative antiquity and independence of the two readings of the MT of Ps. 18:44 and 2 Sam. 22:44. It is not clear, though, what the "venom

in the context: the conqueror who steps on their necks, just below their heads, has become the "head" of their nations! Just as the Assyrian kings were wont to boast of piling up skulls of defeated enemies,[88] so the Judahite king boasts of the slaughter he led. The disembodiment of his enemies is the result of his own bodily strength, and the display of his body in war is accentuated by the display of the dead bodies of the foes. His is one body among many, but at the same time it is different from others. Curiously, the male bodies of his fellow Judahite warriors are not in view here, as if their part in the war would somehow obscure his. He does not lead an army here, but defeats one singlehandedly. While this is obviously a literary fiction, it does serve to place his body in the foreground.

To pull the elements together, this psalm draws a radical contrast between the king and his enemies, not in terms of inward psychological states or ontological moral conditions, but in terms of bodily states. Because of Yahweh's help, the king is physically strong, skilled in warfare, and therefore safe from danger.

The choice of bodily imagery for creating this idealized kingly figure seems highly intentional. We see here a body in motion, its parts perfectly suited for activity. Notably, too, certain features of the body are not emphasized, including the hair, genitalia, and internal organs. The reason for this is not entirely clear, but the parts that are singled out are just those that are visible to an observer of the king (or one seeing him depicted on a relief), and they are just those that figure in the narratives that we shall examine in successive chapters.

Military Anthems: Psalms 20 and 21

Still another genre of royal psalms is the military anthems appearing in Pss. 20 and 21. Typically regarded as a pair—the first invokes a blessing for military success, success that the second celebrates— the psalms contribute fairly significantly to this discussion. In view of the reference to the crown (עטרת; 21:4) and the triumph over

---

of nations" would mean. Moreover, the locution "head of nations" is perfectly intelligible. Yahweh in Ps. 18:44 makes the king the overlord of other countries. 2 Sam. 22:44 may imply that this position predates the victory imagined in the psalm and is an ongoing reality.

[88] See, e.g., RIMA 0.102.2.53.

enemies (21:9–13; cf. Ps. 2), one might argue that Ps. 21 formed part of the coronation liturgy.[89] On the other hand, the use of coronation imagery in the epithalamium that is Ps. 45 should caution one against too readily making this leap. For the present, then, I will follow the scholarly consensus and treat the psalm straightforwardly as a thanksgiving hymn for victory.[90] Ps. 20, meanwhile, has an interesting history: it was (probably) eventually translated into Aramaic and syncretized in the direction of Egyptian religion.[91]

Psalm 20

Ps. 20 is, then, a blessing of a king about to go to war. The priest (?) offering the prayer has already received the king's offerings (v. 4), which evidently are intended to prompt Yahweh's favorable attention. Presumably, the expectation that Yahweh will "remember" (יזכר) these sacrifices (עולה, מנחה) refers not to past acts of piety, but to ones accompanying the preparations for battle. In this case, v. 4 is an illocutionary performative utterance. As Austin points out, how-

---

[89] As does Werner Quintens, "La vie du roi dans le Psaume 21," *Bib* 59 (1978) 516–41. Craigie (*Psalms 1–50*, 190) suggests that it may be a liturgy of a celebration of the "anniversary or renewal of the king's coronation," but this is highly speculative.

[90] See Weiser, *Psalmen*, 133–37; Dahood, *Psalms 1–50*, 131; Hossfeld and Zenger, *Psalmen I*, 139–41.

[91] See Charles F. Nims and Richard Steiner, "A Paganized Version of Psalm 20:2–6 from the Aramaic Text in Demotic Script," *JAOS* 103 (1983) 261–74; K. A. D. Smelik, "The Origin of Psalm 20," *JSOT* 31 (1985) 75–81; and Ingo Kottsieper, "Anmerkungen zu Pap. Amherst 63," *ZAW* 100 (1988) 217–44. Kottsieper has argued that Ps. 20 in its current form can have originated no earlier than the Hasmonean period. This argument rests on his assertion that חר in Papyrus Amherst 63 is אל, not Horus (since non-Semitic deities should not be part of a list of Semitic ones), that Ps. 20 is less vivid than Papyrus Amherst 63, and especially that Ps. 20:8 reflects "die prophetische Kritik am ... falschen Vertrauen auf militärische Stärke in Jes 31,1–3" (243). Each leg of this stool is shaky, however. The critique of reliance on military might probably dates back to the seventh or even eighth centuries or even earlier (Deut. 17:14–20; see Hamilton, "Past as Destiny," for a thorough discussion and bibliography), and one could expect a non-Israelite to edit out such a theologoumenon. In addition, it is not clear that Ps. 20:8 is a critique of reliance on the normal accoutrements of war at all. Since there is no obvious contradiction between trusting in weapons and trusting in a deity—one could always assume that the deity guides the weapons, as is common in Assyrian inscriptions, for example—v. 8 merely draws a comparison between people who trust in mere weapons and those who trust in Yahweh. Certainly other royal psalms have no qualms about using chariots and horses, and it may be that reading v. 8 in the light of the Deuteronomic and prophetic critique of such reliance is a *mis*reading.

ever, such statements succeed only when the audience understands them.[92] The psalm ensures such understanding by repeating the appeal to God with יתן לך כלבבך ("may he give you your heart's desire"), and this quest for Yahweh's attention continues with the paean in v. 6: the entire worshiping community (the court, army, priests) uses music to impress the deity with the gravity of the situation. That this is such an appeal becomes clear in v. 10b: יעננו ביום קראנו ("he will answer us in the day we call"). This does not refer to some day in the unknown future, but to the war of the psalmist's present. The community is performing before its god in order to make victory certain.[93]

The mention of the king's heart in v. 5, meanwhile, marks a shift of focus away from the bodies of sacrificed (indeed, incinerated in the עולה) animals to that of the monarch himself. Here the heart is the organ used in intellection (עצה). The psalmist alludes in these few words to the elaborate plans necessary for warmaking.

Psalm 21

Ps. 21 is a finely balanced hymn with vv. 2–7 and 9–14 forming two sections of six bicola each, with v. 8 as a pivot verse. There is some question as to whether vv. 9–14 refer to the king[94] or to Yahweh.[95] The solution depends upon how one reads v. 10: is יהוה a vocative in the first colon (as the Masoretes place the *athnach*) or the implied subject of the second (as a more prosodically balanced reading of the line would indicate)? Since resolution is impossible, I will not consider this section in discussing the psalmist's depiction of the human king. This very ambiguity, however, is telling: the royal psalms slide between Yahweh and his vicegerent with remarkable ease.

Turning, then, to vv. 2–7, one notes that the king's body is the subject of discussion. V. 3 thanks Yahweh for granting the desire of the king's heart and lips (תאות לבי וארשת שפתיו). The concatenation

---

[92] J. L. Austin, *How to Do Things With Words* (2d ed.; Cambridge: Harvard University Press, 1975) 116.
[93] Accordingly, I cannot agree with Dahood (*Psalms 1–50*, 128), when he sees a switch in time in v. 7 (taking the prefix conjugation verbs to be preterites), and conjectures that a "priest or prophet has received word that the king has scored a military triumph...." This wild guess is entirely unnecessary and misses the ritual background of the psalm.
[94] Mowinckel, *Psalms in Israel's Worship*, 1. 70; Craigie, *Psalms 1–59*, 188–90.
[95] Weiser, *Psalmen*, 136; Dahood, *Psalms 1–50*, 131.

of the interior and exterior organs implies that the king's words and thoughts are congruent. The proper disposition of the king's body (specifically, the heart) is a condition of divine acceptance of his requests.

Vv. 4–6 recall the coronation scene, again focusing upon the royal body. In v. 4a, Yahweh (through his priest, or is this the procession of his image?) comes to greet the king with blessings and places a crown on his head as a sign of those blessings. The crown is part of the royal regalia (cf. Jer. 13:18), but its exact appearance is unknown. Perhaps it resembled the so-called Phrygian cap that appears on Jehu on the Black Obelisk, or the Assyrianizing crown of Kilamuwa of Sam'al.[96] In any case, the placement of the crown points toward the king's head as the locus of divine honor.

While it is not obvious from this verse alone that crowning a king was part of the coronation, the context hints that this was the case. V. 5 is obviously reminiscent of Ps. 2:8. In the coronation ceremony, the king must have requested various blessings of Yahweh. As in Ps. 2, the gift is immortality, if not for the king himself, then for the King, the dynasty.

For the pair הוד והדר, see the comments on Ps. 45, above.

To summarize, then, Ps. 21 evokes the royal coronation as a way of saying that subsequent victories are part of the gifts bestowed upon the king at the beginning of his reign. These gifts find visible expression in the royal body itself: the king becomes successful in war, his lips and heart find divine approval, and his adornment attracts the attention of others.

A Royal Oracle: Isaiah 11:1–9

The final royal oracle to consider is Isa. 11:1–9. Its inclusion here will doubtless be controversial, since many scholars regard the reference to the נזע ישׁי ("Jesse's stump") as an indication of the cessation of the Davidic dynasty.[97] As Wildberger has argued, however,

---

[96] The Assyrianizing crown is also attested on a Judahite bulla from a seal belonging to the שׂר הע[י]ר ("governor of the city"); seal 402a–b in Nahman Avigad and Benjamin Sass, *Corpus of West Semitic Stamp Seals* (Jerusalem: Israel Academy of Sciences and Humanities, 1997) 171.

[97] E.g., Martin Rehm, *Der königliche Messias im Licht der Immanuel-Weissagungen des Buches Jesaja* (Kevelaer, Butzon & Bercker, 1968) 192; Jochen Vollmer, *Geschichtliche*

there is no reason to assume that a promise of a future king need presume the cessation of a dynasty: insuring a smooth succession is the first order of royal business.[98] In addition, one should note the importance of succession in the Immanuel oracle of Isa. 7:14. The death of any king would leave the dynasty a "stump." Accordingly, it is not surprising that the text sees Jesse, who was not a king—and not David, who was—as the stump, since the new king is a new David. Sweeney is probably right to date the surrounding oracle complex in its current form to the reign of Josiah, though with extensive content from the eighth-century wars with Assyria.[99]

Turning now to the text, one finds references to the royal body concentrated in vv. 1–5. V. 2 promises him wisdom and skill, much in the manner of the promise to Solomon in 1 Kings 3. This promise finds physical form in v. 3b–5. Vv. 3b–4a contrast the actions of his eyes and ears with judging the poor בצדק ("with loyalty," with a sense of his proper responsibility toward them). Mere eyes and ears will not provide adequate information for his administrative decisions: he must operate on the basis of the spirit given him.

This is important because it expresses an awareness of the limitations of the king's human body and simultaneously of his transhumanness. We are close here to a conception of the king's two bodies, if not in the medieval senses explicated by Kantorowicz,[100] then at least in the sense that the inadequacies of any given king's body are completely obscured by the perfections of the King's body.

V. 4b calls attention to the king's mouth (פי) and lips (שפתים), which are said to be able to slay enemies and wield a rod of justice (שבט; cf. Ps. 2:9).[101] Compare here Ps. 33:6:

Rückblicke und Motive in der Prophetie des Amos, Hosea und Jesaja (BZAW 119, Berlin: de Gruyter, 1971) 181; Otto Kaiser, *Isaiah 1–12* (OTL; 2d ed.; London: SCM, 1983) 253; Blenkinsopp, *Isaiah 1–39*, 263–64.

[98] Wildberger, *Jesaja*, 1. 440–41. See the literature review in Paul D. Wegner, *An Examination of Kingship and Messianic Expectation in Isaiah 1–35* (Lewiston, NY: Mellen, 1992) 231–32.

[99] Marvin Sweeney, *Isaiah 1–39 With an Introduction to Prophetic Literature* (FOTL 16; Grand Rapids: Eerdmans, 1996) 204–7.

[100] See n. 1 above.

[101] See also the argument of Ian Ritchie for find allusions to the olfactory function in v. 3 (Ian D. Ritchie, "The Nose Knows: Bodily Knowing in Isaiah 11:3," *JSOT* 87 (2000) 59–73.

בדבר יהוה שמים נעשו וברוח פיו כל־צבאם

At the word of Yahweh the heavens were made; by the breath of his mouth, their hosts.

Still more relevant is Ps. 18:9aβ:

ואש מפיו תאכל

And fire emanates from his [Yahweh's] mouth.[102]

The king's vocal equipment, like Yahweh's, is itself a way of expressing his power. But the burden of Isa. 11:4 is not merely the jejune observation that the king gives commands that his subordinates must obey. Rather, that which emanates from his mouth, his breath, like Yahweh's, has destructive power. Indeed, his breath *is* the gift of Yahweh.

In addition to these body parts that appear in other royal psalms, v. 5 introduces the king's thighs and loins (חלצים, מתנים), which wear a breechclout (אזור) of "loyalty" and "fealty" (צדק, אמונה, which are not to be translated as "righteousness" and "truth," later theological language that obscures the political dimensions of the words). As already noted, צדק[ה] is an important theologico-political notion in the Levant. That the king, and specifically his genitals, should be "clothed" with it is very important. This is a way of saying that the king's power of reproduction is guaranteed by Yahweh (who thereby keeps his obligations), and conversely that the royal offspring will also be loyal. So, this brings us back to the same idea also seen in the eighth-century text from Anatolia, KAI 216.4–7:

בצדק אבי ובצדקי הושבני מראי רכבאל ומראי תגלתפליסר על כרסא אבי

On account of the loyalty of my father and my loyalty, my lord Rākib-il and my lord Tiglath-pileser [III] placed me upon the throne of my father [= made me king].[103]

"Loyalty" was a transgenerational characteristic, an expression of long-standing relationships among monarchs; in Isa. 11 these monarchs are the Davidides and their patron deity, Yahweh.

---

[102] For a discussion of the imagery, see Mark S. Smith, "The Heart and Innards in Israelite Emotional Expressions: Notes from Anthropology and Psychobiology," *JBL* 117 (1998) esp. 431–32.

[103] Cf. KAI 215.19.

This explicit mention of the king's reproductive organs is unique in the Judahite royal psalms. It appears to indicate that the oracle does not reflect the same rituals evidenced in other texts; that is, it is probably not from the royal coronation. Rather, it must have to do with the birth of the crown prince[104] and may accompany rituals designed to insure the fertility of the king and queen.

To summarize, then, Isa. 11:1–9, especially vv. 3–5, envisions the body of the crown prince at the time he becomes the king. The coronation (via anointing?) has given the king a new רוח and a more powerful vocal mechanism. This reconfiguration of the royal body effected ritually during the coronation will prove to be an important feature in the narratives that we consider in Chapters 4 and 5.

The Semiotics of the King's Body

With the foregoing texts and interpretation in evidence, it is now possible to ask how everything fits together. Certain patterns of conceptions about the king's body, its actions and display, emerge. It is possible, then, to articulate at least part of the code of signs that circulate around the body.

By "code," I mean to refer to the language of semiotics. As Umberto Eco puts it, "codes provide the rules which *generate* signs as concrete occurrences in communicative discourse. Therefore the classical notion of 'sign' *dissolves* itself into a highly complex network of changing relationships."[105] These relationships can be complex nestings of denotation and connotation, with one semiotics "whose expression plane is another semiotics."[106] Thus, to take a popular example, "rose" denotes a plant in the genus *Rosa* and its flower. Yet, "rose" also can be a sign intelligible in a semiotics of love. A bunch of red roses may signal definite attitudes that the giver hopes to find reciprocated by the recipient. In some cultures, and therefore in some codes, definite rules determine the appropriateness or

---

[104] Wildberger (*Jesaja*, 1. 445–46) discusses the question of whether Isa. 11:1–9 envisions a crisis in succession (the king's childlessness?). This is a possible explanation for the psalm, but not a necessary one. Insuring fertility is always a problem to be addressed ritually, even when not a problem medically.

[105] Umberto Eco, *A Theory of Semiotics* (Bloomington: Indiana University Press, 1976) 49; emphasis in the original.

[106] Ibid., 55.

otherwise of such a gift, and great embarrassment (and in extreme cases, even violence) can result from a violation of those rules. Codes, then, are culturally conditioned choices among all the possible "meanings" of signs. To understand and employ codes—that is, to manipulate them, meaning that the sharers in a code are not passive transmitters of it, but more or less skillful users of it[107]—requires a "cultural competence."[108] If we are talking specifically about the king's body, this principle means that persons in a given society will work with a set of conceptions about the body, which they may then turn about, undercut, subvert, or sustain to serve various purposes.

In this study, the multivalent signs under consideration are first of all linguistic signs. They appear in literary texts. At the same time, they often point toward a set of gestural signs occurring in ritual, or even codes of signs (conventions) in plastic art.[109] For example, in Ps. 110 the reference to the king's birth from the womb of dawn appears, I have argued, to refer to his movement from the east side of the temple precinct toward its center. The textual utterance points toward patterned behavior that in turn draws significance from prior significations of, say, the temple, priests or soldiers in the temple, the deity's presence in the temple precincts, and so on. Or, similarly, Ps. 132 envisions a procession of the Ark (like the processions of images in Babylonia) that finds linguistic expression in the psalm itself. At times, the layers of semiosis are deeper still, as in Ps. 45 when the king's marriage to a foreign queen is expressed in terms of military conquest, which is expressed in terms of the coronation, and that in terms of bodily actions appropriate to Yahweh.

Now, this hunting for multiple levels of semiosis obviously presents problems that have been the topic of much recent theoretical

---

[107] As Herzfeld (*Cultural Intimacy*, 143) puts it, "Skilled social performers are not necessarily dramatic or even particularly impressive; on the contrary, some of the most effective performances are among the least palpable."

[108] Ibid., 64.

[109] As when the king is depicted in the manner of a striding god (e.g., Ps. 18). On images as signs, see Jan Assmann, "Die Macht der Bilder: Rahmenbedingungen ikonischen Handelns im alten Ägypten," *Visible Religion* 7 (1990) 1–20. In the article's opening section, which Assmann cleverly and with a nod toward Austin entitles "How to do things with images: Elemente einer 'Bildakt' Theories," he notes that in reality there is a finite number of scenes portrayed in images, that the scenes are based on everyday life: "Die Situationen sind typisiert und in verschieden hohem Grade organisiert oder geformt. . . ." (1). This notion is important in the context of the larger discussion of infinite semiosis, to which I shall return.

discussion. Peirce proposed that semiosis is infinite, that is, that every sign leads to every other sign.[110] This important insight has led some interpreters of his work to assume that semiotic interpretation of a text was essentially the creation of the interpreters, that there could be no "wrong" interpretation.[111] In its most radical forms, this notion coincides with Barthesian deconstructionism. However, infinite semiosis is itself a kind of fiction. The constellation of signs conveniently called a culture itself acts as a brake on interpretation. So, one knows, for example, that Ezek. 1 is not about flying saucers because it is possible to argue that his baroque imagery of wheels in wheels has a referent in the iconography of the late Iron Age. Texts may mean many things, but not *any* thing.

As I argued in Chapter 1, this point is important because it means that understanding these ancient Israelite texts requires piecing out a code that has referents in antiquity. For example, one cannot reduce even military imagery in the psalms to discussions of "power," as if that word denoted a single entity, readily identifiable across cultural boundaries, that analysis could recover with intense self-critique and careful attention to the relevant evidence. For example, it may not be correct to say that the gesture of the queen's kneeling before her husband in Ps. 45 says anything about her status in marriage, since the entire ceremony evokes a semiotics of conquest of foreign enemies, whom the queen embodies and yet does not embody. The kneeling before the king apparently marks her transition from outside the Israelite community, where she could legitimately (according to the Israelite royal ideation) be booty, to inside the community, where she is the bearer of the community's hope for a smooth succession. The extreme subtlety of the signification of this action should caution us against facile readings of the evidence.

---

[110] For a discussion of Peirce and the paradox of infinite semiosis, see Eco, *Theory of Semiotics*, 68–69; idem, *The Limits of Interpretation* (Bloomington: Indiana University Press, 1990) 23–43.

[111] See, e.g., the articles by Richard Rorty, Jonathan Culler, and Christine Brooke-Rose in Umberto Eco, ed., *Interpretation and Overinterpretation* (Cambridge: Cambridge University Press, 1992). The point I argue (in agreement with Eco) is not that the creator of a text has determined how we read it, but that the cultural code that the real author has used to create an implied author for an implied reader is the control for interpretation. The Bible is not an open work in the sense that it means whatever the reader, however ignorant, wishes. See also Eco, "The Poetics of the Open Work," in idem, *The Role of the Reader: Explorations in the Semiotics of Texts* (Bloomington: Indiana University Press, 1979) 47–65.

In his own explication of semiotic codes, Eco differentiates among the sign, its denotation, and its connotation.[112] The sign does not merely exist in itself, but takes significance from its relationship to other signs in a code. It takes on further signification (connotation) when its "expression plane is another semiotics."[113] To take the signs surrounding the king's body in the royal psalms as a case in point, one notices, say, that the king's arm (זְרוֹעַ) denotes military prowess, but it also connotes his resemblance to Yahweh (since it is the Lord's arm that saves, e.g., at the Reed Sea). Moreover, the arm connotes the peace and security of the nation that results from successful warfare.

In the space that remains, then, I wish to sketch the code(s) that generate the signs applicable to the king in these poetic texts. This summary will, among other things, serve as a basis from which to discuss the manipulation of the code in biblical prose narrative.

The place to begin this summary is with the recognition of what is absent from the royal psalms. First, the texts say nothing about some features of the royal body that figure prominently on Iron Age Syrian, Anatolian, and Mesopotamian sculpture:[114] these include the king's beard, hair,[115] and torso. Second, these psalms are virtually silent about women, except to the extent that they are icons of groups of foreigners (including, perhaps primarily, males). This stands in sharp contrast, as will become evident, to Israelite prose narrative texts and even poetry embedded therein. In the official propaganda as evidenced in the royal psalms, the king's maleness is defined in relationship to, and contrast with, other males. This may be an important mark distinguishing the official from the unofficial portrayals of the royal body and its self-display. Third, the texts are reticent about sex, even when the royal marriage is their subject. The king's sexual prowess is not foregrounded, even when his obligation to carry on the dynasty is a topic of discussion. Sexuality finds its place in the semiosis of religion (Yahweh as the one who continues the ruling family), or warfare (the queen as the embodied foreign vassal). Fourth, the king's death is never demonstrably mentioned, despite the important ritual issues that his demise must have pre-

---

[112] Eco, *Theory of Semiotics*, 54ff.
[113] Ibid., 55.
[114] See, e.g., Madhloom, *Neo-Assyrian Art*, esp. pls. xl–xli; Winfried Orthmann, *Untersuchungen zur späthethitischen Kunst* (Bonn: Habelt, 1971).
[115] See Daniel Schlumberger, "La Coiffure du Grand Roi," *Syria* 48 (1971) 375–83.

sented, from disposal of the body, to purification of the royal chambers, to the funeral.

What is in the code, then? The most noticeable thing is that the king is often portrayed as being like Yahweh. Like the deity, the king acts as a warrior, and indeed Yahweh is his mentor in warfare. This warlikeness requires that the king's body be strong, supported in battle, and skilled. Bodily discipline is an essential part of being like Yahweh, of having access to his[116] blessings. The martial skill of the king, described in how he displays and manipulates his body, thus expresses itself on the semiotic plane typical of the deity.[117]

Simultaneous with the king's likeness to Yahweh is his vulnerability, which I take to be a condition of humanity.[118] This vulnerability may be physical illness (Isa. 38) or danger in battle (Ps. 89?). The danger may be expressed on a different semiotic plane: thus the sick king is at risk of being dragged into Sheol, or is unable to swim in deep waters. (Conceivably, the kings of Judah, like Mauss's French sailors, did not learn to swim, or perhaps the imagery is to be taken less literally.) Or his life is about to be rolled up like a rug. This resort to simile allows a reticence or euphemism about sickness. Not so with danger in battle, however, even if here it is not necessarily the king's somatic body that is at risk, but the state itself, which the body of the king signifies, since both are created and sustained (through covenant) by Yahweh. Even here, though, the code does not allow the legitimate king to flee—he never has "pursuers" (רדפים) after him—he must fight to the death. Yet his bravery is insufficient if Yahweh has betrayed him (Ps. 89). Without divine aid there is no victory; the royal body's military training thus has an all-important cultic dimension that must be proper (hence Ps. 20's reference to the king's sacrifices).

---

[116] I use the masculine pronoun for Yahweh, who is a male deity in the Bible.

[117] For a somewhat different view, see Stephen Geller, "The God of the Covenant," in Barbara N. Porter, ed., *One God or Many? Concepts of Divinity in the Ancient World* (TCBAI 1; Casco Bay: Casco Bay Assyriological Institute, 2000) 285; I agree with Geller that some metaphors for Yahweh in the Hebrew Bible derive from kingship, but it seems clear that reflections on deity and monarch worked in a complex, not unilinear, way.

[118] Of course, this is not obvious, for an older line of scholarship understood many penitential psalms to refer to the king's ritual abasement during the New Year's festival, when he took on attributes of a dying and rising god; the king was Yahweh as a simulacrum of Dumuzi/Baʻl. See, e.g., Mowinckel, *Psalmenstudien II*; Johnson, *Sacral Kingship*; Ahlström, *Psalm 89*.

It is striking, finally, how pervasive the military imagery is in these psalms, how it influences every aspect of the king's life, shaping even the depiction of sexuality (in Israel [Ps. 45]; and similarly in Judah, though the evidence is sketchier [Isa. 11:3–5; perhaps Ps. 72 if it refers to a crown prince]). This raises two complementary issues. First, why does violence so thoroughly overwhelm other aspects of a potential poetics of kingship in Judah and Israel, at least in these psalms? Does the answer lie in the political instability and military insecurity of the Israelite dual monarchies, in a deep structural feature of the local religion, or in some combination of the two? It may be that we should look to the consolidation of the state of Judah during the ninth-seventh centuries as part of the answer. Jerusalem grew in the late eighth century owing in part to immigration from areas devastated by Assyria. The theology of the invincibility of Jerusalem also flourished during this period (though it may have had earlier antecedents), and a bellicose understanding of kingship would have been comprehensible during this period.

This raises the second, and to my mind much more interesting question. How persuasive was the presentation of kingship in these psalms, and how pervasive was this view in the society? How persuasive was the portrayal of a petty ruler as a universal sovereign? In what ways could Israelites (mis)understand, (mis)use the code (disemia) to suit various political, religious, or even gender issues? What happens when the monarch is impotent, either sexually or militarily? To answer this, we take up the narrative texts addressed in Chapters 4 and 5.

APPENDIX A

The King's Body in Iron Age Levantine Inscriptions

Body part (of the king or queen [marked ⁕])	Inscription (KAI number)	Comments
דם ("blood")	43.11;[119] 224.11, 12	Equals "offspring"
פי ("mouth")	11⁕	
פם ("mouth")	214.29, 30; 222A30, 31; 223A9	
עצם ("bone")	9A5	Here equals corpse (cf. 191B2 עצמה with the same meaning)
פעם ("foot")	26A1.16	Enemies under the king's feet
רגל ("foot")	215.16	Panammuwa dies at feet of Tiglath-pileser III, his overlord; the feet are the place of honor where a loyal warrior dies
עין ("eye")	214.30, 32 224.3[120]	
ראש ("head")	224.11	
יד ("hand")	24.6, 7, 8; 202A11, 12; 202B15; 214.2, 4, 8, 12, 25, 29; 222B25, 27, 34	The hand holds the scepter, can be raised against an overlord, and is in short the body part signifying the mastery of one person over another

---

[119] The sponsor of the inscription is a petty ruler, a vassal of the Ptolemies, but his title רב ארץ qualifies him for this list. The spelling here is אדם with a prothetic aleph (see KAI vol. 2, p. 61). דם parallels זרע ("seed, descendant[s]").

[120] In addition add here KAI 226.5, a epitaph for a high priest in Nerab from the seventh century BCE.

CHAPTER FOUR

STORIES OF THE CORONATION OF THE KING

> ... an ideology is never a simple reflection of a ruling class's ideas: on the contrary, it is always a complex phenomenon, which may incorporate conflicting, even contradictory, views of the world.[1]

If the royal psalms portray the political ritual of coronation as the creation of a new human being who leads a revivified nation, other, non-official (though not necessarily non-elite, as Eagleton would remind us) texts offer alternative views. While these narrative, prophetic, and wisdom texts share many of the theological views evinced by the state liturgy, they also at times deconstruct the official views or draw implications latent within them, thus both critiquing and revitalizing the royal traditions.[2] The complex relationships of these views apparently shifted somewhat in response to externally induced crises (read: invasions) as well as to the ongoing theological and political reflection of various "elite" groups within Israelite society.

The chief Iron Age texts offering views of the royal body alternative to that of the royal psalms appear in the Deuteronomistic History. While numerous contemporary scholars argue with varying degrees of plausibility for a date for much of this work within the Achaemenid period,[3] the nihilistic dismissal of the existence of very extensive, recoverable, and plausibly dateable earlier sources does not survive careful analysis of the texts. I agree with Halpern and Vanderhooft that much of the DH as a coherent work dates to the eighth century,[4] and with Cross that most of the work was in place

---

[1] Terry Eagleton, *Marxism and Literary Criticism* (Berkeley: University of California Press, 1976) 6–7.
[2] See the discussion in J. J. M. Roberts, "The Enthronement of Yhwh and David: The Abiding Theological Significance of the Kingship Language of the Psalms," *CBQ* 64 (2002) 675–86.
[3] E.g., John Van Seters, *In Search of History: Historiography in the Ancient World and the Origins of Biblical History* (1983; repr. Winona Lake: Eisenbrauns, 1997) 322–53.
[4] Baruch Halpern and David Vanderhooft, "The Editions of Kings in the 7th–6th Centuries BCE," *HUCA* 62 (1991) 179–244.

by the end of the seventh.⁵ This dating is crucial to much of the analysis that follows in the next three chapters, though many details of this analysis could stand on their own regardless of how one dates the texts.

In any case, the actual procedure of making a king is the subject of several tales in Samuel-Kings. Somewhat different rituals are on view in these cases, perhaps because the ritual developed over time, but also because local differences between Israel and Judah must have existed, even if they remain unrecoverable in detail. None of these rituals fits the Deuteronom(ist)ic prescriptions for coronations in Deut. 17:14–20, so must be dated earlier, to sources not influenced by the concerns of this theological circle, even if they do serve the final editor's overall rhetorical function of exposing the frailty of monarchy.⁶ In part, these stories are concerned with the adornment, presentation, and therefore, the conceptualization of the royal body. Let us examine these coronation stories in some detail.

The Crowning(s) of Saul

The reign of Saul was an important problem in Israelite historiography, one solved most drastically by the Chronicler, who ignored all but that king's final moments, but it was seriously treated also by the Deuteronomists. The presentation in 1 Samuel, which uses older sources perhaps dating back to the reign of Saul himself,⁷ is strikingly full as it exposes the flaws and potentialities of monarchy

---

⁵ Frank Moore Cross, *Canaanite Myth and Hebrew Epic* (Cambridge: Harvard University Press, 1973) 274–89. See also the excellent work of William Schniedewind, *How the Bible Became a Book* (Cambridge: Cambridge University Press, 2004); and the remarks of Richard Elliott Freedman, "An Essay on Method," in Richard Elliott Friedman and William H. C. Propp, eds., *Le-David Maskil: A Birthday Tribute for David Noel Freedman* (Winona Lake, IN: Eisenbrauns, 2004) 10; and Antony F. Campbell and Mark A. O'Brien, *Unfolding the Deuteronomistic History: Origins: Upgrades, Present Text* (Minneapolis: Fortress, 2000) 1–29 and infra.

⁶ On the nature of "Deuteronomism," see Norbert Lohfink, "Was There a Deuteronomistic Movement?" in Linda Schearing and Steven McKenzie, eds., *Those Elusive Deuteronomists: the Phenomenon of Pan-Deuteronomism* (JSOTSS 268; Sheffield: Sheffield Academic Press, 1999) 36–66.

⁷ See Marsha White, "'The History of Saul's Rise': Saulide State Propaganda in 1 Samuel 1–14," in Saul Olyan and Robert Culley, eds., *"A Wise and Discerning Mind": Essays in Honor of Burke O. Long* (BJS 325; Providence: Brown Judaic Studies, 2000) 271–92.

that emerged only long after Saul himself, introduces his reign alongside what has seemed to many scholars to be a polemic against kingship that it preserves but does not fully embrace.[8]

Saul's coronation is anomalous in that he has no predecessor. Yet the narrative treatment of this event owes so much to later practice that one must conclude, I think, that the final DH editor (and perhaps some of his sources) wished to use Saul to address certain crucial theological issues regarding kingship. In any case, 1 Sam. 9–12 is structured around the coronation ritual, as Halpern and others have already observed.[9] As has long been recognized, the text also includes two distinct versions of Saul's coronation, which it nevertheless reconciles by subsuming them under the ritual structure of the actual coronation ritual.[10]

In the first version, 1 Sam. 9:1–10:16, Saul appears as a superbly handsome and tall man (9:2: בחור וטוב ואין איש מבני ישראל טוב ממנו). Like his father, he is a mighty warrior (גבור חיל). His physical appear-

---

[8] For a study of this polemic, see most recently Steven L. McKenzie, "Cette royauté qui fait problème," in Albert de Pury, Thomas Römer, and Jean-Daniel Macchi, eds., *Israël construit son histoire* (Geneva: Labor et Fides, 1996) 267–95; Bruce Birch, *The Rise of the Israelite Monarchy: The Growth and Development of 1 Samuel 7–15* (SBLDissS 27; Missoula, MT: Scholars Press, 1976); Timo Veijola, *Das Königtum in der Beurteilung der deuteronomistischen Historiographie* (Helsinki: Suomalainen Tiedeakatemia, 1977); Frank Crüsemann, *Der Widerstand gegen das Königtum* (Neukirchen-Vluyn: Neukirchener, 1978); Rainer Albertz, *A History of Israelite Religion in the Old Testament Period* (2 vols.; Louisville: Westminster/John Knox, 1994) 1. 122–24; and Dennis McCarthy, "The Inauguration of Monarchy in Israel: A Form-Critical Study of I Samuel 8–12," *Int* 27 (1973) 401–12. Note, however, the proposal of V. Philips Long ("How Did Saul Become King? Literary Reading and Historical Reconstruction," in A. R. Millard, James K. Hoffmeier, and David W. Baker, eds., *Faith, Tradition, and History* [Winona Lake, IN: Eisenbrauns, 1994] 276) that the antimonarchical sentiments are expressed in assemblies, and thus the narrator simply recounts what one could expect of such gatherings. This is an important insight, but Long draws the wrong conclusions from it. The opposition to kingship is not incidental to the coronation process, but an integral part of it: after all, it is the great Samuel himself who ritualistically indicts the monarchy. As I will argue below, the opposition to monarchy is a ritualized trope in which "pro-" and "antimonarchic" ideas existed together, not the product of a coherent political party or social grouping.

[9] Baruch Halpern, *The Constitution of the Monarchy in Israel* (HSM 25; Chico, CA: Scholars Press, 1981) 51–148. Edelman (*King Saul*, 30) sees here three stages in the succession ritual: designation of the king, testing of his worthiness, and coronation; for a similar view, see André Wénin, *Samuel et l'instauration de la monarchie (1 S 1–12): Une recherche littéraire sur le personnage* (Frankfurt: Peter Lang, 1987).

[10] On the literary coherence of this passage, see Tryggve N. D. Mettinger, *King and Messiah: The Civil and Sacral Legitimation of the Israelite Kings* (Lund: Gleerup, 1976) 64–79; Long, "How Did Saul become King?"

ance and family connections apparently appeal to Yahweh and Samuel in this version of the selection of Saul. Accordingly, beginning in v. 15, the narrative explains the choice of Saul. First, it is Yahweh who orders the selection through an oracle announcing the arrival of the king the following day (v. 15) and a second oracle upon his appearance. Second, Samuel invites the young man to dinner in a rather offhanded way, offering him the choice place at the table and the best cut of meat from the sacrifice.[11] The physical location of the prospective king signals the role he is about to assume, and thus the banquet is a sign of kingship. The narrative foreshadows what is to come in v. 20 by having Saul offered, prophetically, "whatever is worthwhile in Israel" (כל־חמדת ישראל). Saul's quizzical response— "Am I not a Benjaminite, from the smallest (מקטני; v. 21) of the tribes of Israel"—to an offer so pregnant with meaning takes the form of a reminder that he is a member of a minor clan. This reminder resembles the traditional prophetic response to a divine call, as one sees in the call narratives of Moses (Exod. 3), Isaiah (Isa. 6), Jeremiah (Jer. 1), Samuel (1 Sam. 3), and most germanely the reluctance of Gideon to become king (Judg. 6). The narrative's use of the reluctance theme here, since it echoes the motif of reluctance to assume the throne,[12] serves to underscore Saul's modesty and therefore the appropriateness of Yahweh's election of him to kingship. Despite his warriorly skill (hence the magnificence of his body), his election to monarchy does not depend on his own doing but on his smallness (in regard to clan size and thus power base). Smallness, patently not a characteristic of Saul's own body, nevertheless functions as an index of his status, an index which the ritual of these chapters alters. Several semiotic codes—family, body, and politics—intersect here so that an index on the plane of one (smallness of family) combined with an icon of another (largeness of body) yields a symbol of the third as Saul is made into a person large enough to rule.

---

[11] I will discuss the theme of the king at a meal below. On this topos as a scene in ancient Near Eastern art, see Winfried Orthmann, *Untersuchungen zur späthethitischen Kunst* (Bonn: Habelt, 1971) 366–92; and Dominique Collon, "Banquets in the Art of the Ancient Near East," in R. Gyselen et al., *Banquets d'Orient* (Bures: Groupe pour l'Étude de la Civilisation du Moyen-Orient, 1992) 23–30.

[12] On Gideon, see Crüsemann, *Widerstand gegen das Königtum*, 19; Veijola, *Königtum*, 100–14.

The subsequent anointing of Saul in 10:1 is so casual that one must ask why the narrator proceeds in this way. An older explanation is that this is an ancient folk tale reused by the DH. As McCarter has argued, however, many elements here are not folkloristic, and many elements of prophetic theology are in evidence, implying minimally a thorough reworking of such a folk tale.[13] Alternatively, one might try to understand the anointing politically, but it is hard to offer a political explanation for a secret anointing. Saul is not like Jehu in 2 Kings 9, a usurper. This ritual must draw its meaning from the larger narrative purpose in 1 Sam. 8–12.

This purpose is, I believe, the exoneration of Saul from the charge of tyranny. Note that 1 Sam. 8:10–18 is a litany of royal abuses of power. Samuel in 12:3–5 demands acquittal of just such abuses. Moreover, as scholars have long recognized, the list in 1 Sam. 8 does not describe the reign of Saul, at least as the Bible presents it. Furthermore, the narrative purposely seeks to exonerate Saul of tyranny. Note that the prospective king in 1 Sam. 8 is guilty of excessive self-display (v. 11), and of commandeering resources to support a standing army (v. 12) and to live luxuriously (vv. 13–17). The narrative complex as it stands refutes the charge of excessive taxation and tyranny by having Saul: (1) decline "every pleasant thing of Israel" (כל חמדת ישראל; 1 Sam. 9:20), (2) say nothing when some Israelites ("dirty bastards" [בני בליעל]) refuse him a gift (1 Sam. 10:27), but instead (3) "go down to his house" (הלך לביתו; 1 Sam. 10:26). The first charge, excessive self-display, fails because Saul does not seek the kingdom, tells no one about his being anointed (not even a close relative),[14] and then hides on the day when the king is

---

[13] P. Kyle McCarter, *I Samuel* (AB 8; Garden City, NY: Doubleday, 1980) 186–87; McKenzie ("Cette Royauté," 289) goes so far as to argue that 1 Sam. 8–12 is a composition of the DH (although using older materials). This is probably true of the organization of the chapter, and certainly chapters 8 and 12 form a frame that is Deuteronomistic almost in toto, but much of the intervening material must be older. For example, in Deut. 17:14–20, the "Levitical priest" supervises the king, not the prophet as here. Unless Deut. 17 is a late level in the book of Deuteronomy (as argued by Georg Braulik, "Deuteronomy and the Commemorative Culture of Israel," in idem, *The Theology of Deuteronomy: Collected Essays of Georg Braulik, O.S.B.* [Berkeley: BIBAL, 1994] 194; and Christa Schäfer-Lichtenberger, *Josua und Salomo: Eine Studie zu Autorität und Legitimität des Nachfolgers im Alten Testament* [VTSup 58; Leiden: Brill, 1995] 52–106), for which the evidence is meager, one must assume that much of 1 Sam. 9–11 is non- (i.e., pre-) Deuteronomistic.

[14] The thesis of D. R. Ap-Thomas ("Saul's Uncle," *VT* 11 [1961] 241–45) that the דוד of Saul was the Philstine governor seems gratuitous. The דוד, whether on

to be announced. This man does not seek the throne. Or, put another way, he rises to prominence by playing correctly the game of obscurity and self-effacement.

At this point, one should also inquire into the precise nature of the critique of kingship. Opposition to a monarch took various forms, ranging in scope from a coup d'etat by a few officers to a popular uprising, and in intensity from humble petitions to assassination of the king. Many of these gradations of opposition appear in Samuel-Kings, as well as in literature from elsewhere in the ancient Near East.[15] In particular, the common notion that an antimonarchic party, perhaps drawing on the "egalitarian" ideals of a nomadic past,[16] perdured in Israelite history, putting its head above water at crucial junctures, needs reexamination. Certainly the Deuteronomistic final editor (and his sources) is ambivalent of monarchy, not hostile toward it. Does the description of tyranny in 1 Sam. 8 represent a full-fledged rejection of kingship or a ritualized one? Certainly a ritualization of opposition to kingship did exist in first-millennium Babylonia, where New Year's Day ceremonies saw the priest of the Esagila slapping the king.[17] I can offer no conclusive refutation of the consensus position, but aver that scholars should at least consider the second option.

In his study of kingship in southern Sudan, Simon Simonse records a coronation ritual among the Lulubo. At one point, the presiding priests imprecate the king as follows:

> Let measles be with you!
> Let syphilis be with you!
> Let small-pox be with you!

---

the mother's or father's side, exerted considerable influence. Note, e.g., Amos 6:10 where the דוד is responsible for the burial of a family.

[15] On the range of options in Neo-Assyria, for example, see Paul Garelli, "Les sujets du roi d'Assyrie," in A. Limet, ed., *La Voix de l'Opposition en Mesopotamie* (Brussels: Institut des Hautes Études de Belgique, 1975) 189–213; Hayim Tadmor, "Monarchy and the Elite in Assyria and Babylonia: The Question of Royal Accountability," in S. N. Eisenstadt, ed., *The Origins and Diversity of Axial Age Civilizations* (Albany: SUNY Press, 1986) 203–24, 518–21.

[16] As argued for (rather brilliantly) by, for example, Crüsemann, *Widerstand gegen das Königtum*, esp. 215–19; Ansgar Moenikes, *Die grundsätzliche Ablehnung des Königtums in der Hebräischen Bibel* (BBB 99; Beltz, Athenäum, 1995).

[17] For a discussion of this, see Jonathan Z. Smith, "A Pearl of Great Price and a Cargo of Yams: A Study in Situational Incongruity," in idem, *Imagining Religion: From Babylon to Jonestown* (Chicago: University of Chicago Press, 1982) 90–101.

Let conjunctivitis be with you!
Let scabies be with you!
Let dysentery be with you!

The list continues, and for each item the assembled people add "let it be with you!"[18] This ritual transfers the evil confronting the community onto the king and thus removes it. Or, alternatively, by wishing for these evils, the ritualizers insure that they will not befall their king or themselves. By naming their worst (medical, bodily) fears in ritual, the culture insures that these evils do not come to pass.

Can something similar be behind 1 Sam. 8? The Lulubo see their king as both a victim and a victimizer. 1 Sam. 8 underscores the latter role, but then the narrative goes on to have Yahweh choose a king. Is this choice grudging, as is usually argued? Or is this all staged reluctance, a ritualization that acknowledges and seeks to forestall the possibility of royal tyranny? Nothing in 1 Sam. 8–12, except perhaps for some late glosses, is truly antimonarchic or even anti-Saulide. Indeed, this king is not a tyrant, and so one could argue that the ritual worked (successfully) to forestall tyranny.

The conclusion of the coronation, in any case, comes in 1 Sam. 10:17–27, where the people see Saul's height (v. 23) and then acclaim him king. These verses form a tightly constructed account of a ritual that begins with an oracle,[19] the gathering of the nation and selection of the new king, popular acclamation of him, and the writing of the "rule of monarchy" (משפט המלכה) and its placement in the temple (לפני יהוה).[20] The ritual separates the king from the people—a separation signaled by his superior stature—and consecrates him

---

[18] Simon Simonse, *Kings of Disaster: Dualism, Centralism and the Scapegoat King in Southeastern Sudan* (Leiden: Brill, 1992) 375.

[19] I agree with McKenzie ("Cette royauté," 271) that 1 Sam. 10:19, with its description of the monarchy as a punishment, must be an addition to the narrative, but would argue (against him) that v. 18 must be from an older stratum of the text, since it agrees with the notion of delivery seen in 1 Sam. 9:16, where the clause "the cry [of my people] has come to me" (כי באה צעקתו אלי) parallels Exod. 3:9 (צעקת בני ישראל באה אלי). The linkage of deliverance from the Philstines to deliverance from Egypt created by this identical terminology makes one expect the reference to Egypt in 1 Sam. 10:18 to be part and parcel of the overall conception of deliverance informing 1 Sam. 8–12. On the tight structure of all these chapters, see Dennis J. McCarthy, "The Inauguration of Monarchy in Israel," *Int* 27 (1973) 401–12.

[20] On לפני יהוה as "inside the sanctuary" in P/H terminology, see Jacob Milgrom, *Leviticus 1–16* (AB 3; New York: Doubleday, 1991) 209–10.

to his office when the "rule of monarchy" moves to the most sacred spot on earth, in the temple לפני יהוה.

Having laid out these disparate aspects of the coronation of Saul, how is one to fit them together? How ancient is this material, or put another way, how much of it is pre-Deuteronomistic? Does the king's body change in this ritual? What role does the story of Saul's possession and "prophesying" play in the whole narrative? The answers to these three questions are complementary.

First, the pattern anointing → acclamation is the customary practice in Israel and Judah and must be very ancient. Also, the presiding of a prophet at the coronation does not accord with Deut. 17:14–20 and must, therefore, also predate the seventh century BCE. Furthermore, although Samuel's writing of the משפט המלכה in 1 Sam. 10:25 is reminiscent of the Deuteronomic (Deut. 17:18) prescription for the king at his coronation to "write a copy of this law" (וכתב... את משנה התורה הזאת), the two rituals of writing are quite distinct in terminology and logic. In Deuteronomy, the king writes in order to bind himself to good rule. In 1 Samuel, the prophet writes apparently in order to place the king's reign under the protection of Yahweh. Accordingly, 1 Sam. 10:17–27 envisions a ritual different from that in Deuteronomy at least.[21] This means that one should look for precedents for Saul's coronation, not in the theology of the Dtn/Dtr school, but elsewhere, including, in principle, in royal practice of the Iron Age Israelite kingdoms, even if the text acknowledges the potential dangers of monarchy and thus rejects an equating of the royal will with that of God.

If we accept the argument that, even if the structure of 1 Sam. 8–12 is Deuteronomistic, much of the text's constituent material is not, and concomitantly that this material reflects beliefs extant prior to the seventh century, one must ask how this text understands Saul's body and his use of it. I have already noted the paradox that, while Saul is conspicuous for his height and therefore warriorly qualifications, he is also reticent about claiming the throne. Indeed, his very modesty is an asset, at least for the editor who compiled most of 1 Sam. 8–12.

---

[21] Andre Caquot and Philippe de Robert (*Les Livres de Samuel* [Geneva: Labor et Fides, 1994] 135) also separate the two writing rituals, though without any explanation.

The pivotal point in the transformation of Saul's body occurs after his anointing in 1 Sam. 10:1. The actual ritual had included a kiss ([1 Sam. 10:1] a mark of the king's friendship with Yahweh in the person of Samuel?) and a promise of divine guidance. As Saul leaves Samuel, Yahweh places within his new נגיד[22] "another heart" (לב אחר; 1 Sam. 10:9). The meaning of this expression, unique in the Hebrew Bible, or as far as I can tell, contemporary Levantine literature, is unclear;[23] nor is it clear how it relates to Saul's becoming "another man" (לאיש אחר; 1 Sam. 10:6), since the latter is to occur after Saul prophesies, whereas the "heart transplant" precedes his doing so. Even if this disconnect between vv. 6 and 9 is the result of redaction,[24] the problem remains as to what Saul's change of heart means. I propose to connect it directly to what follows, the story of his possession. The change of heart is a precondition of Saul's reception of the divine spirit, the first step in his becoming another person. Since the heart is the locus of intellection, emotion, and purpose, and hence either clean or dirty, the creation of a new one is a way of saying that Saul must think new thoughts as king. An intimate connection exists between "heart" and "spirit." Indeed, לב and רוח can be in parallel as in Ps. 77:7:

I sang at night with my heart (לבב)
I meditated and my spirit (רוח) investigated.[25]

---

[22] On the title נגיד as "king designate," see Mettinger, *King and Messiah*, 152–62; I am not sure that the title ever really means this, however. It seems to be just a synonym of מלך. See the thorough review of the evidence by Tomoo Ishida, *History and Historical Writing in Ancient Israel* (Leiden: Brill, 1999) 57–67. He argues that the title נגיד described early rulers only (except Hezekiah) who were founders of dynasties. Similarly, Gerhard Hasel, "נָגִיד nāgîd," *TDOT* 9 (1998) 187–202.

[23] Nor is it clear how this fits into Fabry's typology of the usage of לב/ב in the Bible (לבב is the seat of emotions, intellection, or spirituality); see Heinz-Josef Fabry, "לב," *TWAT* 4 (1984) cols. 413–51.

[24] As argued in various ways by Birch, *Rise of the Israelite Monarchy*, 65; and Mettinger, *King and Messiah*, 68–70; see also Christoph Nihan, "'Is Saul also Among the Prophets?' 1 Samuel 10.10–12 and the Reworking of Saul's Story in the Postexilic Era" (paper presented at the annual meeting of the SBL, Nashville, Tenn., 19 November 2000).

[25] My translation follows LXX, moving אזכרה ("I recounted, remembered") to the end of v. 6 (which makes for better colon balance in vv. 6 and 7) and reading נגינתי as a verb נגנתי ("I sang"). MT is not unintelligible, however, and the exact reading is not crucial to the argument here.

Moreover, "spirit" (רוח) also means "wind" and can even be Yahweh's breath.[26] Does the change of Saul's heart mean that it is the receptacle of the spirit/wind, and further, that the heart was thought of as the organ for breathing? In the era before Harvey, such a possibility cannot be ruled out, and it would explain the details of the story.[27]

In any event, one should cite here references in the royal psalms to the king's לב. The heart has desires that Yahweh grants (Ps. 20:5, 21:3). It is to be "pure" (תם; Ps. 101:2), not "crooked" (עקש) or "wide" (רחב).[28] That is, deformities in character are the result of a misshapen heart (much as oddities in animal organs may signal ominous events in Mesopotamian extispicy). Generated by prior significations of heart as the organ of intellection leading to proper actions, heart here is an icon for the kingly capacity to rule. It is thus appropriate that Saul should receive a לב אחר, for this allows him to receive the divine spirit and rule with God's help.

To summarize, then, the coronation narrative about Saul incorporates fairly ancient material, some of which is related to other biblical evidence, as will become clear soon. In this material, the royal body and its transformation through ritual are a major concern. The royal heart changes. Through a carefully structured ritual of avoidance and then acceptance, the Israelite folk accepts its ruler, whom it has constituted as one who does not collect wives and armaments. That is, his body neither engages in sex for political ends, nor does it concentrate fully on war. Moreover, his body's size indicates his qualification to be king, but mere stature in itself is insufficient. Physical size is, in semiotic terms, an index of kingship, but by no means an unambiguous one. The Israelites also looked to other aspects of the body, and especially to its use in battle. Hence, the statement of the בני בליעל in 1 Sam. 10:27: their contemptuous dismissal of "this one" who could not liberate (מה ישענו זה; "how will

---

[26] See Heinz-Josef Fabry, "רוח," *TWAT* 7 (1993) cols. 401–3.
[27] On the shift from premodern to modern medicine and conceptions of human anatomy, see Barbara Duden, *The Women Beneath the Skin: A Doctor's Patients in Eighteenth-Century Germany* (Cambridge: Harvard University Press, 1991).
[28] Note the Assyrian equivalent *libbu rapšu* ("wide heart"), which, however, is positive in meaning ("magnanimous"). See M.-J. Seux, *Épithètes Royales Akkadiennes et Sumériennes* (Paris: Letouzey et Ané, 1967) 150–51.

this one save us") indicates that they, at least, did not believe that coronation worked *ex opere operato*, no matter the suitability of the king's body for his new role. The narrator, on the other hand, denigrates their skepticism, not only by calling them "worthless bastards" (בני בליעל) but also by immediately introducing the story of Saul's defeat of the Ammonites. Saul is modest and lets his actions speak for him; his restraint is itself a very useful political tool.

So, in short, the transformation of his body is efficacious in making him king. When it is changed through anointing[29] (and kissing?) and the subsequent alteration of his heart, he becomes worthy of the people's acclamation.

The Choice of David

The anointing of David in 1 Sam. 16, part of a complex unit of diverse origins,[30] resembles that of Saul in that again (1) a prophet officiates, (2) the ritual is secret, (3) and it brings the divine spirit upon the anointed (v. 13). Moreover, the aftermath of each coronation is a test of strength against a foreign warlord (Saul versus Nahash in 1 Sam. 11 and David versus Goliath in 1 Sam. 17; see below). In contrast to the physically imposing Saul, however, David is the smallest of his family (הקטן; v. 11).[31] However, the first thing Samuel notices about him is his attractiveness: "he was ruddy, having beautiful eyes,[32] and handsome" (v. 12; הוא אדמוני עם יפה עינים וטוב ראי).[33] We get little sense of precisely how he was attractive.

---

[29] See also the brief discussion of this in Mark K. George, "Body Works: Power, the Construction of Identity, and Gender in the Discourse on Kingship" (Ph.D. diss., Princeton Theological Seminary, 1995) 40. In my view, George overemphasizes the extent to which anointing separates Saul from his people. Acclamation reintegrates him into the people (if in a new role), and the separation is a movement standing in creative tension with the movement of integration.

[30] Antony F. Campbell, *1 Samuel* (FOTL 7; Grand Rapids: Eerdmans, 2003) 168–69.

[31] See also the comments of Azzan Yadin, "Goliath's Armor and Israelite Collective Memory," *VT* 54 (2004) 373–95.

[32] Typically יפה applies to women, but it describes David here, Absalom in 2 Sam. 14:25, Joseph in Gen. 39:6, and an anonymous male in Song 1:16.

[33] I have attempted to translate the MT, even though it is linguistically problematic (see McCarter, *I Samuel*, 275). Still I cannot accept McCarter's assertion that since אדמוני עם יפה עינים is similar to 1 Sam. 17:42 אדמוני עם יפה מראה the former must have been the basis of the latter and both must be corrupt. He offers

The narrator, having repudiated Saul, offers new bodily qualifications for kingship. Size no longer matters, but attractiveness does. That is, the reference to David's appearance is not merely a bit of physiognomatic trivia, but a serious attempt to address the question of how a king's body *should* appear. Features of David's self-display position him for this text as a high-status male of the sort who could become king.[34]

A complex feature of this story deserves comment here. In v. 7, Yahweh tells Samuel not to put too much stock in the "appearance and height" (אל מראהו ואל גבה) of Eliab, David's brother, because "Yahweh sees the heart" (יהוה יראה ללבב). Then, ironically, Samuel focuses precisely on David's appearance before he hears the oracle commanding him to anoint this, the youngest child. This irony is surely intentional and reflects the narrator's attempt to work out the same question seen in 1 Sam. 10 and apparently important to Israelites: how should a king appear? Yahweh, whose opinion is that of the narrator here in 1 Sam. 16, looks upon the heart rather than the obviously visible part of the physiognomy. I see no reason to reduce לבב to a metaphor for "attitude" or "inner goodness" or some such. As Ps. 101 makes clear, Israelites thought the shape of the heart to impinge directly on a king's success in his job. By making the heart the crucial body part, the narrator moves the selection of the king entirely into the divine realm, since the human body is transparent only to the deity. Nevertheless, physical beauty, which is accessible public perception, may also indicate the king's readiness to assume his role. Behind this may also lie the notion that physical appearance mirrors the shape and condition of the interior organs, which in turn generate actions appropriate or otherwise.[35] When juxtaposed with the Saul story, then, this exchange on David's

---

the conjecture אדם ונעים ("ruddy and handsome"). This is simply a non sequitur. I propose that עם can mean "with respect to" or some such. Note, e.g., the Ugaritic text KTU 1.14 III.20, ʿimma ʿulāmi ḥayāta ("may you live forever/may you live with respect to eternity") (on this Ugaritic preposition, see Daniel Sivan, *A Grammar of the Ugaritic Language* [Leiden: Brill, 1997] 199–200; he does not, however, offer the precise nuance for which I am arguing).

[34] See the discussion in Steven L. McKenzie, *King David: A Biography* (Oxford: Oxford University Press, 2000) 47–67.

[35] On the connection between physical beauty and moral and ritual purity in Israelite priestly texts, see Saul Olyan, *Rites and Rank: Hierarchy in Biblical Representations of Cult* (Princeton: Princeton University Press, 2000) 103–14.

body is an attempt to deconstruct a simplistic understanding of the royal body in which mere stature and impressive musculature suffice as an icon of kingship.

This part of the David legend differs structurally from the Saul complex in that David assumes the throne only after a long delay marked by contestation that he wins by not seeming to play the games of power at all.[36] The most effective strategem for gaining power is appearing not to seek it. After this long delay, David is once again anointed, this time by the citizens of Judah in Hebron (2 Sam. 2). What is the connection between this anointing and the earlier one of David in 1 Sam. 16? How can we reconstruct ritual from a literary strategy of delaying David's grasping of the reins of power to such a time as he can avoid blame for the death of Saul? The narration in 2 Sam. 2–3 is extremely sparse, focusing upon David's wives and children, his consultation of Yahweh on the location of a capital, and then his embassage to the Jabesh Gileadites. He positions himself as the legitimate guardian of Saul's body, much as a son would, and the point of the tale and its positioning after the lament in 1 Sam. 1:19–27 is to portray David carrying out the filial piety of Levantine kings (as seen, for example, in the Byblian burial inscriptions [KAI 1, 9–11]). His informing the Jabesh Gileadites that "the house of Judah has anointed me as king over them" (v. 7; גם אתי משחו בית יהודה למלך עליהם) indicates his worthiness to be a partner with these non-Israelites in the treaty he proposes at the beginning of the verse.[37]

Contrast this with the treatment of Ish-baal in the following pericope (2 Sam. 2:8–11). Not only is he the creature of Abiner, but he is merely "made king" (ימלכהו), not anointed or acclaimed.[38] The narrator, then, raises the question of who the legitimate heir of Saul

---

[36] On the politics of obscuration, see Baruch Halpern, *David's Secret Demons: Messiah, Murderer, Traitor, King* (Grand Rapids: Eerdmans, 2001) 73–103.

[37] On this see, P. Kyle McCarter, *II Samuel* (AB 9; Garden City, NY: Doubleday, 1984) 85; cf. Alexander Achilles Fischer, *Von Hebron nach Jerusalem: Eine redaktionsgeschichtliche Studie zur Erzählung von König David in II Sam 1–5* (BZAW 335; Berlin: de Gruyter, 2004) 43–98.

[38] A. A. Anderson (*2 Samuel* [WBC 11; Dallas: Word, 1989] 35) argues that the text's reticence on Ish-baal's coronation means simply that we know nothing about it. But, surely, this silence is literarily important. It is impossible to know how much of this story is factual, but what is important is what it reveals about beliefs concerning monarchy in general, not specific kings.

is: his son is not powerful, experiences no ritualized bodily changes, and is thus not truly legitimate. The parvenu David, on the other hand, has been anointed and is powerful and thus can be king. Biology is not destiny.

An important clue to the provenance of this story lies buried, I think, in 2 Sam. 2:9: "And he [Ish-baal] reigned over Gilead, האשורי, Jezreel, Ephraim, Benjamin and Israel—all of it." What does האשורי mean? It is the only gentilic in the list, a fact that, again, identifies it as somehow different in kind than the place names accompanying it. The Syriac and Vulgate read "Geshur," which is northeast of the Golan, and this is the preference of some modern commentators.[39] The LXX θασιρι (A: θασουρ) is a nonsense reading. Another option is to read the MT without the internal mater ו, making it "the Asherite" rather than "the Assyrian." Complicating the matter is the switch in preposition from אל to על and the final summary "Israel, all of it."

The problem with the MT reading has, for many scholars, been that it was anachronistic.[40] No Assyrians lived in Palestine during David's era (and no Israelite king ruled Assyrians, for that matter). This problem vanishes, however, if we hypothesize that the text as we have it was written later. Notice that the first three geographical names in the list are introduced by אל, and the first and third were incorporated as Assyrian provinces in the 730s BCE (by Tiglath-pileser III). The last three places are introduced by על, and all of them were annexed to Assyria in the 720s (by Sargon II). The switch in prepositions signals a change in sources, and the connection of the list to the history of Assyrian expansion seems more than coincidental.

Arguably, 2 Sam. 2 stems, not from the tenth century, but from the late eighth or even seventh. The latter was a period when Israelite territory was under occupation, its political status contested. Judah sought to influence some of its inhabitants to switch allegiances to Jerusalem.[41] Does 2 Sam. 2, with its clean separation of Judah and

---

[39] E.g., McCarter, *II Samuel*, 82; Caquot and Robert (*Livres de Samuel*, 378) present the options but offer no opinion.
[40] Ibid.
[41] The legend of Hezekiah's Passover in 2 Chron. 30 may be a distant trace of that attempt to sway northerners, and certainly the rapid expansion of Jerusalem during this period is also some indication. See Japhet, *I & II Chronicles*, 935–36.

Israel and David's appeal for northern support, serve as a justification for eighth-century Judahite overtures? Ish-baal becomes a cipher for every puppet king that Israel faced.

A problem with this hypothesis lies in the last part of v. 9. Ish-baal is the ruler of Ephraim, Benjamin, and "Israel, all of it." Note again, however, the switch in prepositions from אל to על.[42] This could be a telltale sign of a later retouching of the story, perhaps after the fall of Samaria. The emphasis on "all Israel" refers to the territorial integrity of the northern kingdom before Tiglath-pileser III, not to a fictional (or real) boundary from the beginning of the first millennium (which is not to comment on the historicity of the border for Ish-baal's reign).[43] "All Israel" implies that the narrator knows a political entity that is "part of Israel." In short, the verse in both its 730s version and its post-722 version refers to the territory ruled by Israel before Assyria's conquest. The expansion of the verse reflects the changing geopolitical realities of the eighth century. Ish-baal originally ruled only the Galilee and Transjordan, areas occupied by Assyria in the 730s, but a later editor made him also rule "all Israel."

Thus by the eighth century, and doubtless considerably earlier, anointing was the crucial moment in the constitution of Judahite kingship, the moment at which the royal body became such. The stories of David serve as a kind of dynastic foundation story in which their hero's actions and bodily conditions validate the policies of his successors. By claiming that anointing was the prerogative of the Davidic dynasty, they assert their claims (in contrast to Saul's) to sole rulership of Yahweh's heritage.[44] The anointed body in its whole-

---

More broadly, see Halpern and Vanderhooft, "Editions of Kings," 179–244; and on the expansion of Jerusalem, Baruch Halpern and Deborah Hobson, *Law and Ideology in Ancient Israel* (JSOTSS 124; Sheffield: JSOT Press, 1991). On the history of Hezekiah's reign, see Andrew G. Vaughn, *Theology, History and Archaeology in the Chronicler's Account of Hezekiah* (Atlanta: Scholars, 1999) esp. 169–81.

[42] This distinction is lost in the LXX and Targum of Jonathan (which reads על דבית). As the harder reading, MT probably preserves the original text on this point.

[43] Cf. מצרים כלה ("Egypt, all of it"; Ezek. 29:2); גוים כלם ("the nations, all of them"; Ezek. 23:12); עמים כלם ("the peoples, all of them"; Ps. 67:4, 6); כל מלכי גוים כלם ("all the kings of the nations, all of them"; Isa. 14:18); and כל אדום כלה ("all Edom, all of it"; Ezek. 35:15). Ezekiel also uses the phrase כל בית ישראל כלה ("all the house of Israel, all of it"; Ezek. 11:15, 20:40, 36:10) to describe the reunited people he envisions worshiping at the temple in Jerusalem.

[44] And, incidentally, they continue the use of stories about past figures as polit-

ness functions for Israelites experiencing the rending of the nation as a symbol of a nation made whole, even in the face of foreign domination.

Now, the conclusion of, so to speak, David's coronation comes in 2 Sam. 5:1–3. After the assassination of Ish-baal, the staff-bearers (šōḇ'ṭê)[45] of Israel ask David to become their king. The basis of the choice is threefold: (1) kinship; (2) success in battle; and (3) a divine oracle. Calling themselves David's "bone and flesh" (עצמך ובשרך) allows the elders of Israel to associate themselves with the king's body, to become his body indeed. The merism bone/flesh turns the king's body into the body politic and vice versa. This bodiliness renders intelligible the defection of Israel to David.

The appeal to ethnic and religious commonality in this text, which leads to the making of a covenant between people and king and then his anointing, is a new touch in the coronation accounts. If it has any claim to date to the tenth century, then it signals the fictive understanding of Israel coming into being with the Davidic dual monarchy itself. Even if it is later, from the eighth century, it still reveals that Judahite (and Israelite?) political ideas included notions of the king as "literally" embodying the nation in his own body. Descriptions of the royal body serve political arguments, whether they be for the essential unity of the two Israelite kingdoms or the legitimacy of the Davidides (two sides of the same coin!). The king's physiognomy, self-presentation, and ritual treatment all figure in Israel's understanding of monarchy.

Before passing to the post-Davidic coronations, one may consider another text, 2 Sam. 23:1–7. This poem, allegedly an oracle of David confirming his divine right to rule, bristles with textual problems, which I will not try to sort out here.[46] The text's basic features are clear, however. The king speaks by means of the divine spirit (רוח; v. 2). He is also the נעים/משיח of God.[47] As in the coronation stories of Saul and David, the connection between anointing and the

---

ical allegory (see David Sperling, *The Original Torah* [New York: New York University Press, 1998]).

[45] On this vocalization, see McCarter, *II Samuel*, 130.

[46] The best treatment may be that of Cross, *Canaanite Myth and Hebrew Epic*, 234–37.

[47] Cf. the Akkadian title *migir ilāni* ("favored of the gods"); for references see Seux, *Épithètes Royales Akkadiennes et Sumériennes*, 163–64.

possession by the spirit is close. Here, the divine רוח places on the tongue of the king the words of the deity. These words invite the king to rule (מֹשֵׁל) in resemblance to natural forces, such as rain and sunshine (v. 3).[48] Just this association is also present in Ps. 72:5–6:

> May they fear you along with the sun (עִם שֶׁמֶשׁ)
> and before the moon, forever (דּוֹר דּוֹרִים).
> May he [the king] descend like rain upon the mowing,
> like downpours watering the land.

Ps. 72:8ff. also speaks of the king's universal rule, again a parallel to 2 Sam. 23:5ff.

Now, I argued in the previous chapter that Ps. 72 is probably a coronation hymn.[49] Is the same true of 2 Sam. 23:1–7? Certainly the language of this latter song lends itself to such an interpretation, even if the editor has placed the hymn among David's last words and described it as דברי דוד האחרנים. Minimally, this hymn must reflect upon the coronation (much as Ps. 45 does). The command to rule is a performative utterance, making rule begin. So, the hymn displays David as one speaking prophetically about his own election to kingship by God, perhaps in order to mitigate the boastfulness of his remarks.[50] These are, after all, the words of the divine רוח placed on the tongue of David. Even if the king speaking prophetically does not lose control of his body (as Saul and *only* Saul does) when the Spirit falls upon him, still, the royal ideology of Judah insisted that the monarch spoke the words of God. Yahweh, in some sense that the texts do not explicate, controls the royal body in a way peculiar to kings.

To summarize the treatment of David's body in these stories, it has become clear that one must (modifying Kantorowicz) speak of two or even three bodies of his: his biosocial body (David), the body politic (David the king representing Israel and constituted by its citizens), and the perpetual body of the King (David as a model for his successors). These bodies come into being during a coronation,

---

[48] This reads v. 3a as containing imperatives rather than substantivized participles (מֹשֵׁל not מוֹשֵׁל) as in 4QSam^a rather than MT.

[49] See also Martin Arneth, *"Sonne der Gerechtigkeit": Studien zur Solarisierung der Jahwe-Religion im Lichte von Psalm 72* (BZAR 1; Wiesbaden: Harrassowitz, 2000) 57–78.

[50] K. L. Noll (*The Faces of David* [JSOTSS 242; Sheffield: Sheffield Academic Press, 1997] 160) understands "David" to be claiming here—falsely—to be a prophet. This mistakes the social setting of the language significantly.

whose chief ritual is anointing of the head. The king's head thus becomes a synecdoche for his entire body and the entire body politic of which he is the "head."

The texts play with the idea of the proper appearance of a king, rejecting the Saulide vision of a tall, warriorly physique as the ideal. This is very surprising given the bellicose nature of the self-presentation of the Judahite monarchs in Pss. 2, 20–21, and 144, and indeed of the entire David tradition. As the Goliath legend makes clear, though, one aspect of the Davidic ideal was an understated warriorly ability in which talents greatly exceeded expectations deriving from physical appearance, and in which reliance on Yahweh counted for everything. The parade of generals, elders, and assemblies of the people who accept David as king (not to mention Samuel himself) validate the divine choice of David, marking his as the body to be followed in and by Israel. Once again, physical appearance signifies fitness for rule, but not unambiguously so.

The Coronation of Joash

Meanwhile, in addition to the stories of Saul and David, the extant fullest account of a Judahite coronation, and the one most useful to this discussion, is that of Joash in 2 Kings 11. Following Athaliah's murder of the other royal males, only the infant Joash survives and is raised by the high priest, presumably as a member of his own family. (One would like to know how this was kept secret in a city as small as Jerusalem. Does the narrator imply that Athaliah never entered the temple precincts, or at least the priest's house adjoining it?) When Joash is seven years old, the high priest Jehoiada stages a coup in which the boy is acclaimed king by the army, priests, and attendees at the Sabbath services.[51] The pattern selection/investment/acclamation that one sees in the stories of Saul and David is also present here. Two features of this coronation deserve special notice.

First, the investment of Joash with regalia (2 Kings 11:10, 12) seems to involve two steps. In the first (v. 10), the weapons of David

---

[51] On the role of עם הארץ in this coup, see Tomoo Ishida, *The Royal Dynasties in Ancient Israel: A Study on the Formation and Development of Royal-Dynastic Ideology* (Berlin: de Gruyter, 1977) 160–62.

are brought from the temple and presented to the שָׂרֵי הַמֵּאיוֹת ("officers of the hundreds"), that is, the officers of the militia.⁵² One might expect the king himself to receive them, but his youth might have necessitated that a surrogate do so. Next, the king himself appears (from the temple?) before the assembly and receives the diadem (נֵזֶר; cf. 2 Sam. 1:10; Pss. 89:40, 132:18) and עֵדוּת, perhaps a written document like that which Saul receives in 1 Sam. 10:25 and the Deuteronomic king does in Deut. 17:14–20.⁵³ The investment with these last two objects marks Joash's transformation from crown prince (בֶּן הַמֶּלֶךְ) to king, a change formalized in the anointing. The two-stage investiture must have a ritual purpose, the second presentation of objects serving to intensify and solidify the objective of the ritual, the making of the king.⁵⁴

Why do these objects appear in the coronation ritual? The evidence of the royal psalms (Pss. 89:40, 132:18; cf. 2 Sam. 1:10) is that the נֵזֶר ("diadem") was a traditional part of the Judahite royal iconography. Since it was worn on the head, it recalled to observers that kingship came through anointing, i.e., pouring oil upon the head. The weapons, meanwhile, even if they were not used by Joash, nevertheless marked him as a warrior (as in Ps. 45; and see below) and not just any warrior, but one in the mold of David. If the stories of military prowess were an integral part of the coronation tales of Saul and David, demonstrations of the efficacy and appropriateness of their anointing, then it is hardly surprising that court ritual of their successors should portray the king as a great warrior (even

---

⁵² These specific weapons are otherwise unknown, but presumably were among the temple's greatest treasures. On the precise identity of these objects, see John Gray, *I & II Kings* (OTL; London: SCM, 1964) 517; Mordechai Cogan and Hayim Tadmor, *II Kings* (AB 11; New York: Doubleday, 1988) 127–28 (who convincingly render שְׁלָטִים as "quivers"). Describing them as David's serves an obvious purpose of tying Joash to a past glorious ruler whom he should emulate.

⁵³ As already noted, 1 Sam. 10:25 does not use the Deuteronomic terminology or ideas and so cannot be an anachronism based on Deut. 17. Rather, both texts, along with 2 Kings 11:12 are evidence that the conveyance of a document of some sort from the priest (or prophet in 1 Samuel) was part of the coronation ceremony itself. The content and physical nature of this document are unclear, although one may surmise that possession of it somehow signified the king's entering into a relationship (a contract?) with the people as a whole. See Antti Laato, *History and Ideology in the Old Testament Prophetic Literature: A Semiotic Approach to the Reconstruction of the Proclamation of the Historical Prophets* (CBOTS 41; Stockholm: Almqvist & Wiksell, 1996) 275. For other interpretations of עֵדוּת, see Cogan and Tadmor, *II Kings*, 128.

⁵⁴ On ritual redundancy, see Stanley Tambiah, "A Performative Approach to Ritual," *Proceedings of the British Academy* 65 (1979) 140.

when he was seven years old!). Weapons are an index of bodily power and thus fitness to rule.[55]

The presentation of the king in military regalia was, of course, common in the Iron II Levant, especially in battle scenes riding a chariot. It is therefore unsurprising that Joash receives "quivers" (שלטים), since chariots typically bore at least two quivers for the king as archer.[56] The identification of these weapons as David's is surely an effort at legitimating the new king by making him a worthy bearer of the ancient weapons. He is a new David.

This leads to the second important aspect of the coronation. The narrator goes to great pains to describe this event, not as the result of a coup, but as the reversal of one. The presence of representatives of every social stratum, the anointing and acclamation, the use of sacred space and special objects (weapons housed in the temple) all serve to sacralize this event. One may imagine that the narrator protests too much, as many scholars have argued.[57] The more interesting aspect of the text, however, is its depiction of the display of the king in the temple precincts. Armed soldiers ring the altar court, the line beginning at each corner of the temple (כתף הבית) itself and surrounding the altar (2 Kings 11:11). This cordon of soldiers creates a space in which the king is physically safe (protected from Athaliah and her supporters), but also now marked as a warrior (by the weapons of David).

The use of sacred space for a coronation—a commonplace or nearly universal practice, to be sure—may have specific precedent in the Saul stories,[58] and Ps. 110:3b envisions a stage of the coronation occurring inside the temple temenos (see Chapter 2). While the great narrative detail in 2 Kings 11 may imply that some of the ritual for Joash was innovative—for example, were soldiers always present at the investiture, or was this a precaution against Athaliah's

---

[55] See Burke O. Long, *2 Kings* (FOTL 10; Grand Rapids: Eerdmans, 1991) 151.
[56] See B. Hrouda, "Die Assyrische Streitwagen," *Iraq* 25 (1963) 155–58; Ursula Magen, *Assyrische Königsdarstellungen: Aspekte der Herrschaft* (Mainz: von Zabern, 1986) Fig. 2.7, 12.
[57] E.g., Lowell K. Handy, "Speaking of Babies in the Temple," *Eastern Great Lakes and Midwest Biblical Societies Proceedings* 8 (1988) 155–65; Patricia Dutcher-Walls, *Narrative Art, Political Rhetoric: The Case of Athaliah and Joash* (JSOTSS 209; Sheffield: Sheffield Academic Press, 1996) 110–12.
[58] See above, on 1 Sam. 10:25 (in which Samuel places the book of kingship לפני יהוה, i.e., in a sanctuary).

intervention?—the basic structure of the ritual must have been traditional. Otherwise, it would have been infelicitous.

The location of the coronation in the space between the temple entrance and the forecourt altar is also surely significant. On account of its proximity to the holiest spot on earth and the place at which Yahweh came into contact with humankind, this space is an appropriate site for the transformation of the royal body that coronation effects.[59] Ps. 110 apparently envisions the temple precincts as the site of the coronation, as well. Since it is also near the royal tombs (see above), this space associates the new king with his ancestors, warriors all. The use of sacred space for a ritual with heavy military overtones must serve to associate the warlike deity with the young king and indeed to signify divine election and approval of Joash. As Catherine Bell puts it in another context, "ritualization . . . temporally structures a space-time environment through a series of physical movements . . . thereby producing an arena which, by its molding of the actors, both validates and extends the schemes they are internalizing."[60] The actors here are the soldiers and priests who make the king and make themselves his subjects and fellow warriors, just as they induct him into the company of men. Their actions create the king and will extend his rule to the entire kingdom and his reputation to those hearing the story later. This is also why the coronation precedes the seizure of government and the execution of Athaliah: the warrior king must be created before he can rule, before he can defeat his enemies (cf. Ps. 2).[61]

Aside from the mention of Sabbath worshipers in 2 Kings 11:9, the narration says nothing about temple rituals, whether sacrifice or purification. Nor do the words of the liturgy (except the acclamation, יחי המלך ["may the king live!'], a performative utterance; v. 12) interest the narrator.[62] In other words, the locale of the coronation is taken for granted; of course, the king is crowned in the temple.

---

[59] In Israel, the sacrality of space is not inherent, but derivative from the presence of a deity; see Sara Japhet, "Some Biblical Concepts of Sacred Place," in Benjamin Z. Kedar and R. J. Zwi Werblowsky, eds., *Sacred Space: Shrine, City, Land* (New York: New York University Press, 1998) 55–72.

[60] Catherine Bell, *Ritual Theory, Ritual Practice* (Oxford: Oxford University Press, 1992) 109–10.

[61] Cf. Long, *2 Kings*, 151–52.

[62] Mettinger (*King and Messiah*, 133) argues plausibly that the phrase "may the king live" granted the king a higher form of life than most humans enjoyed.

This implies that the temple was the normal location of at least some of the coronation ceremony in Judah. One should expect this, given the insistence in Pss. 2, 45, and 110 and Isa. 9:6 that the new king is the scion of Yahweh, one who takes on a new body.

Before passing from this story, one should note three further points that illuminate the way in which the coronation creates the king's body. The first is the emphasis on silence and noise. Athaliah "hears the noise" (קול את עתליה ותשמע; v. 13) of the acclamation and clapping of hands. Then there is the blast of a trumpet (הצצרה)[63] and the din of rejoicing people.[64] This noise creates an environment that clearly demarcates the line between legitimacy and illegitimacy, embodied by Joash and Athaliah. The unexpected noise is the "striking of the hands" by the soldiers. The expression יכו כף is, as far as I can ascertain, a *hapax legomenon* in the Bible and Levantine inscriptions. While it is normally translated "they clapped [their] hand[s]," this is not entirely obvious, and it is conceivable that they struck their hands with the spear they carried or some other object. Nor is it obvious that this is a gesture of applause. Rather, since the verb נכה usually takes an object that is the name of an enemy person or place, it may be that the striking was a kind of imitative ritual whose meaning might be, "just as we strike our hands, so may we, under the leadership of this king, strike our enemies." The ritual is an icon[65] for the role that the king will take on as a warrior who strikes

---

[63] The הצצרה is usually in the Bible an instrument for the priests (Num. 10:3, 4, 7, 8; 31:6; 1 Chron. 13:8; 15:28; 16: 6, 42; 2 Chron. 15:14; 20:28; 29:26, 27; 29:28; Ezra 3:10; Neh. 12:35, 41; Ps. 98:6). Hos. 5:8 is especially interesting: "Sound the *shofar* in Gibeah, the הצצרה in Ramah." The context makes it clear that these are instruments used to sound military alarms, not just for festivals (as in Numbers), but Hosea's evocation of the old Benjaminite sites associated in the tradition with Samuel and Saul is interesting. Wolff's explanation of these as the first objectives of a Judahite invasion seems inadequate (Hans Walter Wolff, *Hosea* [Hermeneia; Philadelphia: Fortress, 1974] 112). On the instrument, see Joachim Braun, *Music in Ancient Israel/Palestine: Archaeological, Written, and Comparative Sources* (Grand Rapids: Eerdmans, 2002) 14–16.

[64] Ritualized rejoicing (שמח) also appears in 1 Kings 1:40 at the coronation of Solomon. Presumably, this rejoicing was part of the overall coronation ritual throughout the monarchic period.

[65] An icon, a sign of something else by reason of intrinsic similarity, need not be visual; see Michael Herzfeld, "On Some Rhetorical Uses of Iconicity in Cultural Ideologies," in Paul Bouissac, Michael Herzfeld, and Roland Posner, eds., *Iconicity: Essays on the Nature of Culture* (Tübingen: Stauffenberg, 1986) 401–19.

enemies.⁶⁶ This would accord well with the aftermath of the ritual, namely the execution of Athaliah.

I cannot demonstrate conclusively this understanding of the "clapping" or "striking" noise, but can only indicate it as one interpretive option. What does seem clear—and this is the second facet of the ritual worth considering—is that Joash here becomes not only a king, but a man. Note that the participants in the ritual are apparently all males, or at least that the cordon demarcating the ritual space consists of males, soldiers. Joash begins the ceremony as the בן המלך ("crown prince") and ends as מלך.

The presence of David's weapons, now Joash's, transfers the latter into the company of males old enough to bear arms (even if he is literally still a boy). When the soldiers surround the king here, they do so as his army, whom he must lead into battle (even if, at the present stage of his life, through surrogates). The coronation ritual, then, recognizes the martial role of the king, and, even if the day's events cannot literally turn Joash into a warrior (any more than would be true for other adolescent males initiated into manhood), it can mark him as a candidate for the role and serve to commence his training for it. All of this appears in the ritual in extremely condensed form in its kinesic and spatial dimensions.

The third point worth observing here is that after becoming king, Joash stands "at the pillar according to custom" (עמד על העמוד; כמשפט v. 14). This tidbit indicates that Judahite kings after their unction and acclamation stood somewhere in the temple precinct (before Jachin and Boaz? near a stele in the courtyard?) to present themselves to the people (cf. 2 Kings 23:3). The narrator skillfully introduces the custom, otherwise unknown, by having Athaliah see Joash, realize what has occurred, and label it treason. Her verdict, of course, is not the readers', because the narrative has already branded her a murderess and Joash the rightful heir to the throne. But it is his standing at the pillar that signals his assumption of power. If the pillar is part of the Yahweh iconography,⁶⁷ this would be a case of

---

⁶⁶ Cf. Ezek. 21:19: "And you, son of man, prophesy and clap hand against hand (כף אל כף), and for a third time the sword will be doubled—a sword for the slain (חרב חללי) it is!" Greenberg (*Ezekiel 21–37* [AB 22A; New York: Doubleday, 1997] 424) calls the hand-clapping here "a gesture of vexation," but I note that it precedes a description of slaughter in battle, which, again, it may be imitating magically (cf. also Ezek. 21:22 and 22:13).

⁶⁷ Is this connected to the stele (מצבה) that was almost certainly an (aniconic)

the king representing himself in an attitude of piety before God, much as Assyrian kings were wont to do, for example.[68] One may also observe that he is a male seen by the female Athaliah, who also willy-nilly labels him king (just as women do for David and Saul), but the text does not expatiate upon this point.

The Joash tale, to reprise, is a highly compressed account of a coronation ceremony during the period of the two monarchies. While the overwhelming presence of soldiers *might* be peculiar to the crowning of a minor who must contest his throne, the structure of the ritual (presentation in the temple, investiture, anointing, acclamation, presentation at the sacred spot for kings) must be more or less the common practice in Judah (and like that in Israel) because parts of it also appear in the Saul and David stories and Pss. 110 and 132. Though somatically still a boy, Joash at his coronation becomes a new man with a newly invigorated body.

Retrospects and Prospects

What is true of Joash is true of the kings of Judah and apparently Israel, though here the evidence is sparser. Certainly the combination of military, religious, judicial, paterfamilial, and other facets of monarchy inform the coronation ritual. Anointing transforms the king's body; acclamation recognizes the transformation; self-presentation confirms it.

Why do the coronation rituals of the Israelites encapsulate a view of a changed body? There may be many reasons. At one level, this ritual marks a change in the man on the throne himself—he changes from a crown prince into a king (and 2 Kings 11 lays this out very carefully). The roles assumed by this new man involve fighting against internal and external enemies, with even his legal judgments being lines in a quasimilitary drama. Ritual serves to create the environment of such a change (whether there really is a biological one or not).

On the other hand, the coronation ritual also changes the community. It reaffirms its commitment to the monarchy, even if, as the

---

icon of Yahweh? See Tryggve N. D. Mettinger, "Israelite Aniconism: Developments and Origins," in Karel van der Toorn, ed., *The Image and the Book: Iconic Cults, Aniconism, and the Rise of Book Religion in Israel and the Ancient Near East* (Leuven: Peeters, 1997) 173–204, esp. 195–98; Ronald S. Hendel, "Aniconism and Anthropomorphism in Ancient Israel," in van der Toorn, *Image and the Book*, 205–28.

[68] See Magen, *Assyrische Königsdarstellungen*, 45–64.

story of Saul's coronation with its denunciations of royal abuse of power shows, part of the ritual involved the stylized critique of the institution. Yet, it also affirms its loyalty to a new wearer of the crown. "The king is dead; long live the king!" The community's relationship to the person who is now king changes, and with it the community itself. Heroic tasks require a heroic body, and this could come to be through ritual.

How does this impinge on the question of the king's body? The king must present his body in ways that the society finds acceptable. His body is not merely a biological given (though it is obviously that), but also a social construction. He must lead in warfare, and this dictates that he must learn to drive a chariot, shoot a bow, and look respectable doing so. This, in turn, requires rigorous bodily disciplines the outlines of which are unfortunately now lost to us. But beyond the acquisition of physical skills, the king must also adorn and display his body in a fitting way if his kingdom is to flourish. The king has two bodies, as Kantorowicz would have it, or perhaps three: his biological body, his socially constructed body, and the larger body politic of which the first two are icons.[69]

Before drawing wider conclusions, we make two final, related points just now. First a question: what would create an infelicitous coronation ritual? Although the three examined here seem paradigmatic in some respects, and we must assume that the basic pattern of presentation in the temple, investiture, anointing, acclamation, and presentation at the sacred spot for kings that appears *mutatis mutandis* in all three informed all or most Israelite and Judahite coronations, we lack direct evidence of a failed ritual. In principle, though, infelicity could arise through the choice of the wrong candidate (not a Davidide in Judah; cf. 1 Kings 1–2), the execution of the ritual in the wrong place, and the employment in it of the wrong words or gestures or

---

[69] See Ernst Kantorowicz, *The King's Two Bodies: A Study in Mediaeval Political Theology* (Princeton: Princeton University Press, 1957); on two bodies, see Mary Douglas, *Natural Symbols* (New York: Vintage, 1973); on three, Nancy Scheper-Hughes and Margaret Lock, "The Mindful Body: A Prolegomenon to Future Work in Medical Anthropology," *Medical Anthropology Quarterly* 1 (1987) 6–41; for a summary of various numerations of the body, see Thomas J. Csordas, "Introduction: the body as representation and being-in-the-world," in idem, *Embodiment and experience: The existential ground of culture and self* (Cambridge: Cambridge University Press, 1994) 5–6.

even of the wrong preritual purificatory disciplines.[70] Any of these infelicities could result in the failure to create the royal body and thus the body politic.

The second point is that despite the appearance of solidity in these coronation rituals, an impression confirmed by the absence of evidence for infelicitous ones, the meaning of the coronation was in fact open to debate. Apparently, 1 Sam. 8–12 embeds within the ritual itself the contest for meaning: the constitution of the royal body does not license the king to dominate the bodies of his subjects by taking their surplus produce, making them slaves or corvee laborers, using cultivable land to support chariot horses, or accumulating wives. Rather, as the coronations of David and Joash also evince, the ideal was cooperation of subjects in the making and support of the king.

Moreover, since the king was a warrior first of all, and thus the leader of other warriors and the protector of women and children who could not fight, the fitness of his body for war was a subject of interest. Size does not ultimately matter, since a child can carry the arms of David! What matters is attractiveness, but even more the experience of anointing and acclamation and presentation. The body royal that counts is not that of the king, but that of the King created by ritual.

As Catherine Bell argues, political rituals serve a society in two ways:

> [F]irst, they use symbols and symbolic action to depict a group of people as a coherent and ordered community based on shared values and goals; second, they demonstrate the legitimacy of these values and goals by establishing their iconicity with the perceived values and order of the cosmos.[71]

Israelite coronations created a royal body that could, through its use of such indexes of power (and of divinity) as weapons, choreographed movements, and so on, signify the basic structure of a cosmos in which Yahweh brought order in the form of justice to the vulnerable and security to all those whose bodily actions (see Ps. 101) coincided

---

[70] On various types of infelicities in performative utterances and thus implicitly rituals, see J. L. Austin, *How to do Things With Words* (2d ed.; Cambridge: Harvard University Press, 1975) esp. 14–45.

[71] Catherine Bell, *Ritual Perspectives and Dimensions* (Oxford: Oxford University Press, 1997) 129.

with the proper order of things. By connecting the king's body to his notional parent, tutor, and model Yahweh, these rituals anchored kingship in the cosmic order. And on this point the narratives embedded in the DH and the royal psalms agree.

Yet, as we have seen, the narratives reflect the knowledge that society is not entirely of one piece, and therefore the depictions of these rituals in texts embedded in the DH encode the awareness of competing sign systems. The king's bodily self-display does not always satisfy divine requirements. Ritual does not correspond neatly to the real world, or to be more precise, the code of signs embedded in ritual coexist with conflicting codes outside the ritual and indeed within the ritual itself.[72] Or to put matters differently still, both the royal rituals included in the Psalter and the unofficial narratives included in the DH share basic assumptions about the structure of the universe but differ on the degree to which kingship, or at least any given king, reflects in his own body that structure. This tension between the official and non-official views of the royal body becomes still more evident in the narratives to be considered next, those revolving around the death of the king.

---

[72] On simultaneous encoding of multiple signs in ritual, see Roy Rappaport, *Ritual and Religion in the Making of Humanity* (Cambridge: Cambridge University Press, 1999) 236–76.

CHAPTER FIVE

WHILE HORSE AND HERO FELL:
ROYAL DEATH AND SICKNESS

> ... For the head
> Lies at Gilboa. The sky
> Is above it, and
> The ant has entered
> The eye arch.[1]
> I have forgotten, literally, God, and through
> The enormous hollow of my head, History
> Whistles like a wind.
> How beautiful are the young, walking!
> If I could weep.

In the biblical narratives about kings, one finds many of the same themes as in the royal psalms, especially the pervasiveness of military life and the impinging of that life, with its simultaneous contest among males for dominance and quest for fellowship and bonding, on other moments in the king's existence. There are differences in these narratives, however, for not only are they less reticent about the monarch's sexuality (at least in the case of David and Solomon), but they also take seriously criticisms of kings. How could there be a greater contrast in outlook between two texts than that between, say, Ps. 2 and its assumption that foes of the king of Judah are raving fools, and the brutally honest middle chapters of 2 Samuel?[2] Laying out those perspectives, their interworkings, and their connection to issues in Israelite culture (where discernible) is the task at hand.

---

[1] Robert Penn Warren, "Saul at Gilboa," in idem, *The Collected Poems of Robert Penn Warren* (ed. John Burt; Baton Rouge: LSU Press, 1998) 214.

[2] On the Succession Narrative and its complex view of David, see Leonhard Rost, *Die Überlieferung von der Thronnachfolge Davids* (Stuttgart: Kohlhammer, 1926); and the critique in Steven L. McKenzie, "The So-Called Succession Narrative in the Deuteronomistic History," in Albert de Pury and Thomas Römer, eds., *Die sogennante Thronfolgegeschichte Davids* (OBO 176; Göttingen: Vandenhoeck & Ruprecht, 2000) 123–35; cf. Otto Kaiser, "Some Observations on the Succession Narrative," *OTWSA* 27/28 (1986) 130–47. It would be difficult to improve on Kaiser's characterization of this text: "The reader gets the impression at last that it was the intention of the narrator to tell his story in such a manner as to provoke different opinions in regard to the motives of the actors in this drama" (140–41).

The Death of the King

The most problematic moment in a monarchy occurs with the death of the incumbent on the throne. The very preservation of the social and political system depends on a smooth succession; hence the frequent wish in the royal psalms for the perdurance of the dynasty, and the deafening near silence in those same texts about royal death. The Psalter apparently contains no trace of the funerary liturgy of an Israelite king, though it is difficult to imagine that such a liturgy (or multiple versions thereof) did not exist. Nothing like the Egyptian "Book of the Dead,"[3] the Mesopotamian *kispu* ritual,[4] or even the Ugaritic coronation or funerary prayer by the king to his ancestors seen in KTU 1.161 and 1.113 survives for Israel or Judah.[5] While this gap in the evidence may, again, be part of the loss of data that we face always for Levantine states of the Iron Age, it nevertheless forces us to account for it. The propaganda that survives in the royal psalms seems to be very reticent about royal death. Not so the narratives embedded in the DH. Apparently, the mention of death in court ritual was thought to open up the possibility of such an event occurring. The narratives' *Sitze im Leben* needed no such reticence.

The demise of the monarch thus calls for elaborate ritual responses, as well as intellectual efforts at legitimation of the succession. As William Hallo has put it, "... the death of kings is a fact of life,

---

[3] On the Pharaoh's role in this, see Friedrich Abitz, *Pharao als Gott in den Unterweltsbuchern des Neuen Reiches* (OBO 146; Göttingen: Vandenhoeck & Ruprecht, 1995); *RÄRG* 824–28.

[4] On which, see Akio Tsukimoto, *Untersuchungen zur Totenpflege* (kispum) *im alten Mesopotamien* (AOAT 216; Neukirchen-Vluyn: Neukirchener, 1985).

[5] See Gregorio del Olmo Lete, *Canaanite Religion According to the Liturgical Texts of Ugarit* (Bethesda, MD: CDL, 1999) chaps. 3–4; and Paolo Xella, *I Testi Rituali di Ugarit I* (Rome: CNDR, 1981) 279–80. These Ugaritic texts are prayers that the king utters to invite his dead ancestors to be present at the ritual. Here the deceased monarchs are also *'ilu* ("god"), a label that in the Bible only applies to living rulers (Ps. 45; Isa. 9). See also Wayne T. Pitard, "The Ugaritic Funerary Text RS 34.126," *BASOR* 232 (1979) 65–75; Theodore S. Lewis, *Cults of the Dead in Ancient Israel and Ugarit* (HSM 39; Atlanta: Scholars, 1989) 5–46; Gregorio del Olmo Lete, "Royal Aspects of the Ugaritic Cult," in J. Quaegebeur, ed., *Ritual and Sacrifice in the Ancient Near East* (Leuven: Peeters, 1993) 57–58; and David Toshio Tsumura, "The Interpretation of the Ugaritic Funerary Text KTU 1.161," in Eiko Matsushima, ed., *Official Cult and Popular Religion in the Ancient Near East* (Heidelberg: Winter, 1993) 40–55, and his bibliography. On possible Israelite ancestor cults, see Lewis, *Cults of the Dead*; and Karel van der Toorn, *Family Religion in Babylonia, Syria and Israel: Continuity and Change in Forms of Religious Life* (Leiden: Brill, 1996).

but a problem for ideology."⁶ This is especially true when the succession is contested or somehow irregular, but even when it is not (as a Maria Theresa of Austria or an Assurbanipal of Assyria discovered) much institutional energy must be expended to insure harmony.⁷ Not surprisingly, then, biblical narrative (as opposed to psalmody) topicalizes the death of the king. The dead king's body, or, rather, its proper care and burial, becomes an important object of consideration. The royal corpse signifies danger to the state and its people, and often stands as a sign of divine judgment against the policies of the king.

Israelite narrative often reports this death in formulaic ways. The Deuteronomistic historians developed a set pattern that could be varied depending on whether the king died peacefully or not. A peaceful death is recorded with the rubric "and he lay with his ancestors (וישכב עם אבותיו) and was buried (ויקבר) in Samaria/the city of David."⁸ A violent death, in battle or during a coup d'etat, causes the narrative to omit וישכב עם אבותיו, even when it mentions the king's burial.⁹ This means that the idiom לשכב עם אבותיו does not mean

---

⁶ See William W. Hallo, "The Death of Kings: Traditional Historiography in Contextual Perspective," in Mordechai Cogan and Israel Ephal, eds., *Ah, Assyria . . .: Studies in Assyrian History and Ancient Near Eastern Historiography Presented to Hayim Tadmor* (Jerusalem: Magnes, 1991) 163.

⁷ On Mesopotamian treatments of regicide, see D. J. Wiseman, "Murder in Mesopotamia," *Iraq* 36 (1974) 249–60; an especially difficult problem was the death of Sargon II (705 BCE) and the loss of his body, on which see Hayim Tadmor, "The Sin of Sargon," *EI* 5 (1958) 150–62 [Hebrew]; J. A. Brinkman, *Prelude to Empire: Babylonian Society and Politics, 747–626 BC* (Philadelphia: Occasional Publications of the Babylonian Fund, 1984) 54 n. 252; and Hayim Tadmor, Benno Landsberger, and Simo Parpola, "The Sin of Sargon and Sennacherib's Last Will," *SAAB* 3/1 (1989) 1–51 (a revision of earlier articles by the first two principals).

⁸ 1 Kings 14:30; 15:8, 24; 2 Kings 2:51; 8:24; 15:7, 38; 16:20; 20:21; 21:18 (Judah); 1 Kings 16:28; 2 Kings 14:16, 29. The expression also reflects the practice of laying out the bodies of aristocrats on bedlike shelves in tombs in which multiple generations were interred. The headrests of Judahite tombs of Iron II create the illusion of a bed; hence the phrase "lying with the ancestors" is literally true. See David Ussishkin, *The Village of Silwan: The Necropolis from the Period of the Judean Kingdom* (Jerusalem: Israel Exploration Society, 1993) esp. 294–317; Gabriel Barkay, Amihai Mazar, and Amos Kloner, "בית הקברות הצפוני של ירושלים בימי בית ראשון," *Qadmoniot* 8 (1975) 71–76; and Eric M. Meyers, *Jewish Ossuaries: Reburial and Rebirth* (BibOr 24; Rome: Biblical Institute Press, 1971) esp. 3–11.

⁹ 2 Kings 12:22; 21:26; 23:30. Problem texts include 2 Kings 14:22, where an unnamed king is said to "lie with his ancestors," and 1 Kings 22:40, where Ahab does "lie with his ancestors" in spite of the text's apparent prior notice of his death in battle. In the first case, the identity of the king who "lies" is unclear: it could be Jeroboam II. On the death of Ahab, see below.

simply "he died," but "he died in his ancestral home," or "he died of natural causes." The cause of death is thus a crucial concern for biblical narrative, to which we will return momentarily. This concern is not unique to the Deuteronomists, however, for their sources also evince it (as will become clear presently).

This formulaic material does offer one important insight, however. This concerns royal burial. There is no reason to treat these short notices in the DH as anything but historical reminiscences reflecting ancient tradition, for they show no traces of being fictions serving the higher ends of the DH. In fact, while the formula of "lying with the fathers" is Deuteronomistic, the underlying sources relating royal death sometimes reflect points of view divergent from that of the work as a whole, as, for example, with the peaceful death of Ahab envisioned in 1 Kings 22:40.

Both the DH and its sources agree, however, that for Judahite kings, the place of burial was in the city of David, apparently because it lay in the patrimonial estate of the royal family[10] (just as Samaria was for the Omrides), until the reign of Manasseh. That ruler was buried (as is his son Amon) in the גן עזא ("garden of Uzza"; 2 Kings 21:18, 26).[11] Presumably, this change reflected a broader shift in the royal self-understanding of Manasseh, although whether this change involved new notions of purity (no burying in cities) or perhaps (conversely) a denigration of Jerusalem is unclear. What does seem clear from the burial of the dead king within the capital city, physically near the palace and symbolically near the actions of government, is that his body is linked metonymically with the living body of his successor. Just as the deceased lies with his ancestors, so does he lie near his successors, still living. (While it is not clear what, if any, ongoing rites connected the dead king to his living successor, one can hardly believe that no such rites existed.) The practice of extramural burials did not obtain for the king.[12] The tomb of the dead king is an icon of the ever-living monarch.

---

[10] On patrimonial estates in Israel, see Lawrence Stager, "The Archaeology of the Family in Ancient Israel," *BASOR* 260 (1985) 1–35.

[11] According to 2 Kings 23:30, Josiah was also buried simply "in his grave" (בקברתו). The LXX addition "in the city of David" ('εν πόλει Δαυιδ) is almost certainly a harmonization to the rest of 1–2 Kings.

[12] On Israelite burial practices, see J. W. Ribar, "Death Cult Practices in Ancient Palestine" (Ph.D. diss., University of Michigan, 1973); Elizabeth Bloch-Smith, *Judahite Burial Practices and Beliefs about the Dead* (JSOTSS 123; Sheffield: JSOT, 1992). Methods

The most interesting feature of these formulaic death reports, though, may be that they exist at all. Why report the location of burial when it does not change? Presumably, that is just the point: the royal corpse lies just where its predecessors do and its successors will. The death formula, that is, points to the continuity of the dynasty in time *and* space. It is probably not too much to say that the text recites these death and burial notices in order to remind its audience that the kings reside with their subjects, in the capital, always.

So, the stories of royal death that are reduced to formula do offer something to the present study.[13] Offering much more, though, are the cases that receive ampler treatment, which are worth careful examination, especially when they show evidence of a process of literary reworking over time. Most of these, with the exception of David's last scene, involve the violent death of the monarch, a situation that presented a standing problem to the monarchic system. In Samuel-Kings, not counting Saul or various pretenders, seventeen rulers of Israel and Judah meet a rough end.[14] A violent death obviously has more narrative potential than a peaceful one. These protracted stories involve violent death, the maltreatment of the body, and perhaps its display in sacrilegious ways. The body under duress, the body dismembered—this is the stuff of these stories. We examine now each in turn, beginning with the death of Saul, which is paradigmatic in this regard.

The Death of Saul (1 Samuel 31–2 Samuel 1)

As background to the Saul stories, let us recognize that the violent death of kings figures prominently in ancient Near Eastern narrative, and not least in Israel. This is unsurprising, since the demise

---

of burial included simple graves, cist graves, jar burials, coffin burials, shaft and cave tombs, and bench and arcosolia tombs, the last being the "typical, official Judahite form of burial" (Bloch-Smith, *Judahite Burial Practices*, 137).

[13] But for other uses of the formula, see Baruch Halpern and David Vanderhooft, "The Editions of Kings in the 7th–6th Centuries BCE," *HUCA* 62 (1991) 170–244.

[14] These include: Ish-baal (2 Sam. 4:7), Nadab (1 Kings 15:28), Elah (1 Kings 16:10), Zimri (1 Kings 16:18), Tibni (1 Kings 16:22), the anonymous "king of Israel" (1 Kings 22:37), Joram of Israel (2 Kings 9:24), Ahaziah of Judah (2 Kings 9:27), Athaliah (2 Kings 11:16), Joash (2 Kings 12:20), Amaziah of Judah (2 Kings 14:19), Zechariah (2 Kings 15:10), Shallum (2 Kings 15:14), Pekahiah (2 Kings 15:25), Pekah (2 Kings 15:30), Amon (2 Kings 21:23), and Josiah (2 Kings 23:29).

of the king marks a crisis in a traditional monarchy, one demanding elaborate political, cultic, and military precautions. With few exceptions, this tragic event was perceived as the result of divine judgment, as in the cases of Shulgi and Naram-Sin in first-millennium retellings of events of the third millennium,[15] and then in the case of Sargon II, whose body was lost on the battlefield.[16] This view also informs the covenant curse formulas in the Sefire inscriptions and in Esarhaddon's vassal treaties, to name a few examples; these texts take great delight in recounting the destruction of the royal body of a disloyal vassal of the great king. In particular, the curses in Esarhaddon's vassal treaty envision the rebellious vassal facing the destruction not only of his power, but also of his very body, including:[17]

414–16	Failure to see old age
417–18	Word of mouth bad
418a–c	Various ailments
419–21	*saḫaršubbû* sickness, wandering in steppe
422–24	Blindness
425–27	Being wounded by arrows, eaten by vultures
449	Eating one's own children owing to hunger
453–54	Enemies binding arms and legs
455–56	Sword destroying innards
461–63	Sickness in heart, bathe in own blood
469–71	Blood flowing like rain
519–20	Being eaten by eagles and vultures
521–22	Drinking "dead" water
540–44	Seeing one's offspring dead
547–50	Experiencing hunger

The inescapable physicality of this political discourse reminds us of the dangers awaiting a malfeasant ruler. Clearly, the notion of a glorious royal death in battle goes against the prevailing currents of royal ideation.

---

[15] A convenient edition of these texts and discussion thereof appears in Joan Goodnick Westenholz, *Legends of the Kings of Akkade* (Winona Lake: Eisenbrauns, 1997) esp. Section B on Naram-Sin.

[16] See the evolving discussion of Sargon's death in Tadmor, Landsberger, and Parpola, "Sin of Sargon and Sennacherib's Last Will," 3–51. An echo of this death may appear in Isa. 14:4b–21, according to H. L. Ginsberg, "Reflexes of Sargon in Isaiah After 715 BCE," *JAOS* 88 (1968) 47–53.

[17] From the edition of Kazuko Watanabe, *Die adê Vereidigung anlässlich der Thronfolgeregelung Asarhaddons* (Baghdader Mitteilungen 3; Berlin: Mann, 1987).

A prominent exception (or brilliant innovation in the semiotic code of kingship) to this comes from the southern Anatolian kingdom of Samal (modern Zençirli), which has yielded inscriptions dating from the mid-ninth to the late-eighth centuries. Here, perhaps uniquely in Western Asia, death in battle allowed glorious self-display (KAI 215). Panammu died in an attack on Damascus, falling "at the feet" (ברגל; l. 16) of his overlord, Tiglath-pileser III. He received a state funeral and monument, and was mourned by his fellow vassals ("brother kings; איחה מלכו; l. 17) and the army. Or so claims his son, Bir-rakib, who must defend his parent's honor, perhaps against claims that submission to Assyria brought about such a horrible end. While this inscription bespeaks the subalternity of the petty rulers under Assyrian rule, with their sycophancy and shrewd self-aggrandizement, it also points up the need of Levantine monarchs to place death in battle in the best possible light and the resources available to them for doing so. For Panammu, death was an opportunity to attract his overlord's attention. It was the ultimate act of male self-display, eliciting the favorable attentions of his peers and superior. For Bir-rakib his son and eulogist, it also proved, or at least did not disprove the support of the gods (ll. 22–23). The readers of the inscription, Bir-rakib's subjects, can feel fortunate to serve such brave and respected rulers! This story appears to be an ad hoc rationalization of an otherwise disconcerting event, but it does show that Levantine rulers and their subjects could sometimes conceive of royal death by violence in positive terms. Or to put it differently, this Samalian portrayal of regal death works because it depicts the event not by reference to the code of kingship and warriorliness, but by switching (brilliantly) to the codes of family and funerary practices.

Now, let us return to the stories of Saul's death. It is true that no Israelite royal stele survives to commemorate this event or any similar one. Conversely, the songs and narratives in 1 Sam. 31–2 Sam. 1 lack a parallel in Samal, although presumably such oral depictions of Panammu's death existed, just as a memorial stele for Saul could have existed.[18] In other words, while the texts about the

---

[18] And a propagandistic literature from the Saulide regime may also have existed; see Marsha White, "'The History of Saul's Rise': Saulide State Propaganda in 1 Samuel 1–14," in Saul Olyan and Robert Culley, eds., *"A Wise and Discerning Mind": Essays in Honor of Burke O. Long* (BJS 325; Providence: Brown Judaic Studies, 2000) 271–92.

deaths of Panammu and Saul are of different genres, they reflect a similar life situation, here a funeral in which performances by the successor kings (David and Bir-rakib) not only judge the deceased monarch as a valiant warrior, but now mark the performer as a worthy successor to such a brave soldier. The dead body of the king becomes, as it were, the raw material out of which the living king constitutes himself as a male, a warrior, and a fit ruler.

A closer examination of 1 Sam. 31–2 Sam. 1 reveals evidence of great intellectual struggle regarding Saul's death, a struggle that finally assumes literary dress.[19] The two understandings of violent royal death—as tragedy and as triumph—collide. After a long narration of Saul's fall from grace, his descent into madness and ignominy culminating at the séance at Endor, 1 Sam. 31–2 Sam. 1 thrice recounts the king's demise.[20] The three versions (1 Sam. 31, 2 Sam. 1:1–17, and 2 Sam. 1:18–27) are not entirely consistent with each other and contain unmistakable evidence of distinctive concerns and origins in separate traditions.[21] For example, taken on its own, the hymn in 2 Sam. 1:18–27 assumes that Jonathan died alongside his father (v. 22), a detail absent in the other tellings of the tale. Or again, the Amalekite who claims to have killed Saul also presents his diadem (נזר) to David (2 Sam. 1:10). Or again, 1 Sam. 31 situates the battle at הר הגלבע, while 2 Sam. 1:17–27 puts it at הרי בגלבע (this construct form occurring apparently only in poetry). As Caquot and de Robert recognize, this part of the royal regalia was a feature of the self-presentation of the Davidides,[22] and so this claim by the Amalekite is both an anachronism from the point of view of the author of the tale and a discrepancy over against the other tales in

---

[19] See the discussion in Baruch Halpern, *David's Secret Demons: Messiah, Murderer, Traitor, King* (Grand Rapids: Eerdmans, 2001) 78–81.

[20] Not just twice as argued for by ibid., 22–26.

[21] See P. Kyle McCarter, *I Samuel* (AB 8; Garden City, NY: Doubleday, 1980) 440–44; idem, P. Kyle McCarter, *II Samuel* (AB 9; Garden City, NY: Doubleday, 1984) 55–79. McCarter tends to view these tales harmonistically and to date them quite early. But see Andre Caquot and Philippe de Robert, *Les Livres de Samuel* (Geneva: Labor et Fides, 1994) 366–67. Diana Vikander Edelman (*King Saul in the Historiography of Judah* [JSOTSS 121; Sheffield: Sheffield Academic Press, 1991] 18–19) dates the Saul complex to the seventh or perhaps eighth century BCE. As I will note below, this makes sense of many details of the death stories. But see the discussion in J. P. Fokkelman, *Narrative Art and Poetry in the Books of Samuel: A Full Interpretation Based on Stylistic and Structural Analyses*, vol. 2: *The Crossing Fates (I Sam. 13–31 and 22 Sam. 1)* (Assen: Van Gorcum, 1986) 622–82.

[22] Caquot and de Robert, *Livres de Samuel*, 367. See Pss. 89:40; 132:18.

1 Sam. 31–2 Sam. 1 (which mention neither diadem nor Amalekite). Going behind the narrative triptych that the pre-DH, prophetic editors created out of older material[23] by identifying and analyzing these discrepancies promises to reveal important aspects of Israelite conceptions of the dead and dying royal body. Proceeding counter-canonically in order to highlight differences among the tales, let us begin with the קינה of David.

David's קינה

I begin with the third version, the song attributed to David (2 Sam. 1:18–27). As Steven Weitzman has shown, this poem—a lay rather than a lament perhaps—is not original to this context.[24] The reference in v. 18 to David's using this song to teach Judahites archery (ללמד בני יהודה קשת) seems to relate this text to training in martial arts, with Saul serving as an inspiration for would-be warriors. The mention of archers in training from Judah is one piece of evidence that points toward the origin of the song in that kingdom. I begin here because the poem, though appropriate to its present literary context,[25] does not share the view of the prose material around it, for it views Saul's death as a glorious (or at least not disgraceful), if tragic, event, in sharp contrast to the two prose accounts. While this song, like the foregoing accounts of his execution of the Amalekite and his dismissal from battle by Akish of Gath, serves to vindicate David of regicide, it also places him in the role of a king who must see to the proper obsequies for his predecessor.[26] In the narrative as

---

[23] See the analysis of Antony Campbell and Mark O'Brien, *Unfolding the Deuteronomistic History: Origins, Upgrades, Present Text* (Minneapolis: Fortress, 2000) 24–32.

[24] Steven Weitzman, "David's Lament and the Poetics of Grief in 2 Samuel," *JQR* 85 (1995) 341–61. Weitzman understands all of 2 Sam. 1 as a "type-scene" of mourning that serves to position David within Israel. On the rough transition to the song, see Fokkelman, *Crossing Fates*, 648.

[25] See McCarter, *II Samuel*, 78. His claim that the psalm must date to the tenth century because "The composition of an elegy for Saul and Jonathan generations after their death would be pointless" (ibid.) is dubious. Witness the ancient case of the Alexander legends, the medieval *Morte d'Arthur* or, closer to home, the first millennium BCE revival (or continuation or intensification) of interest in Naram-Sin of Agade (see the remarks of Westenholz, *Legends of the Kings of Akkade*, esp. 1–29), or the modern retellings of the David story. In all but the last case, oral tradition about a royal death survived for centuries, and the same may well be the case for the stories of Saul's demise.

[26] See Weitzman, "David's Lament and the Poetics of Grief," 341–61. Weitzman understands all of 2 Sam. 1 as a "type-scene" of mourning that serves to position David within Israel.

it currently stands, other Levantine options for honoring a dead king, such as the son's sponsorship of the dead king's coffin (Byblos),²⁷ or his erection of a funerary statue (Zençirli), are out of David's reach because Saul has already died and been buried. The קינה of David allows him to pay his respects, but it also serves notice in the narrative that he has done the kingly duty of ritually marking the end of his predecessor's reign. The warrior exalted here is not really Saul, but David.

In his study of ritual regicide among tribes in southern Sudan, Simon Simonse notes that the murder (euthanasia) of the king during times of distress and the subsequent rituals of purification serve, among other things, to (1) transfer "discontent in the group onto the victim," and (2) eliminate "the victim as a collective mimetic drive in which the group experiences a new sense of unity and a relief from internal violence."²⁸ Using Girard's notion of the scapegoat,²⁹ Simonse argues that the death (or murder, in this case) of the monarch can serve to focus the tensions within a society, be they humanly or divinely originated, on one body, and then to eliminate them with that body's demise. Because the death occurs in the context of ritual, evil consequences do not result. It seems to me that something similar has happened for the narrator's audience in 2 Sam. 1:18–27. By recalling Saul's valiant death, by praising him and Jonathan, David removes the nation's shame stemming from their death (and his own shame at not being there to fight alongside Saul) and the defeat by the Philistines. David's lament imitates Saul's death, repeats it ritually, and thus blunts its sting. Or, to put it differently, the song imitates the death that imitates the national death avoided. This removal of anxiety is expressed in one form in the mention of the communal singing of the בנות ישראל in v. 24. The women who sing of war (cf. Exod. 15:21; 1 Sam. 18:7, 29:5) define the community's attitude toward Saul (and thus his own status as a גבור). Its positive evaluation of his גבורה contrasts with that of the Philistine women,

---

²⁷ On which see below and William F. Albright, "The Phoenician Inscriptions of the Tenth Century BC," *JAOS* 67 (1947) 153–62.

²⁸ Simon Simonse, *Kings of Disaster: Dualism, Centralism, and the Scapegoat King in Southeastern Sudan* (Leiden: Brill, 1992) 18.

²⁹ See Rene Girard, *Violence and the Sacred* (Baltimore: Johns Hopkins University Press, 1977); idem, "Generative Scapegoating," in Robert G. Hamerton-Kelly, ed., *Violent Origins* (Stanford: Stanford University Press, 1987) 73–105.

ROYAL DEATH AND SICKNESS   155

whom David expects to celebrate Saul's death. While maleness is worked out against other men (in battle in this case), it is validated by women. Moreover, the validation of women can even overcome (or revalue) the decision of the battlefield.

The striking thing here is that, as I have already noted, in contrast to the two preceding prose accounts in 1 Sam. 31 and 2 Sam. 1:1–17, David's קינה does not mention Saul's death as being ignominious. Here, Saul fights alongside Jonathan, and both are effective warriors (v. 22) until the end. Here, too, Saul fights with a sword (חרב), not a spear (חנית) as in the Amalekite's tale and elsewhere in 1 Samuel (see below). This means that the poem originates in circles other than those of the narrative death reports, and since the incipit of the poem cites it as an excerpt of the "Book of Yashar" (cf. Josh. 10:13; 2 Kings 8:53 LXX), it must have had an earlier life independent of its present prose setting. This means, further, that the poem preserves a tradition of Saul's death independent of those of the prose accounts, and that this tradition apparently included no mention of Saul's "suicide." Here, there is no reason to think otherwise than that Saul falls in battle.

The verses salient to the current discussion are 21b and 22:

כי שם נגעל מגן ³⁰גבורים מגן שאול בלי משיח בשמן
מדם חללים מחלב גבורים קשת יהונתן לא נשוג אחור וחרב שאול לא תשוב ריקם

For there the heroes' shield was besmirched, Saul's shield lacked the one anointed with oil.
From the blood of the pierced,³¹ from the fat of the heroes, Jonathan's bow did not recoil; Saul's sword did not retract clean.³²

The king and crown prince appear as skilled warriors, even in defeat. Their physical prowess allowed them to destroy the bodies of other males, indeed, of heroic males. Gone entirely is Saul's pathetic cry for mercy killing or his sinister séance at Endor. Gone is the melancholy

---

³⁰ I take this as a plural with MT, not as a singular with an enclitic *mem* (but McCarter, *II Samuel*, 71). Saul is among the heroes, however.
³¹ Reading חלל I. On the connection of חלל III ("to defile") to the Phillistines, see most recently Saul Olyan, *Rites and Rank: Hierarchy in Biblical Representations of Cult* (Princeton: Princeton University Press, 2000) 65, 153 n. 17. The poem may be using double entendre here: the "defiled" Philistines are also the pierced.
³² Literally, "empty," but here in the sense of "without blood and gore on it," hence, "clean."

that Robert Penn Warren so brilliantly captures in his poem "Saul at Gilboa":

> ... For the head
> Lies at Gilboa. The sky
> Is above it, and
> The ant has entered
> The eye-arch.[33]

2 Sam. 1:18–27 breathes a different atmosphere from the prose accounts of Saul's death.

Again, this poem seems to reflect a tradition in which Saul and Jonathan died side-by-side in battle, their bodies undesecrated. This description of the king as warrior follows the apostrophe of the now drought-stricken הרי בגלבע in 21a ("O peaks in Gilboa, there is neither dew nor rain upon you"). Now, the connection of rain and dew to the prosperity of the king is a theme in the Davidic royal propaganda (Ps. 72:6).[34] There, the lifegiving rain comes when a king can subdue his enemies. In the Judahite royal propaganda (Ps. 72, esp. v. 6) rain and royal victory go hand-in-hand (though in Israel, prophets control rain [1 Sam. 12:17–18; 1 Kings 17:1, 18:1]). This same notion also appears in the treaty curses in Esarhaddon's Vassal Treaty (lines 530–532): "Just as rain does not fall from the bronze heavens, may no rain or dew come to your fields and meadows! Instead of rain (*zunnu*), may charcoal rain upon your land!"[35] This may indicate a broader Levantine connection between kingship and rainmaking (which the Assyrians picked up). However this may be, in 2 Sam. 1, the connection between rain and fertility, on the one hand, and military prowess, on the other, is not fortuitous. Both are conditional upon the success of the king as warrior, and therefore upon his martial training and generalship.

Moreover, the attribution of the song to David, while it is explicable in terms both of the narrative flow of 1–2 Samuel and of the evolving tradition of David as a psalmist, may also be a clue that "Yashar" arose in the Jerusalem court. This is admittedly difficult

---

[33] *Collected Poems of Robert Penn Warren*, 214.
[34] The same connection between the monarch's death and the loss of fecundity appears in a funerary text (K. 7856, col. IV') for a Neo-Assyrian emperor (probably from the reign of Esarhaddon or Ashurbanipal); see John McGinnis, "A Neo-Assyrian Text Describing a Royal Funeral," *SAAB* 1/1 (1987) 1–13.
[35] In the edition of Watanabe, *Die adê-Vereidigung*. Translation mine.

to prove, but there is some reason to think that this poem reflects in some measure the state propaganda of Judah.[36] The lament, in short, portrays Saul (and his demise) in terms characteristic of the historically later kings of Judah.

In 2 Sam. 1:18–27, however, the defeat of the king leads to a failure of rain (and, consequently, to infertility; v. 21a): הרי בגלבע אל טל ואל מטר עליכם ("O peaks in Gilboa, there is neither dew nor rain upon you!"). While the restriction of rainfall has a long mythic background,[37] it seems difficult to understand v. 21a as a curse. Why would David curse part of his own kingdom?[38] Rather, it is the death of the king at the הרי בגלבע that has caused drought; David merely recognizes this (and so this is not a performative utterance as one might expect). The dead royal body becomes a symbol of the dying land, and vice versa.

Since, as Gressmann showed seventy years ago in his *Messias*,[39] the Judahite courtly propaganda has Near Eastern antecedents and parallels, one might expect the accounts of neighboring states of the violent death of a king to offer useful information. We have seen already that the account of the death of Panammu II of Samal recorded in the name of his son Bir-rakib (KAI 215) illustrates the option of understanding royal death in battle as a glorious achievement, at least when in it the king fights bravely in a higher cause against the right foe.

Similarly, as David's קינה has it, Saul is one of the "heroes" (גברים; perhaps even "males"), mourned by the women he has clothed in finery, whose very death is the final successful self-presentation. For both David and Bir-rakib, it is appropriate for a king as a warrior to mourn the death of another soldier, and this in the presence of both men and women. Royal mourning was one aspect of an important dimension of royal self-display, that of the king as speaker and maker of reputations.[40] Thanks to David, Saul's death attracts the

---

[36] On the connection of the hymn to 2 Sam. 22, see Ulrich Berges, *Die Verwerfung Sauls: Eine thematische Untersuchung* (Würzburg: Echter, 1989) 272.
[37] McCarter, *II Samuel*, 75–76; KTU 5–6.
[38] *Contra* Edelman, *King Saul*, 308.
[39] Hugo Gressmann, *Der Messias* (FRLANT 43; Göttingen: Vandenhoeck & Ruprecht, 1929) esp. chap. 1.
[40] On the king as speaker, see Dale Launderville, *Piety and Politics: The Dynamics of Royal Authority in Homeric Greece, Biblical Israel, and Old Babylonian Mesopotamia* (Grand Rapids: Eerdmans, 2003) 149–67.

attention of his subjects—if not of Yahweh!—who must mourn his loss and the loss of their own source of self-display through clothing (as booty). Moreover, as K. L. Noll has recently suggested, based on the mention in v. 18 that David wished to teach Judah the use of the bow, the lament serves in the narrative to point toward the new king's attempt to stir up his subjects' martial spirit.[41]

Now, this analysis has moved in two seemingly different directions. On the one hand, I have argued that the poem in 2 Sam. 1:18–27 serves to release anxiety about the death of Saul. On the other, I have proposed that it celebrates his valor. Are these contradictory? They would not be if the קינה dated from the reign of David or shortly thereafter, when sound politics would dictate the need to placate Saul's partisans.[42] Even later, when David's reputation was more secure, the need to forestall any diminution of his reputation would be desirable.[43] Thus portraying him exhibiting the piety of a subject for his king, and of one great warrior for another, would serve to elevate him and remove the odor of complicity in regicide from his reputation. These two lines of interpretation reflect different literary levels of the text as it exists today. For the characters in the narrative created by 1–2 Samuel, the removal of anxiety is important. David must prove his worthiness as a successor of Saul, who is heroic because all dead kings are heroic. It may not follow that the removal of anxiety was a priority for later tellers of the tale, although one still cannot exclude that possibility altogether. The succession of David demanded great literary and intellectual efforts at justification. The hymn, whatever its date of origin, reflects how its composers, who knew that kings die and that their successors and others mourn them, thought a living king should defuse such anxiety.

---

[41] K. L. Noll, *The Faces of David* (JSOTSS 242; Sheffield: Sheffield Academic Press, 1997) 160. This suggestion appears in a list of explanations for the placement of the song here, many of which are unpersuasive. Cf. Fokkelman, *Crossing Fates*, 659. On the possibility of emending the text to delete קשת, see McCarter, *II Samuel*, 68. Removal of the word simplifies the text, perhaps, but the MT is well attested and to remove קשת, one must explain how it came to be part of the received text.

[42] See the discussion of the date of this material in general in Halpern, *David's Secret Demons*, 57–72.

[43] On ancient Near Eastern royal apologies, see Hayim Tadmor, "Autobiographical Apology in the Royal Assyrian Literature," in Hayim Tadmor and Moshe Weinfeld, *History, Historiography, and Interpretation: Studies in biblical and cuneiform literatures* (Jerusalem: Magnes, 1983) 36–57.

What, then, can one say about the other two accounts of Saul's death? Clearly, they are radically different from the poem because Saul's self-presentation is self-abnegation. Let us examine the versions in the reverse order of their appearance in the canonical text, because the first account (1 Sam. 31) appears to correct aspects of the second (2 Sam. 1:1–16) and thus must be redactional.

The Amalekite's Tale

2 Sam. 1:1–16 presents the case of an Amalekite who claims to have killed Saul at the latter's behest, and then to have removed the diadem and armlet from the corpse and brought them to David. As it stands, this story is plausible in the context of ancient warfare, where the stripping of corpses was acceptable.[44] Given Saul's earlier treatment of Amalekites (1 Sam. 15), 2 Sam. 1 presents a deeply ironic version of his death.[45] The narrator presents this as a believable account of Saul's end, and the only clues that the Amalekite is lying come from the version in 1 Sam. 31, which portrays Saul's death as self-inflicted. Certainly, David believes, or appears to believe, or wants to appear to believe the foreign toady and executes him for regicide. This aura of credibility is important because it again argues that we are dealing here with a tradition different from that of 1 Sam. 31.

This tradition also shows awareness of the self-presentation of the kings of Judah in one and probably two instances. Note first that Saul wears a נזר ("diadem"), part of the regalia of that state (2 Kings 11:12 = 2 Chron. 23:11; Pss. 89:40, 132:18). An ancient Israelite audience for this text would have recognized Saul as a king in the mold of the Davidides. Second, Saul's חנית ("spear") is also a leitmotif in narrative depictions of him (1 Sam. 18:10, 11; 19:9, 10; 20:33; 21:9; 26:7, 11, 12, 16, and 22), where it is a prop connoting simultaneously his skill as a warrior and lack of skill as a king (see below). No other king appears in biblical narrative bearing a חנית. None, that is, except Joash (2 Kings 11:10), who receives one that the text claims belonged to David. 2 Kings 11 treats this חנית

---

[44] See, for example, 1 Sam. 17:53–54.
[45] Note also that in 1 Sam. 30, David campaigned against the Amalekites. See the discussion in Jakob H. Grønbaek, *Die Geschichte vom Aufstieg Davids (1. Sam. 15–2. Sam. 5): Tradition und Komposition* (Copenhagen: Prostant apud Munksgaard, 1971) 201–24.

in a very offhanded way, as if its history were public knowledge, offering no explanation about its origins or purpose. The spear must, therefore, have been part of the martial equipment that Judahites associated (correctly or not) with David and subsequently his successors. Saul, then, resembles the later monarchs of Judah. The Jerusalemite historical traditions understood the use of a spear to be a feature of Saul's self-display (and perhaps, since the weapon of choice of a charioteer was the bow, this reflects the military tactics of an era before Israelites used chariots extensively or had a state apparatus that could support them; this would be an accurate memory of early-tenth-century conditions).[46] At the same time, the Jerusalemite coronation ritual and its attendant legends also preserved a memory of David using a חנית. I will explore the implications of this further below, but suffice it to say here that the use of a spear requires the king to be a vigorous warrior skilled in single combat (as in Ps. 144), and this is how the tradition depicts Saul.

The Narrator's Version[47]
This takes us, then, to 1 Sam. 31 and its divergent portrayal of Saul's death. This version differs in important ways from the other two. It also appears to be intended as a corrective of them. Note the narrator's emphasis on the fact that Saul was dead at his own hands, not that of another: "and Saul took the sword and fell on it" (ויקח שאול את החרב ויפל עליה; v. 4); "Now when his armorbearer saw that Saul had expired" (וירא נשא כליו כי מת שאול; v. 5); "Saul died together with his three sons and his armorbearer... together" (וימת שאול ושלשת בניו ונשא כליו... יחדו; v. 6). Why this repetition? The simplest explanation seems to be that the composer of chapter 31 wished to refute a version of the story in which Saul's end came in some other way. In short, the suicide tradition is already present

---

[46] On chariots and their evolution, see Wolfram Nagel, *Der mesopotamische Streitwagen und seine Entwicklung im ostmediterranen Bereich* (Berliner Beiträge zur Vor- und Frühgeschichte 10; Berlin: Hessling, 1966); B. Hrouda, "Die Assyrische Streitwagen," *Iraq* 25 (1963) 155–58; J. E. Reade, "The Neo-Assyrian Court and Army: Evidence from the Sculptures," *Iraq* 34 (1972) 103; and Mary A. Littauer and J. H. Crouwel, *Chariots and Related Equipment from the Tomb of Tut'ankhamen* (Oxford: Griffith, 1985).

[47] "Narrator" here indicates that 1 Sam. 31 is told in the third person from the perspective of an omniscient narrator. The text bears no stamp of the Deuteronomistic school, and therefore must be older; the "narrator" is thus the voice of the person or group who constructed the story of Saul's death out of disparate materials.

in the Amalekite's tale, precluding the possibility of death at the hands of the Philistines. (I leave to one side the question of the origins of the suicide story itself, a problem I can see no way of solving unless one assumes the antiquity and probable reliability of the biblical traditions.) Yet, having a hated Amalekite kill Saul, while it creates a delicious literary irony, since Saul had been the sparer of Agag (1 Sam. 15), seems too shocking. 1 Sam. 31 softens this—if one may describe it so—by having Saul do the deed himself. By reworking the story in this way, the narrator turns the Amalekite's tale into a lie.

The portrayal of Saul's death as a suicide occasioned much discussion among later biblical interpreters,[48] but the Bible itself does not moralize on the event. Instead, it insists that the king did not die as a conquered warrior, either hero or coward.[49] His actions short-circuit the contest with the Philistines in which he was engaging.

The rest of this version of the tale contains at least two serious problems related to the conceptions of the royal body. They are, how and why did Saul die; and why did his corpse receive the treatment it did?

The first problem begins with Saul's request that his armor bearer slay him. The request for a mercy killing parallels the Amalekite's tale in 2 Sam. 1, though the potential executioners are different persons. Saul's motivation in 1 Sam. 31 is his fear that the Philistines will "make [sexual] sport" of him (v. 4). The verb התעלל may have a sexual connotation, as in Judg. 19:25:

> And they had intercourse (וידע) with her
> and "made sport" of her (התעלל) all night.

התעלל for Saul must mean something more than taunt—this would be a small problem for a badly wounded man—though it undoubtedly includes a belittling of his maleness. Note that the same root refers to Yahweh's mockery of Philistine warriors in 1 Sam. 6:6 and of Pharaoh (Egypt) in Exod. 10:2. The successful warrior (God in

---

[48] For references, see Fred Rosner, "Suicide in Jewish Law," in Kalman J. Kaplan and Matthew Schwartz, eds., *Jewish Approaches to Suicide, Martyrdom, and Euthanasia* (Northvale, NJ: Aronson, 1998) 63–65; Sidney Goldstein, *Suicide in Rabbinic Literature* (Hoboken, NJ: KTAV, 1989) 11–12, 22–24.

[49] Contra Fokkelman, *Crossing Fates*, 630: "The narrator has given his character Saul a dignified and even heroic death...."

these cases) uses what moderns would call psychological warfare to help dispirit an enemy, invigorate his own retainers, and frame the audience's understanding of what has taken place. Similarly, Saul's success as a warrior can be erased by the taunts of more successful men, his enemies. But, again, the Judges passage seems to imply something more than verbal abuse, apparently some kind of sexual abuse. If this abuse includes sexual torture, it must be something other than penetration (which is the meaning of ידע in Judg. 19:25), but it must also involve significant, slow, and painful mistreatment or even mutilation of Saul's body. The MT explanation ודקרני ("and they will pierce me"; 1 Sam. 31:4) is thus a correct, if inadequate, interpretation of התעלל.⁵⁰ A range of verbal and physical actions by the Philistines would render the dying Saul a sexual plaything, and if we read his plea in light of the Judges story, he becomes almost a woman to be raped. Suicide is preferable.

The connection between sexual torture (emasculation) and death in warfare is not unique to this passage. For example, a relief from Carchemish published by Akurgal[51] portrays a type scene of a chariot and team crushing enemy soldiers. Such a scene is common in Neo-Assyrian and in Assyrianizing Syro-Anatolian (Neo-Hittite) art,[52] but the image I cite here is distinctive in that the trampled man's penis is clearly visible and obviously erect (as is that of the horse above him). Normally, the victim lies face down, his derriere elevated, arrows piercing his body (presumably the ones from the king's bow, for the king is shooting in the scene as well). Sometimes the victim is exposed from the waist down. In this case, though, the nudity of

---

[50] Less adequate is the Targum of Jonathan's יתלעבו ("they will mock me"; in the edition of Emiliano Martínez Borobio, *Targum Jonatan de los Profetas Primeros en Tradicion Babilonica*, vol. 2: *I–II Samuel* [Madrid: Instituto de Filología, Departamento de Filología bíblica y de Oriente Antiguo, 1987]).

[51] From Ekrem Akurgal, *Spaethethitische Bildkunst* (Ankara: Archaeologisches Institut der Universitaet Ankara, 1949) p. xxiib.

[52] On the presentation of power in battle in Assyrian inscriptions, see Luc Bachelot, "La Fonction politique des Reliefs Neo-Assyriens," in D. Charpin and F. Joannes, eds., *Marchands, diplomates et Empereurs* (Paris: ERC, 1991) 109–28, esp. fig. 3.8. The portrayal of the Assyrian king in battle also relates to depictions of him as a hunter (especially of lions) (ibid., 111; cf. Ursula Magen, *Assyrische Königsdarstellungen: Aspekte der Herrschaft* [Mainz: von Zabern, 1986] 29–36 and pls. 3–4). In the hunting scene, the wounded lion is trampled in precisely the manner of the enemy warrior in the battle scene.

the enemy soldier is obvious and calls for explanation. The artist may use the erect member to convey the fear inspiring the warrior who is about to die, but this portrayal also serves to point out that defeat means loss of maleness. In contrast to the powerful king who is charging forward, the dying enemy has been fleeing. His nudity serves notice that even the male member, whose erection one expects to connote fecundity and successful performance of male roles, can also signify ignominious death. Death can be an act of emasculation. The end of sexual function is an index of death itself: highlighting the gender of the dying by displaying his useless genitalia ironically points to his maleness and simultaneously his loss of maleness in the face of a superior (male) warrior.

This association of defeat with loss of maleness, I suggest, underlies Saul's desire to die. Even if no actual sexual torture were to take place, defeat in itself is loss of male status for the benefit of other males. This is doubly true if sexual torture does take place. The purpose of such acts is clearly not to pleasure the abuser, but to mark the abused as someone outside the realm of the vigorous male warrior. Saul is not afraid of death because that allows him to retain his status—even great warriors die in battle—but he fears disgrace and so seeks death.

Curiously, however, Saul's companion refuses to kill him. Why? The text says merely that he was "very afraid" (כי ירא מאד). Since the נער soon commits suicide himself, one can exclude fear of human punishment or Saul's resistance as a factor. One possibility is that he, like David in 2 Sam. 1 and elsewhere (e.g., 1 Sam. 24 and 26), respected God's anointed (משיח) and feared divine retribution, or even the loosing of powerful, inimical (superhuman) forces embodied in the anointed king.[53] Unfortunately, the text does not say this explicitly. It is just as possible that the relutance of the נער was owing to his adherence to a code of warriorly camaraderie that demanded every possible act of aid. Admittedly, in a world in which kings assumed the posture of invincibility examples of such a code are difficult to find outside of epic (one thinks of Gilgamesh and Enkidu), but a few parallels do exist. One occurs, for example, in a letter to Esarhaddon from a courtier:

---

[53] See Edelman, *King Saul*, 284 (with bibliography).

The talk (*dabābu*) which the king, my lord, had with his servants about the former kings (*ša šarrāni maḫrūti*) who had fallen ill, "How their servants did sit up with them all nights (and) carry them on litters! How they did keep watch for them!"⁵⁴

In addition to the use of the reference to a past reality as an argument about how the present should be, the Assyrian text gives a glimpse into an ethic of care for the royal body (here a sick one, not a dying one, admittedly) that was supposed to be the concern of courtiers. The case of Saul and his נער differs from this in detail, but 1 Sam. 31 shares the notion that a retainer of the king should care for him in times of physical duress.

In any event, the text does not pass judgment on the armor bearer's actions: was this a case of refusing an unreasonable, impious request,⁵⁵ or simply a prelude to a noble death?⁵⁶ Should he have killed Saul? With characteristic reticence, the biblical text does not decide the issue for the reader. Saul has done what no one else could or dared do, and his comrade followed suit.

The second issue surrounding Saul's body concerns what happens next: the description of the dismemberment of his and his sons' corpses. Just as David is said to have decapitated the dead Goliath (1 Sam. 17:51),⁵⁷ so do the Philistines behead Saul.⁵⁸ They apparently do not sexually violate his body (התעלל), as he had feared, because his suicide preempted that terrible fate. They then display his body on the wall of nearby Bethshean. The purpose of this dis-

---

⁵⁴ Letter 247 ll. 9–15 in Simo Parpola, *Letters from Assyrian Scholars to the Kings Esarhaddon and Assurbanipal*, vol. 1: *Texts* (AOAT 5/1; Neukirchen-Vluyn: Neukirchener, 1970) 190–91.
⁵⁵ Edelman, *King Saul*, 284–85.
⁵⁶ David Gunn, *The Fate of King Saul: An Interpretation of a Biblical Story* (JSOTSS 14; Sheffield: Sheffield Academic Press, 1980) 111.
⁵⁷ As pointed out by Berges, *Verwerfung Sauls*, 257.
⁵⁸ The beheading of enemies is, of course, well attested in the ancient Near East, notably in Neo-Assyria, where mention of the practice figures prominently in many royal inscriptions. However, beheading after single combat, the practice in 1 Sam. 31 (and 17), has specifically Aegean precedents and may therefore be a Philistine innovation introduced into the Levant; see, *Iliad* 17.125–128, "Now Hektor, when he had stripped Patroklos of his glorious armor, sought to drag him away in order to decapitate him with his sharp bronze, drag off the corpse and feed it to the Trojan dogs" ("Ἕκτωρ μὲν Πάτροκλον 'επεὶ κλυτὰ τεύχε' 'απηύρα "ἐλχ̣ 'ιν' 'απ' ὤμοιιν κεφαλὴν τάμοιε' ὀξέϊ χαλκῷ τὸν δὲ νέκυν Τρῳῆσιν 'ερυσσάμενος κυσὶ δοίη). Since the Philistines hale from the Aegean, it is at least possible that they introduced the practice of beheading a corpse and stripping off its armor.

memberment and display are not made clear in the biblical text, which, despite its hostility toward Saul, is reluctant to describe his death in detail. However, in similar situations, Neo-Assyrian kings erected piles of heads of enemies before the walls of conquered cities, apparently in order to intimidate would-be foes.[59] The Philistines likewise used the body as both a warning to their enemies and an encouragement of their allies. This grisly trophy of war also must have marked them as successful warriors (hence, males), worthy of the praise of their womenfolk (just as David calls for the praise of women for the warriors Saul and Jonathan). The removal of the head ironically signals the reality that the national *corpus*, the incipient Israelite state, is now without its head. The head, the anointed part of the royal body, is a synecdoche for the king's body as a whole, and the entire national body.[60] Again, to borrow the medieval rubric studied by Kantorowicz,[61] the king—in this case Saul—possesses two bodies, one biosocial and the other sociopolitical. Both died at Gilboa, and the display of the royal body as a war trophy desecrates it and signals the demise of the body politic.

This desecration of Saul's corpse surely impinges upon the subsequent fate of Saul's body. The denizens of Jabesh Gilead rescue the headless body, burn it, and bury the bones beneath a tamarisk tree in their village (1 Sam. 31:12–13).[62] At an earlier stage, this part of the tale may have been part of an aetiology of a local landmark or even holy site, but 1 Sam. 31 focuses upon this appropriate rescue of the body (as an act of fealty). The burial of the body and the seven-day mourning period are unsurprising (cf. Gen. 50:10). Yet very surprising is the cremation of the royal body, since in the Bible burning a body typically is the punishment for defilers of sancta.[63]

---

[59] See, for example, RIMA 0.102.1.60'; 102.2.i.16, 34; 2.ii.53, and many others.

[60] This is a case of the king's having two bodies, much in the manner discussed in Ernst Kantorowicz, *The King's Two Bodies: A Study in Mediaeval Political Theology* (Princeton: Princeton University Press, 1957).

[61] See ibid.

[62] See the comments of Fokkelman, *Crossing Fates*, 628–29.

[63] Gen. 38:24 knows the practice of burning for adultery; Lev. 21:9 marks a special case of this practice, one nuanced with a view toward the sacredness of the priestly father of the adulteress; see Baruch Levine, *Leviticus* (Philadelphia: JPS, 1989) 144. (This use of burning the corpse to remove miasma has an interesting parallel in the Mesopotamian practice of burning witches; see Tzvi Abusch, "Ghost and God: Some Observations on a Babylonian Understanding of Human Nature," in A. I. Baumgarten, Jan Assmann, and G. G. Stroumsa, eds., *Self, Soul and Body in*

Moreover, Amos 2:1 thinks of the exhumation and cremation of a royal body as a sacrilegious act. True, cremation seems to have been practiced in Iron Age Syria-Palestine primarily outside the borders of Israel and Judah, though examples do exist within them.[64] Yet the difficulty of explaining the Jabesh Gileadites' action remains.

Their action does not reflect Canaanite customs for practice for disposing of royal bodies (since, at least along the Phoenician coast, inhumation was the custom; see the Byblian inscriptions).[65] Nor is this burning somehow a mimicking of Philistine practice, since in the Aegean homeland cremation became the rule only during the Iron Age.[66] Ostensible Hittite parallels are too widely removed in time to be probative.[67] We must seek, therefore, a local, intra-Israelite explanation.

The answer may lie in the fact that, as noted, a few biblical texts, widely variant in age, point to cremation as the punishment for defilers of sacra (Josh. 7:15; Lev. 21:9). Strictly speaking, burning is unnecessary—stoning an adulteress would suffice to kill and even to relieve the community's anxiety over defilement. Incineration has a

---

Religious Experience [SHR 78: Leiden: Brill, 1998] esp. 273–75). The detail of Saul's cremation is absent from the parallel passage in 1 Chron. 10:12, probably because the Chronicler was offended by the cremation (*contra* McCarter [*I Samuel*, 442], who thinks "the notice...secondary and late").

[64] See Bloch-Smith, *Judahite Burial Practices*, 52–55, 244–45.

[65] See Edith Porada, "Notes on the Sarcophagus of Ahiram," *JANES* 5 (1973) 355–72.

[66] See Walter Burkert, *Greek Religion* (Cambridge: Harvard University Press, 1985) 211. Cremation was common during the Mycenaean (second millennium) and the Late Geometric (post 760 BCE) eras, but not during the Protogeometric period contemporaneous with Saul. See Carla M. Antonaccio, *An Archaeology of Ancestors: Tomb Cult and Hero Cult in Early Greece* (Lanham, MD: Rowman & Littlefield, 1995). Note, too, that it is in the eighth century that a revival of hero cult occurs in Greece side by side with the creation and formalization of the "Homeric" epic (see Gregory Nagy, *The Best of the Achaeans: Concepts of the Hero in Archaic Greek Poetry* [2d ed.; Baltimore: Johns Hopkins University Press, 1999] 115); many of the alleged Greek parallels to the Saul story may, therefore, be eighth-century parallels rather than older ones. This would mean that, in order to make the details of this story fit tenth-century or earlier Aegean antecedents, one would have to posit continued trans-Mediterranean influence, a more difficult task. On the connection between hero cult and the performance of the Homeric epic, see Jane B. Carter, "Ancestor Cult and the Occasion of Homeric Performance," in Jane B. Carter and Sarah P. Morris, eds., *The Ages of Homer: A Tribute to Emily Townsend Vermeule* (Austin: University of Texas Press, 1995) 285–312.

[67] The Hittite emperors (mid-second millennium BCE) were cremated during the night preceding the third day of a fourteen-day mourning ritual (see Volkert Haas, *Geschichte der hethitischen Religion* [Leiden: Brill, 1994] 221).

ritual function, however: it purges the community of the impurity created by sacrilege. The ashes of the malefactor absorb, so to speak, the impurity, and burning the body prevents the spread of miasma to the community as a whole.[68]

True, Saul's case does seem different, in that he is not a criminal and the desecration involved is not necessarily the result of his decision-making. Everything in the text, moreover, suggests that the denizens of Jabesh Gilead burned his body as an act of piety, and as an expression of their warriorly skill. The point of contact with the tales of ritual incineration is that the human body was the focal point of desecration, which only burning could counteract. Achan and the sexually nonconforming daughter of a priest committed acts that desecrated sancta and indeed persons other than themselves. Burning their corpses protected the community from the evil effects of such defilement. So, too, with Saul. Since the king was a superhuman figure created at his coronation, his death demanded certain ritual precautions. Later these included the burning of spices (Jer. 34:5 apparently),[69] but Saul's case, because of the dismemberment and display of his body, was special. I argue, therefore, that the cremation of it was an attempt to limit the spread of miasma caused by the king's terrible death.

What evidence might support this admittedly speculative explanation? First, the death of the king in battle in various biblical stories requires ritual treatment of his body and/or the accoutrements of war. Second, the royal corpse uniquely can be buried inside a city, even near the temple. In this regard, note Ezek. 43:9, in which Yahweh says in an oracle, "Now let them put far away from me their whoredom [i.e., idolatry] and the corpses of their kings" (עתה ירחקו את זנותם ופגרי מלכיהם ממני). This indicates that the royal tombs

---

[68] This assumes that the older view of sancta contagion, in which the human body (and not just objects) was susceptible to contagion, was in place. On the P polemic against such an idea, see Jacob Milgrom, *Leviticus 1–16* (AB 3; New York: Doubleday, 1991) esp. 270–78.

[69] The text, an oracle urging Zedekiah to surrender to Nebuchadrezzar, reads, "You will die in peace, and as your ancestors, the former kings who preceded you, had things burned (for them), so too, they (i.e., your subjects) wiill burn for you. And they will mourn (יספדו) 'Woe for the lord' (הוי אדון) for you...."

This shows that the mourning ritual for the king included lamentation and the burning of something (משרפות); 2 Chr. 16:14 and 21:19 indicate that the something was spices. See William L. Holladay, *Jeremiah* (2 vols.; Hermeneia; Minneapolis: Fortress, 1989) 235.

lay inside the capital city and, as David P. Wright observes, near the temple.⁷⁰ Ezekiel thus seeks to alter an early practice and therefore an earlier conception of the royal body, according to which the king's corpse should lie near the sanctuary. According to this ancient (pre-Ezekielian, pre-P) viewpoint, the royal body thus differs from others in that it does not transmit impurity to denizens of a city in which it lies.

Third, the display of royal corpses may serve as indexes of the removal of curses. Proper burial of them is necessary to avoid widespread problems for the culture. The crucial piece of evidence comes from the story of what happens to Saul's body sometime later.⁷¹ 2 Sam. 21:1–14 seems chronologically out of place in its present context, where it fits into a kind of appendix in which the redactor includes various stray tales about David.⁷² There is no reason to assume that this pericope's view of Saul's end should accord precisely with those represented in 1 Sam. 31–2 Sam. 1. In any case, this text tells the story of how David ended a famine by executing Saul's offspring to satisfy a vendetta by the Gibeonites, with whom Israel had a treaty that Saul had broken. In the logic of such treaties, the grandchildren of the offender were liable to punishment.⁷³ Accordingly, David executes them and exposes their bodies. Next, Saul's concubine Rizpah keeps watch over their bodies for an unspecified period of time until David decides to bury them. The relevant part of this story comes at the end (vv. 13–14):

> So [David] brought up from [Jabesh Gilead] the bones of Saul and the bones of Jonathan his son, and they gathered the bones of the executed (המוקעים). And they buried the bones of Saul and Jonathan his son in the land of Benjamin, in Sela, in the tomb of his father Qish—so they obeyed the king's commands fully. Then God could be entreated concerning the land.

---

⁷⁰ David P. Wright, *The Disposal of Impurity: Elimination Rites in the Bible and in Hittite and Mesopotamian Literature* (SBLDS 101; Atlanta: Scholars, 1987) 123–24.

⁷¹ This story may originally have followed 2 Sam. 9 (McCarter, *II Samuel*, 443; cf. Timo Veijola, *Die ewige Dynastie: David und die Entstehung seiner Dynastie nach der deuteronomistischen Darstellung* [Helsinki: Suomalainen Tiedeakatemia, 1975] 107–8) or have come even earlier in the narrative of David's reign. See Campbell and O'Brien, *Unfolding the Deuteronomistic History*, 315; J. P. Fokkelman, *Narrative Art and Poetry in the Books of Samuel*, vol. 3: *Throne and City (II Sam. 2–8 & 21–24)* (Assen: van Gorcum, 1990) 283–84.

⁷² See Caquot and de Robert, *Livres de Samuel*, 578–87.

⁷³ Hence, part of the treaty curses in, say, the Sefire steles or Esarhaddon's vassal treaty, includes a curse on descendants of treaty-breakers.

Understanding the story requires understanding why David reburied Saul and Jonathan, what Rizpah's solicitude for the corpses of her family had to do with David's actions, and why the eventual interment removed a divine curse?

The simplest explanation is that the slaying of the Saulides also allows the ancient audience of the story to reinterpret the death of Saul himself (and Jonathan) as a punishment for treatybreaking. The entire family died on account of Saul's deeds, and the whole family must share in a common burial. Like Saul's, his descendants' bodies must be exposed to the elements for all to see. The divine oracle in v. 2, which explains the famine as the result of Saul's crime against the Gibeonites, combined with the eventual burial of his body, points in this direction. Why bury the bodies of Saul and Jonathan unless this in some way marked the end of the expiation of their sins brought on by the execution of the king's male descendants as a virtual sacrifice (note the cultic language לפני יהוה in v. 9)? This is why the bodies of the Saulides are mutilated[74] and exposed, just as Saul's was, and why all receive a common burial in the family tomb. Rizpah's role is crucial here, too, for she protects the corpses from scavengers, and thus prevents the spread of more impurity.

If this is correct, it means that the dead body of a king or even one of his male descendants improperly buried can have ill effects on the king's domain. (To contextualize this belief, note that this was certainly the case in Neo-Assyria, as the anxious contemplations of the loss of the corpse of Sargon II show.)[75] Other biblical texts show some interest in the problem, as well. The stories of the Jabesh Gileadites' cremation of Saul's corpse and of David's (re)interment of it both evince concern with the proper disposal of a royal body treated as Saul's was.

Summary

In tying these disparate threads together, then, one finds in the accounts of Saul's death different views thereof. 2 Sam. 1:18–27 and probably 1:1–16, reflecting Jerusalemite conventions, are reticent about the ultimate fate of his body, focusing instead upon its successful self-display in life and then its tragic death. By contrast,

---

[74] יקע (v. 9); on the meaning of the root ("crucify"? "hang"?), see McCarter, *II Samuel*, 442.
[75] See n. 14 above.

170   CHAPTER FIVE

1 Sam. 31 is interested in the events following his death. Here, he is not (unequivocally) the brave warrior, but rather the one who may be mocked and tortured, and is so in death. His נבורה is lost.

All these accounts share, however, an interest in Saul as a contestant in battle. For the קינה, his contestation is successful, if tragic in the end. In the Amalekite's tale, Saul is a failed contestant in battle, while for 1 Sam. 31, he short-circuits the contest by killing himself out of fear that the contest will take an unacceptable course, namely sexual torture and emasculation. All of these views share a vision of the king as a warrior who defines his maleness by bodily exertions against, or alongside, other males. Like that of the ideal king in Pss. 2, 20, 21, and 144 (and reversedly in Ps. 89), Saul's body must be fit for warfare, else he fails to be a king. The text both in its constituent layers and as a whole operates by switching subtly between the code of warriorly bravery and that of purity and the cult. The dead body of the king is a symbol of the potential death of the nation as a whole.

The Death of the "King of Israel" (1 Kings 22)

1 Kings 22:1–38 recounts the death of an anonymous "king of Israel." In its Deuteronomistic setting (identified by the regnal summary in v. 39), the tale relates to Ahab, but originally it may have referred to Joram.[76] The latter king was injured at Ramoth-Gilead according to 2 Kings 9:15, while the report of Ahab's death in 1 Kings 22:39ff. does not envision his violent death.[77] Nor is it clear that vv. 1–38 are themselves a unity.[78] For the purposes of this discussion, in any case, the identity of the king is less important than the ideas shaping the depiction of his death and the subsequent treatment of his body.

---

[76] Ahab is mentioned by name only in v. 20, where it may come from the redactor. On the LXX versions of these chapters, see James Donald Shenkel, *Chronology and Recensional Development in the Greek Text of Kings* (Cambridge: Harvard University Press, 1968) 61–64 and 82–83. But for counter-arguments, see Mordechai Cogan, *I Kings* (AB 10; New York: Doubleday, 2000). The identity of the king is not crucial for the present discussion.

[77] As many have observed. See, e.g., Stefan Timm, *Die Dynastie Omri* (FRLANT 124; Göttingen: Vandenhoeck & Ruprecht, 1982) 49–50.

[78] See Ernst Würthwein, "Zur Komposition von 1 Reg 22,1–38," in F. Maass, ed., *Das ferne und nahe Wort* (BZAW 105; Berlin: de Gruyter, 1967) 245–54; Simon DeVries, *1 Kings* (WBC 12; Waco, TX: Word, 1985) 265–66; and Steven McKenzie,

Like Saul in 1 Sam. 15:35 and elsewhere, this king has been abandoned by Yahweh, who conspires to deceive him by sending a lying prophetic spirit (רוח שקר). Also like Saul, the king disguises himself (התחפש; v. 30; cf. 1 Sam. 28:8) in order to circumvent the divine plan.[79] Saul does this before the battle and the king of Israel during it, but the trope of disguise serves in both tales to point out the royal body by hiding it. Both rulers must deny that they are themselves in order to try to retain their thrones or their very lives, and both disguises fail. Moreover, the king of Israel dies from an arrow wound but only after fighting to the end, just as Saul fights to the end. These points of similarity can hardly be accidental, though each death story has its own literary integrity. With these parallels, we may be in touch with a literary convention about reporting the violent death of a king that involves the mutilation of his body.

The core of the death report is in vv. 29–38. With their armies at Ramoth-Gilead facing the Aramaeans, the "king" and Jehoshaphat both disguise themselves, the first as a common soldier, and the second as the first, and therefore as the head of the expeditionary force. Again, the disguise serves literarily to draw attention to the royal body, just as in the story time the goal that the king has in mind is precisely the opposite. Moreover, since the vassal Jehoshaphat takes on the appearance of his overlord, the bodily alteration that the two men undergo signal a reversal of their power relationship and, indeed, a notion of Judahite political superiority.

The story proceeds when the Aramaean troops attack what they believe to be the unit under the command of the "king of Israel"—presumably the vanguard of the army or the center of the line—until Jehoshaphat utters a cry (ויזעק יהושפט; v. 32). They encircle him,[80] prompting this cry. Is it a cry for (divine?) help or a battle cry, as Montgomery argues?[81] If the former, this piece of the story

---

The Trouble with Kings: The Composition of the Book of Kings in the Deuteronomistic History (VTSupp 42; Leiden: Brill, 1991) 91–92.

[79] This theme of disguising oneself for battle after ignoring a divine warning against engagement also informs the Chronicler's retelling of the death of Josiah in 2 Chron. 35:22. See Sara Japhet, *I & II Chronicles* (OTL; Louisville, KY: Westminster/John Knox, 1993) 1042–43.

[80] Reading ויסבו (with LXX 'εκύκλωσεν) for MT ויסרו in v. 32. It is important that he not be depicted as fleeing (as in RSV etc.), since in the royal psalms the king of Judah (and Israel?) never flees from pursuers (רדפים).

[81] James A. Montgomery and Henry Snyder Gehman, *The Book of Kings* (ICC; Edinburgh: T. & T. Clark, 1951) 340.

may connect to the convention in Judah of depicting its kings as seeking divine aid in battle (Ps. 144:11), in which case the Judahite ruler's cry is not an act of cowardice or despair but of piety. Since he avoids death, one could assume that the deity heeded him, and this would confirm Jehoshaphat's standing as a fit ruler. On the other hand, if we understand the cry as a battle cry, a less likely solution since זעק usually means a cry for aid,[82] then again the cowardice of the king of Israel comes into focus in contrast with Jehoshaphat's bravura.

The battle maneuvers of the Aramaean king are likewise difficult to understand from this story. According to v. 31, he orders his troops to fight only with the king of Israel while ignoring all other soldiers ("the small and the great" [אֶת קָטֹן וְאֶת גָּדוֹל]), a very high-risk tactic indeed. Unfortunately for a historian of ancient military tactics, 1 Kings 22:29–38 merely sketches the battle in order to focus upon the "king's" death and simultaneously the character of Jehoshaphat. The Israelite narrator understood the Aramaeans to believe that they could recognize the Israelite king by his dress and his cry (hence by his self-display both sartorial and auditory). This recognition would lead to the king's death and the defeat of his nation. The monarchs' disguises become a way of attempting to cheat death. Both monarchs fight bravely, and both must place their bodies forward to encourage their men. Jehoshaphat's act of self-display (the cry) itself undoes his earlier act of disguise so that he alone acts like a king. Meanwhile, in a supreme irony in which the avoidance of self-display cannot prevent death, the "king of Israel" falls to a stray arrow. He has thrown off the visible signs of kingship and this leads to his demise, contrary to his own intentions.

To continue, the tale draws the death scene with great literary skill. The wounded "king of Israel" orders his driver to leave the battlefield, but the fighting comes to him. He finally dies in his own pooled blood, whereupon the Israelite army melts away. Then the chariot itself is taken to Samaria, where it is washed (presumably to remove ritual impurity), but dogs lick the blood and harlots bathe in it (note again the connection between sex and death) "according

---

[82] See Judg. 3:9, 15; 6:6, 7; 10:10; 1 Sam. 7:8–9; 8:18; 12:8, 10; 15:11; Isa. 30:19; Jer. 11:11; Hos. 7:14; 8:2; Mic. 3:4; Jonah 1:14; Hab. 1:2; Ps. 22:6; 107:13, 19; 142:2; 142:6; Neh. 9:4, 28; 2 Chron. 20:9; 32:20 etc.).

to the word of Yahweh."[83] This gruesome scene is calculated to point to the dissolution of the royal body, and the failure of the ritual washing by the king's retinue to remove impurity underscores the destruction of the body. The postmortem rituals are infelicitous because impure humans (harlots) and animals (dogs) defile the dead man's chariot. Thus the story simultaneously recognizes the social conventions under which the royal corpse received suitable obsequies, and radically subverts those conventions by noting how these rituals fail to allow for an honorable burial of one whose failure to display himself properly in life led to a tragic defeat and death.

It is instructive at this point to contrast the mention of dogs consuming the king's blood in this text with a similar feeding of a witch's corpse to dogs in Mesopotamia.[84] There such a gruesome end meant that the witch could not return to life. Her body simply ceased to exist. In the biblical text, the king of Israel is buried in his patrimonial estate, Samaria (1 Kings 22:37), and so his postmortem existence near the seat of royal power continues. Yet his body is associated with sexual deviance and wild animals, and hence with the world outside the boundaries of order that, as king, he was supposed to be part of in life. By playing out the story in terms of the semiotics of impurity, the narrator subverts the royal conventions of self-display in which even the royal tomb was an index of dynastic endurance and power.

What is one to make of this tale, then? Does the "king" disguise himself in order to confuse the Aramaeans or Yahweh (or his heavenly minions)? If the latter, does this imply that Israelites believed that a substitute king could attract the divine wrath intended for the real monarch, much in the manner of the Assyrian substitute kings?[85] Why does the disguise fail, because Yahweh saw through it or the

---

[83] LXX adds pigs to dogs and has the harlots wash in the blood. In MT, they may merely bathe in the pool.

[84] See Abusch, "Ghost and God," 273–75.

[85] The Assyrian *šar pūḫi*, or "substitute king," was a person who stood in for the real king around the time of an eclipse, which indicated divine displeasure and danger to the ruler (see the discussion in Simo Parpola, *Letters from Assyrian Scholars to the Kings Esarhaddon and Assurbanipal*, vol. 2: *Commentary and Appendices* [AOAT 5.2; Neukirchen-Vluyn: Neukirchener, 1983] 123–24). It may be that the king of Israel has an idea similar to this in which a lesser personage can stand in for him when the deity has threatened him. I am not arguing for a direct borrowing of Assyrian ritual into Israel, however.

Arameans did—or merely the narrator and readers do? Does the story seek to make Jehoshaphat—and therefore the Davidides in general—seem more heroic, a truer embodiment of kingship, than his presumed overlord? The failure of the king of Israel to display his body appropriately (bravely)—which Jehoshaphat did—presaged its ultimate humiliating dissolution.

Again, as in the Saul story and, as Chapter 7 will show in stories about foreign rulers, the kings of Israel and Judah in 1 Kings 22 are involved in contestation for successful male, warriorly self-display. In the present story, the struggle operates at several levels: Micaiah versus the king of Israel; the king of Israel versus his Aramaean counterpart; both of them versus Jehoshaphat (though in different ways); and the king of Israel (and surprisingly not that of Aram!) against Yahweh. The tale operates in a very complex way to point to the multivalency and contingency of the self-descriptions that the rulers of the dual monarchies made when they called themselves Elohim or "son of Yahweh"[86] and consequently laid claim to divine protection. Yahweh can destroy even the body of a king whom he has rejected, and can even treat that ruler as a foreign foe like that in Ps. 2.[87]

The Death of Joram, Jezebel, and the Family of Ahab

The aforementioned theme of dogs eating royal bodies also appears in the tale of Jehu's coup d'etat in 2 Kings 9–10, the author[88] of which understood the execution of Joram, Jezebel, and the rest of the royal family as divine retribution for the murder of Naboth, prophets, and assorted servants of Yahweh (כל עבדי יהוה; 2 Kings 9:8). If Joram was the original king in 1 Kings 22, as I have suggested above, then 2 Kings 9–10 is simply a continuation of the previous story, or rather a different version of it. However this may be, here Joram is hunted down by his former lieutenant, Jehu. The

---

[86] A royal self-predication that this story appears to ignore. Although, since Ps. 82:6 indicates an Israelite belief in deicide, it is possible that a faint notion of royal "deicide" is not entirely absent even in 1 Kings 22.

[87] See Jeffries M. Hamilton, "Caught in the Nets of Prophecy? The Death of King Ahab and the Character of God," *CBQ* 56 (1994) 649–63.

[88] For my purposes, the redactional history of chapters 9–10 is not crucial. On this, see Timm, *Dynastie Omri*, 136–37; Martin Mulzer, *Jehu schlägt Joram* (St. Ottilien: EOS, 1992).

narrative pays little attention to Joram's actions in flight, concentrating instead on the disposition of his corpse and that of his Judahite colleague Ahaziah (2 Kings 9:26-29). The former remains unburied as a punishment for his family's murder of Naboth. The concurrent murder of Ahaziah is perplexing, though. Why kill him at all? One possibility is that as a grandson of Ahab, he was culpable or at least politically a potential dynastic enemy,[89] but this is uncertain, even if the fate of Athaliah makes it a tempting explanation. The text offers no explanation. It does, however, note that Ahaziah's retinue transported him by chariot to Jerusalem.[90] Even in death—or rather especially in death, since the living Ahaziah had fled Jehu fecklessly—the king of Judah is a warrior before all others. The movement of the royal body presumably needed Jehu's permission and must have involved some ritual activity that the narrator does not mention.

The use of a chariot in funerary ritual is reminiscent of the heroic burials in contemporary Cyprus,[91] albeit there the distances covered in the funeral parade are much shorter. We do not know whether the chariot was actually interred with the royal corpse. Yet, the explanation for the use of a chariot must lie in Judahite court language with its emphasis on the king's warlike qualities. The chariot functions as an icon of royal skill in battle, even though events render its use in this case deeply ironic. The fact that Ahaziah fails as a warrior creates within the report of his cortege a deep and unresolved irony.

Assassination: Joash of Judah (2 Kings 12:21-22)

The story of the reign of Joash of Judah begins and ends with regicide, with the murder of a queen thrown in for good measure. Since

---

[89] T. R. Hobbs, *2 Kings* (WBC 13; Waco, TX: Word, 1985) 117-18.
[90] The LXX adds 'ἐπὶ τὸ ἅρμα ("upon the chariot"; = על המרכבה or על הרכב). This plus is surely a gloss, but a contextually appropriate one. See also Mulzer, *Jehu*, 111-13.
[91] See David W. Rupp, "The 'Royal Tombs' at Salamis (Cyprus): Ideological Messages of Power and Authority," *Journal of Mediterranean Archaeology* 1 (1988) 111-39, esp. 121; the use of Cypriot-style architecture in tombs around Jerusalem points to a connection between Judah and the Islands (see Ussishkin, *Village of Silwan*, 312-16 [although tombs in both Judah and Cyprus were part of an international style partially inspired by Egyptian architecture]). See also Gabriel Barkay and Amos Kloner, "Jerusalem Tombs from the Days of the First Temple," *BAR* 12 (1986) 22-39; David Ussishkin, "The Necropolis from the Time of the Kingdom of Judah at Silwan," *BA* 33 (1970) 34-46.

176   CHAPTER FIVE

I have discussed the coronation of Joash, let me focus but briefly upon his death. 2 Kings 12:21–22 reports his assassination by his courtiers at the בית מלא ("house of the fill").[92]

Assassination: Amaziah (2 Kings 14:17–20)

In contrast to the two previously discussed assassination reports, that of Amaziah of Judah does not report the names or fates of his killers. Indeed, the fact that he could be killed in Lachish after fleeing Jerusalem indicates some popular support for the assassination. His burial in the capital city and coronation of his son by the people of Judah (עם־יהודה) seem to indicate that the society was able to minimize the political and social disruption caused by Amaziah's untimely death. V. 20, moreover, has his corpse transported by horses (in a chariot or on horseback?) back to Jerusalem. His executioners also carried out proper funeral rites.[93]

The narrative in 2 Kings 14 reaches this acceptance of regicide in several ways, most focusing upon the royal body. After cataloging Amaziah's successes, the text recounts his foolish efforts at attacking Israel, a much more powerful state. This conflict finds expression in an exchange of diplomatic messages in which Jehoash of Israel rebuffs Judahite overtures with a bon mot obviously reminiscent of, though not necessarily dependent upon, Jotham's fable in Judg. 9:8–15 (v. 9):

> A thorn plant (חוח) in Lebanon sent a message to the cedar in Lebanon saying,
> 'Give your daughter to my son as a wife.' Then a wild beast (חית השדה) in Lebanon trampled (ותרמס) the thorn plant.

The point of the proverb is obvious: a mere thorn cannot ask for a cedar princess for his son (if anything, a thorn princess should marry out). The Israelite king is a cedar, the Judahite king a thorn. And, at still another level of double entendre, the Lebanon in which the thorn dwells is the palace in Jerusalem (cf. 1 Kings 7:2ff.).

As if the meaning were not clear enough, v. 10 makes it brutal:

---

[92] Interestingly, this notice follows the Deuteronomistic summary statement in v. 20, of which it must be part.

[93] Accordingly, there is no reason to think that the text implies a coup d'etat by a small coterie of noblemen (*contra* John Gray, *I & II Kings* [OTL; London: SCM, 1964] 554).

You have certainly struck (הכה הכית) Edom, and your heart (לבך) has lifted you up. Be glorious, stay home [in the Lebanon palace!]. Why should you stir up trouble (תתגרה ברעה) so that you have a downfall and (take) Judah with you?

Here the level of signification moves from a code of plants and animals (as in v. 9) to a more direct referentiality to the royal body. Amaziah's heart has deceived him into attacking a more powerful state. He should keep the sort of glory proper to him, one belonging to a stay-at-home king whose Lebanon is a building. Jehoash's diplomatic message mocks the bodily, warriorly pretensions of Amaziah. This message is an interesting case of the refusal (by Jehoash) to accept the Judahite king's claims—see Pss. 2, 20–21, and 144—to be an all-conquering ruler. This refusal centers upon an understanding of the Judahite royal body as inadequate: heart and muscles do not match.

This episode lays the groundwork for the assassination of Amaziah. He next attacks Israel, becomes a prisoner of war, and returns to power only years later (vv. 8–14). His assassination follows next in the narrative, as if to say that his subjects punish him for this defeat.[94] Or, to put it in bodily terms, they destroy the body that has destroyed them because it believed its own pretensions.

The difficulty with this understanding of events appears in v. 17: "Amaziah b. Joash, king of Judah, lived fifteen years after the death of Jehoash b. Jehoahaz, king of Israel" (ויחי אמציהו בן יואש מלך יהודה אחרי מות יהואש בן יהואחז מלך ישראל חמש עשרה שנה). Cogan and Tadmor propose that the verse refers to Amaziah's life after losing his throne following the lost battle of Beth-shemesh.[95] Azariah, they propose, became the Israelite's puppet king after the war. However, the biblical synchronisms between Israel and Judah do not correlate at this point,[96] and so may be of little historical value. Still, the chief point is not what "really" happened but how the text portrays events. And of this we can be fairly certain. In Judah, failure on the battlefield

---

[94] Roland de Vaux (*Ancient Israel: Its Life and Institutions* [1961; reprint ed. Grand Rapids: Eerdmans, 1997] 377) suggested that the priests revolted at Amaziah's looting of the temple, but 2 Kings does not explicitly claim this.
[95] See Mordechai Cogan and Hayim Tadmor, *II Kings* (AB 11; New York: Doubleday, 1988) 154.
[96] See Gershon Galil, *The Chronology of the Kings of Israel and Judah* (Leiden: Brill, 1996) 60 n. 47.

could lead to assassination. Few members of society were apparently bothered by this fate for the king whose defeat had led to economic and political loss. The powers within the state could conspire to carry out the murder and then provide the proper obsequies without any sense of the irony of doing so. This would explain, as de Vaux hypothesized,[97] the ease of Azariah's accession.

Josiah (2 Kings 23:29–30)

The death of Josiah, though reported dispassionately in 2 Kings 23:29–30, called for elaborate explanation in 2 Chron. 35 and may have necessitated the ongoing revision of the DH itself.[98] 2 Kings 23:26–27 explains this death as the result of Manasseh's impieties, but this does not explain the motivation for, or mode of, his death. It reports merely that he died at Megiddo and was transported back to Jerusalem by chariot (וירכבהו; cf. 2 Kings 9:28) and then buried.

The expansion in 2 Chron. 35:20–25 may or may not contain authentic data independent of 2 Kings, but it does portray this death as: (1) a just punishment for disobedience to divine commands to keep treaty obligations, and (2) a contest between two powerful males (Necho taunts Josiah before killing him in battle).[99] Like Saul and the "king of Israel" before him, Josiah assumes a disguise (ויתחפש; v. 22) before going into battle, apparently doing so in order to counteract the divine indictment that Necho had uttered. Again, therefore, we are in touch here with a widespread literary motif about the royal body about to die.

---

[97] De Vaux, *Ancient Israel*, 377.

[98] See most extensively Marvin Sweeney, *King Josiah of Judah: The Lost Messiah of Israel* (Oxford: Oxford University Press, 2001); Cross, *Canaanite Myth and Hebrew Epic*, 274–89; Gary N. Knoppers, *Two Nations Under God*, vol. 1: *The Reign of Solomon and the Rise of Jeroboam* (HSM 52; Atlanta: Scholars, 1993) 36–56; H. G. M. Williamson, "The Death of Josiah and the Continuing Development of the Deuteronomistic History," *VT* 32 (1982) 242–47; idem, "Reliving the Death of Josiah: A Reply to C. T. Begg," *VT* 37 (1987) 9–15; Christopher T. Begg, "The Death of Josiah in Chronicles: Another View," *VT* 37 (1987) 1–8. On the contradiction between the facts of Josiah's death and the promises by Huldah in 2 Kings 22:20, and the implication that the two pericopes are from different hands, see Gary Knoppers, *Two Nations Under God*, vol. 2: *The Reign of Jeroboam, the Fall of Israel, and the Reign of Josiah* (HSM 53; Atlanta: Scholars, 1994) 150, 221.

[99] On the theological notions informing the Chronicler's construction of the events, see Japhet, *I & II Chronicles*, 1056–57.

Another expansion is interesting, namely, the report specifying that Josiah's cortege used his *second* chariot. Why this and not his first chariot became part of the grave goods is not clear: perhaps his successor inherited the first chariot. This small added detail may or may not reflect the normal practice of the Judahite monarchy, but it does fit nicely with the previous notices of chariots (first or second) serving in funeral processions that we have just seen. Again, the chariot signifies royal prowess on the battlefield.

Summary of the Death of Kings in the DH

So far, then, the various reports of the violent death of the king contained in the DH reveal certain recurrent patterns. The first is that these texts highlight the king as a contestant with other males, sometimes including the male deity, Yahweh. That violent ends come in a contest may seem a banal point, but the pervasiveness of contestation deserves recognition. Sometimes this takes the form of artifacts with semiotic (iconic) functions (chariots, crowns). At stake in these contests is not only survival, but often (Saul, Amaziah) a pre- and postmortem reputation as a skilled warrior. The respect of others causes more concern than mere physical existence.

Second, the body is the focus of the contest. A loser in battle can become a sexual plaything. His blood may fill a chariot and feed dogs. Sex outside the limits of social norms can defile his remains. The heart may lead one astray, the muscles and cardiovascular systems fail to deliver sufficient strength in the heat of battle. Kings may adorn their bodies with crowns or disguise them. Yet, in every case we cannot understand the story without some awareness of how the royal body is playing a role.

Third, proper mourning rituals for the dead king insured his reputation as a warrior, or, not to put too fine a point on it, the survival of his male body in the memories of the people. The successor king played an important role in this creation of the past, as did women, who validated the maleness that kings won against and alongside other males.

Fourth, traces of the ideas about the king's body seen in the royal psalms survive in these narrative texts just examined as well. However, the narratives frequently subvert the "official" lines, playing out possible ramifications of any given self-presentation of the king, often choosing the one least congenial to the maintenance of royal power and dignity. This is a world of disemia; signs (words, artifacts, gestures, rituals) mean different things in different contexts.[100]

In summary, then, the violent death of kings was a well-developed motif in Israelite narrative (though not in the royal psalms), since this event was a moment of grave political and even theological or intellectual concern. The king's body, because it was anointed (see below), required carefully ritualized disposal. This leads me, then, to consider the next transition, the coronation.

The King in Narrative

To conclude the discussion of the narratives so far, the tales of the violent deaths and coronations of kings of Judah and Israel make for exciting reading. Yet, more crucially, they also reveal the intricate conceptions of the roles of the monarch extant in the two kingdoms. Without having discussed other biblical narratives about kings, it would be premature to say too much. At this point, though, some issues can be adumbrated.

We noted earlier the heavily martial overtones of the royal psalms, even those that centered upon the coronation, temple building, and other events that at first blush seem unconnected to military life. We also asked whether the claims to military prowess and even universal sovereignty in this royal propaganda met with criticism, disbelief, skepticism, mockery, or other forms of dissent in the larger culture. Now we can add the fact that the biblical narratives about the violent death of kings (obviously) and coronations (less obviously) share the same interest in violence. These stories do, however, expose the royal psalms and the code of monarchy in them as a *strategy*, as propaganda, put forth by the monarch and state apparatus to argue for his and its divine origin and raison d'etre. Some Israelites and Judahites could question various aspects of royal self-presentation. In extreme cases, this could result in a coup d'etat. In most instances, however, other forms of resistance, cooptation, or criticism could transpire.

---

[100] On disemia, see Michael Herzfeld, *Anthropology Through the Looking Glass: Critical Ethnography at the Margins of Europe* (Cambridge: Cambridge University Press, 1987) 111–17.

Nevertheless, this modification of the claims of the royal psalms is also a strategy, and in the narratives we have, mostly a case of competition among males—the king, nobles, warriors, and prophets—for status. The kings who play the game best are those who seem not to be playing it at all, who live out the ideals of the royal psalms without overtly calling attention to that fact. Hence Saul's or David's modesty when summoned to the throne. Hence the failure of Ahab, at least in the eyes of the Deuteronomist. Yet, modesty cannot be traduced into self-effacement, for this leads to death, as in the case of the "king of Israel."

Now, much of the narrative that this chapter has explored has concerned itself with ritual, narrowly conceived. The coronation of the king was a highly structured event fraught with significant actions and words, the performance of which made a king. Much of this language and ritual movement is martial in tone. Witness the military cordon around Joash, the mention of warfare immediately following the acclamation of Saul. This ritual also, however, sought to contextualize warfare, to insure that the burdens for it, whether economic or mortal, did not fall unduly upon the king's subjects. The king is enjoined in ritual to avoid excessive taxation and the corruption that comes from standing armies. Or, rather, ritual makes him into a person who is both militarily strong and capable *and* unrapacious. (The ritual may be infelicitous if the king does not follow up on its ideal behaviors, of course, but this is a different issue.)

Finally, one should ask how the narratives connect to the royal psalms. I will return to this question in greater detail. For now, let me make an argument that needs further exploration. The ritualized protest against kingship in 1 Sam. 8:5 introduces the people's request for a king: "Appoint over us a king to 'judge' (שפט) us like all the nations (ככל הגוים)." This famous verse conceals a less than obvious notion: Israelites worked with a conception, a stereotype really, of how kings governed. Their own rulers were instantiations of that larger set /king/, and yet as the narrative's development makes clear, were also different from other members of the set. Unlike foreign kings, who were rapacious in Israel's experience (since they mostly encountered them in battle!), Israel's kings were to behave differently. This different behavior was assured by anointing and acclamation.

At this point, we should step back from the myriad details of this analysis and examine the larger chains of signification that the details reveal. In his exposition of semiotics, Umberto Eco discusses the phenomenon of "overcoding," in which "on the basis of a pre-established rule, a new rule was proposed which governed a rarer application of the previous rule."[101] Much of the biblical narrative about royal deaths and coronation is, I propose, a working out of just such overcoding. The coronation rituals embed a series of claims about the king, claims that take linguistic form in the royal psalms, which must then be negotiated against other claims about the king and his body originating in other social environments. Rules about royal behavior were shared with other cultures (hence the *Hofstil*; hence the phrase ככל הגוים in 1 Sam. 8:5) and spread by rituals, in which many subjects might participate or observe, at the royal center. Yet, narratives about these same kings could and did manipulate these official codes in ways that the originators of the codes could not control. And, since the king did not rule mindless automatons but human beings, they were forced to shape their message to these countermessages, in turn. I will return to this argument later. The narratives examined here evince the complexity of the negotiations that Israelite society undertook around the significations of the royal bodies, somatic and sociopolitical. The very elaborateness of the narratives witness to the extreme complexity of intellectual engagement with the question, what is the proper training, actions, and display—in short, use—of the royal body.

---

[101] Umberto Eco, *A Theory of Semiotics* (Bloomington: Indiana University Press, 1976) 133.

CHAPTER SIX

THE BODY OF THE KING IN WAR AND PEACE

> The warrior hero is admired by both sexes for running real risks; but the man of solidierly temperament... will run risks whether admired by the outside world or not.[1]

Israelite society used a royal body as a symbol of itself, an icon of God, and an index of the divine-human relationship. This complex, always uneasy usage becomes most important (that is, most semiotically complex and most troublesome for other human actors) when the king engages in warfare, but also when he speaks and builds, that is in his exercise of kingship as a system of communicating sovereignty. All of these items are tropes of kingship in royal inscriptions and graphic art throughout the ancient Near East, and all feature body imagery prominently. In all of them, as well, Israel's beliefs and practice bear fruitful comparison with those of neighboring states.

The Endangered and Dangerous King

The bodily complexity at which the coronation ritual hints becomes still more obvious in stories about the king who is either endangered or dangerous. Danger may result from warfare, a failure to eliminate potential rivals, or from sickness or curses, among other sources. Danger manifestly involves the body, and the narrative depiction of danger reflects decisions about the significations of the body. Portraying the king as dangerous engages a network of icons (the king in battle, horses on the move), indexes (weapons, beards, spittle, bodily decrepitude), and symbols (the divine realm, Zion; regions from which Yahweh works in the king's warfare or sickness).

In Samuel-Kings, as in other texts from the Iron Age Levant, many surviving royal stories depict kings at war. Aside from its ability

---

[1] So John Keegan, *A History of Warfare* (New York: Vintage, 1993) 226.

to entertain a reader, warfare figured centrally in the king's life because it allowed the consolidation or dispersal of power, and not a little because going on campaign was the most dramatic (and exciting) event in the life of males (even if actual warfare is often months of drudgery punctuated by moments of terror).[2] War bonded males together in ways otherwise impossible to achieve, and defined their roles in a community they defended. Not only was warfare sometimes politics by other means, as von Clausewitz had it, but it was life in another key.

In a monarchy, too, the health of the king is a pressing concern, and although the Bible says less than we might like about ill monarchs, what it does say is telling.[3] So, this chapter will consider the illnesses of Ahaziah and Hezekiah. Moreover, the healthy king can legitimate and extend his power, and construct a reciprocally beneficial relationship with his subjects and the deity by building monuments, again a theme in biblical texts. All of this deserves attention.

First a caveat: it would be impossible in the following pages to work thoroughly through every story in the Bible about a king at war. This would require another book in its own right. However, certain key stories highlight the king's body, its display and (real or imagined) anatomy. These stories fall into two convenient groups: those in which the king is in danger, and those in which he presents a danger to others. The focus is upon the narratives involving Saul and David, David as conqueror (2 Sam. 8), David and Absalom, Ahaziah of Israel and Hezekiah of Judah in illness, and the "king of Israel" encountering siege and starvation (2 Kings 6:24–33). Most of the evidence comes from the David cycles, the so-called "History of David's Rise" and "Succession Narrative" (or collectively, the "Court Narrative"), where his relationship with Saul in some ways mirrors that with Absalom.[4]

---

[2] On male (and female) approaches to war, see Jean Bethke Elshtain (*Women and War* [New York: Basic Books, 1987]), who accentuates the camaraderie and group love of soldiers (perhaps exaggeratedly so, but still properly, in my view).

[3] Witness, e.g., the letters between the Assyrian monarchs and their doctors and diviners collected by Simo Parpola in his book, *Letters from Assyrian Scholars to the Kings Esarhaddon and Assurbanipal*, vol. 1: *Texts* (AOAT 5/1; Neukirchen-Vluyn: Neukirchener, 1970); and the *bīt rimki* series of ritual texts, published by Jørgen Læssøe, *Studies on the Assyrian Ritual and Series bīt rimki* (Copenhagen: Munksgaard, 1955).

[4] Through this analysis, I bracket the question of sources behind these narratives, since delineations of such sources vary widely, and since all of them fall within

Is the distinction between dangerous and endangered king ultimately arbitrary? After all, a king going into battle risks his life by definition. Yet royal narratives from other ancient Near Eastern cultures conventionally ignore this risk, focusing instead upon the invincibility of the king. In Neo-Assyrian royal inscriptions, for example, danger to the king recedes far into the background, and only his bravery merits the readers' attention.[5] Narrating risk to the king is not inevitable, but a decision that the storyteller makes, perhaps depending upon the norms of culture. More importantly, the biblical texts themselves worry at length about dangers to the king as well as his danger to others (Israelites and foreigners), indicating again the texts' sensitivity to the multiple viewpoints in play in Israelite society and the king's need to negotiate among them in order to rule. The contrasting rubric dangerous/endangered thus convincingly explains details of the texts themselves. Here, then, the focus is sharply on those stories in which the king is at risk but does not die.

The Dangerous King

Although 2 Sam. 8[6] and other pericopes emphasize the dangerous king, the definitive set of Israelite stories about the dangerous monarch concerns the interactions between Saul and David, in 1 Sam. 18:6–2 Sam. 1. Saul, the dangerous king who becomes endangered, seeks

---

the period of the Israelite monarchies but cannot be dated much more precisely. Hence, little is to be gained here from elaborate source-critical hypotheses. For recent proposals for the "History of David's Rise" in its pre-Dtr^G phases, see, e.g., François Langlamet, "'David-Jonathan-Saül' ou le 'Livre de Jonathan': 1 Sam 16,14–2 Sam 1,27," *RB* 101 (1994) 326–54; idem, "De 'David, fils de Jessé' au 'Livre de Jonathan'," *RB* 100 (1993) 321–57. The "narrator" is thus the point of reference in the following discussion.

[5] This aspect of the Neo-Assyrian inscriptions is so egregious that it needs no documentation; it is even embedded in the royal titularies with such titles as *šarru dannu* ("strong king") (see Paul Garelli, "La Conception de la Royauté en Assyrie," in *Assyrian Royal Inscriptions: New Horizons in literary, ideological, and historical analysis* [ed. F. Mario Fales; Rome: Istituto per l'Oriente, 1981] 1–11; see the epithets listed in Barbara Cifola, *Analysis of Variants in the Assyrian Royal Titulary from the Origins to Tiglath-pileser III* [Naples: Istituto Universitario Orientale, 1995]). On Neo-Assyria and the ideology of warfare, see R. J. van der Spek, "A Comparative Study of War and Empire in Assyria, Athens, and Rome," in *The Tablet and the Scroll* (ed. Mark E. Cohen, Daniel C. Snell, and David B. Weisberg, Bethesda, MD: CDL, 1993) 262–70; cf. Hayim Tadmor, "History and Ideology in the Assyrian Royal Inscriptions," in Fales, *Assyrian Royal Inscriptions*, 13–33.

[6] On the historicity of the passage and its sources, see Gösta Ahlström, *The History of Ancient Palestine* (Minneapolis: Fortress, 1993) 480–84.

to kill David, the one whom the narrator portrays as the worthy successor. Though often known as the "History of David's Rise,"[7] this narrative complex could well be called the "History of Saul's Fall." Despite its obvious apologetic nature,[8] the text's sophisticated portrayal of the dangerous royal body invites extended investigation. This narrative of veritable *Doppelgänger* explores how the display and skill of the body of the one declines as that of the other increases. Although David is to be king, he has not yet attained that role, and indeed the narrator masterfully insists that he neither seeks the crown nor considers himself king. True, these chapters do show, in part, how testing in warfare and peace prepares David's body for kingship,[9] yet they also insist upon his refusal to claim the throne for himself. David is not the king, but at most the king in waiting.

How, then, does the reader know to expect a dangerous king? As such texts as Exod. 15:1–18, Judg. 5, 2 Sam. 1:17–27, and others show, and as we have earlier noted, male prowess in battle is frequently the subject of the songs of women, and the biblical narrators often use these songs to point toward a male's ability to endanger other males. The women, functioning as commentators much in the manner of the chorus of Greek drama, delimit the boundaries of manhood.[10] A good place to begin the discussion of the dangerous

---

[7] For recent discussion of the nature and content of this source, see Otto Kaiser, "David und Jonathan: Tradition, Redaktion und Geschichte in I Sam 16–20, ein Versuch," *EthL* 66 (1990) 281–96; Thomas Römer and Albert de Pury, "L'historiographie deutronomiste (HD): Histoire de la recherche et enjeux du débat," in Albert de Pury, Thomas Römer, and Jean-Daniel Macchi, eds., *Israël construit son histoire* (Geneva: Labor et fides, 1996) 106–7; Antony Campbell and Mark O'Brien, *Unfolding the Deuteronomistic History: Origins, Upgrades, Present Text* (Minneapolis: Fortress, 2000) 1–37 and passim; and Antony Campbell, *1 Samuel* (FOTL 7; Grand Rapids: Eerdmans, 2003) 310–17.

[8] On which see Baruch Halpern, *David's Secret Demons: Messiah, Murderer, Traitor, King* (Grand Rapids: Eerdmans, 2001) 14–53. But see the cautions of Stuart Lasine, *Knowing Kings: Knowledge, Power, and Narcissism in the Hebrew Bible* (Atlanta: Society of Biblical Literature, 2001) 121–25.

[9] As explicated by Mark K. George, "Body Works: Power, the Construction of Identity, and Gender in the Discourse on Kingship" (Ph.D. diss., Princeton Theological Seminary, 1995) 62–90. George contrasts the constructions of the bodies of Saul and David, Jonathan and David, and especially Goliath and David. David becomes the king with the proper body by competing with, or fighting against, these other males.

[10] On the chorus in Greek plays, see Claude Calame, *Choruses of Young Women in Ancient Greece: Their Morphology, Religious Role and Social Function* (Lanham: Rowman and Littlefield, 1997); on similar choruses in biblical texts, see Klaus Baltzer, *Deutero-Jesaja* (KAT 10/2; Gütersloh: Gütersloher Verlagshaus, 1999) 48–49.

monarch is with the ditty, sung by women, that was famous enough to appear three times in 1 Samuel:

הכה שאול באלפיו ודוד ברבבתו

Saul has struck his thousands, David his myriads!¹¹

Taken on its own, the song does not obviously draw an invidious distinction between David and Saul.¹² The pair אלפ(ים)/רבבות occurs eleven times in the Bible, usually as a synonymous pair.¹³ Consider, for example, Deut. 33:17, "And they are the myriads of Ephraim and the thousands of Manasseh" (והם רבבות אפרים ו[ה]ם אלפי מנשה).¹⁴ Just as x/x+1 parallelism is a well-known feature of Israelite and Ugaritic poetry (3:4 or 7:8 being the usual number pairs), so also thousands/myriads is a trope of superaddition rather than contrast. The ditty may, therefore, conceivably have originally been part of a poetic cycle, perhaps even part of the same one a fragment of which also appears in 2 Sam. 1:17–27 pairing David and Saul as equally skilled warriors.

Still, the line is ambiguous and open to multiple construals. That Saul in the narrative chooses one possible meaning among several, that he applies to himself the sign *inferior warrior* rather than *equivalently heroic warrior* is a byproduct of the nature of signs, which may convey "many intertwined contents" and are therefore "text[s] whose content is a multileveled discourse."¹⁵ That is to say, even within an ancient Israelite setting the ditty was open to multiple, competing interpretations chosen to serve larger rhetorical ends. For the narrator, Saul's very negative interpretation allows the portrayal of this

---

¹¹ 1 Sam. 18:7, 21:12, 29:7. On poetry snippets in biblical prose, see James W. Watts, "'This Song': Conspicuous Poetry in Hebrew Prose," in Johannes C. de Moor and Wilfred G. E. Watson, *Verse in Ancient Near Eastern Prose* (AOAT 42; Neukirchen-Vluyn: Neukirchener, 1993) 345–58.

¹² This point is also made by Stanley Gevirtz (*Patterns in the Early Poetry of Israel* [Chicago: University of Chicago Press, 1963] 15–24), who does not, however, work out the use of the ditty in the prose narrative.

¹³ Gen. 24:60; Num. 10:36; Deut. 32:30, 33:17; Judg. 20:10; 1 Sam. 18:7–8, 21:12, 29:5; and Ps. 91:7.

¹⁴ ו omitted in Samaritan, Syriac, Vulgate, according to BHS apparatus.

¹⁵ Umberto Eco, *A Theory of Semiotics* (Bloomington: Indiana University Press, 1976) 57. On poetry embedded in biblical prose, see Steven Weitzman, *Song and Story in Biblical Narrative: The History of a Literary Convention in Ancient Israel* (Bloomington: Indiana University Press, 1997).

ruler as one who, in a moment of realistic self-evaluation or paranoia, according to one's lights, foresees his own demise.

In the narrative context of 1 Samuel this little fragment serves several purposes, all of them aiming to elevate David at Saul's expense. The narrative chooses one set of possible meanings (*Saul is inferior to David*) rather than another (*Saul and David are both heroic*). At one level, Saul's reaction foreshadows the comparison between himself and David that the reader will draw at the end of the story of David's reign, but such a reaction is not inevitable for Saul the literary character. His decision to react in this way profoundly alters his relationship with David. With the great artistry typical of biblical narrative prose, the text does not make this point in the narrator's voice, but in those of various characters who utter the line in response to David's deeds.[16] These characters debate, as it were, what it means to be a heroic (male) monarch. They do not finally decide the issue, but leave the question open in order to allow him to practice, as appropriate, the subterfuges and acts of bravery necessary to mark him as a hero. Saul, who wants to be dangerous to both the myriad enemies of the song and David, fails to menace anyone but himself.

The words of the song first appear as the women of Israel (who name the successful male warriors with song, as in 2 Sam. 1:24) greet the soldiers returning from the slaughter of the Philistines (1 Sam. 18:7).[17] Saul has made David his army commander, an appointment that garners universal approval. Saul turns on David, however, after hearing the ditty "Saul has struck his thousands, David his myriads." The narrator here plays on the ambiguity of the line to denigrate Saul, even though other characters in the tale do not necessarily share Saul's construal of it, David least of all.[18]

Saul's angry response to the song is curious: "They have ascribed myriads to David and (only) thousands to me; only kingship is left for him." (נתנו לדוד רבבות ולי נתנו האלפים ועוד לו אם המלוכה; 1 Sam. 18:8 MT).[19] This is interesting on several fronts. First, an objective

---

[16] On minor characters in Samuel, see Adele Reinhartz, "Anonymity and Character in the Books of Samuel," *Sem* 63 (1993) 117–41.

[17] On the origins of this alternative story of the early relationship of David and Saul, see Campbell, *1 Samuel*, 175.

[18] See J. P. Fokkelman, *Narrative Art and Poetry in the Books of Samuel: A Full Interpretation Based on Stylistic and Structural Analyses*, vol. 2: *The Crossing Fates (1 Sam. 13–31 and 22 Sam. 1)* (Assen: Van Gorcum, 1986) 213–16.

[19] LXX^B omits v. 8b, though Saul's actions in the shorter text implies the judg-

body count of Philistines is not what is at stake here. Rather, the opinion of others—notably women!—is central. Saul's reputation is at issue, and as king he can allow no one to be more heroic than he is. Warfare here is not conceived of primarily as the maneuverings of armies led from a distance by generals, but rather as hand-to-hand combat in which the king as generalissimo takes a major part. Not merely his generalship, but his physical prowess is decisive, and Saul's has come into question.

Second, the attribution of physical prowess is an indispensable ingredient of rulership, so much so that a king who has lost it has lost his ability to rule. Instead of taking credit for a wise choice in generals, Saul must fear for his position. He feels that the song of others is the first stage of a possible coup d'etat by David.[20] At this point, Saul begins to "eye" David with suspicion.[21] While this need not be a reference to an "evil eye," a malevolent, spellbinding glare that wreaks evil willy-nilly, it is an allusion to an aspect of royal power.[22] In this connection, note that the royal psalms (and therefore Israelite royal propaganda) were concerned about the king's gaze. According to Ps. 101:3, the king is not to "put a dastardly deed before his eyes (אשית לנגד עיני דבר בליעל), but is instead (v. 6) to gaze upon and employ the "loyal of the land" (נאמני ארץ) and the "walker in the straight way" (הלך בדרך תמים). An Iron Age Jerusalemite with access to traditions behind 1 Samuel would probably have known this psalm or at least the ideas behind it. The king vows to avert his gaze from evil in any form. His eye passes moral judgment in the psalm and in the story about Saul. It is an organ that signifies

---

ment that the expansion in the MT implies (see the text critical analysis of Campbell, *1 Samuel*, 174–75). The LXX[B] version heightens the contrast between David and Saul by making the latter's actions seem all the more paranoid, though, again, the expansion in MT does portray him equating reputation with power in a direct way.

[20] Especially in the MT version, though also in the LXX[B] version. Steven McKenzie (*King David: A Biography* [Oxford: Oxford University Press, 2000] 86–88) has plausibly proposed that David did attempt such a seizure of power. Minimally, the narrator feels a need to exonerate David of someone's belief, well founded or not, that he had attempted a coup d'etat. As Halpern argues, this fact probably indicates a very early date for the work (*David's Secret Demons*, 94–103; for 2 Samuel, though his arguments apply to 1 Samuel as well).

[21] Reading with the Qere and LXX (ὑποβλεπόμενος) the participle עוֹיִן (though admittedly a *hapax legomenon* in the Bible) for עָיִן (MT). See P. Kyle McCarter, *I Samuel* (AB 8; Garden City, NY: Doubleday, 1980) 312; Caquot and de Robert, *Livres de Samuel*, 217.

[22] See McCarter, *I Samuel*, 312–13.

danger for the king's foe. The irony in the Saul story then becomes delicious, for Saul in his eyeing David intends to mark him as what he is not, an evildoer, and yet along the way marks him as the opposite, as a "loyal one." Saul fears David's success and newfound prestige, and thus makes an attempt on David's life. "Eyeing" David marks him, inaccurately, as an evildoer who must be harried out of the land. For the narrator, Saul's misuse of his royal body contributes to his own unfitness for rule, the opposite of his intentions.[23]

However, Saul does not reveal his jealousy to anyone. He must intrigue to eliminate David. Conceivably, this reluctance simply to execute a rival may be a function of the primitive governmental organization of Saul's realm in which the ruler simply lacked a monopoly on the use of force,[24] but since David attempts to hide his murder of Uriah and Ahab his of Naboth, a more probable explanation of Saul's behavior is that Israelites even later—especially later—shunned the open execution of rivals.[25] The king must at least appear not to be involved in murder.[26] Saul, therefore, must hide his anger in order to portray himself in a kingly way.[27] Saul's lack of skill in the social poetics of kingship costs him dearly.

Saul's suspicion seems well founded, as becomes clear in the second appearance of the ditty. 1 Sam. 21:12 bears examination:

> Whereupon the retainers of Akish (עבדי אכיש) said to him, "Is this not David, the king of the land (מלך הארץ)? Is it not he whom they sing (יענו) about in their dances: 'Saul has struck his thousands, David his myriads'?"

---

[23] On the conflicting views of Saul in 1 Samuel, see Eben Sheffler, "Saving Saul from the Deuteronomist," in Johannes C. de Moor and Harry F. van Rooy, eds., *Past, Present, Future: The Deuteronomistic History and the Prophets* (OTS 44; Leiden: Brill, 2000) 263–71.

[24] On the organization of Saul's chieftainship (?), see Gösta W. Ahlström, *The History of Ancient Palestine* (Minneapolis: Fortress, 1993) 421–54; Hermann Michael Niemann, *Herrschaft, Königtum und Staat: Skizzen zur soziokulturellen Entwicklung im monarchischen Israel* (FAT 6; Tübingen: Mohr/Siebeck, 1993) 3–7.

[25] An exception to this might be David's command to Solomon to slay various enemies and potential rivals (1 Kings 2:1–5). The attempt to hide royal murder did not always succeed. Moreover, this testamentary command may stem from a Solomonic defense of the purge.

[26] On the royal cover-up of murder, see Halpern, *David's Secret Demons*, 73–103.

[27] Contrast this with the Assyrian convention, which considered the display of royal anger at rivals appropriate and worthy of reportage on royal inscriptions; witness, e.g., the use of the epithets *ekdu* ("fierce"), *palḫu* ("fearsome"), *šitmuru* ("fierce"), *uzzu dannu* ("fierce anger") *inter alia* (see the list in Cifola, *Analysis*, 181–88).

This question operates at multiple levels. It uses non-Israelites to label David king, and to do so by explicitly recognizing his skill at killing their own people. From the point of view of the story time, the question is anachronistic, since David is not yet king. The ditty does not at this point reflect some secret or partial rule by David, but is purely anticipatory. The reader knows, however, that David will soon be king, and so this is a case of foreshadowing. The narrator signals that everyone knows David to be the rightful ruler of Israel (even if David himself is in the dark; else why would he flee to Gath, a dangerous move for the future king of the Philistines' enemy, Israel, and one obviously embarrassing to David's later defenders?).[28]

Again, we find the prowess of the warrior recognized by singing, and here, dancing.[29] (This verse nicely complements, again, the reference to Philistine women singing in victory celebrations in 2 Sam. 1:20.) Yet this very recognition forces David to alter his appearance in order to avoid disaster. V. 14 reads: "So he went out of his mind (טעמו)[30] in their eyes and acted like a lunatic (ויתהלל) in their hand (בידם). He made marks[31] on the doors of the gateway and spittle (ריר)[32] was running down on his beard." That is, rather than protesting his innocence, David radically alters his behavior to illustrate his powerlessness. Madness obviously disqualifies one for kingship, a fact that the narrator also plays upon when having Saul lie naked when under spirit possession (1 Sam. 19:24). David does not allow himself to be the brave warrior of the ditty—at least not in Gath.

---

[28] See Halpern, *David's Secret Demons*, 302–6.

[29] See J. H. Eaton, "Dancing in the Old Testament," *ExpTimes* 86 (1975) 136–40; C. L. Seow, *Myth, Drama, and the Politics of David's Dance* (HSM 44; Atlanta: Scholars, 1989).

[30] For √טעם meaning "discretion," "judgment" see Ps. 34:1; Prov. 26:16; KAI 233.8 (Aššur Ostracon). See also the cognate Akkadian idiom *ṭēma šenû* ("to change an opinion, change one's mind" or "to go out of one's mind") in, e.g., the "Tukulti-ninurta Epic," 5.10, and SAA III 33r2 (+K4730+Sm1816) on the "Sin of Sargon." The word also appears in Amarna texts; see Pinhas Artzi, "Rationality in Ancient Near Eastern International Relations in the 'Extended Age of the Amarna Archive,' ca. 1460–1200 BCE: The Force of *ṭēmu* 'Mind'," in *Sefer Moshe: The Moshe Weinfeld Jubilee Volume* (ed. Chaim Cohen, Avi Hurvitz, and Shalom Paul; Winona Lake: Eisenbrauns, 2004) 339–50.

[31] Or, "he spat," reading חפף II rather than חוה I; so McCarter, *I Samuel*, 355. ריר means an egg white in Job 6:6, thus a thick, slimy liquid. The more common word for spit, רק, signifies contempt (Isa. 50:6; Job 30:10), but only when one is spat upon. Here we know that spit on the beard signifies madness, loss of physical control, and thus a loss of status because (1) the Philistines call David a madman, and (2) he adopts this bodily state in order to prompt them to do so.

[32] The pair טעם/ריר also appears in Job 6:6, though with different denotations.

What purpose does this tale serve? Surely it does not cast the erstwhile hero David in a heroic light, even though it does show that David can use his body to feign madness, whereas Saul cannot control his body or, through it, his environment. The use of the idiom *ṭēma šešnû* in Assyrian texts to describe frenzy in battle contrasts strongly with the use of the Hebrew וישנו את טעמו, the former describing the behavior of warriors in battle, the latter of a warrior who cannot fight even against those who, at this very moment, recognize his prowess. The irony of David's position folds back in on itself. Frenzy does not lead to defeat of enemies but to acceptance of their tutelage. On the other hand, the Hebrew idiom does preclude one possible interpretation of the comparison with Saul: David cannot slay Israelites on behalf of the Philistines if he is mad, and so his myriads of victims are foreigners. David is not responsible for Saul's demise.[33] Yet the narrator solves the problem of David's apparent collaboration with the enemy more successfully later by having the Philistines remove David from their army before the battle of Gilboa (1 Sam. 29:6–11).[34] The purpose of this feigned madness becomes clearer in the next three verses.

First, vv. 15–16 label David a משגע ("lunatic") and have Akish crack the joke, "Do I have a shortage of lunatics? Is this why you have brought this one to act like a lunatic before me?" This joke at the expense of Philistines in general and Akish's courtiers in particular has a serious purpose. At one level, it marks all of them as madmen unworthy of consideration as warriors. At another level, an implied reader knows that משגע can also designate an ecstatic, a prophet. 2 Kings 9:11, Hos. 9:7, and Jer. 29:26 both use the word in connection with prophecy. Without getting into the complex question of the role of ecstasy or, better, possession trances[35] in Israelite prophecy, I observe simply that some prophets could behave in ways that observers of them could brand "lunacy," much in the manner of David's feigned madness. They might lose control of their facul-

---

[33] See McKenzie, *King David*, 101–4; Halpern, *David's Secret Demons*, 287–94.

[34] This latter solution is very adroit: the dismissal by the Philistines exonerates David of breaking his treaty with Akish, as well as washes Israelite blood from his hands!

[35] On which see, Simon B. Parker, "Possession Trance and Prophecy in Preexilic Israel," *VT* 28 (1978) 271–85; Robert R. Wilson, "Prophecy and Ecstasy: A Reexamination," *JBL* 98 (1979) 321–37.

ties or appear to do so, and this could lead to bodily movements or self-presentation that Israelite (and Philistine) culture ordinarily stigmatized.[36] On the other hand, Saul himself fell into such behavior in 1 Sam. 10 and 19:20–24. Although the text remarks upon the unexpectedness of this behavior in a king—"Is Saul also among the prophets?" (הגם שאול בנביא)[37]—one does not get a sense that the behavior is invariably considered either positive or negative. That depends upon how the possessed ecstatic performs both during and after ecstasy. When, therefore, 1 Sam. 21 describes David in this way, the text's audience must decide if David is (1) a charismatic or (2) a madman. His outward behavior can be socially construed in either way. The narrator and reader understand David's actions as a ploy, or perhaps even a sign of his fitness for kingship, even if the option of understanding David as a prophet is left to one side. For Akish, though, the answer is clear: David is mad.

Here the most obvious sign—and I use the term in its semiotic sense—of David's derangement is his inability to control his spittle. The beard was an important index of heroism as well as an icon of manhood (hence the embarrassment of the shaved ambassadors to Ammon in 2 Sam. 10:4).[38] To foul it with spit is to index a loss of manhood. This behavior thus well serves David when he wants to refute the charge from the ditty "Saul has struck his thousands, David his myriads." He poses no threat to the Philistines.

And yet, of course, he does. By portraying the king who radically endangers the Philstines as deliberately manipulating the icon of his own body to feign innocence, the text paradoxically underscores the very danger to Israel's enemies that David, for the moment, seeks to downplay. Israelites and other Levantines accustomed to portrayals of kings sporting magnificent beards would recognize in David's spittle-covered one the erosion of his power and manliness.[39] David manipulates, as it were, the visible aspects of his own body to portray

---

[36] This behavior was Hosea's own, not that of his opponents; see Hans Walter Wolff, *Hosea* (Hermeneia; Philadelphia: Fortress, 1974) 156–57.

[37] 1 Sam. 10:11 and 19:24.

[38] See also Daniel Schlumberger, "La Coiffure du Grand Roi," *Syria* 48 (1971) 375–83.

[39] For bearded kings from Syria-Palestine, see Rüdiger Schmitt, *Bildhafte Herrschaftsrepäsentation im eisenzeitlichen Israel* (AOAT 283; Münster: Ugarit-Verlag, 2001) 365 figs. 141–44.

himself as a non-hero, all for the sake of a better self-presentation. The narrator, through Akish's overcoded joke, indicates that this merely makes David at home in Philistia, where everyone can act this way (as the Israelite narrator and his audience have it).[40] This bit of ethnocentricity has a larger purpose, for it allows David to survive to fight another day, and it allows Saul momentarily to be the one endangering the Philistines. Moreover, it casts Saul's earlier actions as an ecstatic in a new light: the king who uses his body properly does so as David does, not as Saul does. Ecstatic behavior serves the political ends of the king, potential or real, not the indeterminate plans of the deity, who may indeed seek to destroy the royal body to which he has given birth. Also, in the scheme of the overall narrative of his ascent to power, David's actions allow him to be the one who eventually slays myriads of Philistines. Heroes may be afraid (וירא; v. 13), but they must not be stupid.

Meanwhile, the third use of the ditty occurs in 1 Sam. 29:5, where it serves to justify the Philistines' dismissal of their vassal and thus to exonerate David of complicity in Saul's death. The narrative plays with the question, "who is David?" When the Philistine שׂרים[41] demand his ouster from the army, his satisfied overlord Akish defends him as the "servant[42] of King Saul of Israel ... in whom I find no fault from the time of his 'fall' until now" (v. 3; ... עבד שאול מלך ישראל ולא מצאתי בו מאומה מיום נפלו עד היום הזה). This defense concedes what cannot be denied (David's past), but insists that David has not acted like a servant of Saul. The narrator suggests, that Saul has threatened to kill David, and that the latter has entered Akish's service only to avoid death. It is thus Saul who has not behaved like a proper overlord, though, and so one should read the Philistine ruler's

---

[40] In other words, the joke is a case of what Michael Herzfeld calls "rhetorical uses of iconicity": the narrator wishes the reader to think *madman* whenever he or she hears *Philistine* (see Michael Herzfeld, "On Some Rhetorical Uses of Iconicity in Cultural Ideologies," in Paul Bouissac, Michael Herzfeld, and Roland Posner, eds., *Iconicity: Essays on the Nature of Culture* [Sebeok Festschrift; Tübingen: Stauffenburg, 1986] 401–19).

[41] Are these to be distinguished from the סרנים or paramount chiefs of Philistia? See Caquot and de Robert, *Livres des Samuel*, 343; Diana Vikander Edelman, *King Saul in the Historiography of Judah* (JSOTSS 121; Sheffield Academic Press, 1991) 255.

[42] Edelman (*King Saul*, 254–56) sees here a possible connection to the Nabal story, in which David's servanthood is also at issue. This may be, however, a demonstration of the flexibility of the word עבד rather than an intended narrative link.

claim at two levels in tension with each other. On the other hand, David is Saul's servant and therefore has faithfully discharged all his duties; yet, Saul has not reciprocated this fealty, having removed David from office ("his fall" [נִפְלוֹ], not necessarily "his defection").[43] At the level of this episode, Akish defends David on the basis of his loyalty to him since his departure from Saul's court. At the level of the narrative of David's ascent to power, the defense is based on David's relationship to Saul.

The generals, meanwhile, retort that David is the hero of the ditty, and therefore his band is a potential fifth column. They thus present a second viewpoint on David and Saul. The latter is not their real worry, for he is not the mighty warrior of the song. Yet, simultaneously, they imply that David is untrustworthy: has he not betrayed Saul? Akish argues, contrariwise, that David presents no danger to his hosts, despite his past. He has perhaps struck his myriads, but that is a thing of the past (or the future, as the reader knows!). For the narrator, though, David has struck his myriads, but they are not Israelites.[44] He remains altogether blameless, from everyone's point of view, rightly considered. Interestingly, though, David in all this exchange remains passive. The narrator allows the other characters to argue the major themes of the text: David is loyal to Saul despite his master's betrayal (Akish's point), yet he is also the mighty hero who poses a powerful threat to Israel's enemies (the generals' point).[45]

To summarize, the narrator uses the line comparing David and Saul three times in order to explore David's relationships with other males, not only Saul, but also the Philistines. Is David the dangerous king or not? That is the question. The text slyly answers, yes and no. Yes, he will be king, one who slays Philistines in droves, one whose military prowess excels everyone else's and is comparable only to Saul's. Yet, also no. David, the text insists, does not gain the throne by plotting with Israel's enemies against Saul (even though the narrator and his audience know of an undoubtedly historically accurate tradition of David's involvement with the Philistines). David,

---

[43] *Contra* ibid., 254.
[44] But see the remarks of McKenzie, *King David*, 89–90.
[45] On the complex unfolding of these themes through the end of 1 Sam., see Tomoo Ishida, *The Royal Dynasties in Ancient Israel* (BZAW 142; Berlin: de Gruyter, 1977) 57.

in short, performs the role of the mistreated but still admirable warrior and subject of his king to the end. Still the ancient Israelite who knows the story of David must entertain reservations. David does ultimately endanger not only the Philistines, but even his own subjects. His manipulation of the display of his own body ultimately serves to build his power. He uses spit and clawing and babbling to show that he is not the threatening king but a future king presently under threat. And it is precisely in this self-effacement, this obscuration of power, that legitimate power resides.

This threat comes decisively from Saul. His role is under consideration along with David's. The various uses of the ditty about thousands and myriads point to Saul's increasing inability to endanger the enemies of Israel, the Philistines, and so mark his gradual loss of the throne to a superior candidate.[46] He is an inferior warrior, an overlord who abuses his subordinates—and soon he will no longer be king. David, meantime, avoids killing his enemies, and his self-effacement that seems to give the lie to his reputation as killer of myriads actually reinforces it by telling the reader that, unlike Saul, he depends upon Yahweh, whose gracious provision allows David to become the king. The conflict with Saul revolves, then, around each man's bodily self-display. How has the text brought us to this point?

Saul's Hunt for David

1 Sam. 18–2 Sam. 1 deals with Saul's pursuit of David on account of the hatred provoked by the ditty. The narrative as it stands recounts an escalation of violence against David, beginning with subterfuge in 1 Sam. 18, and leading to David's exile and Saul's pursuit in the succeeding chapters. Several episodes are of particular moment.

The first comes in 1 Sam. 18:9–30. After hearing the ditty, Saul "eyes"[47] David, a point on which I have already touched. Saul's misuse of the royal body becomes more pronounced in the next verses,[48]

---

[46] On this point, see Mark K. George, "Yhwh's Own Heart," *CBQ* 64 (2002) 442–59.
[47] See n. 14 above.
[48] McCarter (*I Samuel*, 306–9) argues that this material is part of a later interpolation, since it is apparently missing from OG (being absent from B). But the numerous literary niceties that would be obliterated by excising this text, as well as

or rather the narrator seeks to explicate his behavior by saying that Yahweh dispatched an evil spirit (רוח אלהים רעה) to cause Saul to act deranged (ויתנבא [!]; v. 10). Saul throws a spear, the weapon he always bears in 1 Samuel.

What is the connection between the arrival of the evil spirit and Saul's actions? Mettinger points out that the removal of the spirit from Saul and its transference to David are a sign of the passing of the divine charisma from one king to another.[49] Saul still is possessed by a divine spirit, though unfortunately it is now "evil" (רעה). Does the spirit *cause* his murderousness? Does Saul's misuse of his eyes somehow make him susceptible to spirit possession? In other words, how does a spirit enter an Israelite body? What, moreover, makes the spirit "evil": is it so because Saul's actions are evil? The text raises these questions without answering them. Clearly, however, just as the divine spirit received at his coronation empowered Saul to be king, and therefore to menace Israel's enemies, the arrival of an evil spirit (also from God!) allows him to threaten his imagined domestic enemies. Spear-throwing is part of the self-display of a mighty warrior, but here in 1 Sam. 18:9–30, such a feat of prowess only emphasizes Saul's impotence (at least in his own mind) before the rising David. Again the narrator uses iconicity ironically. Rather than being an index of a great warrior, the spear signifies a king who fails precisely as a warrior in the eyes of his subjects.

The king's ineffectuality takes a new turn later in 1 Sam. 18 when he offers to make David his son-in-law. After David's aborted engagement to Merab,[50] the two men agree that David will marry Michal. Curious is the text's explanation of Saul's motivation: upon learning that Michal loves David, Saul found the idea of their marrying to be "right in his eyes" (וישר הדבר בעיניו; v. 20), but not because of fatherly affection for his daughter. Rather, just as he misused his eyes to mark David as an evildoer, so now he "sees" this love as an opportunity for mischief. "For Saul thought, 'I shall give her to

---

the absence of clear MS. evidence (since OG could be a shortening of MT, as Wellhausen argued) militate against this. See John T. Willis, "The Function of Comprehensive Anticipatory Redactional Joints in 1 Samuel 16–18," *ZAW* 85 (1973) 294–314; Julius Wellhausen, *Der Text der Bücher Samuelis untersucht* (Göttingen: Vandenhoeck & Ruprecht, 1871) ad loc.

[49] Tryggve N. D. Mettinger, *King and Messiah: The Civil and Sacral Legitimation of the Israelite Kings* (Lund: Gleerup, 1976) 247–48.
[50] Possibly a later addition; see Campbell, *1 Samuel*, 196–98.

him, and she will be a snare to him, and the hand of the Philistines will be upon him'" (ויאמר שאול אתננה לו ותהי לו למוקש ותהי בו יד פלשתים; v. 21). The connection between marriage to the princess and danger from the Philistines is not obvious, and it becomes so only when Saul comes to demand the bride price (מהר) of one hundred Philistine foreskins (ערלות; v. 25).[51] David walks into this trap by protesting his poverty and unworthiness to be part of the royal family (though perhaps this modesty was a conventional negotiation tactic). David acknowledges his and his family's inferiority, but then turns around and demonstrates his martial superiority to Saul. He comes out the winner when he collects the grisly *mohar*.

The story of the slaughter of the Philistines presumes David's extraordinary ability to endanger Israel's enemies. Whereas Saul must depend on David's generalship, David himself kills more Philistines than anyone else (1 Sam. 18:30). Interestingly, too, his removal of the foreskin paves the way for his right to marry, and therefore to have sex with, Michal. Not to put too fine a point on it, his genital power increases by means of the mutilation of the genitals of other males. This can hardly be accidental to the story, since Saul might easily have asked for one hundred heads of Philistines or their entire corpses. Admittedly, the foreskin proves an attractive trophy of war in this case because David could not cheat by killing Israelites, or women or children, that is, noncombatants.[52] Still, the focus is upon the genitalia of the warriors involved, David's and his victims.[53]

If the narrator wishes to show the potential dangers that a king poses—through the use of his eye or through plotting or even the use of women as sex objects—this theme takes a sharp turn when David overcomes every trial. Saul cannot use other males to kill David and so falsify the ditty comparing the first two Israelite kings.

---

[51] On Philistines as sexual aggressors, see Meir Sternberg, *Hebrews Between Cultures: Group Portraits and National Literature* (Bloomington: Indiana University Press, 1998) 195–96, 245–48.

[52] On the Philistines as ערלים, see Judg. 14:3; 15:18; 1 Sam. 14:6; 17:26, 36; 31:4; 2 Sam. 1:20; and 1 Chron. 10:4.

[53] Note also that when Saul discovers that Jonathan is loyal to David, he curses his son by calling him the son of a "perverse, treacherous woman" (בן נעות המרדות; 1 Sam. 20:30). If Jonathan is literally a bastard, then Saul is a cuckold and implicitly one whose genitalia failed to produce the crown prince (even granting that Saul's imprecation "reproduisent probablement des expressions courantes" [Caquot and de Robert, *Livres des Samuel*, 251]). Again, then, the proper nature of the king's member is an issue of discussion.

In 1 Sam. 19, this exploration of the dangers a king may pose takes on still more dimensions. Two more times (19:9 and 23–24), Saul falls into a trance on account of the evil spirit. Again he seeks to spear David (19:10), and the intended victim finally recognizes his peril quits Saul's court. On the second descent of the spirit, Saul lies naked all night: this display of his body exposes Saul (so to speak) as one no longer fit to be king, since he can no longer control his self-presentation. The king possessed by an evil spirit is a threat to his foes, but also to himself. Moreover, Saul no longer has access to the sort of divine knowledge otherwise obtainable in a state of ecstasy, or rather, his access only endangers him. Thus the loss of bodily control signifies to the knowing onlooker, Saul's erstwhile subjects, the loss of a major aspect of kingship, access to the divine realm's knowledge.[54]

These two episodes involving the evil spirit's influence over Saul bracket an enigmatic one (1 Sam. 19:11–17). Here Michal saves David's life. A woman is thus a vigorous actor who thwarts the dangerous king Saul (even after he had hoped she would help him endanger her husband). Just as women singers help define the maleness of successful warriors in songs after battle, so too does Michal define who is a successful male (David) and who not (Saul). A curious aspect of this is her use of the teraphim to effect a diguise for David (on other disguises, see above). How this worked is unclear: Gen. 31:30–35 reports Rachel hiding her father's teraphim in her saddle bags, thus indicating that they were small cult objects easily transportable and therefore probably part of the repertoire of (anthropomorphic) religious figurines common to Palestine throughout the Iron Age (and earlier).[55] Yet, Michal covers them with a כביר העזים[56] in order to disguise David's escape through the window.

---

[54] On knowledge as a feature of the king's life, see Lasine, *Knowing Kings*; and Dale Launderville, *Piety and Politics: The Dynamics of Royal Authority in Homeric Greece, Biblical Israel, and Old Babylonian Mesopotamia* (Grand Rapids: Eerdmans, 2003) 209–19.

[55] For a handy summary of the evidence, see Ora Negbi, *Canaanite Gods in Metal: An Archaeological Study of Ancient Syro-Palestinian Figurines* (Tel Aviv: Tel Aviv University, Institute of Archaeology, 1976); Christoph Uehlinger, "Anthropomorphic Cult Statuary in Iron Age Palestine and the Search for Yahweh's Cult Images," in Karel van der Toorn, ed., *The Image and the Book: Iconic Cults, Aniconism, and the Rise of Book Religion in Israel and the Ancient Near East* (Leuven: Peeters, 1997) 97–155.

[56] כביר is a *hapax* in the Bible; the root כבר II denotes woven or lattice-like work of some kind. But see KTU 1.6.V.15–16, where *ba-kabarāti* (fem. pl. "sieves" in J. C. L. Gibson's translation [*Canaanite Myths and Legends* (Edinburgh: Clark, 1978)

This action has puzzled some commentators because it seems to them to indicate that Michal's teraphim were more or less life-size representations of human beings: the covered teraphim, these scholars believe, looked like a man sleeping.[57] This understanding appears unlikely, however, since there is no Iron Age evidence for such large figures used outside temples in Palestine (and how could Michal have moved such an object in any case?). As Rouillard and Tropper have argued, the more economical explanation is that she used teraphim in a healing or apotropaic ritual.[58] When she then says to the soldiers who have come to kill her husband, "He is sick" (חלה הוא; v. 14), she offers a reason for not entering the room, which the soldiers accept. Michal's lie[59] portrays David's body as one needing the care of a woman (as it did, though only to escape!). She can use ritual practices to thwart the dangerous king, and she is the one whose decisions define the success and failure of the powerful males around her.

David's escape, then, leads to two final episodes regarding the dangerous king. They are 1 Sam. 24 and 26, a diptych framing the story of David's shady dealings with Nabal and marriage to Abigail. The stories share a common pattern: (1) Saul pursues David into the desert; (2) while Saul is vulnerable, David and/or his men perform a daring feat that allows (3) David to reveal himself to Saul and his army as a loyal vassal. While there are differences in logic and outlook between the stories,[60] there can be no doubt that they form a pair (even if they may originally have been two versions of the same incident). Both stories are concerned with the treatment of the royal body by a rival, a subject that may have worried Judahites

---

79], but seems hard to understand, for how can Ba'lu mistreat Môtu with a sieve?) parallels *ba-bvriḥīma* ("bars"?).

[57] E.g., Henry Preserved Smith, *The Books of Samuel* (ICC; Edinburgh: Clark, 1899) 180; Ralph W. Klein, *1 Samuel* (WBC 10; Waco: Word, 1983) 197. But see Campbell, *1 Samuel*, 204.

[58] Hedwige Rouillard and Josef Tropper, "*trpym*, rituels de guérison et culte des ancêtres d'apres 1 Samuel 19:11–17 et les textes parallèles d'Assur et de Nuzi," *VT* 37 (1987) 340–61; Edelman, *King Saul*, 150. Note LXX^B of 1 Sam. 15:23, which renders תרפים as θεραπέιαν ("healing") instead of transliterating it as θεραφιν/μ as in LXX^{AL}. This variant may be the result of an inter-Greek transmission process, but it may also witness to an aspect of the usage of the teraphim in addition to its use in divination (see Ezek. 21:26).

[59] If it is a lie, that is; but see Edelman, *King Saul*, 148–49.

[60] On which see Caquot and de Robert, *Livres des Samuel*, 290.

familiar with the serial coups d'etat in the northern Israelite kingdom, in particular. The notion of the inviolability of the royal person finds expression in the claim of David that only Yahweh can slay the king, and that without the aid of his fellow Israelites.

The first exchange is in 1 Sam. 24. Here the narrative opens by presenting Saul as the quintessential dangerous king. He fights the Philistines and then leads his crack regiments (שלשת אלפים איש בחור מכל ישראל; v. 3) against David and his band hiding near Engedi. He seeks (בקש) to capture and kill David. Then, as luck would have it, Saul chances to relieve himself inside a cave in which his prey is hiding. David's companions interpret this accident as a sign that Yahweh has offered David a chance to kill Saul, but the former is content with cutting off the hem (כנף) of the king's robe. Even this limited invasion of the royal body causes David remorse (ויך לב דוד; v. 6), and perhaps a more tangible physical reaction,[61] and he forbids his men to kill Saul.

The first scene in this little drama ends on an unexpected note. V. 8 has David "tearing up" (וישסע) his men in order to prevent their murdering Saul. Many commentators have thought this verb "too strong,"[62] since it also describes Samson's dismemberment of a lion, for example (Judg. 14:6). Yet this interpretive discomfort may be unjustified, since the overall tone of the scene is comedic, even burlesque. A man falling into the clutches of his enemies while he is defecating is hardly the stuff of sober historiography, though it does seem to be a feature of comedic scenes about threats to kings (cf. Judg. 3). So, why should not the text also depict a fight among David and his companions? David must exert great force to prevent his men from slaying the king who is also hunting them.

Still, there is much here that is serious. For example, David removes a piece of Saul's garment. Why? Does he do so in order to acquire the proof he will later use to demonstrate how close Saul came to death? Or is more at issue? One possibility is that David intended to use this piece of fabric in a ritual of cursing. While little direct Israelite evidence for such a practice exists, it is worth noticing that one of the means of witchcraft counteracted in the first-millennium

---

[61] As Fokkelman (*Crossing Fates*, 458) suggests.
[62] E.g., BDB; Smith, *Books of Samuel*, 218; McCarter, *I Samuel*, 381; Caquot and de Robert, *Livres des Samuel*, 293.

Assyrian[63] *bīt rimki* ritual, an apotropaic ritual on behalf of the monarch, involved the making of an image using the victim's hair and the "fringe" (*sissiktu*) of his garment.[64] I am not proposing that Israelites borrowed this Mesopotamian ritual, but merely that the use of a hem of a garment could serve as a point of contact between a sorcerer and her (in the *bīt rimki* ritual, at least) victim. It is at least possible that David planned to use this fabric in a ritual cursing Saul, or that the narrator at leasts wants to tease the reader with that possibility. Also, this implies that an object that the king wore could serve as a point of contact between a sorcerer (in David's employ?) and Saul himself. Perhaps David in the story considers the possibility of using the cloth in a ritual that would endanger Saul without risking violation of the taboo on harming his body directly. If so, he eventually rejects even this option.

His explanation for failing to murder Saul may lend support to this hypothesis, for David objects to killing Yahweh's מָשִׁיחַ. As I argued earlier, anointing transformed the Israelite king into a more than human personage. Yet, as the case of the Amalekite in 2 Sam. 1 also makes clear, this unction did not work *ex opere operato*. Persons could circumvent the ritual, as the troops sought to do here, though at their own peril. David here chooses not to do so, but rather to offer a display of bravura that would win Saul over to him. This he does in the rest of the story.

The conversation between David and Saul in 1 Sam. 24:10–23 explores how one whom the king threatens may escape that threat.[65] David's petition is very artistic: addressing the king in the third person according to the polite style of the court, and pulling out all rhetorical stops,[66] he appeals to the witness of Saul's eyes (v. 11)

---

[63] On the origins of the ritual, see Walter Farber, "*Bīt rimki*—ein assyrisches Ritual?" in Hartmut Waetzoldt and Harald Hauptmann, eds., *Assyrien im Wandel der Zeiten* (Heidelberg: Heidelberger Orientverlag, 1997) 41–46.

[64] Line 19 in the edition of Læssøe, *Studies on the Assyrian Ritual and Series*, 45.

[65] See also the analysis of Fokkelman, *Crossing Fates*, 461–73.

[66] Note, e.g., his use of a *mashal* in v. 14: מֵרְשָׁעִים יֵצֵא רֶשַׁע ("from evil people, evil comes"). David claims that he is not evil, and by appealing to a known saying, he links his claim to the common assumptions of his audience. He also demonstrates his skill in choosing the pithy, and apposite, apophthegm for the moment. Such use of proverbs in self-defenses before a king also appears in Neo-Assyrian texts and may therefore be a broad Near Eastern convention. See, e.g., Letter 12 (r. 3–6) in Parpola, *Letters from Assyrian Scholars*, 8–9: *la mudê šipri dayyānu ušannaḫ; lā mudê amāti ušanzaqa dannu* ("the ignorant frustrates the judge; the unlearned agitates

rather than the rumors spread by others (v. 10). David is the victim of the slanders of other males who are competing with him for their sovereign's favor. He protests his innocence of rebellion (רעה/פשע; v. 12), and addresses Saul as "father" (אבי). And, he simultaneously displays Saul's severed hem as proof of his own power over the king (v. 12) and then paradoxically describes himself as a "dead dog, a flea" (כלב מת . . . פרעש אחד; v. 15). This masterful performance, which draws in part on the conventions of the lament,[67] permits David to come off as simultaneously a brave hero and a self-effacing subject of his king.

Perhaps the centerpiece of this speech is v. 12:

> So, my father, see, yes, see the hem of your robe in my hand; for I cut off the hem of your robe yet did not kill you. Know and see that there is no treachery or rebellion in my hand, and I have not revolted against you. Yet you hunt my life to take it!

ואבי ראה גם ראה את כנף מעילך בידי כי בכרתי את כנף מעילך ולא הרגתיך
דע וראה כי אין בידי רעה ופשע ולא חטאתי לך ואתה צדה את נפשי לקחתה

Saul must "see" the evidence of David's innocence.[68] The fabric in his hands testifies to the absence of any signs of rebellion there. The emphasis here, as in chapter 18, is on Saul as the one who sees. Since the royal eye is a sign connoting royal justice, as we have seen, the plea here is for Saul to carry out his duties properly.

The king's response is striking. He is no longer the threatening king, but the one who accepts David's defense, repents of his own behavior, and blesses his erstwhile enemy. The threats of the king can be overcome by a brave protestation of innocence.

Now, this brings us to the final story of Saul as the dangerous king to be considered here: 1 Sam. 26. Though clearly a doublet of chapter 24, this second version of the story also adds a few new wrinkles.[69]

---

the mighty"). With this saying, the diviner Ištar-šumu-ereš defends his prognostication before the king and against a rival. For commentary, see Simo Parpola, *Letters from Assyrian Scholars to the Kings Esarhaddon and Assurbanipal*, vol. 2: *Commentary and Appendices* (AOAT 5/2; Neukirchen-Vluyn: Neukirchener, 1983) 14–16.

[67] On which see Ulrich Berges, *Die Verwerfung Sauls: Eine thematische Untersuchung* (Würzburg: Echter, 1989) 148–51.

[68] Note that David also must see (v. 12), though I think Edelman (*King Saul*, 231) is wrong to see in his case a distinction between the eye and the heart: both here are instruments of perception.

[69] On the differences, see Fokkelman, *Crossing Fates*, 529; Campbell, *1 Samuel*, 265.

David and Abishai sneak into the enemy encampment, spot Saul lying asleep and surrounded by his army, and then steal his water flask (צפחת המים) and spear (חנית), ironically the weapon with which the king had earlier threatened David.[70] The spear stands in the ground at Saul's head (מעוכה בארץ מראשתו; v. 7). This placement is not the best for a warrior who needs his weapon in a hurry: he should have placed it near his hands. Rather, this fine literary touch points the reader once again to the importance of Saul's head, the part that is anointed, and so this anticipates David's refusal in v. 11 to harm the משיח of Yahweh. At another level, we remember that Saul's head is a synecdoche for Saul as head, king of Israel (just as in 1 Sam. 31). The head of the kingdom, the king himself relies on a weapon that cannot protect it, and thus cannot protect the realm as a whole. Only because another man, here David, forswears harming the king does he remain safe. As with the story of Saul's first attempt on David's life, here the spear becomes not an index of successful warriorhood, but of just the opposite.[71]

Again, as in 1 Sam. 24, the narrative here portrays Saul as a dangerous king, the anointed one leading his army (as in Pss. 2, 20, and 21), and then shows how he is not dangerous because he cannot live up to his kingly roles. This is true because he attacks the wrong foe, and, because it is true, everything goes wrong for Saul in the contest of manhood with David. Noteworthy are the multiple forms of male contestation here. First, David chooses two men to help him, and only the native Israelite Abishai (his relative, to boot) dares to accompany him into camp. Second, after the expedition into Saul's camp ends with the dawn, David taunts, not Saul, but Abiner and his troops (v. 14):

> Are you not a man without equal in Israel (הלוא איש אתה ומי כמיך בישראל)? So, why have you not guarded your master the king? Somebody came to destroy (להשחית) the king, your lord! This is not a good thing you have done, by God (חי יהוה); so you (pl.) deserve to die[72] (כי בני מות אתם), (you) who have not guarded your lord, the anointed of

---

[70] As Gunn (*The Fate of King Saul* [JSOTSS 12; Sheffield: JSOT Press, 1980] 102) notes.
[71] See also the remarks of Campbell, *1 Samuel*, 266–67.
[72] On this translation, see McCarter, *I Samuel*, 408. The shift from second person singular to second person plural in David's address spreads the blame from Abiner to all Saul's retainers.

Yahweh. Now, see the king's spear and the water flask that were near his head! (1 Sam. 26:15–16)

This mockery of Abiner focuses upon his utter helplessness, blaming him for neglect or perhaps even treachery ("what you have done"; הדבר הזה אשר עשית). Abiner has not lived up to his reputation as a great warrior and skillful commander, yet David frames this failure as a failure of his opponent's very identity as a male. On the other hand, David himself has bested other warriors and thus shown his superiority.

Third, there is a contest involving Abishai, whose bravery is unimpeachable (he dares to accompany David, while Ahimelek the Hittite[73] does not). Yet, David must restrain him from killing Saul with one lunge of the king's own spear (v. 9bα; ועתה אכנו נא בחנית[74] ובארץ פעם אחת). In discussing earlier the refusal of Saul's armorbearer to kill him,[75] I raised the possibility that the soldier's actions owed less to a fear of breaking a taboo against harming the king than of violating a code of warriorly conduct. Abishai is willing to take the risk of harming Yahweh's anointed and argues that the deity must have offered the opportunity to do so to him and David. Yet David refuses to acquiesce. The warrior must not take advantage of every opportunity offered to him, for who can be sure that the chance came from Yahweh? Who can preclude the possibility of divine punishment for such a deed? No, the true warrior must play by the rules, must be daring but must also risk the possibility that his opponent will not be. David allows Saul to remain the dangerous king.

Fourth, this brings us to the climax of the story, the tête-à-tête between David and the king. Vv. 17–21 portray the two men in conversation, the one pleading his innocence and his loyalty (אדני, עבדו/עבדך), the other acknowledging his guilt (חטאתי; v. 21) and more surprisingly his paternity (בני). David carefully portrays himself as the victim of the dangerous king, who pursues (רדף), seeks to kill (לבקש), and exiles to a pagan land (v. 19). Saul is the skilled warrior, the relentless pursuer whom the speech evokes. David, to be sure, has evaded these actions by his cleverness and piety, and yet

---

[73] Is the ethnicon a foreshadowing of Uriah the Hittite, who is too brave for his own good?
[74] With the LXX omit ו here (see McCarter, *I Samuel*, 405).
[75] In 1 Sam. 31; see above.

he downplays his skills even as he displays the spear that is the token and proof of them. He plays the role of the resourceful warrior while appearing to be the opposite. And by doing this, he exposes Saul as something less than he pretends to be. Moreover, while David does not accept the king's claim of (quasi-) paternity—"son" implies "father," which in turn implies that Saul has acted as a benevolent overlord and patron, though he has done nothing of the sort—David does not respond coldly,[76] but rather as one who seeks royal protection if not patronage at court (the due of a "son"). David asks for only the most fundamental rights of a loyal subject. At the same time, the rejection of fictive paternity is a claim to be dissimilar from Saul.

This leads to the final point about the dangerous king. Ultimately, the contest between David and Saul explores the ways in which Israelite culture expected a king to menace others: through warfare, police actions, curses, and so on. This exploration focuses repeatedly on the appropriate display of the body, which seems manipulatable. What it signifies is largely context-driven. For example, David can act like a madman by scratching and clawing and letting his spittle run into his beard, and this action appears as a clever ruse for saving his life from those who see him as a threat. Saul can genuinely lose control of his body (in ecstasy), and this marks him as one unfit to rule. Saul can pursue his enemy or hurl a spear at him, and these actions which mark him as a skilled warrior signify his manifest unfitness to rule. David can slay myriads or mutilate their genitalia, and this signal of his prowess marks him as a fit warrior, and eventually king. The dangerous king trope thus ultimately was concerned with the proper actions of the royal body and of the bodies around it.

Sometimes, to be sure, the victim could escape the royal wrath, often by playing the role of a superior male. Being more pious, more brave and daring, even quicker to honor responsiblities to the king who endangers one—all these could help one avoid danger. If I may put it this way, this message is encapsulated in the sign that is Saul's spear. Its placement by his head points to the fact that he is the head of the realm and that his head is anointed in order to protect him and his realm. The spear also signifies the fact that the monarch

---

[76] *Contra* Gunn, *King Saul*, 104.

can endanger even his own subjects. Yet, finally, David's theft of it also reminds one that signs sometimes are ways of lying,[77] and such is the case here. The spear is not an icon of Saul's power in battle, but the loss thereof. It is not Saul's body that is invincible or even a serious threat to others. It is David's, for he will soon become king.

The Endangered King

Complementing the story of Saul's pursuit of David is that of Absalom's revolt against the latter. While the literary relationship between 1 Sam. 16–2 Sam. 1, on the one hand, and 2 Sam. 15–19, on the other, remains an unsolved problem,[78] there are enough echoes between the two narrative complexes to suggest that they form a matching pair, at least in their present form. Some parallels include:

David	Absalom
Has a beautiful body	Has a beautiful body
Flees Saul's court	Flees David's court
Wins popularity by generalship	Wins popularity by jurisprudence

The equation David:Saul::Absalom:David becomes explicit in Shimei's curse of David in 2 Sam. 16:8:

> Yahweh has recompensed you for all the blood (דמי) of the family (בית) of Saul in whose place you rule (מלכת). And may Yahweh place the kingdom in the hand of your son Absalom. Your ruin is upon you, for you are a man of blood (איש דמים).

Shimei's curse helps the narrator to explain Absalom's revolt by asking whether it is somehow linked to Saul's relationship with David. Ultimately, this linkage fails to convince, but this is so because David plays successfully the role of the endangered king who thus escapes danger. But let us keep the investigation in its proper order.

While one may explain Absalom's revolt as owing to naked ambition or even an oedipal resentment of his father—certainly justified

---

[77] See Eco, *Theory of Semiotics*, 58.
[78] For a close link between the "Succession Narrative" and the "History of David's Rise" in general, see Otto Kaiser, "Some Observations on the Succession Narrative," OTWSA 27/28 (1984–85) 130–47; John van Seters, *In Search of History* (2d ed.; Winona Lake, IN: Eisenbrauns, 1997) 285; Ishida, *Royal Dynasties*, 54–80; but see Leonhard Rost, *Die Überlieferung von der Thronnachfolge Davids* (Stuttgart: Kohlhammer, 1926) 2–3. On 2 Sam. 15–20 as a unit, see Caquot and de Robert, *Livres des Samuel*, 525–26.

by David's failure to discipline Amnon[79]—the text does not explicitly embrace such explanations. It does, however, explore the nature of proper royal self-display. In doing so, it offers a sort of apology for David, who remains in spite of everything the model monarch.[80]

This exploration begins even before the mention of Absalom's plot. Just as 1 Sam. 10:23 describes Saul as the tallest man in the nation, and 1 Sam. 16:12 emphasizes David's beauty, so too does 2 Sam. 14:25 introduce Absalom as "the most handsome man in all Israel, exceedingly praiseworthy, from the sole of his feet to his head; there was no defect in him" (לא היה איש יפה בכל ישראל להלל מאד מכף רגלו ועד קדקדו לא היה בו מים). V. 26 emphasizes his luxuriant hair, which, in addition to marking him as virulent male in the manner of Samson (esp. Judg. 16), surely must be a merism for his entire head, and hence a sign pointing toward his worthiness to receive the royal anointing and thus to rule. What is more, the merism מכף רגלו ועד קדקדו ("from the sole of the feet to the crown of his head") invites the reader to think about every part of the prince's body. This implied *wasf* or poetic description of a human frame,[81] which is similar to texts from Song of Songs that I discussed earlier, understands Absalom's body as the locus of the contest between him and his father. At another level, the narrative in the rest of chapters 15–18 works out the implied comparison between his and everyone else's (including his father's) body. For example, his having sex with his father's concubines (2 Sam. 16:21–22) both asserts a claim to the throne and expresses the superiority of his penis to his father's.[82] Likewise, his head proves to be the instrument of his death (2 Sam. 18:9), his heart receives the fatal blow from Joab (2 Sam. 18:14), and his eyes approve the plan of Ahithophel but only temporarily (2 Sam. 17:4). His body fails him in the end.

---

[79] But on the motives of the characters, see Halpern, *David's Secret Demons*, 358.
[80] See McKenzie, *King David*, 172.
[81] I owe this genre identification, derived from Arabic poetry, to R. A. Carlson, *David, the chosen King: A Traditio-Historical Approach to the Second Book of Samuel* (Uppsala: Almqvist & Wiksell, 1964) 185.
[82] For (unconvincing) arguments against the older view that this represented a claim to the throne, see A. A. Anderson, *2 Samuel* (WBC 11; Dallas: Word, 1989) 214; following Ernst Würthwein, *Die Erzählung von der Thronfolge Davids* (Zurich: Theologischer Verlag, 1974) 39.

Though a dandy, Absalom shrewdly assumes the trappings of a proper king before launching his revolt.[83] The story of the revolt opens in 2 Sam. 15:1–6 by explaining his success at attracting a following: he parades about in a chariot leading an entourage of fifty troops; he settles cases for Israelites, allegedly on the king's behalf; and he greets his potential subjects with a kiss, eschewing the etiquette of the royal court, which demanded obeisance. In other words, Absalom manages to portray himself as one who has power and uses it innovatively and well, but does not allow it to make him proud. He becomes a grander version of the ordinary person.[84]

Upon launching his revolt, he forces David to beat a strategic retreat. Then, everything goes wrong, for Absalom makes a classic military blunder of failing to exploit his enemy's weakness. In the meantime, however, the narrator addresses the nature of the threatened king and his foes, not only through the detailed description of David's retreat in 2 Sam. 15:13–16:23, but especially through three speeches.

The first is the already mentioned curse by Shimei in 16:7–8. Here the narrator, through this hostile witness, offers one possible explanation for David's discomfiture, his alleged usurpation of Saul's throne. Anticipating the Chronicler's (1 Chron. 22:8) apologia for David's failure to build the temple, the narrator uses Shimei to define David by his unquestioned military prowess, but argues that this success has come back to haunt him. To be a warrior has consequences. The important point, however, is the king's response to Abishai: "Perhaps[85] Yahweh said to him, 'Curse David.' So who can say, 'Why have you done this?'" (v. 10; וכי יהוה אמר לו קלל את דוד ומי יאמר מדוע עשיתה כן). David has also retained his role as the ultimate interpreter of the divine will, just as he was when facing Saul (1 Sam. 24 and 26). It is tempting to cite here the Israelite proverb (Prov. 25:2): "God's province (lit. glory) is hiding a matter; the king's

---

[83] See Halpern, *David's Secret Demons*, 364.

[84] On this "poeticity of the commonplace," that is, the presenting of oneself as "ordinary," see Michael Herzfeld, "The Poeticity of the Commonplace," in Michael Herzfeld and Lucio Melazzo, eds., *Semiotic Theory and Practice: Proceedings of the Third International Congress of the IASS Palermo, 1984* (2 vols.; Berlin: de Gruyter, 1988) 1. 383–91.

[85] On כי at the beginning of a conditional sentence, see GKC §159aa–bb.

province is searching out a matter" (כבד אלהים הסתר דבר וכבד
מלכים חקר דבר).⁸⁶ David is not yet ruler when Saul pursues him,
but he is king in waiting and a fitter one than the present incumbent. Now in 2 Sam. 16, he again exercises his royal prerogative of
defining Yahweh's will.⁸⁷

What is more, the mention of Abishai here points the reader
toward 1 Sam. 26:20, where David, similarly menaced by a king,
calls himself a flea (פרעש) before Saul, and this in turn recalls 1 Sam.
24:15, where David similarly refers to himself as a "dead dog ... a
flea" (כלב מת ... פרעש אחד). So, when Abishai calls Shimei "this
dead dog" (הכלב המת הזה; 2 Sam. 16:9), the reader can hardly miss
the intertextual linkages. Shimei has assumed David's earlier role,
implicit to be sure, as the accuser of a king. Will David also assume
Saul's role as the dangerous monarch?

This he does not do, for he refuses to kill Shimei, raising the possibility that the latter's curses are divinely inspired, and simultaneously disarming them. David's response, in other words, belies the
description of the curse and thus removes him from the category of
the menacing king. In bodily terms, he refuses to use his warriorly
skill to remove a problem. What is at stake here is, then, not so
much David's personal piety (his willingness to seek the divine will
even when uncomfortable), but rather his ability to deal with his
Israelite subjects in a nonthreatening way. His innocence in question, David passes the first test. This becomes still more explicit in
vv. 11–12, where David describes himself as the king under threat
from his own son, who (like Saul!) "seeks my life" (מבקש את נפשי)
and then wishes for divine favor.

The second speech of importance is that of Hushai in 2 Sam.
17:8–10. A spy, this counselor offers the advice against which good
generals have often raged: "your enemy is too powerful; attack him
only when you are assured of success."⁸⁸ He frames his advice by
portraying David as the threatening king:

---

⁸⁶ On the connection of the "Succession Narrative" in general to "Wisdom" traditions, see R. N. Whybray, *The Succession Narrative: A Study of II Sam. 9–20 and 1
Kings 1 and 2* (SBT 9; Naperville, IL: Allenson, 1968) 56–95; Larry Lyke, *King David
with the Wise Woman of Tekoa: The Resonance of Tradition in Parabolic Narrative* (JSOTSS
255; Sheffield: Sheffield Academic Press, 1997).

⁸⁷ The narrator confirms David's analysis (or fond wish!) by noting in 2 Sam.
17:14 that Yahweh contravened Ahithophel's counsel "because he wished to bring
evil upon Absalom" (לבעבור הביא יהוה אל אבשלום את הרעה).

⁸⁸ Note, e.g., the words of Ulysses S. Grant to his generals during the 1864 cam-

You [Absalom] know that your father and his men are warriors (גברים) and that they are enraged like a bear bereft (of its cubs) in a field, or a sow snared in the wild[89] and your father is a man of war who does not lodge with troops (העם). Even now he is hidden in some pit or some place.... And even the valiant man with a heart like a lion's will melt with fear, for all Israel knows that your father is a warrior, as are the troops with him (2 Sam. 17:8–9a, 10).

This extraordinary bit of deception succeeds because it plays on David's well-deserved reputation as a wily and fearless warrior skilled in single combat ("does not lodge with the troops"). He can survive in the field without the supply train and servants he would have had when with the army. This means, further, that his body is physically fit, trained (cf. Ps. 144), and thus appropriate for a king. Hushai's deception also succeeds because it draws upon the stories of David's encounters with Saul, in which he was forced to hide in caves.

Ironically, too, Hushai contrasts David with all other males, and implicitly therefore Absalom himself. If a man with a lion's heart fears David, this must be because as king he has a different, and superior kind of heart. He is the dangerous king nonpareil, whose menace only the entire nation in a levee en masse can overcome. Under the circumstances of the moment, of course, this picture of David is absurd: he is on the run and dares not slay even an unarmed man cursing him. Although he is, in fact, the endangered king against whom the entire people has revolted, his reputation is such that Absalom fears to seize the initiative. Hushai overcomes the realities of dangers to the king by evoking past successes and portraying David's as the body of a warrior.

This blunder leads inevitably to Absalom's defeat and death at the hands of Joab (2 Sam. 18:14–15). David lives up to his reputation as the dangerous king, but he does so because he plays the role of the endangered one flawlessly. He submits to the divine will but also shrewdly plants spies in the right places. He shows mercy to opponents and generosity to friends. He does not even seek the death

---

paign in Virginia: "Oh, I am heartily tired of hearing what Lee is going to do.... Go back to your command, and try to think what we are going to do ourselves, instead of what Lee is going to do." (In Mark E. Neely, *The Last Best Hope on Earth: Abraham Lincoln and the Promise of America* [Cambridge: Harvard University Press, 1993] 76).

[89] The reference to the sow has fallen out of MT but survives in LXX (καὶ ὡς ὗς τραχέια ἐν τῷ πεδιῷ), perhaps owing to haplography (McCarter, *II Samuel*, 382) or to a deliberate omission of reference to swine (but see Smith, *Books of Samuel*, 351).

of his rebellious son. If the story of Absalom is about David under the curse,[90] it is a reversible curse.

Yet, at this point his performance almost fails, as does the narrator's apology. He weeps loudly and openly before his troops, demoralizing them (2 Sam. 19:4). While public mourning has its place in a warrior's life,[91] here David does so for the wrong reasons and with a surfeit of emotion (בכה... ויתאבל... לאט את פניו ויזעק [19:2, 5]). And, here the third crucial speech occurs: in 2 Sam. 19:6-8, Joab demands that David stifle his grief and show himself to his troops. He accuses David of preferring his enemies to his friends and of wishing the latter dead. He even threatens to abandon David, thus exposing him to the worst calamity of his life (הרעה אשר באה עליך מנעריך עד עתה; v. 8b), that is, implicitly a danger greater than those he faced from Saul and Absalom. In short, Joab says, David has become a danger to his supporters rather than his foes and has failed to present himself with the restraint and gratitude proper to a king. Still, for the narrator, this infelicitous self-display by David at his moment of triumphant transition from the dangerous to the endangered king serves paradoxically to exonerate him of charges of profiting from the death of his own son.

To summarize this section, I note that the presentation of the endangered king is much less expansive than that of the dangerous one. Here, as in the royal psalms, Israelites emphasized the dangers that a king presented to his enemies and downplayed any risks to himself that he might take (hence, e.g., the fact that no one ever pursues [רדף] the king). In the books of Kings, meanwhile, kings in danger usually die, as we have seen. The trope of the endangered king, then, finds fullest expression in the story of Absalom's revolt, where the tension between David the menacing and David the menaced is a prime engine of narrative movement.

The body of the endangered king inverts that of the dangerous king. The former runs, hides, fails to have sex with the right people, and may appear less attractive than someone else's body. Yet, as the

---

[90] Carlson (*David, the chosen King*) divides all of 2 Samuel 2-24 into two sections: David under blessing and David under curse. This seems a considerable oversimplification, since David here avoids the worst results of the curse. Rather, one should say that the narrator toys with the notion of David's being cursed but ultimately lets him off the hook.

[91] See Ps. 89; more broadly, Launderville, *Piety and Politics*, 242-51.

Absalom and David story makes clear, who is dangerous and who endangered is open to interpretation, precisely because the display of the body is variable in the hands of a skilled performer of gendered display (like David and unlike Absalom). Absalom's famous physical beauty, his sexual exploits with his father's concubines, his self-presentation with a chariot and retinue—all of this cannot create for him the proper royal body, which must also be hardened by war but above all submitted to the training of Yahweh. Such a body comes into being at the coronation and is reinforced by acts of piety, as well as warfare and self-display.

The King as Medical Patient

A special case of the dangerous/endangered king is the monarch as a medical patient. Since royal illness was an index of the sickness of the body politic, it was understandably a less popular topic in the ancient Near East than warfare was, but nevertheless was the subject of epic, as in the Ugaritic story of Kirta, or in the massive correspondence of an Esarhaddon.[92] Stories of past royal illnesses also apparently circulated at the Neo-Assyrian royal court during the seventh century BCE, at least.[93] This is hardly surprising, since the king's health is a central political concern of a monarchy. A few stories in Samuel-Kings speak to this problem.

It is noteworthy that here the monarch does not fall victim to an evil spirit in the manner of Saul. With the notable exception of the "leprosy" (צרעת, מצרע) of Uzziah/Azariah in 2 Kings 15:5 and especially the expansion in 2 Chron. 26:19–21,[94] sickness is not necessarily of divine origin, though the deity does take interest in healing or intervenes in other ways.[95] The king must seek Yahweh's aid, and failure to do so results in tragedy, for the sick ruler and his subjects. Two stories, those of Ahaziah and Hezekiah, illustrate these points.[96]

---

[92] See the letters in Parpola, *Letters from Assyrian Scholars* (vol. 1); Steven Cole and Peter Machinist, *Letters from Priests to the Kings Esarhaddon and Assurbanipal* (SAAS 13; Helsinki: Helsinki University Press, 1999).

[93] See Letter 247, ll. 8ff., in Parpola, *Letters from Assyrian Scholars*, 1. 190–91; see also (later) Dan. 4:19–36.

[94] The Chronicler expands the story of Kings, making the ruler's fate the result of cultic violations. The king who would stand before Yahweh receives the ultimate bodily disqualification for such an undertaking.

[95] See the discussion of Yahweh in 2 Kings 1:2–17 in Burke O. Long, *2 Kings* (FOTL 10; Grand Rapids: Eerdmans, 1991) 12–15.

[96] See also the tale of Uzziah/Azariah in 2 Kings 15:5.

The first tale of illness appears in 2 Kings 1:2–17. Here Ahaziah of Israel accidentally falls through a lattice on the roof of his palace (apparently a *bīt ḫilāni*)[97] and is mortally wounded. He seeks the aid of the god Baal-zebul of Ekron, much to the dismay of Elijah, who rains fire upon the hapless messengers of the king. The king dies, as the prophet promises. He dies out of physical and religious clumsiness: physical in that he falls out of his own house (while intoxicated? but the text does not say), religious because he seeks aid from the wrong deity. His religious mistake also brings divine vengeance upon his subjects, the military messengers. That is, the endangered king who does not play his role correctly becomes the dangerous one who may hurt the innocent. Royal sickness or injury demands the intervention of Yahweh lest the sickness of the royal body become an index of the sickness of the body politic.

The second sickness story concerns Hezekiah. 2 Kings 20:1–11 has a parallel in Isaiah 38, discussed previously. As Blenkinsopp notes, the two versions differ somewhat in that the Isaiah version decouples the Kings version's linkage between sickness and sin. Royal illness is not necessarily an index of past or future royal failure, and thus has limited signification to the state.[98] Here it suffices to examine v. 6aβ–b: "... and from the grasp (וּמִכַּף) of the king of Assyria shall I rescue you and this city. And I will protect this city for my own sake and for the sake of David my servant" (וּמִכַּף מֶלֶךְ אַשּׁוּר אַצִּילְךָ וְאֵת הָעִיר הַזֹּאת וְגַנּוֹתִי עַל הָעִיר הַזֹּאת לְמַעֲנִי וּלְמַעַן דָּוִד עַבְדִּי). Cogan and Tadmor are probably correct to suggest that this verse argues for an original placement of the pericope before 2 Kings 18:13.[99] As Blenkinsopp notes, the Isa. 38 and 2 Kings 18 versions of the story differ in that the former decouples the latter's linkage between sickness and sin.[100] The royal body may become ill through no fault of its own. Sickness is not necessarily an index of royal failure, though it may be. Even in its current position, however, the text retains the close linkage between two ideas: danger to the king in illness par-

---

[97] On the architecture, see James A. Montgomery and Henry Snyder Gehman, *The Book of Kings* (ICC; Edinburgh: T. & T. Clark, 1951) 349; Jean-Claude Margueron, "Palace," in Eric Meyers, ed., *Oxford Encyclopedia of Archaeology in the Near East* (5 vols.; Oxford: Oxford University Press, 1997) 4:197–200.

[98] Joseph Blenkinsopp, *Isaiah 1–39* (AB 19; New York: Doubleday, 2000) 482–83.

[99] Mordechai Cogan and Hayim Tadmor, *II Kings* (AB 11; New York: Doubleday, 1988).

[100] Blenkinsopp, *Isaiah 1–39*, 483–83.

allels that to his people from foreign invaders. Healing Hezekiah will allow Yahweh to rescue his city (note, not Judah as a whole!) from foreign occupation.

While the oracle of reprieve explains Yahweh's action as a case of his keeping his promise to David (cf. 2 Sam. 7; Ps. 89), this does not occur until Hezekiah has appealed to divine honor by recounting his own actions as king (v. 3). When Isaiah calls Yahweh the god of David (אלהי דוד; v. 5) and has the deity appeal to the covenant with the ancestral king in v. 6, all this means is that Hezekiah in v. 3 has invoked the Davidic covenant and offered a specific interpretation of it. The promise of dynastic survival becomes one of the long life of the incumbent on the throne. Hezekiah thus says that his present illness belies his own loyalty to the covenant, his own public acts of rule (whether temple restoration or the administration of justice), and thus his own self-display. Yahweh is obliged to rectify the disjuncture between the king's actions and his present bodily limitations. Since Hezekiah has disciplined his body properly and has acted justly, Yahweh must heal his illness. The royal bodies, the biosocial one and the body politic, must be whole at the same time, and the health of one is a precondition of the health of the other.

Summary

In their treatment of the dangerous and endangered king, and a subspecies of the latter, the king who is ill, the tradents of Samuel-Kings both acknowledge and radically subvert the exploration of these same themes in the royal psalms, where the king pursues but is never pursued, where he may menace his foes but not his righteous subjects, where rectitude and prowess go together. That is, the stock of motifs present in the royal psalms, and perhaps antedating all the biblical texts, informs these narratives almost completely, but the narrators are free to manipulate the motifs to tell their stories.

The endangered body is one whose meaning is under negotiation. Will the king live or die? Will he be sexually humiliated? His inferior physical appearance signals his danger, as may his sickness. The negotiation takes place as the king and other actors seek to shape their society.[101] The royal body could either menace his enemies or

---

[101] See Launderville, *Piety and Politics*, 93–99.

his subjects, or it could be in danger itself. The last two options endangered society at large and thus the successful king must enact the menacing role with just the right touch.

The King as Eulogist

As we saw in the discussion of Ps. 45 in Chapter 2, an important part of the public role of the kings of Israel and Judah was oratory.[102] In the royal propaganda expressed in that psalm, this oratorical gift found expression by means of an altered mouth and lips, which Yahweh created especially for the king.

In the narratives in Samuel-Kings, this feature of kingship also plays a prominent role, especially in the stories of the dangerous and endangered king. The monarch who builds also orates. But one story explores this royal function and the use of the body that it requires especially well. It is the story of David's supervision of, and oration at the funeral of Abiner in 2 Sam. 3:31–39.[103]

The only extended biblical description of a funeral, this text seeks to exonerate David of wrongdoing in the death of Abiner, and to shift blame to Joab.[104] V. 37 makes this explicit: "On that very day, all the army (כל העם) and all Israel knew that it was not the king's doing (לא ... מהמלך) to kill Abiner son of Ner." How did they know?

David achieves this through the manipulation of his and his followers' bodies. First, he orders a change of raiment, weeping, and breast-beating[105] for his followers, and he himself leads the funeral bier.[106] While David does not himself join in the mourning practices,

---

[102] See also the discussion in ibid., 57–98.
[103] Alexander Achilles Fischer (*Von Hebron nach Jerusalem: Eine redaktionsgeschichtliche Studie zur Erzählung von König David in II Sam 1–5* [BZAW 335; Berlin: de Gruyter, 2004] 126–65) takes the funeral oration to be a later addition, though his rather mechanical redaction-critical analysis offers no conclusive reason for that claim. I follow here Campbell and O'Brien, *Unfolding the Deuternomistic History*, in taking 2 Sam. 3 as basically a well-knit unit from a pre-DH strand.
[104] *Contra* James Vanderkam, "Davidic Complicity in the Deaths of Abner and Eshbaal: A Rhetorical and Redactional Study," in idem, *From Revelation to Canon: Studies in the Hebrew Bible and Second Temple Literature* (JSJSup 62; Leiden: Brill, 2000) 31–52.
[105] On ספד ("to beat the breast") as a mourning custom, see Mayer Gruber, *Aspects of Nonverbal communication in the Ancient Near East* (Studia Pohl 12/1–2; 2 vols.; Rome: Biblical Institute Press, 1980) 2. 437–56, esp. 447.
[106] On the possibility that David's "going (הלך) before the bier" implies dancing, see Eileen F. de Ward, "Mourning Customs in *1, 2 Samuel*," *JJS* 23 (1972) 20–21.

he does lead the cortege. Second, at the gravesite he makes an oration that praises Abiner as a great warrior who deserved to die in a more fitting way.[107] At the same time, he labels the killers criminals: "You fell as one falls before a criminal" (כנפול לפני בני עולה נפלת; v. 34aγ). I think that McCarter misses the point here when he proposes to emend the text to delete לפני and read, "you fell like a criminal."[108] MT makes good sense and as it stands it serves David's purpose of turning blame from himself to others. The oration not only rehabilitates Abiner as a warrior who deserves the praise of the king, but it presents the king as one who deserves to eulogize a warrior.

David's third and final bodily manipulation is his refusal to eat (v. 35), which apparently is his way of keeping the mourning going. He avoids the meal following the obsequies in order to show his grief or, since fasting was also a penitential rite, his remorse for the death. In any case, this led to his popular approval.

This episode closes with one last royal speech, in which David blames the "sons of Zeruiah" for Abiner's death (v. 39). With evidence of their wrongdoing, he could either lead a coverup or punish the guilty parties. The first alternative was unbefitting a king, as well as impractical; the second was politically inexpedient, especially if a case could be made that Joab was merely avenging his brother's death. David takes neither option: he blames his minions but does not punish them. Far from being a sign of his fecklessness,[109] this is evidence of his political adroitness and his royal bearing. Notice that 2 Sam. 3:31–39 refers to David five times as המלך, emphasizing the new status and dignity he has acquired as a result of besting the house of Saul. As king, his words of judgment have power (they are performative utterances), and so Joab does not escape punishment even though he remains in power.

David's oratory, finally, works because it is part of a series of felicitous ritual actions that his audience regards as successfully conveying

---

[107] See the analysis by J. P. Fokkelman, *Narrative Art and Poetry in the Books of Samuel*, vol. 3: *Throne and City (II Sam. 2–8 & 21–24)* (Assen: van Gorcum, 1990) 111–13.

[108] McCarter, *II Samuel*, 111. On the other hand, the reading of 4QSam^a in v. 34 might support this interpretation. I would argue, however, that this longer reading deliberately alters the older text, represented by MT both to clarify it and to push more of the blame onto Abiner. For the text critical issues, see Donald W. Parry, "The Aftermath of Abner's Murder," *Textus* 20 (2000) 83–96.

[109] *Contra* Caquot and de Robert, *Livres des Samuel*, 382.

his message. He disciplines his body in public and labels the body of a fallen foe as one similarly disciplined. Fasting, parading, and speaking are bodily actions that mark him as the worthy king. He is not the menacing ruler, nor is he any longer endangered. He is the monarch whose words are gracious, to friend and foe alike.

The King as Builder

Although ancient Near Eastern monarchs regularly portrayed themselves as builders of palaces and temples,[110] and such buildings served to educate the populace in the ways of subordination,[111] the Israelite evidence for the king as builder centers almost exclusively around the construction of the temple in Jerusalem. Since the primary temple-building narrative (1 Kings 5–9) is overwhelmingly Deuteronomistic with even later retouchings,[112] it is difficult to use this material as evidence for beliefs and practices prior to the seventh or eighth century. In any event, these stories impinge on the conceptions of the

---

[110] For the Assyrian expression of convention of the king as builder, see Sylvie Lackenbacher, *Le roi bâtisseur: Les récits de consruction assyriens des origines à Teglatphalasar III* (Paris: ERC, 1982); for Palestine see Jan-Waalke Meyer, "Tempel und Palastbauten im eisenzeitlichen Palästina und ihre bronzezeitlichen Vorbilder," in Bernd Janowski, Klaus Koch, and Gernot Wilhelm, eds., *Religionsgeschichtliche Beziehungen zwischen Kleinasien, Nordsyrien und dem Alten Testament* (OBO 129; Göttingen: Vandenhoeck & Ruprecht, 1993) 319–28. On temples, see Victor (Avigdor) Hurowitz, *I Have Built You an Exalted House: Temple Building in the Bible in Light of Mesopotamian and Northwest Semitic Writings* (JSOTSS 115; Sheffield: Sheffield Academic Press, 1992).

[111] John Malcolm Russell, *Sennacherib's Palace Without Rival at Nineveh* (Chicago: University of Chicago Press, 1991) on one dramatic case of a palace being an instrument of royal self-presentation.

[112] For a Dtr.² date, see Jon Levenson, "From Temple to Synagogue: 1 Kings 8," in Baruch Halpern and Jon Levenson, eds., *Traditions in Transformation: Turning Points in Biblical Faith* (Winona Lake: Eisenbrauns, 1981) 143–66. On possible post-Deuteronomistic additions to this text, see Sebastian Grätz, *Der strafende Wettergott: Erwägungen zur Traditionsgeschichte des Adad-Fluchs im Alten Orient und im Alten Testament* (BBB 114; Bodenheim: PHILO, 1998) 276–79; but see Hurowitz (*I Have Built*, 285–310), who argues (310) that the composer of the prayer of Solomon "was familiar with a literary pattern (known to us almost exclusively from Assyrian inscriptions) according to which a building story was concluded with conditional blessings and curses addressed to a future king who would find the current building in ruins." This is not to deny, however, a basic historical core to the story of Solomon's building the temple; see William G. Dever, "Archaeology and the 'Age of Solomon': A Case-Study in Archaeology and Historiography," in Lowell K. Handy, ed., *The Age of Solomon: Scholarship at the Turn of the Millennium* (Leiden: Brill, 1997) 217–51, esp. 229.

king's body only in incidental ways. 1 Kings 8, for example, portrays Solomon standing before the altar with hands raised to draw public attention. The chapter portrays a king as one who can stand before God (not necessarily as a priest)[113] and receive divine favor.

As is well known, 2 Sam. 7 and the reworked parallel text in 1 Chron. 28 seek to explain David's failure to build the temple as an act of obedience to the divine mandate. The secondary literature on these texts is vast, and rehearsing all the issues involved would serve no purpose here.[114] The stories become relevant, however, when one considers the explanations they offer for David's failure to build the temple. As part of a strategy of rewriting its source,[115] 1 Chron. 28:3 supplements 2 Samuel's simple divine fiat with the statement, "You shall not build a temple in my honor, for you are a warrior and you have spilled blood" (לא תבנה בית לשמי כי איש מלחמות אתה ודמים שפכת). This explanation seems very strange when one recalls that Near Eastern kings routinely boasted of both their temple building and their war-making, often in the same text. Indeed, Ps. 144:1 envisions Yahweh training the king in martial arts (המלמד ידי לקרב אצבעותי למלחמה). Moreover, in the context of 2 Samuel-1 Kings, the Chronicler's explanation would appear absurd, since Solomon begins his reign with a bloody purge of his enemies. This is true, even though the Chronicler bases his argument on an exegesis of his sources: David's preoccupation with fighting changes from an unfortunate necessity to a simple vice.[116] Note, however, that the Chronicler

---

[113] That the king may preside in the cult as a priest *ex officio* is clear even from the Assyrian practice, where the monarch is a temple sponsor or administrator (*šangu*), patron, and even sacrificer (see Brigitte Menzel, *Assyrische Tempel* (Studia Pohl Series Maior 10; 2 vols.; Rome Biblical Institute Press, 1981) 1. 173.

[114] Among recent studies, see e.g., Manfred Görg, *Gott-König-Reden in Israel und Ägypten* (BWANT 105; Stuttgart: Kohlhammer, 1975) 178–268 (on Egyptian parallels); Lyle Eslinger, *House of God or House of David: The Rhetoric of 2 Samuel 7* (JSOTSS 164; Sheffield: JSOT Press, 1994); Stephen Pisano, "'2 Samuel 5–8 et le Deutéronomiste: critique textuelle ou critique littéraire?" in Albert de Pury, Thomas Römer, and Jean-Daniel Macchi, eds., *Israël construit son histoire* (Geneva: Labor et Fides, 1996) 237–63; and B. Renaud, "Un oracle prophétique (2 Samuel 7, 1–17) invalidé? Une approche du Psaume 89 (88)," in Jean-Georges Heintz, *Oracles et prophéties dans l'antiquité* (Paris: de Boccard, 1997) 215–29.

[115] On which see Sara Japhet, *I & II Chronicles* (OTL; Louisville: Westminster/John Knox, 1993) 485–87.

[116] See Roddy Braun, "Solomon, the Chosen Temple Builder: the Significance of 1 Chronicles 22, 28, and 29 for the Theology of Chronicles," *JBL* 95 (1976) 581–90; Mark A. Throntveit, *When Kings Speak: Royal Speech and Royal Prayer in Chronicles* (SBLDS 98; Atlanta: Scholars, 1987) 86–87; the choice of Solomon for

completely recasts the Succession Narrative, both by making David a vigorous king until the end, one who chooses Solomon well in advance of his own death, and then by omitting all mention of the purges. In 1–2 Chronicles, Solomon does begin as a man of peace, even if he does create a military apparatus (2 Chron. 1:14–17). This is to say that the Chronicler is consistent in his view of David as a bloody king and Solomon as a peaceful one, though this picture is won at the expense of fidelity to the author's sources. Since Chronicles, as William Riley has recently argued, sought to explain the end of the Davidic dynasty and the paradoxical perdurance of the Davidic promise in the form of the temple cult itself,[117] the recasting of Solomon as a man of peace befitting his name allows the author to explore the different options of royal self-presentation and to show how each fails to insure the survival of monarchy. Nevertheless, the author continues, Israel endures through its temple.

The Chronicler's (brilliant, but idiosyncratic) rethinking of the connection between king and cult merely highlights, however, the fact that during the Iron Age, the warrior king could also be a temple builder. His body's training for war and then the use of that training did not render him impure or unfit to build the house of Yahweh, which, of course, lay in proximity to his own. It was only during the period of Israelite statelessness that blood on his hands disqualified him from the job, at least for the Chronicler.

To summarize, narratival evidence of the Israelite or Judahite kings as builders is rare for the preexilic period, but this very silence is telling. The military aspects of the kingly ideal apparently overwhelmed all other considerations. The king was a warrior first and last.

---

the Chronicler reflects his larger conception of "rest" (מנוחה), on which see Gerhard von Rad, "There Remains Still a Rest for the People of God: An Investigation of a Biblical Conception," in idem, *The Problem of the Hexateuch and Other Essays* (New York: McGraw-Hill, 1966) esp. 97–98.

[117] William Riley, *King and Cultus in Chronicles* (JSOTSS 160; Sheffield: JSOT Press, 1993) esp. 203.

Conclusions

To conclude, this and the previous chapters' exploration of biblical narratives about kings has argued that these tales drew upon a fairly well-defined stock of motifs, adumbrated in the royal psalms and paralleled elsewhere in the ancient Near East, and then manipulated them for various purposes. The proper nature of the royal body, its display and care, and the response of subjects to it were important topics because, in part, they allowed Israelites to reflect on their ideals and experience of human governance and politics.

This body, while it was constituted ritually at the coronation, also was the subject of constant negotiation and contestation involving the king, his subjects and foes, and the deity. A given bodily display might mean several different things (such as mad behavior disqualifying one for kingship or a clever ruse permitting survival), depending on what it signified to actors other than the king. That is, *body* exists always within a network of signs that give it meaning.

Although the royal psalms (with the exception of Ps. 89) present the Judahite king as an all-conquering hero, the narratives about these kings present them as dangerous or endangered. The narrative texts do not do this by rejecting the courtly notions of the royal psalms outright, but by telling tales about how those notions took shape in the course of complex events. Thus, for example, Saul pursues David rather than being pursued by him, and this type of chase is what the psalms make us expect of an Israelite king trained for war by Yahweh. Yet Saul's pursuit does not demonstrate his prowess, but rather the cleverness of his foe, which is not what the psalms lead us to anticipate. In other words—and one may multiply examples here—the "proper" motions and display of the royal body derive their propriety, not from a static ideology (adumbrated in the psalms) that one either accepts or rejects, but from a set of conventions (sign relationships) that various actors use for their own purposes.

Now, when we say *body*, we inevitably also mean *gender*, and one subtext of these narratives is the manliness of the monarch. How does he compare to other men (and to women *mutatis mutandis*)? Mere physical strength or size does not a man or a king make, as the Saul stories illustrate. The king, as a male and a warrior, must also show by turn slyness, remorse, compassion, or grief, as well as boldness. David is the exemplary model of all of this, as we have seen, and later rulers referred themselves to him (as in the case of Hezekiah in 2 Kings 20, for example). Like all models, he is also inimitable; none of his successors can equal his skill at self-display and bodily self-control.

Finally, most of the attention here has been on the Saul and David cycles in 1–2 Samuel because these stories with their unparalleled sophistication include most of the moments in a king's life when the signification of the body is important. As will be seen in the following chapter, many of these moments and the themes surrounding them continue to inform the discussion of foreign kings and eventually of Israelite males in general as the society works out what the king as male means within the network of meanings that is Israelite culture.

CHAPTER SEVEN

THE BODY OF THE FOREIGN KING

In the propaganda of the Israelite states, the foreign king figures as a vulnerable enemy, weak in body and mind, a foolhardy braggart whose incessant threats will come to naught. Thus in Ps. 2, these rulers rage (רגש) and take up arms against the deity and his משיח. Put another way, the foreign king's body is not prepared for warfare, his public boasting about his skills is wrongheaded and thus his self-display is infelicitous. Some non-official Israelite texts also take up this view, while in others this stereotype of the foreign king disappears, in part under the pressure of external political events, and in part owing to the collision of the official ideal with other views of reality.

The biblical tradents knew of rulers of countries other than their own, as far afield as Nubia and Mesopotamia, whom they called מלכים and whose exploits (read: ravages) they sought to understand. Thus biblical texts preserve pieces of the self-presentations of these kings, but also reconfigure them to fit preexisting pictures of kings deriving from the Israelite monarchs and their self-presentation. Israelites, notably the prophets, fitted knowledge about the bodily self-presentation of foreign kings into a mythic matrix in which the foreign king was always a failed warrior (as seen in Ps. 2). To be sure, many texts talk about all too real foreign victories over Israel and Judah, but in these texts by and large the foreign royal body does not come into view except in the most superficial way.

Though diverse in genre, date, point of origin, and historicity, the mentions of foreign kings in the Bible exhibit certain patterns. First, the extent of description varies with the date of encounter. The conquest tradition contains only the barest traces of the humanity of the Iron I petty Palestinian kings. (This probably is yet another indication of the chronological remove of the texts from the events they report.) Rulers of neighboring Iron Age Syro-Palestinian kingdoms receive more extensive treatment, and the self-display of the emperors who overran the Israelite kingdoms still more.

Second, the focus is, not surprisingly, on the martial aspects of kingship, though not exclusively so and not always in the same ways.

The foreign rulers' self-predication as builder or priest and purifier mostly disappears, probably because Israelites experienced these kings primarily as invaders.[1] Although Israel and Judah at times allied themselves with neighboring polities (as against Shalmaneser III, for example), allied kings receive no detailed attention in the Bible. The foreign king is *ipso facto* the dangerous king in Israelite tradition (exceptions include Hiram of Tyre and the Edomite king in 2 Kings 3). On the other hand, in comparison to some Neo-Assyrian inscriptions with their baroque invective against the enemy king,[2] the biblical narratives tend to be almost restrained, as if the text wished to give the foreigner his due. This state of affairs doubtless owes something to the Deuteronomistic (mostly) distrust of Israelite monarchy, but the restraint also exists in the inscriptions of other Levantine states,[3] and so must be part of a broader mindset and thus a literary convention.

Third, the warrior facing the foreign king is typically not the Israelite ruler, but Yahweh. This disappearance of the human Israelite king presents a theological problem. While it is true that the royal psalms certainly emphasize divine leadership and aid in battle,[4] so much so that the triumph comes even when the human king's generalship fails (Ps. 144:10–11), the failure to present the king of Israel as a co-combatant in many non-official texts is very striking. Nor can we resort to dating all of the texts late.[5] Rather, it should be clear that in the prophetic circles that produced both the so-called "oracles against the nations" and many of the tales of defeat of for-

---

[1] Another possible (complementary, not contradictory) reason for the disappearance of these motifs is that non-Israelite texts depicting the king as purifier, priest, sponsor of temples, builder, etc., emphasize his relationship with various deities, whom Israelites also saw as enemies of Yahweh.

[2] To take one of many possible examples, consider the case of Ahunu of Bit-Adini, whom Shalmaneser III describes as "swaggering about with might and main" (*šipsu u danānu iltakanu*; RIMA 0.102.20 ll. 8; cf. 0.102.5 iii 4), and in summary inscriptions (in the paragraph concerning the third year's campaign) as being fearful. The Assyrians' enemies are craven, not shrewd or fearless.

[3] See for example KAI 24 (noting opposition to Kilamuwa's rule); 202 A 4; and see below.

[4] E.g., Pss. 20; 21; 89; 144; see Martin Klingbeil, *Yahweh Fighting from Heaven: God as Warrior and as God of Heaven in the Hebrew Psalter and Ancient Near Eastern Iconography* (OBO 169; Göttingen: Vandenhoeck & Ruprecht, 1999); William P. Brown, *Seeing the Psalms: A Theology of Metaphor* (Louisville: Westminster John Knox, 2002) 199–203.

[5] See the arguments of William Schniedewind, *How the Bible Became a Book* (Cambridge: Cambridge University Press, 2004).

eign rulers now embedded in the DH, the human king of Israel and Judah, if he did not drop out of consideration altogether, at least receded far into the background before the warriorly skills of Yahweh. The circles that produced these texts were not slavishly following the government line, but were in many cases subverting it.

Now let us examine these traditions about the bodies of the foreign king, beginning with those ruling in the land eventually claimed by Israel, then proceeding outward, first to neighboring polities, and then beyond to the ancient superpowers of Egypt, Assyria, and Babylonia. The goal is the recovery of narrative conventions about the body of the foreign king and then the general political realities lying behind them.

Kings in the Conquest Tradition

For Israelite storytellers of Iron II, the ancient foes of the era of national formation appeared as mighty warriors whose ultimate failure before the onslaught of Yahweh symbolized the divine reordering of the world as a place in which power concentrated in the hands of those trained for it by the deity. The failed royal body indexed the failed opposition of the forces of chaos to the deity.

To begin, Josh. 10 and 12 present lists of local Cis- and Transjordanian rulers allegedly conquered by Moses and Joshua. Whatever the historical value of these lists,[6] they indicate Israel's willingness to recognize that ritual creation of a royal body was not efficacious in the face of Yahweh's military opposition (a theme of the royal propaganda as well). The two notices, often repeated, that do offer something concern Og and Sihon, rulers in Transjordan. The two form an inseparable pair in Israelite tradition.[7] Og retained the

---

[6] On which, see, e.g., John Van Seters, *In Search of History: Historiography in the Ancient World and the Origins of Biblical History* (reprint ed.; Winona Lake: Eisenbrauns, 1997) 329–30 (who attributes the lists to Dtr. and P respectively); on the nonexistence of a unified conquest, see e.g., J. Maxwell Miller, "Israelite History," in Douglas A. Knight and Gene M. Tucker, eds., *The Hebrew Bible and its Modern Interpreters* (Chico, CA: Scholars, 1985) 10–12; Israel Finkelstein, *Archaeology of the Israelite Settlement* (Jerusalem: Israel Exploration Society, 1988); William Dever, *What Did the Biblical Writers Know & When Did They Know It?* (Grand Rapids: Eerdmans, 2001) 119–22.

[7] Num. 21:21–30; Deut. 1:4; 2:24–3:11; 29:6; 31:4; Josh. 2:10; 9:10; 12:2ff.; Pss. 135:11; 136:20.

reputation of being a giant, a vestige of the Rephaim (מיתר הרפאים; Deut. 3:11; Josh. 12:4), whose gigantic iron bed (ערש)[8] survived for centuries in Rabbath Ammon.[9] His gigantism is unique among kings in the Bible,[10] an interesting fact indicating that Israelite writers in describing other rulers resisted any tendency toward understanding outsized power in terms of an outsized body.[11] Put another way, the mythic grid into which the ancients could squeeze history did not permit the creation of oversized human beings except in this one case, where a physical artifact (a bed) offered evidence of gigantism. The bed was an index of the king's massive body but paradoxically of his failure as a warrior—the chief artifact of his reign remains precisely his place of repose from warfare.

Sihon, meanwhile, remains a mighty warrior in the war song in Num. 21:27b–30, which does not easily fit into the conquest tradition itself. This ancient,[12] fragmentary poem apparently celebrates Sihon's destruction of cities throughout Moab.[13] In its narrative setting, the poem functions as an *a minore ad maius* argument: if Sihon conquered Moab, and Israel subdued Sihon, Israel can conquer Moab. In using an older song apparently against its own internal logic, Israel does not denigrate the warriorly skills of this foe, but rather sees those skills as proof of its own virtue. The foreign king is not always merely a "monster."[14] The king's self-display as a mighty

---

[8] Was this "bed" a sarcophagus? For arguments pro and con, see A. R. Millard, "King Og's Bed and Other Ancient Ironmongery," in Lyle Eslinger and G. Taylor, eds., *Ascribe to the Lord: Biblical and Other Studies in Memory of Peter C. Craigie* (Sheffield: JSOT Press, 1988) 481–92; T. C. Mitchell, "Furniture in the West Semitic Texts," in Georgina Herrmann, ed., *The Furniture of Western Asia, Ancient and Traditional* (Mainz: von Zabern, 1996) 59.

[9] Deut. 3:11. The bed was 9 X 4 cubits (ca. 4.5 X 2 m). It is conceivable that the enormity of this trophy led to the tradition that Og was a giant.

[10] Though it is part of a larger tradition, on which see Lothar Perlitt, "Riesen im Alten Testament: Ein literarisches Motiv im Wirkungsfeld des Deuteronomismus," in idem, *Deuteronomium-Studien* (FAT 8; Tübingen: Mohr/Siebeck 1994) 205–46.

[11] Nor does the case of Saul constitute an exception, since he is tall but not a giant.

[12] On its literary origin and use, see Martin Noth, *A History of the Pentateuchal Traditions* (trans. Bernhard W. Anderson; Atlanta: Scholars, 1981) 73–74; Horst Seebass, "Einige vertrauenswürdige Nachrichten zu Israels Anfängen: Zu den Söhnen Hobabs, Sichon und Bileam im Buch Numeri," *JBL* 113 (1994) 579–80.

[13] See Paul Hanson, "The Song of Heshbon and David's *Nîr*," *HTR* 61 (1968) 297–320; Jacob Milgrom, *Numbers* (JPSTC; Philadelphia: Jewish Publication Society, 1990) 462–63; for other views, see Hans-Christoph Schmitt, "Das Hesbonlied Num. 21,27aβb–30 und die Geschichte der Stadt Hesbon," *ZDPV* 104 (1988) 26–43.

[14] *Contra* Cristiano Grottanelli, "The Enemy King is a Monster," in idem, *Kings*

warrior puts him in the category of king that one expects from the royal psalms and elsewhere.

Moreover, in the poem of Sihon appears the word pair אש/להבה (Ps. 83:15; cf. Ps. 29:7 אש להבות ["flames of fire" or "lightning"])[15] or אש alone (Ps. 18:9, 13, 14; 97:13) appears in hymns praising Yahweh as the divine warrior. Yahweh rains fire (or lightning, since lightning from heaven produces fire on earth) on his enemies. The song portrays Sihon as a king imitating the divine warrior (here Kemosh?).[16] This, in turn, would connect the poetic image of him to the larger convention, seen in Ps. 144 and also in many Neo-Assyrian royal inscriptions, of the king whom the deity trains in the martial arts. And this, further, would imply that Sihon's body fits him for warfare. If this seems too much to hang on the single word pair אש/להבה, one notes that the Song of Heshbon is full of "holy war" imagery (such as the ruler marching out to war, with lightning as his harbinger).[17]

Kings of Neighboring States

More numerous and extensive in the Bible are the tales of rulers of countries neighboring Israel. At times, only the names and realms of the kings appear, without useful information about their ideas of kingship in general, and the royal body in particular.[18] For rulers of Tyre, Aram/Damascus, and Moab, however, it is possible to discern local Israelite knowledge of the royal bodily self-presentation of these foreign states.

---

and Prophets: Monarchic Power, Inspired Leadership, & Sacred Text in Biblical Narrative (New York: Oxford University Press, 1999) 47–72.

[15] See Klingbeil, Yahweh Fighting from Heaven, 87 n. 197.

[16] On Kemosh as a divine warrior, see the discussion in Gerald Mattingly, "Moabite Religion and the Mesha‛ Inscription," in Andrew Dearman, ed., Studies in the Mesha Inscription and Moab (Atlanta: Scholars, 1989) 223.

[17] See Hanson, "Song of Heshbon"; Frank Moore Cross, Canaanite Myth and Hebrew Epic (Cambridge: Harvard University Press, 1973) 105.

[18] Note mentions of rulers of Geshur (Josh. 13:13; 2 Sam. 3:3; 13–14; 1 Chron. 2:23; 3:2); Philistia (Gen. 26:1; though Iron Age rulers thereof are סרנים); and Edom (Num. 20:14 [= Judg. 11:17]; 2 Kings 3:9, 12, 26; Jer. 27:3; Amos 2:1 [the king of Moab exhumed an Edomite ruler's corpse and burned it]).

The King(s) of Tyre

Unlike the Palestinian rulers in the conquest tradition, Tyre's king was never the overt foe of Israel or Judah.[19] Yet the Jeremiah tradition predicts the city's destruction at Yahweh's behest (Jer. 25:22; 27:3), and Ezek. 28 offers important insights into what seems to be the Tyrian royal self-presentation (or propaganda). This self-display draws on very ancient motifs and shapes them to the king's ends.[20] Here, the king is an index of his kingdom, and the defeat of that state finds expression in the degradation and destruction of the royal body. As in the narratives about Israelite kings previously discussed, politics takes the form of contests in self-display between a human monarch and Yahweh. The king of Tyre engages in a foolhardy attempt to equal the deity, and this results in his horrible death. A detailed examination of Ezek. 28 is in order.[21]

The chapter's taunt against the Tyrian prince falls into two sections, 28:1–10 and 11–19, the second section being a lament (קינה) proper.[22] Each section has a separate background and perhaps redactional history, although attempts to attribute their linkage only to the final editorial stage fail because of the many verbal connections between them.[23] Rather, the two closely related pericopes present a kaleidoscope of images about the body of the Tyrian monarch. Several

---

[19] Israelite-Tyrian relations were, "Aucune guerre, aucun affrontement militaire ne les a marquées pendant quatre siècles" (F. Briquel-Chattonet, *Les Relations entre les Cités de la Côte Phénicienne et les Royaumes d'Israël et de Juda* [OLA 46; Leuven: Peeters, 1992] 375).

[20] On the antecedents of this chapter, see Julian Morgenstern, "The King as God among the Western Semites and the Meaning of Epiphanes," *VT* 10 (1960) 152–55; H. Jacob Katzenstein, *The History of Tyre: From the Beginning of the Second Millennium B.C.E. until the Fall of the Neo-Babylonian Empire in 538 BCE* (Jerusalem: Schocken Institute, 1973) 161–62; Martin Alonso Corral, *Ezekiel's Oracle Against Tyre: Historical Reality and Motivations* (BibOr 46; Rome: Pontifical Biblical Institute, 2002).

[21] For a treatment of this chapter's use of metaphor, see Carol Newsom, "A Maker of Metaphors: Ezekiel's Program of Restoration," in James Luther Mays and Paul Achtemeier, eds., *Interpreting the Prophets* (Philadelphia: Fortress, 1987) 188–99.

[22] On the structure of the lament, see Ilana Goldberg, "העיצוב האמנותי של הקינה על מלך צור," *Tarbiz* 58 (1989) 277–81.

[23] As in Robert R. Wilson, "The Death of the King of Tyre: The Editorial History of Ezekiel 28," in John H. Marks and Robert M. Good, eds., *Love & Death in the Ancient Near East: Essays in Honor of Marvin H. Pope* (Guilford, CT: Four Corners, 1987) 211–18, who believes the two sections arose separately and that 28:11–19 originally referred to the Israelite high priest. Note equivalent expressions in each: ויגבה לבבך (28:5), גבה לבך (28:2), חכמה (28:5, 17); רכלתך (28:5, 16); and גבה לבך (28:17).

questions demand attention: (1) how does the text conceive of the king's anatomy; (2) what does his divine self-predication mean; (3) how does his adornment or self-display figure into the picture; and (4) how much of this is Tyrian and how much an Israelite ethnocentric polemic?

To begin, Ezekiel mocks the Tyrian's claim to possess חיל ("power, might"; used three times in vv. 4–5). Wealth serves as an index of חיל, and loss of wealth of its loss (v. 7), a shrewd recognition of the connection between the Tyrian state's economic centrality to the emerging Mediterranean economy.[24] Yet the sign system with which Ezekiel operates is not that of trade goods, of manufactured objects and money, but that of the body. The failure of the royal body and its pretensions draw his attention.

A crucial part of Ezekiel's criticism of the king centers upon the nature of the latter's heart, which he claims is like the "heart of Elohim" (vv. 2 and 6) and is "high" or "haughty" (וינבה; vv. 5 and 17). In a clever turn of phrase, moreover, the prophet describes Tyrian maritime power and geographical position as being "in the heart of the sea" (בלב ימים; v. 8; cf. Prov. 30:19). That is, the basis of the city's prosperity and power thus relates metonymically to the part of the king that overrelies on that prosperity. The plasticity of bodily imagery here should already alert the reader to the existence of multiple levels of meaning within Ezekiel's oracles.

What does it mean, then, to have a heart כלב אלהים? Commentators usually interpret this as a phrase describing arrogance, haughtiness, or some other inappropriate attitude.[25] This is correct, as far as it goes, but insufficient. The expression occurs only here in the Bible, and I can find no example of it in Phoenician, although the literary corpus (and notably from Tyre) is so limited that this may mean little. That is, Ezekiel may well know Tyrian propaganda on this point, though we cannot be certain. In principle, כלב אלהים could mean either "like the heart of Elohim" or "like a superlative, extraordinary heart" (cf. רוח אלהים in Gen. 1:2). While Yahweh's internal organs play no role in the biblical traditions (unlike his external

---

[24] See Maria Aubet, *The Phoenicians and the West* (Cambridge: Cambridge University Press, 2001); Corral, *Ezekiel's Oracles*, 66–141.
[25] For example, Walther Zimmerli, *Ezekiel* (2 vols.; Hermeneia; Philadelphia: Fortress, 1983) 2. 74.

ones),[26] it is not difficult to envision an ancient Levantine like Ezekiel speculating on precisely this part of the divine anatomy. The first is more likely in view of the king's claim to divinity in vv. 2 (אֵל אָנִי) and 9 (אֱלֹהִים אָנִי). Here, then, is a notion that the king's heart differs from that of ordinary humans, just as Saul's "different heart" did (1 Sam. 10:9).

This anatomical difference leads to the monarch's allegedly superior wisdom (28:4–5, 17) and consequent prosperity, and it must link to the claim of a divine nature of some sort in vv. 2 and 9, even if there the prophet uses this claim only as part of his polemic. Assuming that Ezekiel's attribution of a claim to some kind of divinity by the Tyrian ruler is not mere hyperbole—and the Israelite king's identification as אֱלֹהִים in Ps. 45:7 demonstrates that some Levantine rulers could wear such a label—one must then ask what Tyrians would have meant by such a claim. In what sense is the king "divine"?

Not enough is known of Tyrian royal self-predication to decide this question from the inside. Greenberg cites a passage in the second-century CE historian Aelian to prove that the "Phoenician royal family claimed descent from the gods."[27] The text in question, *Varia Historia* 14.30, describes a Carthaginian named Hanno who trained birds to say, "Hanno is a god" (θεός ἐστιν ʺΑννων). However, since Aelian cites this case amidst a list of rulers he regards as foolish or worse, and since Hanno is not certainly either Tyrian or royal, this evidence does not prove, as Greenberg hopes, that Tyrians attributed divinity to their rulers. Even if behind Aelian's snide polemic lurks hard facts, this would prove only that some Phoenicians (and their western colonists) could claim divine status. Hypothetically, one could argue that kings are the most likely humans to do so, and this would reinforce the impression that Ezekiel, two or three centuries before Hanno, bore witness to genuine claims of Phoenician leaders. Yet even this is speculative.

In short, then, the assumption of the Tyrian king's divinity based on evidence deriving from inside that culture is tantalizing but inconclusive, and we must still depend entirely on Ezek. 28. Since the Israelite king is אֱלֹהִים during the coronation rite and his wedding

---

[26] For a brief treatment of Yahweh's body in Psalms, see Brown, *Seeing the Psalms*, 169–87.

[27] Moshe Greenberg, *Ezekiel 21–37* (AB 22A; New York: Doubleday, 1997) 577.

(Ps. 45), Ezekiel certainly may be imposing the self-predication of the Israelite king on the Tyrian ruler. This option seems improbable for several reasons, however. First, since Ezekiel does not make up features of royal self-presentation out of whole cloth for other rulers and since he knows a great deal about other kingdoms (see below), the burden of proof lies with anyone who would claim that he invented the first oracle's central basis of criticism of the Tyrian king. Second, other features of Tyrian kingship and society (such as seafaring) as he describes it seem specific to that state, which after all lies very near his own.[28] It is more than conceivable, then, that Ezekiel knows something about Tyrian royal self-presentation.

What, then, did Tyrians mean when they said their king was אל or אלהים? One should assume, lacking other evidence, that like his Israelite neighbor and the Egyptian pharaoh,[29] the Tyrian ruler's divinity was provisional and contextual, not a condition inherent at birth or transcending death. V. 9, by offering the king's violent death as proof of his mere humanity ("you are a man/Adam and not a god"; ואתה אדם לא אל),[30] may imply that some notion of immortality was part of the royal claim to divinity (cf. Ps. 82:7). Otherwise, the attribution of humanity would be a banality. Still, though, what did such immortality entail? In Israelite court ritual, the king received "immortality" as a gift from the deity, apparently at his coronation.[31] It is tempting to think that the Tyrian state conceived of royal immortality in a similar way. That is, the coronation ritual effected a change in the royal body that guaranteed some sort of immortality, hence invulnerability to attack, hence health, hence perhaps care of the corpse post mortem. Ezekiel, of course, repudiates the appropriateness of such a view for the king of Tyre, but the fact that he takes pains

---

[28] See also Newsom, "Maker of Metaphors," 188–99.
[29] See n. 95 below.
[30] On connections between this chapter and Gen. 2–3, see Ed. Noort, "Gan-Eden in the Context of the Mythology of the Hebrew Bible," in Gerard P. Luttikhuizen, ed., *Paradise Interpreted: Representations of Biblical Paradise in Judaism and Christianity* (Leiden: Brill, 1999) 24; on ties to the Canaanite ʾIlu/Baʿlu theomachy, cf. also Marvin Pope, *El in the Ugaritic Texts* (Leiden: Brill, 1955) 97–103.
[31] Ps. 21:5: חיים שאל ממך נתתה לו ארך ימים עולם ועד ("He asked life from you and you gave it to him; endurance forever and ever"). V. 4 refers to the coronation, and although the temporal sequence connecting this to v. 5 is not spelled out, the simplest explanation of it is that the victory hymn in Ps. 21 is referencing the coronation in both verses. The message is, "well begun is half (or more) done." The coronation encapsulates the entire reign of the king. The wish for royal immortality is also a greeting in the Judahite royal etiquette (1 Kings 1:31).

to refute it lends credence to the idea that he thought that the Tyrians believed in royal "immortality" and acted upon that belief.

Now, again, Ezekiel does not explicitly reject the notion that a king could be in some sense אלהים, only that the king of Tyre is. Indeed, when the second oracle calls him a כרוב (v. 14), it acknowledges his place in the celestial menagerie, if not in the pantheon. So, while Ezekiel's is a religious as well as political polemic, it is not an overt rejection of the "divinity" of a king. The Tyrian fails in playing his role, but this does not eliminate the role itself.

If Tyre shared with Israel a view of the monarch as a figure possessing a godlike body, and if Ezekiel demolishes this view, it is striking that the second section of chapter 28 (11–19) extends the prophet's polemic with material relevant to the Tyrian royal body that seems to differ from Israelite notions. In this second oracle, the king lives in Eden and wears precious jewels (28:13). He is "perfect in his ways" (בדרכיך ... תמים; 28:15), an epithet comparable to the Israelite king's promise to follow "a perfect path" (בדרך תמים; Ps. 101:2, 6b).

According to v. 14 MT, he is also a cherub in the garden, thus evoking the signs associated with the primal human beings and the idyllic setting for humankind. The verse is textually problematic, however. LXX reads the first words as μετὰ τοῦ χερουβ ἔθηκά σε ("With the cherub I placed you"). This differs from MT in two ways: first, it reads את as the preposition rather than as a defectively spelled second masculine singular pronoun, and, second, it deletes the problematic ממשח הסוכך. Certainly the simpler LXX reading entices, yet it must be wrong on the principle of *lectio difficilior potior*. The second masculine pronoun can be spelled defectively in the Hebrew Bible,[32] and this is the normal spelling in Phoenician inscriptions.[33] (Perhaps Ezekiel's very spelling is designed to evoke a Phoenician ambience.) Greenberg plausibly translates ממשח הסוכך as "great, overshadowing," deriving ממשח from a root attested in Aramaic.[34] That is, Ezekiel calls the king a sphinx guarding the holy mountain of God.

---

[32] The second masculine singular pronoun is spelled defectively also in Num. 11:15 and Deut. 5:24. See also the discussion in James Barr, "'Thou Art the Cherub': Ezekiel 28.14 and the Post-Ezekiel Understanding of Genesis 2–3," in Eugene Ulrich et al., *Priests, Prophets and Scribes* (JSOTSS 149; Sheffield: Sheffield Academic Press, 1992) 213–23; but T. Stordalen, *Echoes of Eden: Genesis 2–3 and Symbolism of the Eden Garden in Biblical Hebrew Literature* (Leuven: Peeters, 2000) 342–43.
[33] KAI 13.3; 14.4, 20.
[34] Greenberg, *Ezekiel 21–37*, 583–84.

This extraordinary imagery makes sense once one realizes that stone sphinxes stood guard at entrances to ancient Near Eastern palaces, themselves surrounded by gardens and thus symbolizing the divine abode and serving as an index of royal power under the aegis of the divine realm.[35] Sphinx thrones were well-attested throughout Syria-Palestine during the Iron Age, and on an Iron Age II seal depicting a king or god from Tyre itself,[36] and thus the king as sphinx becomes an icon of the throne on which he disposes his body before the gaze of his subjects, the throne itself being an index of royal power.[37] Ezekiel's funeral taunt has transformed a human, no longer a god, into a superhuman (but also stone) figure. The sphinx is a symbol of royal power, and now it becomes an icon of the royal body itself. Conversely, the royal body has been transformed into an index of a paradisiacal world now under threat from the divine conqueror and creator, Yahweh. Thus it is too simple to say, with Dale Launderville, that this beast functions in the book of Ezekiel as a boundary marker between the human and divine realms, a boundary that the king of Tyre has trespassed.[38] Rather, it is a bridge between the realms that can no longer be crossed.

In using this imagery, the prophet acknowledges the place of the king in the celestial menagerie, if not in the pantheon. While Ezekiel's is a religious as well as political polemic, it is not an outright rejection of the divinity of the king. The Tyrian fails in playing this role,

---

[35] See Lawrence Stager, "Jerusalem and the Garden of Eden," *EI* 26 (1999) 183*–94*

[36] See Fig. 41 in Eric Gubel, "The Iconography of Inscribed Phoenician Glyptic," in Sass and Uehlinger, *Studies in the Iconography*, 119; idem, *Phoenician Furniture* (StPh 7; Leuven: Peeters, 1987) esp. 75–84. If this figure is the king, then Ezekiel's imagery depends on a metonymic chain: king → throne → sphinx throne → sphinx/cherub. The imagery works because only a king sits on a sphinx throne (on the working of such metonyms, see Umberto Eco, "The Semantics of Metaphor," in idem, *The Role of the Reader: Explorations in the Semiotics of Texts* [Bloomington: Indiana University Press, 1979] 80–81). On Phoenician sphinx thrones, see Eric Gubel, "The Influence of Egypt on Western Asiatic Furniture and Evidence from Phoenicia," in Herrmann, *Furniture of Western Asia*, 142–44; Martin Metzger, *Königsthron und Gottesthron* (AOAT 15/2; Neukirchen-Vluyn: Neukirchener, 1985) figs. 1181–1217. Achaemenid era seals from Tyre also associate a deity's (Baal's?) throne with a freestanding sphinx; see Eric Gubel, "Cinq Bulles inédites des Archives tyriennes de l'époque Achéménide," *Semitica* 47 (1997) 58–62.

[37] There is thus no reason to assent to the claim of Stordalen (*Echoes of Eden*, 348) that MT must reflect a late (Hellenistic era) angelology.

[38] Dale Launderville, "Ezekiel's Cherub: A Promising Symbol or a Dangerous Idol?" *CBQ* 65 (2003) 165–83.

but this does not eliminate the role itself. He fails precisely because he forgets that Yahweh (says Ezekiel) has placed him in the garden. Here is where the connection with the previous oracle becomes important. If we read Ezek. 28:1–19 as two closely related units, or as one unit with two subunits, then the actions of the cherub/king become part of the Tyrian king's larger claim to be אל, and then they figure in his contest with the true אל, Yahweh. The king claims invincibility but will experience degradation, perhaps even mutilation (v. 10). His merchandising leads to his destruction (v. 18), but more importantly, Yahweh will subvert his self-display (as rich and wise) and publicly humiliate him. Others will pass judgment on the cherub's value (v. 19), just as others will kill the king (v. 10). The contest between Yahweh and the king is one for the acclaim of others (apparently warriors, and hence males, since these are the ones who kill the king). Royal bodily self-display fails to rival successfully that of the divine warrior. By understanding the fall of Tyre's ruler in this way, in short, Ezekiel has fitted Tyrian royal self-understandings into an Israelite mythic matrix in which Yahweh contests with the foreign ruler for the (implicit) approval of other warriors, just as one sees in the royal psalms.

Moreover, the Tyrian king is a "jeweled"[39] seal full of wisdom" (חותם תכנית מלא חכמה; 28:12).[40] This imagery is striking and clever. A royal seal bears the king's name or title and signifies his power exercised at a distance. The seal is ordinarily a sign for the king, but here the king is his seal. As with the sphinx, an index of royal power becomes an icon of the royal body. Like a fine seal, he is exquisitely crafted. The wisdom aspect of the seal is harder to explain, but may refer to the use of seals in religious rites, the point being that the king is a skilled mystagogue.[41] However that may be, the

---

[39] The lexeme תכנית has never been satisfactorily explained. For a discussion of the options, see Zimmerli, *Ezekiel*, 2. 81. The translation I propose here is apparently new and understands the word to be a cognate of the Akkadian *tiqnu*, "jewel." See, e.g., the expression *tiqnāti simāt šarrūti* ("jewels befitting kingship") in VAT 10057 ln. 8 (= SAA 3.32 ln. 8). Ezekiel's "jeweled seal" is a construct chain with a pleonastic sense and refers to an especially fine seal, one fit for a king. I read *hôṭām* ("seal") with the LXX instead of MT's *hôṭēm*.

[40] H. J. van Dijk (*Ezekiel's Prophecy on Tyre [Ez. 26,1–28,19]: A New Approach* [BibOr 20; Rome: Pontifical Biblical Institute, 1968] 113–16) emends the text to חוה תכנית, "a serpent of perfection," a very unlikely (and unnecessary) alteration.

[41] See the comments of Christoph Uehlinger, "Northwest Semitic Inscribed Seals, Iconography and Syro-Palestinian Religions of Iron Age II: Some Afterthoughts and

focus of the text is on the exquisiteness of the jeweled seal as an icon of the sphinx's garden itself.

Among others, Robert Wilson has argued that the list of gems in v. 13 is based on that of the high priest's pectorale in Exod. 28:17–20 and 39:10–13.[42] Undoubtedly, Ezekiel knew these P texts, and he may be alluding to them here. David Noel Freedman offers a better explanation when he asserts that "Ezekiel is indicating that these stones go back to the beginning of things—the Creation story and the high priest's breastplate."[43] That is, the mention of the stones does not necessarily imply that the Tyrian king was a priest, though we know from other evidence that he was,[44] much less that Ezekiel has invented a feature of Tyrian royal display modeled on the Israelite high priest! Rather, the text offers a genuine picture of the splendor of the Tyrian court and its self-understanding and self-display.

Is "Eden" the royal palace,[45] or perhaps all of Tyre?[46] Given the small area of the pre-Alexandrian city, perhaps the answer does not matter. Both material and clear, though, is the movement throughout Ezek. 28:1–19 between the iconography of royalty and the body

---

Conclusions," in Benjamin Sass and Christoph Uehlinger, eds., *Studies in the Iconography of Northwest Semitic Inscribed Seals* (OBO 125; Göttingen: Vandenhoeck & Ruprecht, 1993) 273–75. On the later use of seals in magic, see Rebecca Lesses, *Ritual Practices to Gain Power: Angels, Incantations, and Revelation in Early Jewish Mysticism* (Harrisburg, PA: TPI, 1998) 275 n. 429. Interestly, some surviving Phoenician seals draw on Egyptian imagery, including portrayals of the scribe god Thoth, among other scenes (see CWSSS, nos. 735, 741 [cf. 716, 733]), and so I propose that the iconography of the seal could point toward the supposed wisdom of its owner. Ezekiel is comparing the king of Tyre to the image of the seal itself.

[42] Wilson, "Death of the King of Tyre," 214.

[43] Editorial note, in Greenberg, *Ezekiel 21–37*, 582.

[44] On Ittobaal as a priest, see Katzenstein, *History of Tyre*, 162. The evidence is from the Balawat Gate, an Assyrian portrayal of tribute-bearers (see L. W. King, *Bronze Reliefs from the Gates of Shalmaneser King of Assyria BC 860–825* (London: British Museum, 1915) pl xiii.

[45] The Tyrian palace was already noteworthy in the Amarna period (EA 09), and it is possible that by the Iron Age it was surrounded by enclosed gardens supplying an Edenic character. On palace and temple gardens (which could be the same thing since temples often adjoined palaces), see Stager, "Jerusalem and the Garden of Eden."

[46] Ezek. 28:18 claims that the king defiled his sanctuary (מקדשׁיך) through iniquitous trading, though it is not quite clear why trade or even successful trade is evil. In any event, this defilement must occur where the trade occurs, hence the city or even the royal palace, either of which could be Eden. The specific commercial infractions Ezekiel has in mind (if any) are unknown (see Zimmerli, *Ezekiel*, 2. 94–95). It is possible that רכל refers to sorcery, though not probable (see Ann Jeffers, *Magic and Divination in Ancient Palestine and Syria* [Leiden: Brill, 1996] 122–23).

of the king itself. Seals and sphinxes and gardens signify royal power and perdurance. Thus the builder of the garden can emulate primeval times and thus index his own immortality to those who might otherwise doubt it.

Also clear and material is the fact that Ezekiel's text seeks to destroy this king, making his bodily suffering a symbol for the Israelite audience of the suffering of the entire city-state. The קינה is a funeral hymn. Elsewhere in the Bible קינות celebrate the martial prowess and the bodily beauty of a king (2 Sam. 1:17–27 for Saul) or great hero (2 Sam. 3:31–33 for Abiner). Here, Ezekiel inverts that, acknowledging the Tyrian royal claims to an extraordinary body that led to the prosperity of his state, but then systematically subverting those claims. Ezekiel attacks icons of the king's body, not his state, not his economic structure,[47] not even his *institutions* of governance. Rather, Ezekiel portrays the king's downfall as a reversal of his previous grand self-display, with the king piteously claiming godhood to those killing him (28:9). Vv. 18–19 make this explicit: "I [Yahweh] turned you into ashes on the ground in the presence (לעיני) of your audience" (כל ראיך). All among the peoples knowing[48] you were appalled (שממו). . . ." The distinction between those "seeing" and "knowing" the king may be one between courtiers and more distant retainers. Together, the two groups are a merismus: everyone will witness the fall of this arrogant monarch!

This reversal of fortune goes so far as to mean "the death of the uncircumcised" (מותי ערלים; 28:10) for him. Since Phoenicians practiced circumcision,[49] this must be an insult to the king.[50] Yet, do uncircumcised persons die harder deaths than others, or more disgraceful ones? As noted already, sometimes both art and texts from the Levant depict the exposed erect genitalia of defeated enemies. Here Ezekiel echoes that tradition, calling attention to the penis as

---

[47] Thus the use of wealth as a symbol of royal power and rich goods decorating the royal body as indexes of such is secondary to Ezekiel's basic point. Wealth as a corrupting influence is not crucial to Ezekiel's argument (contra Stuart Lasine, *Knowing Kings: Knowledge, Power, and Narcissism in the Hebrew Bible* [Atlanta: SBL, 2001] 150–51).

[48] ידע may have covenantal overtones, hence, "your allies," "your clients/vassals."

[49] Herodotus 2.104. H. J. van Dijk (*Ezekiel's Prophecy*, 113) translates ערלים as "castrated," a tempting but not technically accurate reading.

[50] As noted in Greenberg, *Ezekiel 21–37*, 576.

a sign of the royal ineffectualness and now emasculation. Through the presentation of the Tyrian's state's conception of the royal body as an icon of a divine body and an index of Tyrian might, and then the utter obliteration of that bodily image, ending in mutilation and the termination of reproductive ability, Ezekiel creates a vision of the fall of Tyre itself.

To conclude the discussion of the king of Tyre, one should ask how much Ezekiel knew about Tyrian royal self-presentation. Scholars have offered varying opinions. On one extreme, Greenberg thinks that Ezekiel utilizes "whatever components of tradition would add color" to build his portrayal.[51] On the other, Katzenstein, following Mazar, thinks that Ezekiel employed a Tyrian poem, otherwise unknown.[52] The truth undoubtedly lies somewhere in the middle. Ezekiel does present what seems like a ragbag of mythological images, from Danilu to Eden, but his apparent opportunism is illusory and may well reflect the heterogeneous character of the royal theology that he seeks to undermine. The simplest way to make his polemic convincing was to draw on common knowledge about the Tyrian crown's language about itself. The prophet drew on the popular image of the city of Tyre as a wealthy trading center, and of its king as the prime beneficiary of that pan-Mediterranean trade. Creating the most sophisticated mental manipulation of the royal body in the Hebrew Bible, Ezekiel demonstrates the mortality and vulnerability of the king who challenges Yahweh.

The Kings of Aram/Damascus

Another set of stories about kings concerns the rulers of Aram/Damascus. Part of a network of states that grew prominent after the beginning of the first millennium,[53] Damascus took center stage in

---

[51] Ibid., 593; cf. Wilson, "Death of the King of Tyre."
[52] Katzenstein, *History of Tyre*, 323–24.
[53] On the history of the Aramean polities in Syria after 1000 BCE, see Abraham Malamat, "The Aramaeans," in D. J. Wiseman, ed., *Peoples of Old Testament Times* (Oxford: Clarendon, 1973) 134–55; Hélène S. Sader, *Les États Araméens de Syrie: Depuis leur fondation jusqu' à leur transformation en provinces assyriennes* (BTS 36; Wiesbaden: Steiner, 1987); Wayne Pitard, "The Arameans," in Alfred Hoerth, Gerald Mattingly, and Edwin Yamauchi, *Peoples of the Old Testament World* (Grand Rapids: Baker, 1994) 207–30; and P.-E. Dion, *Les Araméens à l'âge du Fer* (Paris: Gabalda, 1997). Hamath (2 Sam. 8:9; 2 Kings 19:13 [= Isa. 37:13]; 23:33; 25:21; Jer. 39:5; 52: 9, 27; Amos 6:2; Zech. 9:2 etc.) and Sobah (2 Sam. 8; 10:16; 1 Chron. 18; 19:16) appear in the Bible, though with little useful ethnographic or historical information.

the Bible as the bête noir of Israelite foreign policy.[54] The contest between Israel (the northern kingdom) and Aram could be understood, at least in prophetic circles, to fit into the machinations of Yahweh, who makes kings even in foreign states. One episode in 1–2 Kings in particular reveals how this works, and especially how the royal body figured into it. The focus is upon the sick king. A second story, though more about the Israelite king, sheds light on the sick king motif.

The first story comes from 2 Kings 8:7–15, which describes Yahweh's selection of Hazael, the generalissimo of Ben-hadad, as king. The story begins with Ben-hadad's serious illness, which prompts him to dispatch Hazael with gifts to Elisha (cf. 2 Kings 5). Though Ben-hadad's solicitude of Yahweh exceeds that of the Israelite king in 2 Kings 1, Elisha reveals that he will die and that his general will succeed him and wreak havoc on Israel (8:12).

The final scene is crucial to the current discussion (8:14–15). Ben-hadad anxiously asks for the prophet's diagnosis. Hazael returns to the palace with the news, "The prophet says, 'You shall surely live'" (חיה תחיה). This response to his lord's question sounds reassuring but is actually ambiguous: is it an indirect quote with Ben-hadad as the subject or a direct quote with Hazael as the subject? Who will live, Ben-hadad or Hazael? Elisha has instructed Hazael to lie in this way (8:10), or rather to offer a verdict open to multiple interpretations. This "double-talk" seems a deliberate[55] attempt at the sort of information management Stuart Lasine has described in other biblical texts, in which a monarch (here Hazael) controls the boundary between public and private to his own advantage.[56]

The tale climaxes with the asphyxiation of Ben-hadad with a cloth (מכבר). The text offers no clue as to how the narrator would have known of the means of the king's death (such as a citation of archives or a reference to rumors), so we cannot be sure whether this detail is an Israelite invention or a report of a genuine Aramaean custom.

---

[54] The locution מלכ(י) ארם appears in Judg. 3:10; 1 Kings 10:29; 15; 18; 20:1, 20, 22, 23; 22:3, 31; 28:23; 2 Kings 1:17; 5:1, 5; 6:8, 11, 24; 8:7, 9, 28, 29; 9:14–15; 12:18, 19; 13:3, 4, 7, 22, 24; 15:37; 16:5–7; Isa. 7:1; 2 Chron. 16:2, 7; 18:30; 22:5, 6; and 28:5; cf. Amos 1:4.

[55] Rather than as the result of redactional activity; see Burke O. Long, *2 Kings* (FOTL 10; Grand Rapids: Eerdmans, 1991) 104.

[56] Stuart Lasine, *Knowing Kings: Knowledge, Power, and Narcissism in the Hebrew Bible* (Atlanta: SBL, 2001).

Arguably, Hazael simply commits murder by means of a method calculated to avoid bloodshed and thus overt clues of foul play.[57]

Yet, another possibility is that this may be a form of euthanasia. While undoubtedly Ben-hadad's death benefited his successor, the narrative does not explicitly say that the king would have recovered without human intervention.[58] It is at least conceivable that Hazael's (and Elisha's) lie and then the murder itself had the purpose of easing death for a sick king who had, after all, had the good sense of consulting the god of Israel. The deception of the king could have served to spare his feelings and those of his courtiers. It would also have avoided the spilling of blood and the potential miasmic dangers resulting therefrom. While Near Eastern texts unsurprisingly do not otherwise narrate the euthanasia of a sick king, an act of almost unimaginable risk to the cosmic order, this possibility should not be ruled out.

However this may be, the narrative focuses upon the military prowess of Hazael, and thus of Aram. Other possible aspects of kingship (for example, wealth, wisdom, fame, etc.) do not come into view. Rather, Hazael is the one who will "torch their fortresses, put their young men to the sword, dash their babies to pieces, and rip open their pregnant women."[59] He is only the warrior, and Ben-hadad is only the sick patient. Yahweh has prepared Hazael for war (as in Ps. 144) and slain his predecessor, whose body had become unfit for battle. In this sense, the biblical view of Hazael's Aram coincides with its image elsewhere, namely, in Hamath, whose king Zakkur a generation after Hazael faced down a Damascus-led coalition,[60] and in Assyria.[61] Whereas in Israel, only royal injustice could warrant

---

[57] For a refutation of the notion that this was an accidental death, see Mordechai Cogan and Hayim Tadmor, *II Kings* (AB 11; New York: Doubleday, 1988) 91.

[58] See Long, *2 Kings*, 104–5.

[59] 2 Kings 8:12bβ (מבצריהם תשלח באש ובחריהם בחרב תהרג ועלליהם תרשש והרתיהם תבקע).

[60] KAI 202 A 4.

[61] See, for example, the annals of Shalmaneser III for his eleventh and fourteenth regnal years (RIMA 9.102.8. 35'–41' and 44'–47'a; and parallels). Shalmaneser's foe was a Hadad-ʿidri (= Hebrew הדדעזר, the name of David's foe in 2 Sam. 8; could the latter text be an anachronism?). On the historical discrepancy thus arising, see Wayne Pitard, *Ancient Damascus: A Historical Study of the Syrian City-State from Earliest Times until its Fall to the Assyrians in 732 BCE* (Winona Lake: Eisenbrauns, 1987) 137–38; but Frank Moore Cross, "The Stele Dedicated to Melcarth by Ben-Hadad of Damascus," *BASOR* 205 (1972) 36–42; then Sader, *États Araméens de Syrie*, 255–60.

240   CHAPTER SEVEN

regicide,⁶² only the most chauvinistic interpretation of Hazael's deed could construe it as a legitimate act.

Before leaving Aram, one should note one further story, that of the healing of Naaman in 2 Kings 5. As in 2 Kings 8, here the king sends gifts and a request for medical care to Elisha. Again, the theological theme of the international scope of Yahweh's power shapes the narrative. Again, generals and warfare determine the image of Aram. The new wrinkle here is that Naaman first comes to the anonymous Israelite king, who despairs, "Am I God, (one able to) kill or make alive?" (להמית ולהחיות האלהים אני; 2 Kings 5:7). The narrative is thus referring to the claim of the Israelite king to be אלהים (cf. Ps. 45) and attributing healing powers to that divine status (while simultaneously denying such attributions). Even while referring to this theologoumenon, the text denies one possible implication of it, namely that the king of Israel could heal. Prophets heal. The idea in play here is that of what was later called the royal touch, the belief that the physical contact with the king could cure certain diseases.⁶³ According to the prophetic tradents of this story, Israel's kings lack this charism. Yet, the fact that the king here thinks that the Aramean king attributes this ability to him is striking. Did the kings of Damascus claim to heal some cases, or is the reputation for healing confined to Israel? As before, the story yields more questions than answers, but at least one must consider the possibility that Arameans thought that some kings through their own body could heal.

The juxtaposition of these stories produces two interesting results. First, the DH and before it the prophetic source used the Aramean king and his courtiers to explore the question of the sick king. Since there is no reason to think that Damascus's rulers were more or less often ill than anybody else, we are dealing here with a mental image, a set of signs, in which *sick king* and *Aramean* were somehow connected in a network of signs. Like Hezekiah in Isa. 38 and implicitly Amaziah in 2 Kings 1, the Aramean ruler could consult Yahweh

---

⁶² Dale Launderville, *Piety and Politics: The Dynamics of Royal Authority in Homeric Greece, Biblical Israel, and Old Babylonian Mesopotamia* (Grand Rapids: Eerdmans, 2003) 268.
⁶³ Cf. 2 Kings 5:6, which assumes a version of the royal touch. On the medieval version of the practice, see Marc Bloch, *The Royal Touch: Sacred Monarchy and Scrofula in England and France* (1923; London: Routledge & Kegan Paul, 1973).

and seek his help; unlike Hezekiah he did not receive it. Ben-hadad's death, whether euthanasia or murder, leads to the unambiguous rise of a great Aramean king, Hazael, whose feats bear the sanction of the god of Israel. Even if Hazael is not explicitly trained by Yahweh for war—the biblical narrator does not go so far as to attribute the qualities of Israelite kingship to foreign rulers—his martial activities are backed by that deity. Thus the story nods toward the Israelite mythic signification of the foreign king as the vulnerable king but turns even bodily sickness into an index of Yahweh's power, and indirectly of Aram's.

The Kings of Moab

This brings us to the third case, Moab. Like Aram, Moab was a longtime rival of the Israelite polities and entered statehood contemporaneously with them, in the tenth century.[64] Moabite kings figure in biblical traditions as possessors of distorted bodies or as inadequate warriors who cannot display themselves felicitously.

The biblical tradition contains numerous historical memories and a fair amount of invective regarding the small Transjordanian state.[65] On the other hand, the stele of Mesha portrays Israel as an oppressor that ultimately loses in its contest with the god Kemosh and his agent, Mesha. This ruler's major inscription from Dibon (KAI 181) portrays him as a skilled warrior, a builder of temples, fortresses, reservoirs, and gardens, and a succorer of his people. All of this takes place under the aegis of Kemosh, who guided Mesha's military tactics and who, in turn, received from him various temples. As we saw earlier, the motifs of the king as builder, warrior, and pious agent of the deity are also part of the self-presentation of the rulers of Israel and Judah, and so we are dealing here with a region-wide rhetoric of kingship.[66]

---

[64] See Bruce Routledge, "Learning to Love the King: Urbanism and the State in Iron Age Moab," in Walter Aufrecht, Neil A. Mirau, and Steven W. Gauley, eds., *Urbanism in Antiquity* (JSOTSS 244; Sheffield: Sheffield Academic Press, 1997) 130–44.

[65] For a summary of these traditions, see J. Maxwell Miller, "Moab and the Moabites," in Andrew Dearman, ed., *Studies in the Mesha Inscription and Moab* (Atlanta: Scholars, 1989) 16–40.

[66] And this helps explain the presence of such practices of חרם in Mesha's inscription.

Mesha's immediate audience is Dibon: as Routledge observes, "By associating himself with the built environment of an urban center, the king is inserting himself into the everyday experience of all those oriented towards that center."[67] However, traces of the Moabite version of this rhetoric may survive in Zeph. 2:10's depiction of the king of Moab among weeds and salt pits[68] and especially in the account of the attack on Mesha in 2 Kings 3, though the tradition-history of this text and its relationship to actual events are unclear.[69] Yet, it is worthwhile to observe that the features of the military campaign upon which 2 Kings 3 centers are reflexes of the achievements that Mesha emphasizes. Consider 2 Kings 3:19, Elisha's instructions to Jehoshaphat of Judah:

> So, you shall strike every fortified city, every choice city; every good tree you shall fell; every artesian well (מעיני מים) you shall plug; every plot of ground you shall mar (תכאבו) with stones.

Just as Mesha's stele emphasized his work constructing gardens and waterworks, and building cities, just so are the Israelite armies to destroy these very things. The contest with Moab takes the form of ecological ravaging, just as, for Mesha, the contest with Israel involved the shaping of nature to benefit humans (Moabites) and to enhance his own reputation. The contest is thus a form of royal self-display. And so, implicitly, the Israelite texts can be read as an effort to discredit Moabite royal self-presentation, even if Israelites may not have read the stele we have from Mesha. This means that we should not discount the possibility that the biblical texts had at least some accurate information regarding Moabite kingship, at least for the Iron II period, and hence that the other two texts pertinent now, Num. 22–24 and Judg. 3, may be more than just an intra-Israelite view of how Moabite kings ought to be.

Whatever the importance of these texts, ancient Israelite views most clearly appear in two stories that we will examine now. Each

---

[67] Routledge, "Learning to Love the King," 140.

[68] See the discussion in Marvin Sweeney, *Zephaniah* (Hermeneia; ed. Paul Hanson; Minneapolis: Fortress, 2003) 141–42.

[69] There is also a formal, structural similarity between 2 Kings 3 and the Mesha inscription, on which see, Alviero Niccacci, "The Stele of Mesha and the Bible: Verbal System and Narrativity," *Or* 63 (1994) 244–48. On the historical problems, see Miller, "Moab and the Moabites"; and Klaas A. D. Smelik, "King Mesha's Inscription," in idem, *Converting the Past: Studies in Ancient Israelite and Moabite Historiography* (Leiden: Brill, 1992) 59–92.

portrays the Moabite king as a failed warrior, and each understands this failure to be connected in some way to peculiarities of the Moabite royal body.

The first tale is that of Balaq in Num. 22–24. Though in the narrative logic of the Pentateuch, this character lived during the pre-settlement period, he does not feature in the historico-credal formulae in the same ways other monarchs do (as in D, Ps. 136; but see Mic. 6:5), and thus can properly appear at this point in our study. Much research on these chapters has, properly, focused upon issues of textual evolution and prosody,[70] prophetic origins (including the character type of Balaam),[71] and relationships of traditions to extrabiblical sources (Deir Alla),[72] but few have paid attention to the descriptions of Balaq himself. Admittedly, while the king's fear sets in motion the narrative of Num. 22–24, he is a subordinate character to his hired diviner. The exception to this is in the song in 23:18b–24, of which I cite here vv. 18–19 and 22–24:[73]

¹⁸⁻¹⁹Arise, Balaq, and hear!   קום בלק ושמע
Heed me, son of Sippor!   האזינה עדי בנו צפר
'Il is no man that he should lie,   לא איש אל ויכזב
no human being that he should renege.   ובן אדם ויתנחם
Will he speak and not do?   ההוא אמר ולא יעשה
Or utter and not follow through?   ודבר ולא יקימנה

²²⁻²⁴Il brought them from Egypt   אל מוציאם ממצרים
Like the rampage (?) of a wild bull.   כתועפת ראם לו
So, there is no curse against[74] Jacob,   כי לא נחש ביעקב
no imprecation against Israel.   ולא קסם בישראל

---

[70] E.g., William F. Albright, "The Oracles of Balaam," *JBL* 63 (1944) 207–33.

[71] Sigmund Mowinckel, "Der Ursprung der Bilʿāmsage," *ZAW* 48 (1930) 233–71.

[72] E.g., André Lemaire, "Les Inscriptions sur Plâtre de Deir ʿAllā et leur Signification Historique et Culturelle," in Jakob Hoftijzer and G. van der Kooij, eds., *The Balaam Text from Deir ʿAllā Re-evaluated* (Leiden: Brill, 1991) 33–57; Jo Ann Hackett, "Some Observations on the Balaam Tradition at Deir ʿAllā," *BA* 49 (1986) 216–22; eadem, "Religious Traditions in Israelite Transjordan," In Patrick Miller, Paul Hanson, and S. Dean McBride, eds., *Ancient Israelite Religion* (Cross Festschrift; Philadelphia: Fortress, 1987) 125–36. See Hackett's study of the Deir Alla text, *The Balaam Text from Deir ʿAllā* (HSM 31; Chico, CA: Scholars, 1984).

[73] I print here the text of BHS; for a reconstruction of the pre-Masoretic spelling, see Albright, "Oracles of Balaam," 214–16. For a discussion of the rhythm and prosody of the poem, see Angelo Tosato, "The Literary Structure of the First Two Poems of Balaam (Num. xxiii 7–10, 18–24)," *VT* 29 (1979) 98–106.

[74] For ב as "against," see ibid., 215 n. 49.

244   CHAPTER SEVEN

> For now it will be said of Jacob
> and of Israel,
> "What has 'Il done?"
> Now a people like a lion arises;
> Leonine it rears!
> It does not lie down until it
> has devoured prey,
> And it drinks the blood of the slain.

כעת יאמר ליעקב
ולישראל
מה פעל אל
הן עם כלביא יקום
וכארי יתנשא
לא ישכב עד יאכל טרף
ודם חללים ישתה

This extraordinary poem portrays Israel as an invincible foe and Balaq's as a lost cause. The foreign king's adversary is a deity, just as in Ps. 2, even though God's champion is not a human king here, but is the chosen people as a whole.

A revealing element of the poem is the mention of lions, which signals the king's desired function as a hunter, hence as a virile male with a well-trained and fit body. Lion hunting was an important part of the royal self-image in Assyria[75] and Egypt,[76] as well as in Israel and Judah,[77] and lions lived around the Dead Sea (Jer. 49:19; 50:44), which meant that Moabites would have had firsthand knowledge of their danger. Against this background, Balaq's failure is stark: he cannot slay lions, hence is an untrained hunter and a king who cannot protect his people, and thus one not fit to rule.

On the other hand, Isa. 15:9bα mentions among the curses befalling Moab a lion rampaging among refugees (לפליטת מואב אריה). This verse is notoriously difficult, causing commentators often to label it a gloss (which only pushes the problem to another level of the text's development!),[78] but I propose that it is an interbiblical reference to Num. 23:24, and thus a reference to a relationship between Israel (the lion) and Moab (the prey). Although Isa. 15 does not explicitly

---

[75] See Elnathan Weissert, "Royal Hunt and Royal Triumph in a Prism Fragment of Ashurbanipal (82–5–22,2)," in Parpola and Whiting, *Assyria 1995*, 339–58.

[76] See Walter Wreszinski, *Löwenjagd im alten Ägypten* (Leipzig: Hinrichs, 1932).

[77] See Rüdiger Schmitt, *Bildhafte Herrschaftsrepräsentation im eisenzietlichen Israel* (AOAT 283; Münster: Ugarit-Verlag, 2001) 121–25.

[78] See Otto Kaiser, *Isaiah 13–39* (OTL; London: SCM, 1974) 69–70; Hans Wildberger, *Jesaja* (BKAT; Neukirchen-Vluyn: Neukirchener, 1975) 618–19. Part of the problem arises from the discrepancy between MT and LXX, which reads in this clause καὶ 'αρῶ τὸ σπέρμα Μωαβ καὶ Αριηλ ("and I will lift up the seed of Moab and Ariel" [or, "even Ariel"?] (וישא הפלט מואב ואריאל) or some such). Σπέρμα normally renders זרע, but Mishnaic Hebrew has a verb פלט meaning, among other things, "to discharge semen" (s.v., Jastrow, 1178) and this could explain the LXX's reading.

mention the king of Moab, the destruction of his country that the prophet envisions obviously implies a failure on the part of that unfortunate monarch. His failure to kill a lion signifies (as an index) this broader failure as a warrior. The mention of the rampaging lion generates the sign *unsuccessful king* in both Numbers and Isaiah.

The second Moabite royal story is that of Eglon (Judg. 3:12–30). While the Bible is not squeamish about regicide, this story stands out for its sheer brazenness.[79] A left-handed man named Ehud carries a concealed weapon while presenting tribute to the Moabite king, who has occupied Israelite territory. In an extraordinary performance, he asks for a private audience with the king, to whom he promises to reveal a "word of God" (דבר אלהים; Judg. 3:20). This "word" is nothing less than the murder of Eglon in his private rooftop toilet.[80]

In attempting to understand this story, scholars have recently debated the precise genre to which we should assign it: history[81] or satire.[82] Deciding the question depends to a considerable degree on definitions of these terms and the imagined relationship of the story to the facts of the era it purports to describe. Whatever its origins in the Iron I period, for Iron II hearers of it, it fitted into a larger set of mental associations—networks of signs—labeled *king of Moab* and even *foreign king*.

Brettler has emphasized the latent sexual imagery in the text, and some of the associations he suggests may be convincing.[83] More saliently, however, the royal bodily feature that stands out here is Eglon's extreme obesity. The obsession with excrement reflects this feature: a man who eats so much must produce a great deal of waste. More to the point, notice v. 17: "Next he [Ehud] brought

---

[79] On regicide, see Launderville, *Piety and Politics*, 262–72.

[80] On the architecture envisioned here, see Baruch Halpern, *The First Historians: The Hebrew Bible and History* (San Francisco: Harper & Row, 1988) 47–54.

[81] Ibid., chap. 3.

[82] Marc Zvi Brettler, *The Creation of History in Ancient Israel* (London: Routledge, 1995) chap. 5.

[83] Ibid., 82. But some of his examples seem forced, e.g., that Ehud's sword was a phallic symbol and that "to open" and "to lock" imply sexual intercourse because they do so in Song 5:2 and 4:12 (Brettler's latter association being a case of semiotic drift [when one assumes that since a relates to b and b relates to c, then a relates to c], I think, that could exist only if one had the entire biblical corpus available).

(יקרב) the tribute (המנחה)[84] to Eglon king of Moab; now Eglon was an extremely fat man" (איש בריא מאד). Along with the text's highlighting of the king's name עגל → עגלון ("calf"), its description of the bearing of tribute uses sacrificial language, which is not inappropriate, as Brettler claims,[85] but may reflect a subtle connection between sacrifice and tribute and between the deity as the recipient of the first and the king of the second that appears elsewhere in the Bible.[86] To complicate this aspect of the story more, the narrator states that the public audience with the king takes place near "the images that are near (at?) Gilgal" (הפסילים אשר את הגלגל).

The images (פסלים) may function as witnesses to the tribute-bearing of Ehud, as some have argued,[87] but it is more important that the murder of the king near them suggests that the king's death becomes in some way a sacrifice to the images, much in the manner of Samuel's flaying of Agag in 1 Sam. 15:33, "before Yahweh" (לפני יהוה) and David's execution of Saul's male descendants (2 Sam. 21). The royal body is a fit sacrifice to the Moabite gods. The divine protectors of the royal body, and thus the state that is symbolizes, accept that very body as a sacrifice, thus vitiating their own rule.

The story emphasizes the gruesomeness of the assassination: Ehud disembowels the corpulent king (28:22). And finally the text implies that the servants of Eglon at first believed him to be relieving himself (מסיך הוא את רגליו; 28:24). For a very fat man, defecation might require some time, but the servants are ashamed (בש) to wait as long as they have and thus force their way into the room, only to find their master dead.

This story obsesses over the royal body in a grotesque form. A very fat man cannot be a skilled warrior. He cannot even defend himself even against a lone assassin. His servants readily assume that his bathroom functions require an extended time to complete. His guts swallow a sword and (implicitly) flow on the ground. The narrator seeks to present this king as one unworthy of the name. His

---

[84] On מנחה, see Jacob Milgrom, *Leviticus 1–16* (AB 3; New York: Doubleday, 1991) 196–201.
[85] Ibid., 81.
[86] E.g., Ps. 89:28; see the discussion in Chapter 3 above.
[87] So Robert G. Boling, *Judges* (AB 6A; Garden City, NY: Doubleday, 1975) 86. On the other hand, the text does not say that Ehud contracted a covenant with Eglon, even though the bearing of tribute may imply one.

body betrays him and his cause—the oppression of Israel—at the crucial moment.

To summarize, then, Moabite kings figure in the Bible as dramatic failures, as men untrained for war, unable to discipline their own bodies, and thus unable to protect themselves and their nations from Yahweh. The royal body becomes a symbol of the inadequacy of the foreign people as a whole.

Summary

So far, we have seen that Israelites portrayed rulers of neighboring states, when they considered their bodies at all, as sick and vulnerable, or else overweening. All of the portrayals just discussed depict these rulers, except Hazael, himself an instrument of divine destruction of a failed royal body, as entering into an impossible contest with Yahweh. The narratives and prophecies in question depict this loss in terms of bodily failure and, at least in the case of the king of Tyre and probably of Balaq, of the reversal of the claims made by the king himself (or by actual rulers of his state when the king is legendary as is Balaq). Far from being indexes of royal power, parts of kings' bodies, or the body as a whole, becomes a symbol of sexual, political, and economic impotence. Failed self-display means failure altogether.

The Superpowers: Egypt, Assyria, and Babylon

A different situation obtains for the rulers of the ancient Near Eastern empires. While the Bible recounts the deeds, real or imagined, of nearby kings, it gives its most developed and sustained attention to the leaders of the three great superpowers that the Israelite dual monarchies encountered. Israelites were aware of the rhetorics of these empires,[88] and in some cases, notably, of the features thereof that centered upon the ruler's body, especially in the case of Neo-Assyria. The biblical pictures of them often show fairly extensive knowledge of conditions within the alien realms, not mere stereotypes. A good example of this is Jer. 46, which, as we will see, knows

---

[88] For examples of this, see Peter Machinist, "Assyria and Its Image in the First Isaiah," *JAOS* 103 (1983) 719–37; David Vanderhooft, *The Neo-Babylonian Empire and Babylon in the Latter Prophets* (HSM 59; Atlanta: Scholars, 1999).

names of Egyptian gods and the practices of Egyptian warfare. In short then, Israelite prophets and narrators[89] deformed and reused the sign systems of the empires for new purposes.

Egypt and the Pharaoh

Kingship in Egypt began twenty centuries before the rise of Israel.[90] Over that time, the primary focus of contemplation of the Pharaoh had shifted from his mortuary cult to his leadership of the army and status as priest of the sun-god.[91] His godlikeness had undergone a series of reinterpretations, as had the royal iconography. Thus in the first millennium BCE, the Twenty-fifth (Kushite) Dynasty (ca. 760–656 BCE) repristinated Old and Middle Kingdom mythology and ritual to lend themselves an aura of Egyptianness.[92] Many of these reclaimed forms persisted into the Twenty-sixth (Saite) Dynasty (ca. 664–525 BCE) as well. All along, however, the king is guarantor and embodiment of *maat* ("order," "harmony," "cosmos"), preserved through ritual, warfare, and governance.[93]

This is not the place to trace out in detail the portrayal of the Pharaoh during the period of the Israelite monarchy, but merely to resist the easy generalizations that sometimes populate biblical

---

[89] I avoid choosing as an appropriate label, "historian," "epic writer," or whatnot. See the discussion in John Van Seters, *In Search of History*, esp. 209–48; but Frank Moore Cross, *From Epic to Canon: History and Literature in Ancient Israel* (Baltimore: Johns Hopkins University Press, 1998) 29 n. 21. These two scholars are discussing the Pentateuch, but some of the issues are also relevant for Samuel-Kings.

[90] For a concise history of Egyptian monarchy, see Marie-Ange Bonhême, "Kingship," *Oxford Encyclopedia of Ancient Egypt* (2001) 2.238–45.

[91] See *inter alios* Klaus Koch, *Geschichte der agyptischen Religion: Von den Pyramiden bis zu den Mysterien der Isis* (Stuttgart: Kohlhammer, 1993) chaps. 3 and 13; Jan Assmann, *Der König als Sonnenpriester* (ADAIK 7; Glückstadt: Augustin, 1970); idem, "State and Religion in the New Kingdom," in James P. Allen, et al., eds., *Religion and Philosophy in Ancient Egypt* (New Haven: Yale Egyptological Seminar, 1989) 55–88.

[92] CHA 1 (1982) 890; Karola Zibelius-Chen, "Theorie und Realität im Königtum der 25. Dynastie," in Rolf Gundlach and Christine Raedler, eds., *Selbstverständnis und Realität* (ÄAT 36.1; Wiesbaden: Harrassowitz, 1997) 81–95; on the "presentation of *Maat*" scenes in the art of the Third Intermediate Period, see Emily Teeter, *The Presentation of Maat: Ritual and Legitimacy in Ancient Egypt* (SAOC 57; Chicago: Oriental Institute, 1997) 13–14, 16. Isaiah is apparently aware of the political tensions between the Egyptian nobility and the occupying powers, for Isa. 19:11 represents the former as claiming (foolishly) to be descendants of ancient dynasts (אני בן מלכי קדם) and therefore wise.

[93] See Jan Assmann, *Ma'at: Gerechtigkeit und Unsterblichkeit im Alten Ägypten* (Munich: Beck, 1990); Teeter, *Presentation of Maat* (with qualifications of Assmann).

studies: for example, that the Pharaoh *was* a god in the same way that Re was. Rather, Pharaoh's divinity began at the coronation, when he became an avatar of Horus, and it changed to a new level at death, when he became an extension of Osiris. On the other hand, this divinity did not inure him from all human frailties or protect him from death or defeat.[94] The focus of the discussion here, then, is not upon the theological abstractions of Egyptian kingship, but upon the ways in which Israelite texts depict the Pharaoh moving about or displaying himself to others.

As Donald Redford has observed, "Egyptian influence in the Bible, or specific borrowings by Israelite culture, are remarkably few and certainly do not come to mind immediately."[95] On the other hand, the material culture of Egypt influenced Syria-Palestine during the Iron Age, particularly after the eighth century (even if less than in the second millennium, when the region was often part of the Egyptian empire).[96] What is more, the definitive Israelite story involving Egypt, the exodus cycle, failed to influence some of the most graphic biblical depictions of the Pharaoh. Before turning to the Pharaoh of the exodus and the notorious hardening of his heart, let me examine these other strands of biblical Egyptiana.

The fullest attack on the Pharaoh comes in Ezek. 29–32. This series of seven addresses to the Egyptian ruler shows stages of redactional development, but only limitedly so.[97] There is no convincing

---

[94] A vast literature on this topic exists; see recently Marcelo Campagno, "God-Kings and King-Gods in Ancient Egypt," in C. J. Eyre, ed., *Proceedings of the Seventh International Congress of Egyptologists* (OLA 82; Leuven: Peeters, 1998) 237–43; Friedrich Abitz, *Pharao als Gott In den Unterweltsbuchern des Neuen Reiches* (OBO 146; Göttingen: Vandenhoeck & Ruprecht, 1995).

[95] Donald B. Redford, *Egypt, Canaan, and Israel in Ancient Times* (Princeton: Princeton University Press, 1992) 365. Certain biblical texts recount diplomatic and military relations between Egypt and the Israelite monarchies, but some are hard to corroborate. These include the ceding of Gezer to Solomon as a wedding present (1 Kings 3:1; 9:16); the flight of Hadad of Edom and Jeroboam to Egypt (1 Kings 11:18, 40); Shoshenq's raid (1 Kings 14:25); and the various alliances with Egypt against Assyria (2 Kings 17:4, 7; 18:21). See further Susan Cohen, *Canaanites, Chronologies, and Connections: the relationships of Middle Bronze IIA Canaan to Middle Kingdom Egypt* (Winona Lake: Eisenbrauns, 2002).

[96] See Bernd Ulrich Schipper, *Israel und Ägypten in der Königszeit: Die kulturellen Kontakte von Salomo bis zum Fall Jerusalems* (OBO 170; Göttingen: Vandenhoeck & Ruprecht, 1999) esp. 35–82, 159–85, 247–65; Raphael Giveon, *The Impact of Egypt on Canaan* (OBO 20; Göttingen: Vandenhoeck & Ruprecht, 1978).

[97] Zimmerli, *Ezekiel*, 2. 102–5. Lawrence Boadt, *Ezekiel's Oracles Against Egypt: A Literary and Philological Study of Ezekiel 29–32* (BibOr 37; Rome: Biblical Institute Press, 1980) 10.

reason to locate at least the six dated oracles (29:1, 17; 30:20; 31:1; 32:1, 17) and probably all seven, later than the early sixth century. In principle, then, a coherent picture of the Pharaoh, and precisely of his body, should emerge from these chapters.

The most direct statement of the purposes of these oracles appears in Ezek. 32:9–10, part of a קינה for the king (32:1–16):[98]

> So, I will shake the heart (והכעסתי לב) of many peoples when I bring about your [Pharaoh's] destruction (בהביאי שברך) among the nations in lands you do not know about. And I will make you shocking (והשמותי) to many people, and their kings (ומלכיהם) will shiver in terror (ישערו) before you when I brandish my sword before their face. They will tremble constantly (וחרדו לרגעים), each for his life, in the day of your downfall.

This text adumbrates the key themes of the biblical portrayals of foreign kings: (unequal) contestation with Yahweh, (implicitly) destruction of the royal body, and public humiliation before other males, here the foreign kings. The instrument of divine punishment, Nebuchadrezzar, is another king, whose body is more suited for war.

V. 16 surfaces still another theme familiar from narratives about the Israelite king, namely the validation of royal actions, and therefore the royal body, by women. Just as women sing at the funeral of Saul and the triumphs of David, here they commemorate the death of the Pharaoh. Since a קינה is a funeral song (not always a "lament" properly speaking) that celebrates the achievements of the king, Ezekiel's choice of the genre is deeply ironic. The king's achievements are all disasters, his boasting is empty, his body is ill prepared for kingship.

All the oracles in Ezek. 29–32 unpack, so to say, these themes, not didactically, but by means of a kaleidoscope of images of the Pharaoh, most reflecting some knowledge on Ezekiel's part of Egyptian hydrology, zoology, and possibly theology. To begin, the first oracle describes the Pharaoh as both a sea monster or crocodile (29:3) (תנין [MT תנים]) and a broken reed (29:7). The first metaphor, whatever its mythological overtones,[99] centers upon the ruler's great power, his security in the Nile delta, and his essential inscrutability. The

---

[98] On the tradition history of the pericope (expansions to the core קינה), see Zimmerli, *Ezekiel*, 2. 157–58.

[99] See Greenberg, *Ezekiel 21–37*, 601–2; Boadt, *Ezekiel's Oracles*, 27–28.

hooks with which Yahweh catches him recall the hooks placed in the noses of deported captives by the Assyrians and Babylonians. The zoomorphic icon of the king's body became an index of his defeat.

The penultimate oracle (32:1–16, esp. v. 2), meanwhile, reiterates this analogy and extends it to make the Pharaoh food for the nations (the imagery of Pharaoh as a fallen mighty tree in 31:1–18 makes the same point). While the reference to the תנון could simply reflect a knowledge of Egypt's wildlife, it is also possible that Ezekiel is referring to the god Sobek, a prominent deity of the Saite period (as well as earlier), whose "Erscheinungsform"[100] was the crocodile (and this might explain the claim to having created the Nile that Ezek. 29:3 attributes to the Pharaoh). Also, at least some evidence points toward this beast's being a symbol of the Pharaoh in Egyptian sources, at least in the New Kingdom.[101] In either case, the reference is to an exotic and fearsome animal that Yahweh hunts down and destroys. By analyzing Pharaoh's body, Ezekiel turns it into a sign of a hunted, subhuman creature.

The swarm of metaphors continues with the comparison to a broken reed in Ezek. 29:6–7. Again, the text reflects a very rudimentary knowledge of Egyptian flora, one also picked up by the Assyrian Rab-shakeh in 2 Kings 18:21. The reed staff is also a popular image on Iron Age Levantine seals depicting Egyptian rulers,[102] and thus an index of his power over those seeing the seal, and so it may have been part of the regional mental picture of Egypt (much as a Coke bottle may remind some of the United States, or a bearskin hat and red tunic call to mind Great Britain today). The staff is part of the Pharaonic regalia, an index of the Pharaoh's prowess. If it is a fragile reed, this means that Egypt's king is ineffectual, his realm weak, and his trusting allies foolish.

This becomes still more explicit in 30:20–26. Here, Yahweh promises to break the arm(s) (זרוע[ת]; vv. 21–22) of Pharaoh so that he drops his sword. At the same time, Nebuchadrezzar will take up the sword of Yahweh and thus vanquish his foe. Now, this is noteworthy because one expects the bearer of Yahweh's sword to be the

---

[100] See Koch, *Geschichte*, 457.
[101] *RÄRG* 392–94.
[102] See CWSSS, nos. 738, 741, 1041, 1081, 1090, 1091, 1093, 1096, 1099, 1122, 1130, 1153, 1167, 1179, and 1181.

king of Judah, as in Ps. 144:1–2 (cf. Ps. 20). Ezekiel is too politically realistic to believe that, however, and so he imputes an important part of the Judahite notions about kingship to a foreign ruler. The prophet understands political contest as single combat between two rulers, a contest in which divine intervention is decisive. The endangered Pharaoh's defeat derives precisely from the public failure of his body in warfare.

V. 22aγ is confusing: what does "And I will break his [Pharaoh's] arms, the strong one and the broken one" (ושברתי זרעתיו את החזקה ואת הנשברת) mean? Commentators have tried to unravel the paradox by labeling the explanatory phrase "the strong one and the broken one" a gloss, but this merely pushes the problem one step back in the literary development of the text.[103] Solving this problem demands more evidence, but it is tempting to point to some Egyptian seals depicting the Pharaoh in right profile, with the left arm shown only in part (hence "broken").[104] In this case, the iconic representation of the royal body, signifying to the supporters of the Pharaoh his power, becomes an index of the failure of his power and self-display. The breaking of the royal arms signifies the defeat of the Pharaoh's state. The broken body of the ruler points to the broken body politic.

Later, the failure of Pharaoh's war plans leads to his descent into the Netherworld (32:17–32). (The placement of this oracle following the funeral hymn [קינה] indicates a high degree of planning for the entire oracles against Egypt complex of Ezek. 29–32.) The vision in this Netherworld oracle is of various fallen states (Assyria, Elam, Meshek/Tubal, Edom, and Sidon), each represented by a horde residing in Sheol. The striking repetition of "uncircumcised ones" (ערלים; ten times) and "the falling ones" (הנפלים; 4 times, three of which precede "with a sword" [בחרב]) point toward the bodies of the defeated, slain nations destroyed by Yahweh (who inspires fear among the living by sending mighty warriors to the grave).[105] Bodily defectiveness (uncircumcision) represents to a perfectly-bodied Israelite audience the sad fate—defeat and death—of the foreigners. The end

---

[103] So Greenberg, *Ezekiel 21–37*, 634; Zimmerli, *Ezekiel*, 2. 138; but Boadt, *Ezekiel's Oracles*, 86–87.

[104] See e.g., Schmitt, *Herrschaftsrepräsentation*, fig. 78.

[105] The idea of Yahweh as a fearsome warrior is part of the most ancient layers of Israelite theology (Exod. 15, Judg. 5), and it also figures prominently in the royal theology seen in Pss. 2, 20–21, and 144, as Chapters 2–3 have shown.

of the scene (32:31) contains an especially brutal and delicious bit of irony:

> Them shall Pharaoh see and be comforted—for all his crowd, those slain by the sword—Pharaoh and all his army!
>
> אותם יראה פרעה ונחם על כל המונה חללי חרב פרעה וכל חילו

This grim comfort is, of course, all that is available.

This extraordinary type scene may reflect Ezekiel's knowledge of the importance of the funerary cult in Egyptian theology, though there is little in his Netherworld that seems specifically Egyptian. Indeed, this very absence of Egyptian elements, whatever it says about the prophet's knowledge of Egyptian theology and mortuary practice, serves to reduce the Pharaoh to one member of the species *failed warrior*. Salient aspects of Ezekiel's vision include: (1) the placement of Pharaoh alongside the soldiers of enemy states (notably, Assyria); (2) the silence regarding the kings of Judah; and (3) the brief but tantalizing mention of the warriors' burial with their weapons of war (32:27). This last point indicates Ezekiel's notion that warriors, including kings, retained their status after death. Pharaoh, however, does not lie alongside these warriors who fell honorably and received proper burial, and so he is both part of and not part of their group. While the origins of Ezekiel's picture of the Underworld remain unknown,[106] the use to which he puts the vision is clear enough. He employs it as a commentary on the past, which he can now portray as a series of events in which kings fail to win permanent triumphs on the battlefield. All roads lead to the grave, and to a grave in which the royal self-display becomes a cruel joke.

Like Ezekiel, his older contemporary Jeremiah views the Pharaoh primarily as a failed warrior. Jer. 46 contains two oracles against Egypt, the first dating to just after the battle of Carchemish in 605 BCE (46:1–12) and against Necho, and the second (46:13–26) a generation later and against Apries/Hophra.[107] The first opens with a call to battle describing well-equipped warriors and follows with a

---

[106] For an examination of some of Ezekiel's connections to other texts, see Greenberg, *Ezekiel 21–37*, 660–70.

[107] On the problems of dating the second oracle, see Duane L. Christensen, *Transformations of the War Oracle in Old Testament Prophecy* (HDR 3; Missoula: Scholars, 1975) 220–21; Beat Huwyler, *Jeremia und die Völker: Untersuchungen zu den Völkersprüchen in Jeremia 46–49* (FAT 20; Tübingen: Mohr/Siebeck, 1997) 125–26.

depiction of the rout at the hands of Nebuchadrezzar, or rather, of Yahweh, the power behind the Babylonian king. The second oracle continues the theme of flight but adds a taunt of the Pharaoh himself, whom it cunningly renames שאון העביר המועד, to be translated something like "Loudmouth missed his chance (46:17),"[108] apparently a pun on the name Hophra (w'ḥ-ib-rʿ). The implication is that the king's utterances do not coincide with his actions, and so his self-display is that of a boisterous fool. He pretends to have the body of the skilled warrior, but his frailties render these claims nugatory.

To summarize the findings so far, the picture of Egypt at the end of the Israelite monarchy is that of a state that cannot deliver on its promises. The Pharaoh is an ineffectual warrior, his body incapable of winning battles, his self-display infelicitous. (The same view, by the way, informs the plaintive address of Adon [of Ashkelon or Gaza?][109] to Pharaoh Necho, whom he calls "the lord of kings" (מרא מלכים), and to whom he looks for aid against Nebuchadrezzar.) The one further issue to be considered is the nature of the Pharaoh of the exodus.

Without trying to unravel the many tangled threads in the exodus story that tie into this issue, I will raise two points. First, the parts of the Pharaoh's body that receive attention in Exod. 1–14 are his arm and his heart. Like Ezek. 30, Exodus focuses upon the king's arm, which signifies his strength and martial skill, and by extension his ability to control unruly slaves. This emphasis may reflect knowledge of old Egyptian conventions about the royal arm.[110] More importantly, the text frames this theme in terms of a personal contest between Pharaoh and Yahweh. Yahweh knows that Pharaoh will not release Israel unless compelled to do so by "a mighty hand" (ביד חזקה; 3:19). At the same time, the king will drive Israel out of his land by "a mighty hand," his own (6:1)! In other words, the god

---

[108] So William L. Holladay, *Jeremiah* (Hermeneia; 2 vols.; Minneapolis: Fortress, 1989) 2. 324; so also Huwyler, *Jeremia und die Völker*, 114–16.

[109] KAI 266; on the historical issues involved in the letter, see Joseph Fitzmyer, "The Aramaic Letter of King Adon to the Egyptian Pharaoh," in idem, *A Wandering Aramean* (reprint ed.; Grand Rapids: Eerdmans, 1997) 231–42.

[110] See James K. Hoffmeier, "The Arm of God Versus the Arm of Pharaoh in the Exodus Narratives," *Bib* 67 (1986) 378–87. A problem with his argument, however, is that the arm language declined in the Third Intermediate period, just the age when the Pentateuchal sources (as opposed to the traditions behind them) coalesced.

of Israel will force Pharaoh to use his power and skill against his own best interests.

This contest also underlies the notorious theme of the hardening of Pharaoh's heart (כבד לב חזק לב). Whatever the precise meaning of this phrase,[111] whatever the extent of divine causation for the king's insane behavior, the relevant point worth is that the heart is the seat of understanding. Refusal to listen equals hardening the heart in Exod. 7:19 and 8:15. Yahweh blocks the heart of the king so that he cannot hear and make a sound self-interested decision.

Second, the warlike aspects of the Pharaoh are latent, coming to the fore only in the final catastrophe at the Reed Sea. This contrasts sharply with the Ramesside self-image,[112] and even that of the less grand rulers of the Third Intermediate Period. Previously in the story, he is a builder, a father of a son, an owner of flocks, and a patron of magicians. The narrative presents a range of royal attributes, all of which fail when the king loses the contest with Yahweh. In this sense, then, the Exodus narrative both does and does not mirror the later image of Egypt seen in the prophets.

The Kings of Assyria

Like Egypt, Assyria appeared to Israel as a feared superpower. A large secondary literature exists studying facets of the royal propaganda of Neo-Assyria, its antecedents in earlier Mesopotamian empires, and its influences on the Levant.[113] Assyrian iconography and texts circulated in the Israelite kingdoms, in glyptic, inscriptional, and

---

[111] See Henri Cazelles, "פרעה," *TWAT* 6 (1989) 760–63; John Van Seters, *The Life of Moses: The Yahwist as Historian in Exodus-Numbers* (Louisville: Westminster/John Knox, 1994) 87–91.

[112] See Claudia Maderna-Sieben, "Der König als Kriegsherr und oberster Heerführer in den Eulogien der frühen Ramessidenzeit," in Rolf Gundlach and Christine Raedler, eds., *Selbstverständnis und Realität* (Wiesbaden: Harrassowitz, 1997) 49–79.

[113] For example, see the studies in F. M. Fales, *Assyrian Royal Inscriptions: New Horizons* (Rome: CNR, 1981); and in Parpola and Whiting, *Assyria 1995*; Peter Machinist, "Kingship and Divinity in Imperial Assyria" (unpublished paper); Mario Liverani, "The Ideology of the Assyrian Empire," in Mogens T. Larsen, ed., *Power and Propaganda* (Copenhagen: Akademisk, 1979) 297–317; Peter Machinist, "Assyrians on Assyria in the First Millennium BC," in Kurt Raaflaub, ed., *Anfänge politischen Denkens in der Antike* (Munich: Oldenbourg, 1993) 77–104; Jürgen Bär, *Der assyrische Tribut und seine Darstellung* (AOAT 243; Neukirchen-Vluyn: Neukirchener, 1996); Eva Cancik-Kirschbaum, "Konzeption und Legitimation von Herrschaft in neuassyrischer Zeit," *WO* 26 (1995) 5–20.

probably other media.[114] The body of the Neo-Assyrian king, created ritually and depicted in texts and pictures as one fit for war, hunting, sacrifice, and building, had its own integrity.[115] Israelite texts do not, however, present this bodily imagery in full, but instead choose only certain elements of it that they then fit into an overall understanding of the Assyrian rulers as threatening kings who ultimately lose to Yahweh.

In an important article, Peter Machinist has shown that Isaiah of Jerusalem and his circle were familiar with Assyrian royal propaganda and especially its martial aspects, which they subverted in order to underscore the continuing validity of Yahweh's covenant with Israel and protection of the king of Judah.[116] Here I examine features of the body of the Assyrian emperor as seen in 2 Kings 19:21–28 (= Isa. 37:22–29) and Isa. 10:13–14.

The first poem, an oracle to Hezekiah from Isaiah, follows the taunt of the Rab-shakeh during his unsuccessful siege of Jerusalem, and serves as a retort to it.[117] Although the poem itself describes a contest between God and the Assyrian emperor, without mentioning the king of Judah, the narrative framework brings Hezekiah into the picture. Unlike other biblical texts that describe the struggle as one purely between the god of Israel and the foreign king, here Yahweh's human vicegerent plays a role. This should caution against a too-easy assumption that the prophecies against the nations, in particular, stem from a setting outside, or even hostile to, the royal court and its propaganda (as seen in the royal psalms). Instead, multiple groups within the society share common viewpoints.

Hezekiah in this story must play a role that attracts divine attention. According to 2 Kings 19:1–19 (= Isa. 37:1–20), he does this, not only by going to the temple and inquiring of the prophet Isaiah (actions that must have required ritual purification of some sort, though the text does not explicitly say this), but by donning sack-

---

[114] See Schmitt, *Herrschaftsrepräsentation*, passim; Paolo Matthiae, "The Painted Sherd at Ramat Rahel," in Yohanan Aharoni, ed., *Excavations at Ramat Rahel: Seasons 1961 and 1962* (Rome: Centro di Studi Semitici, 1964) 85–94.

[115] See Ursula Magen, *Assyrische Königsdarstellungen: Aspekte der Herrschaft* (Mainz: von Zabern, 1986).

[116] Peter Machinist, "Assyria and its Image in the First Isaiah," *JAOS* 103 (1983) 719–37; idem, "Kingship and Divinity in Imperial Assyria."

[117] For the historical issues involved in this story, see Cogan and Tadmor, *II Kings*, 223–52.

cloth (וַיִּתְכַּס בַּשָּׂק; 2 Kings 19:1) and appealing to Yahweh to solve the problems facing Judah. Hezekiah's appeal in 2 Kings 19:16 centers upon orienting the divine body toward himself: "Incline, O Yahweh, your ear (אָזְנְךָ) and hear; open, O Yahweh, your eyes (עֵינֶיךָ) and see; and hear the words of Sennacherib which he sent to mock (לְחָרֵף) the living God." This appeal to divine honor depends for its success, in part at least, on Hezekiah's obeisance, demonstrated by the wearing of sackcloth. The king, that is, cooperates in the acts of divine intervention, not as a warrior, but as a pious supplicant. Hezekiah becomes like the pious king who petitions Yahweh in Ps. 144:10c-11, "Rescue me from the evil sword, and deliver me from the hand of the enemies, whose mouth speaks slander, whose right hand is the right hand of treachery" (מֵחֶרֶב רָעָה פְּצֵנִי וְהַצִּילֵנִי מִיַּד בְּנֵי נֵכָר אֲשֶׁר פִּיהֶם דִּבֶּר שָׁוְא וִימִינָם יְמִין שָׁקֶר). Conversely, Sennacherib is now the raging king attacking Zion in Ps. 2.

The text next turns to the taunt against Sennacherib (2 Kings 19:21–28 = Isa. 37:22–29), where the focus is again on the royal body, especially as an instrument of communication. Yahweh, through Isaiah the prophet, quotes Sennacherib as boasting of Assyrian ability to conquer. The citation of Assyrian direct speech may mirror the *oral* propaganda of the Assyrian empire, since direct quotation is rare in Sennacherib's inscriptions, only becoming a feature of the *written* propaganda during Esarhaddon's reign and later.[118] Hence the repeated mention of Yahweh's "hearing" (שָׁמַעְתִּי) of Sennacherib's boasts.[119] Sennacherib and Yahweh enter into a verbal contest, each laying claim to power and thus the praise of onlookers.

Although the Bible never systematically rebuts the Rab-shakeh's speech, here Yahweh focuses upon the king's loud utterances (and hence his mouth): "you have boasted . . . mocked . . . raised your

---

[118] See Pamela Gerardi, "Thus, He Spoke: Direct Speech in Esarhaddon's Royal Inscriptions," *ZA* 79 (1989) 245–60, esp. 245–46 n. 3. Alternatively, one could argue that the speech here dates to the seventh century and reflects written propaganda of that period. The choice between these options matters little for the present discussion, though.

[119] This emphasis on the oral component of the foreign king's self-portrayal and concomitantly the aural dimensions of Yahweh's (negative) response to it appears in the contemporaneous text, Zeph. 2:8: "I have heard (שָׁמַעְתִּי) of the mockery (חֶרְפַּת) of Moab, and the insults (גִּדּוּפֵי) of the Ammonites...." The text understands interethnic struggle as a verbal fight between the foreign nations and the god of Israel.

voice" (2 Kings 19:22; הרפת ונדפת/הרימות). The king's words, through his state apparatus and here the Rab-shakeh (19:23: ביד מלאכים), are blasphemous, since they mock a deity, Yahweh. These words are a "din" (19:28; שאננך)—compare Jer. 46:17's renaming of Necho!—and they irritate Yahweh. The Assyrian king has chosen to enter into a contest with the deity, one he cannot win.

This verbal and soon-to-be martial contest, strikingly, takes place before a female figure, the "Virgin Daughter of Zion/Jerusalem" (ציון בתי רושלם/בתולת בת; 2 Kings 19:21b-c). She mocks (בזה) and derides (לענה) Sennacherib. Here, as at the funeral of Saul or the military triumphs of David discussed in Chapter 4, male vigor must prove itself to a woman. For Sennacherib, this woman is, of course, the personified city that he will fail to capture, but in the context of male contestation in the Bible, the femaleness of the city cannot be gratuitous. The reputations of warriors stand or fall on the basis of the reports of women. Here the report is scornful.

The final point to be made here concerns the feet of the king (19:23), which climb high mountains. This verse reflects a theme of Neo-Assyrian propaganda, the king as conquering adventurer who scales distant mountains.[120] Isaiah, interestingly, does not deny to the king these adventures or the strength, stamina, and skill that they require. Instead, he admits that Yahweh knows all this and consequently will put his hook in Sennacherib's nose and the bit in his lips (ושמתי חחי באפך ומתני בשפתיך; 2 Kings 19:28b), thus transforming this royal body into a captive's visible to the mocking crowds and the feminized, personified city of Jerusalem.

The absence of any reference to Sennacherib's assassination in this description of his fate may indicate that the poem dates to a period during or shortly after the campaign of 701 BCE.[121] Also early may be the prose promise in 19:34: "So, I will defend this city in order to liberate it—*for my own sake and for the sake of David my servant*" (למעני ולמען דוד עבדי). Sennacherib has challenged the divine honor by boasting of his bodily accomplishments. So, his mouth, hands, and feet must fail in the contest with Yahweh, who speaks

---

[120] See Machinist, "Assyria and Its Image," 721.
[121] *Contra* Kaiser (*Isaiah 13–39*, 383–85), who posits a multi-stage redactional process for the text.

and acts in superior ways. This text reflects the official Judahite view of the king, in part. Yahweh will defend the current king because of his ancestor David. On the other hand, the idea of Hezekiah himself fighting or even preparing to do so (as in Pss. 20 and 21) is absent altogether. Isaiah is a political realist who expects divine salvation, but not from the puny Judahite military. Or, to put it another way, he can bend the Judahite royal self-presentation to fit the facts of the case and vice versa.

A similar view informs Isaiah 10, which again shows extensive knowledge of Assyrian royal propaganda. The prophet argues that, while Assyria was an instrument of Yahweh's punishment, it has exceeded its commission, building an empire instead (Isa. 10:5–10). At issue are two different views of the legitimation of Assyrian imperialist expansion: conquest as divine punishment and conquest as display of Assyrian royal glory. This distinction, which informs the entire Isaianic pericope, precisely mirrors two complementary views of expansion within the Assyrian corpus. Many Neo-Assyrian royal inscriptions justify the nation's expansion as, among other reasons, divine punishment of sacrilegious foreigners or a way of demonstrating the magnificence of the emperor (and the gods).[122] Isaiah brilliantly picks up these themes and plays them off against each other.

For this reason, I think that the line of scholarship that understands vv. 10–12 as an interpolation is fundamentally wrong,[123] because it misses the subtlety of the prophet's argument. He slides between a personified Assyria and that nation's king. The divine attack upon that nation takes the form of an attack on the royal body. Thus Yahweh in v. 12 singles out for criticism the royal heart (לבב) and eyes (עיניו), both of which the king uses to boast of his power, and both of which the deity will subvert.

To emphasize the bodily aspects of royal self-display, the text next quotes a boast of the king of Assyria (10:13–14):

---

[122] On the rationales, with relevant texts cited, see Bustenay Oded, *War, Peace and Empire: Justifications for War in Assyrian Royal Inscriptions* (Wiesbaden: Reichert, 1992) 121–37 and 145–62 respectively.

[123] See, for example, Otto Kaiser, *Isaiah 1–12* (2d ed.; OTL; London: SCM, 1983) 237–38; Wildberger, *Jesaja*, 401–3.

¹³By the strength of my hand I have acted,　　בכח ידי עשׂיתי
yes, in my wisdom—for I am discerning!　　ובחכמתי כי נבנותי
I have shifted the boundaries of the peoples,　　ואסיר גבולת עמים
and their treasures I have plundered,　　ועתידתיהם שׁושׂתי
and I have brought down like a bull the sitters (on thrones?).　　ואוריד כאביר יושׁבים
¹⁴My hand has found, like a nest,　　ותמצא כקן ידי
the wealth of the peoples.　　לחיל העמים
As one gathers abandoned eggs,¹²⁴　　כאסף ביצים עזבות
I have gathered all the earth!　　כל הארץ אני אספתי
And no one lifted a wing, opened a mouth, or chirped!　　ולא היה נדד כנף ופצה פה ומצפצף

Along with the homely metaphor of the person gathering eggs from an abandoned nest, this poem includes the expected mentions of military might. Yet perhaps the most interesting feature is one that is missing: the Assyrian king does not attribute his success to Aššur or other deities, as a real Assyrian emperor would have done.

Consider among many possible examples, the introduction to the famous "Black Obelisk" of Shalmaneser III, which lists the deities Aššur, Anu, Enlil, Ea, Sin, Adad, Šamaš, Marduk, Ninurta, Nergal, Nusku, Ninlil, and Ištar before the name of the king, whose patrons they were.¹²⁵ The biblical text clearly picks up on the first-person presentation style of the Assyrian royal inscriptions, but omits this important feature of almost of them. The Assyrian rulers, that is, portray themselves as pious dependents of the pantheon, through whose power the empire's conquests are possible.¹²⁶ The Isaiah tradition, however, decontextualizes the Assyrian emperor's self-presentation, turning it into errant boasting against Yahweh, though not, interestingly, against the Judahite king (*contra* Ps. 2).

Thus the Assyrian king figures in Israelite texts primarily as a conqueror. His roles as ritualizer, builder, and hunter are absent.¹²⁷ What is more, many aspects of the depictions of the royal Assyrian body that one finds in the country's art—the manly beard, well-muscled

---

¹²⁴ Hans Wildberger (*Jesaja*, 400) references here Deut. 22:6–7 with its prohibition of eating both a bird and its eggs. This is far in the background of Isa. 10:14, or perhaps altogether absent, however.
¹²⁵ For the text, see RIMA 0.102.14.
¹²⁶ See also Machinist, "Assyrians on Assyria."
¹²⁷ On the interrelationships of these roles in Assyrian royal self-understanding, see Magen, *Assyrische Königsdarstellungen*.

arms, powerful nose and eyes—also fade from view.[128] Although he is made to claim wisdom in Isa. 10:13, the Assyrian ruler is essentially a braggart who cannot deliver on his boasts. The biblical texts single out the bodily actions of boasting that the Judahite royal psalms attribute to the foreign ruler. For example, while this ruler's feet are powerful, they ironically set him on adventures to faraway lands where his eyes and mouth lead to his downfall. Israelites know the propaganda of the Assyrian empire but deliberately subvert it by reading it through the lenses of their own inherited tradition.

The King of Babylon

The next group of kings are those of Babylon, about whose bodies the biblical texts portray similarly to those of the other emperors as regards the contrast between promise and delivery that appears in depictions of Egyptian and Assyrian emperors also shapes the descriptions of the king of Babylon, Nebuchadrezzar. Although Babel figures in the Primeval History, and Hezekiah allied himself with Marduk-apla-iddinna against Assyria, only with Nebuchadrezzar do detailed Israelite reflections on Babylonia commence. David Vanderhooft has recently examined this material, and much of what follows relies on his work.[129] Leaving aside the late portrayal of Nebuchadrezzar in Daniel,[130] he appears in the Bible as a conqueror (2 Kings 24-25; Jer. 40-44, 46). The sign /conqueror/ generates images of him as a client of diviners (Ezek. 21:18-23), and (paradoxically) as an agent of Yahweh (Jer. 49:28, 30; this feature has antecedents in the portrayal of the Assyrian rulers in the prophets). However, this image of the "king of Babylon" applies only to Nebuchadrezzar. Another king, presumably Nabunaid, hears that his city is surrounded, and he can do nothing about it (Jer. 51:31). Yet the very same chapter juxtaposes the taunt of Babylonia containing this image of the king against another that has Nebuchadrezzar devouring Israel (Jer. 51:34). Not all Babylonian rulers are the same.

---

[128] On the conventions of this portraiture, see Irene Winter, "Art *in* Empire: The Royal Image and the Visual Dimensions of Assyrian Ideology," in Parpola and Whiting, *Assyria 1995*, 359-81.

[129] David Vanderhooft, *Neo-Babylonian Empire*.

[130] For an effort to assess the historical value of the portrayal of Nebuchadrezzar in Daniel, see D. J. Wiseman, *Nebuchadrezzar and Babylon* (Oxford: Oxford University Press, 1985) 81-115.

This contrast between Nebuchadrezzar and his successors is most prominent in Isa. 14:4b–21. To be sure, the date of the oracle is in question: it may be as late as the end of the Neo-Babylonian state or even later.[131] Alternatively, it may be a recycling of a taunt of a dead Assyrian emperor.[132] Either way, it clearly draws on much older literary traditions as it transforms epic into mockery.[133]

This mockery concentrates on the royal body. Helel ben Shahar wields a staff (מטה/שבט) in battle and is thus a king trained for warfare (vv. 5–6). Trees rejoice when he cannot arise, the reclining body becoming an index of failed power (v. 8). He boasts in his heart (לבב; v. 13) that he will ascend to the heavens, hero-like, just as he descends to the underworld, again like the failed hero. His successful self-display before monarchs, a central role of an ancient monarch, as can be seen in many inscriptions, fails miserably as "those seeing you (ראיך) stare; they contemplate you—is this the man making the world shake, causing kingdoms to tremble?" (v. 16). The poem thus inverts the foreign king's intended self-display of triumph over kings (seen in mirror image in Israel's contemplation of its own monarch as triumphant over foreign kings; e.g., Ps. 2), exposing him to the ridicule of other foreign kings. Yet even there the triumph of the foreign remains incomplete, for all the monarchs repose in the underworld!

Thus the taunt of the king resembles those in Ezekiel and Jeremiah we have seen already. Like the Pharaoh in Ezek. 32, this king dies and descends to the underworld. V. 17 describes him as a practicer of scorched earth policies (שם תבל כמדבר ועריו הרס), an accurate description of Neo-Babylonian military tactics. Vv. 18–19 contrast the normal burial of kings at home with his burial elsewhere. This may reflect the deportation of Nabunaid by Cyrus, or it may reflect an older theme, seen in the anguished discussion of the loss of Sargon's body, of the importance of proper burial for a slain king.

---

[131] See Kaiser, *Isaiah 13–39*, 31–33 ("there are no criteria to be found within the poem for its dating" [31]); Wildberger, *Jesaja*, 537–38; but see Vanderhooft, *Neo-Babylonian Empire*, 128–29, who argues that it is a reused oracle against Assyria (following H. L. Ginsberg, "Reflexes of Sargon in Isaiah after 715 BCE," *JAOS* 88 [1968] 47–53).

[132] See Joseph Blenkinsopp, *Isaiah 1–39* (AB 19; New York: Doubleday, 2000) 286–87.

[133] See the comments of R. Mark Shipp, *Of Dead Kings and Dirges: Myth and Meaning in Isaiah 14:4b–21* (Academia Biblica 11; Atlanta: Society of Biblical Literature, 2002).

The poem points to the ultimate failure of foreign kings to defeat Yahweh. This failure results not only in death, which awaits everyone, but also in mockery and burial far from home.

Conclusion

This survey of biblical material on foreign kings has led to several conclusions. First, Israelites were primarily interested in these rulers as military leaders (though the king of Tyre plays the role of merchant prince). The texts are reticent about the rulers' personal appearance, marital life, religious practices, and a host of other features about which one might like to know. The portrayal of the foreign rulers almost exclusively as warriors obviously reflects the realities of Levantine politics of the Iron Age, but it also accepts and then subverts the *self*-portrayals of these kings, who wanted Israelites to see them as warriors.

Second, concentration on the military aspects of kingship implies an interest in arms and legs, which are variously strong or broken, skilled or helpless. Hair, clothing, and other elements of self-display do not play a prominent role in the biblical images of foreign kings. Is the notion that these elements are epiphenomenal, or is the reason deeper? Recall that the fit Israelite ruler in some respects inhabits a body modeled on Yahweh's (see Ps. 110; 144). Precisely these elements of Yahweh's body—hands, feet, eyes, mouth—play the chief role in descriptions of him.[134] The sliding scale between God and king that appears in the royal psalms also underlies the basic attitudes of Israelites toward foreign kings.

Third, the Bible's portrayals of foreign rulers tend to view them through the lenses of the royal Judahite propaganda, namely as kings making wild declamations against Yahweh and Judah and attacking Jerusalem (cf. Ps. 2). To change the optical metaphor, the Bible refracts genuine knowledge of foreign beliefs and practices through the prism of Israelite conceptions of their own king. This is true even when, as in the case of the Tyrian rulers, the foreign king and his state historically posed no threat to the Israelite monarchies. In

---

[134] See Thomas Podella, *Das Lichtkleid YHWHs* (FAT 15: Tübingen: Mohr/Siebeck, 1996).

the texts, the foreign king is always a potential threat, even when Israel is threatening him. This is true whether we are speaking of the great emperors or the Palestinian mayors of the conquest tradition. This reification of the foreign king as a perennial threat constitutes, of course, a kind of argument, not merely a "factual" description of reality. Kings always live in a dense network of political relationships that they must negotiate properly. The "state" does not exist apart from "subjects," who use it for their own purposes.[135] In principle, the biblical authors could have dealt even with imperialists like the Assyrian rulers as saviors (as Ahaz of Judah or Birrakib of Sam'al did). Yet they universally understood foreign rulers as a threat and therefore an object of divine judgment. To push further, the royal body is also an object that subjects and enemies "use," or to speak less oracularly, an object upon which they project their hopes and fears. In the cases examined here, Israel concentrates mostly its fears on the foreign kings, fears which divine intervention overcomes.

Fourth, and most importantly, the Israelite texts we have studied understand the international geopolitics on which they comment in terms of contestation between the foreign king (and usually derivatively, his state) and Yahweh. This notion, which one may call mythological, harks back to the Judahite royal self-presentation in texts like Pss. 2 and 144, where the foreign kings are raving madmen assaulting the divine suzerain. With the exception of 2 Kings 19 (= Isa. 37), this contestation leaves the human Israelite or Judahite king out of the equation. Or alternatively, as with the rulers of Aram and in a different way Assyria (Isa. 10:5ff.), the foreign ruler becomes an instrument of Yahweh's punishment of the king of Israel or Judah. The foreigner threatens Israel (as in Ps. 2), but the threat comes at Yahweh's behest!

This competition between the foreign king and the deity, before it ends in warfare, takes the form of verbal sparring, a major topic of which is the proper display and even characteristics of the royal body. The best example of this is in 2 Kings 19 = Isa. 37, but traces of the same motif appear throughout the texts we have examined. The foreign king's body fails to pass Yahweh's examination, leading to the downfall of the state in question.

---

[135] See Michael Herzfeld, *Cultural Intimacy: Social Poetics in the Nation-State* (New York: Routledge, 1997) esp. 2.

Significantly, however, these unofficial texts alter the Judahite royal propaganda in a significant respect. They sever the relationship between Yahweh and the human Israelite ruler. That is, the signs *foreign king* and *Israelite king* do not function antonymically. The code of the state, in which the royal body is the locus of divine activity, is not deployed by other Israelites, notably the prophets. At one level, the disassociation of royal body and divine body reflects the realities of Levantine politics, yet a functional explanation does not suffice given the vast human ability to manipulate experience to fit an ideational code. Rather, contestation of the state's views was an important feature of Israelite life, even among elites and retainers who had access to the state apparatus. To refer again to Terry Eagleton's dictum, "... an ideology is never a simple reflection of a ruling class's ideas: on the contrary, it is always a complex phenomenon, which may incorporate conflicting, even contradictory, views of the world."[136] The various surviving Israelite views of divine kingship and its human correspondences both cohere and disagree, depending on the issue in question.

Finally, then, one is left with the cry of Ps. 2:1: למה רגשו גוים. The very question posits the illegitimacy of the aspirations of these nations and their rulers, even as it promises their ultimate failure in the face of the triumphant God of Israel. Israelite texts coopt the metaphors of the foreign powers in order to deligitimize them. Along the way, however, the raging peoples will spill much blood, forcing Israel to seek ways to explain the discontinuity between politico-religious rhetoric and reality.

---

[136] Terry Eagleton, *Marxism and Literary Criticism* (Berkeley: University of California Press, 1976) 6–7.

CHAPTER EIGHT

CONCLUSIONS AND IMPLICATIONS

This book began with a puzzle: what happened when Saul received a new heart at his coronation? This tiny conundrum became the starting point of a long investigation into the problem of the Israelite king's body and its function as a sign relating to Israel's conceptions of maleness, rule, and divinity. Many texts in the Bible discuss the royal body and seek to discriminate proper display of it from improper. Understanding the shape and flow of this discussion has required not only the close historical- and literary-critical examination of these texts, but the deployment of newer methods (semiotics, performativist approaches to ritual) that try to understand texts as records of ritual behavior and as reflections of underlying systems of signs. In this final chapter, I summarize what I think we have learned about Israel's reflections on the royal body and also seek an explanation of why the topic was so important to that society. This entire project exemplifies what Ziony Zevit describes as an emerging fourth paradigm of biblical scholarship, one that is keenly aware of both literary and historical questions and their complex interrelationships, of the boundedness of the researcher, and of the need to concentrate on subordinate issues in order to illuminate Israelite society writ large.[1] My hope is that the work succeeds to some degree in illuminating the problem at hand.

As a foundation for this summary, let us also recall the groundbreaking study of the two bodies of the medieval king by Ernst Kantorowicz. He noted that, "Not only is the body politic 'more ample and large' than the body natural, but there dwell in the former certain truly mysterious forces which reduce, or even remove, the imperfections of the fragile human nature."[2] The medieval king, according to this way of thinking (which Kantorowicz explicates),

---

[1] See Ziony Zevit, *The Religions of Ancient Israel* (London/New York: Continuum, 2001) 69–73.

[2] Ernst Kantorowicz, *The King's Two Bodies: A Study in Mediaeval Political Theology* (Princeton: Princeton University Press, 1957) 9.

was both mortal and immortal, both frail and invulnerable, his judgments both fallible and irrefragable. The king was a man, but the King was almost a god. Medieval thinkers spoke, not of kingship as an office separate from the incumbent on the throne, but, mythologically, of two bodies of the king, the two forming one whole person.[3] The distinction derived in part from formulations of the dual nature of Christ, though with important adjustments made for a king who was, after all, not divine. And, insofar as the speculation on the body of Christ has biblical roots,[4] it ultimately traces back to the Hebrew Bible.

The differentiation between the body politic of the King and the biosocial body of the king also proves useful for understanding the biblical texts concerning the Israelite royal body. While a given king could die, the King remained, and this perdurance found expression in various ways, such as burial near the seat of government (in the capital cities), or marriage (hence procreation, hence dynastic succession) in the palace near the temple. In Israelite texts, kingship is not an institution disassociated from the actions of human beings, including their physical movements, their dress and etiquette, their sickness and health. One cannot understand many features of Israelite beliefs and practices impinging upon monarchy without comprehending this fact. Moreover, though in Israelite literature, the frailties of the "natural body"—the words are Kantorowicz's and a biblical writer might not have understood them—might pervade stories about kings, the "body politic" cannot always remove or even ameliorate its inadequacies. The destruction of the "natural body" may result from, or result in, the destruction of the body politic. The endangered king signifies the endangered state and people.

This equation between king and people is true for at least four reasons. First, the term "body" refers not merely to an easily measurable, finite entity. Rather, the king's body is a sign—a code really—that signifies for Israelite spectators at once every male, the society, the cosmos, and even Yahweh. When we speak of the royal body,

---

[3] On which see Caroline Bynum, *The Resurrection of the Body in Western Christianity* (New York: Columbia University Press, 1995).

[4] For a discussion of the body of Christ in the New Testament, see, e.g., Heon-Wook Park, *Die Kirche als 'Leib Christi' bei Paulus* (Giessen: Brunnen, 1992); and Martinus C. DeBoer, *Johannine Perspectives on the Death of Jesus: Contributions to Biblical Exegesis & Theology* (Kampen: Kok Pharos, 1996).

we mean all it stands for. Second, this sign function of the body exists because behaviors and ideas revolve around the body. The king acts, displays himself, trains and grooms himself. His subjects and enemies respond with actions that seem to them commensurate and appropriate. Third, all these behaviors and the ideas with which they exist in a reciprocal relationship generate still more behaviors and ideas, more signs. Kingship exists as part of a self-perpetuating society and vice versa. Hence one can speak of the social poetics of kingship. Fourth, the nature, purpose, and proper use and display of the royal body elicited much discussion among rulers and subjects. All of this was negotiable, mutable, and fluid. One may not speak of the "body" as a fixed datum, but only of it in particular situations, or in particular relationships. Viewers of the king decided over and over again what his body meant. All of these aspects of the body as a (network of) signs come into play.

Here let us be specific. In the royal psalms, the kings of Israel and Judah took on a new body at their coronation. Since harem politics played a role in traditional states in determining who the heir to the throne would be, the coronation rather than physical birth (or, apparently, even the death of the previous king) marked the moment at which the new king became a different person with a different anatomy. Pss. 2 and 110 describe him as the son (בר or בן) of God (cf. Isa. 9:6), and Ps. 45 labels him אלהים; how these titles differed in meaning, if at all, remains unclear. The coronation created a king for whom "dominance is a sort of norm," a ruler set on Zion able to face down all foreign enemies because Yahweh has trained him for war, giving him not only the right anatomy, but the right martial disciplines and weapons for dominating all attackers.

This new king also undertook to reform his own body and those of his subjects. Ps. 101 expresses the obligations of the monarch—and his subjects—in bodily terms, avoiding lists of customary obligations such as one finds in Mesopotamia. The Israelite king must destroy those whose bodies (and thus actions) did not accord with virtue.

An important theme that emerges in the royal psalms is that of the king as a male contesting for status with other males, but under the tutelage of the supreme male, Yahweh. Even at his wedding, he appears as a warrior who "conquers" the foreign powers represented in the person of his wife and the guests bearing tribute to them (Ps. 45). The Israelite king must face down foreign kings, who are, virtually by definition, warriors contesting sovereignty with the ruler of Israel. With the exception of Ps. 89, these texts portray him doing so. Even that psalm, to be sure, recognizes Israelite dominance as a given and merely calls upon God to insure that the natural state of affairs returns. All the royal psalms make much of the king's self-display as a great warrior, as well as a lover and procreator (Ps. 45) and builder (Ps. 132). Never far away is the sense that the disciplined royal body can dominate all comers.

It is striking to what degree the military imagery influences depictions of every aspect of the king's life in these psalms. Violence and the circumscription thereof thoroughly overwhelm other aspects of the poetics of kingship in Judah and Israel. Does the reason for this lie in the political instability and military insecurity of the Israelite dual monarchies, in a deep structural feature of the local religion (e.g., the Yahweh as Divine Warrior theme in the earliest Israelite religion), or in some combination of the two? Perhaps we should look to the consolidation of this state during the ninth-seventh centuries as part of the answer. Jerusalem grew in the late eighth century owing in part to immigration from areas devastated by Assyria. The theology of the invincibility of Jerusalem also flourished during this period (though it may have had earlier antecedents),[5] and a bellicose understanding of kingship would have been comprehensible just at this time.

Whenever one dates the origins of this tendency toward rhetorical violence, its claims raise an important and interesting question. How persuasive was the presentation of kingship in these psalms? How convincing was the portrayal of a petty ruler as a universal sovereign? In what ways could Israelites (mis)understand, (mis)use the code (disemia) to suit various political, religious, or even gender issues? What happens when the monarch is impotent, either sexually or militarily? Or how does his impiety—misuse of the body in ritual—affect how others view him?

Now, the official ideas of states (ideologies) often seem remarkably coherent and irresistible, but in fact, members of a polity often appropriate them in different ways, feeding them into other sets of ideas and practices that exist at local or familial levels. The claims of the

---

[5] J. J. M. Roberts, "The Davidic Origin of the Zion Tradition," *JBL* 92 (1973) 329–44.

political center may elicit a range of rhetorical strategies "entailing the constant renegotiation of stereotypical categories," as Michael Herzfeld puts it.[6] That is, the state line rarely commands unquestioned assent, and various persons may use it for their own purposes.[7]

This principle operates in the many biblical narratives describing the king and thus relating to his body. As we have seen, the royal psalms' presentation of the royal bodies, biosocial and political, did not command universal, unqualified assent, although these bodies did draw universal interest. The narratives contained in the DH portray the king as dangerous and endangered. Danger obviously came from the king trained in warfare rather than merely from the one who seemed most attractive (Absalom) or the most physically imposing (Saul). But even the successful warrior needed to mask his threatening aspect, which he could do by sparing a Shimei, for example. The threatened king must seek to reverse his position by dressing in sack, thus displaying his humiliated body, and by appealing to the deity to ascertain whether his body matched the proper body of a king, as a Hezekiah does.

To take another example, although the coronation ritual described in 1 Sam. 8–12 portrays a king whose will is law—much to the detriment of his subjects—the DH and its sources are well aware of the fragility of any given king. The twin themes of the dangerous king/endangered king inform large narrative blocks, and we see kings and would-be kings manipulating and displaying their own bodies to advance themselves. Male contest shapes the lives of Saul and David, David and Absalom, and then many of their successors. Males and females constantly negotiate understandings of the kings' bodily behaviors: is David's frenzy a sign of valor or madness (or somehow both)? Can Absalom's handsomeness and skill at orchestrating self-display qualify him for kingship? Ancient readers seem to have been fascinated with such questions.

Nor was their fascination limited to Israelite kings. Various biblical writers knew much about the internal royal self-conceptions of foreign powers, but they understood these bits of knowledge in terms

---

[6] Michael Herzfeld, *The Poetics of Manhood: Contest and Identity in a Cretan Mountain Village* (Princeton: Princeton University Press, 1985) 31.

[7] On the state in an agricultural society, see Ernest Gellner, *Nations and Nationalism* (Ithaca: Cornell University Press, 1983) 8–18.

of Israelite conceptions of foreign kings as the dominated ones. Sometimes they reversed the official Israelite line and, in accordance with the realities of current politics, portrayed the foreign king as the triumphant one, even the tool of Yahweh. Sometimes they took the opposite tack. But the point is that these writers took an interest in the self-display, sometimes even the anatomy, of these foreign kings. Hophra becomes "blabbermouth," a reference to the futility of his pompous boasting. Pharaoh takes a tour of the Underworld in which, rather than becoming Osiris after a successful judgment, he merely sees the tombs of the nations that Yahweh has defeated, including his own.

This brings me to several larger-scale findings of this study. First, the king's body resembles that of Yahweh. In a recent study of the *Lichtkleid JHWHs*,[8] Thomas Podella has noted that portrayals of the deity draw heavily on royal imagery, especially regarding the adornment and display of his body. Conversely, he notes that the king draws on divine imagery. Podella thus speaks of "JHWH als Königsgestalt" (186ff.) and "Der königliche Mensch als *imago Dei*" (252ff.). That is, God and the human king are on a sliding scale without clear demarcations between the two. As I will note momentarily, this is an important insight into the Israelite mindset regarding kingship.

Second, however, simultaneous with the king's likeness to Yahweh is his vulnerability, which I take to be a condition of the "body natural." Certainly there is no sense here, *contra* the history of religions school, of the king as a simulacrum of a dying and rising god. This vulnerability may be physical illness (Isa. 38) or danger in battle (Ps. 89). The danger may be expressed on a different semiotic plane: thus the sick king is at risk of being dragged into Sheol, or is unable to swim in deep waters. (Conceivably, the kings of Judah did not learn to swim, or perhaps the imagery is to be taken less literally.) Or his life is about to be rolled up like a rug. This resort to simile allows a reticence or euphemism about sickness. Not so with danger in battle, however, even if here it is not necessarily the king's body that is at risk, but the state itself, which the body of the king signifies. Even here, though, the code does not allow the king to

---

[8] Thomas Podella, *Das Lichtkleid JHWHs: Untersuchungen zur Gestalthaftigkeit Gottes im Alten Testament und seiner altorientalischen Umwelt* (FAT 15; Tübingen: Mohr/Siebeck, 1996).

flee—he never has pursuers (רדפים)—he must fight to the death. Yet his bravery is insufficient because Yahweh has betrayed him (Ps. 89). Without divine aid there is no victory; the royal body's military training thus has an all-important cultic dimension that must be properly carried out (hence Ps. 20's reference to the king's sacrifices).

Third, Israelite kingship both is and is not *sui generis*. The dangerous/endangered king motif appears with modification at Zençirli, although it contrasts sharply with the Neo-Assyrian view of its emperor as the invincible tool of the god Aššur. The idea that the royal body took new form at the coronation may also have parallels in both Mesopotamia and Egypt. And, in numerous smaller details, one can discern within the Bible and Levantine inscriptions, in particular, a common outlook on the royal body. Gressmann was apparently right to discern a regionwide *Hofstil* reflected also in the Bible.

To summarize these three points, then, the tales of kings reflect various conventions, laid out in the royal psalms and transfigured in narrative, that give shape to the ways in which rulers are presented. Bodily functions—from eating, to intercourse, to defecation, to fighting, to mourning, to parading about—constitute the stuff of which kingship consists. The good king is the one who masters these bodily activites, these modes of bodily display, in ways that his society judges appropriate. Understanding kingship in Israel necessitates understanding the dual monarchies' rules for bodily action and inaction and the proper etiquette for dealing with the royal body.

Now we may proceed to the fourth point. Why did the royal body occasion so much story and song in ancient Israel? Beyond the obvious answer that powerful persons and their deeds hold intrinsic interest, whether they directly affect others or not, at least three other factors play a role. First, the display of the king's body signifies the good order of the society as a whole. Note, for example, Ps. 101's interest in the proper body of both king and subject. Conversely, improper bodily display—or the improper body, like Saul's or Absalom's—can lead to national disaster. Second, the royal body offers a norm for other males. The Assyrian proverb has it that "Man is a shadow of god. . . . The king is the perfect likeness of God" (*muššulu ša ili*).[9] The proverb both compares the king to other

---

[9] Letter 145, ll. 9–13 in Simo Parpola, *Letters from Assyrian Scholars to the Kings Esarhaddon and Assurbanipal*, vol. 1: *Texts* (AOAT 5/1; Neukirchen-Vluyn: Neukirchener, 1970) 112–13.

human beings and contrasts them. For Israel, too, the king was both in the same category as other males, and in a transcendent category. Third, and most importantly, the royal body intrigued Israelites because they saw in it a sign of the body of Yahweh. The king's very existence served as a token of divine interest in, and protection of, Israel. Royal sickness or death could be a sign of divine displeasure. Royal health and vigorous self-display could signify divine favor. In short, the royal body was an icon of Yahweh's body and therefore revelatory of the divine realm. Religion and royal cult tended to merge, and the prophets and various biblical narrators took upon themselves the task of limiting this merger.

Finally, before ending this journey, though, let me picture the vistas that lie ahead. Several important questions need reexamination in the light of this study.

First, we need to rethink the notions of the divine body in ancient Israel. I have argued that a sliding scale exists on which king and deity lie close together. Thomas Podella came to much the same conclusion, though on different grounds in a very interesting book on the "luminescent body of Yahweh." It would be important to try to understand how this linkage between king and god originated in Israel (what connection does it have to Egyptian ideas, for example), and then how it transmuted into Second Temple messianism.

Second, I have hinted in various ways about the implications of this study for our understandings of the acceptable limits of male behavior in ancient Israel. This question needs more study. We know a great deal more about conventions of femaleness than we used to, but the male so far has not been studied in the light of contemporary gender theory or with sufficient attention to relevant comparative evidence. We do know that, while Israelite males gained status in competitive self-display with each other, this status was often ratified (signified) by women in song or otherwise. We also know that, not surprisingly, kings did things unacceptable, because overweening, in others (such as riding about in a chariot, as Absalom did). The royal body was a model for other males, but not a fully attainable model.

Third, the setting and function of the prophecies against the foreign kings (and, in general, against the nations) deserve more study. I have tried to note the ways in which these texts talk about the bodies of foreign rulers, but we know too little about (1) how well the prophets understood foreign ideologies (though they clearly did to some degree), (2) when and where these texts were used (were they part of a ritual of which the Israelite or Judahite king figured or not), and (3) how Israelites measured the success or failure of the claims of these texts. All of these questions are intrinsically interesting, even if not fully answerable, but they also bear upon the problem at hand because they speak to the ways in which Israelites also understood the claims of the royal psalms regarding foreign powers.

Let me conclude, then, with a text that Mesopotamians, perhaps satirically, used to understand kingship, the close of the Standard Babylonian Recension of the "Cuthean Legend" of Naram-Sin:

> Read this stele! Hearken unto the words of this stele.... Strengthen your walls! Fill your moats with water! Your chests, your grain, your money, your goods, your possessions, bring into your stronghold! Tie up your weapons and put (them) into the corners! Guard your courage! Take heed of your own person! Let him [the enemy] roam through your land! Go not out to him...! (But) you be self-controlled, disciplined. Answer them, "Here I am, sir"! Requite their wickedness with kindness! (ll. 154–55, 160–66, 170–72)[10]

This obviously ironic portrayal of the fearful, ineffectual king marks the exact inversion of the Israelite ideal. In Israel, the king goes forth to war, his eyes alert to evil, his heart set on good, his limbs trained for war, and his feet supported by Yahweh. Those who see his extraordinary body either run away, if they are his foe, or fall at his feet. Or so goes the state line. Others had different views. Here I have tried to explicate all these views with an end toward understanding more fully an important theme in Israel's societal self-understanding.

---

[10] In the translation of Joan Goodnick Westenholz, *Legends of the Kings of Akkade: The Texts* (Winona Lake: Eisenbrauns, 1997) 327–31.

WORKS CITED

Abitz, Friedrich, *Pharao als Gott In den Unterweltsbuchern des Neuen Reiches* (OBO 146; Göttingen: Vandenhoeck & Ruprecht, 1995).
Abou-Assaf, Ali, Pierre Bordreuil, and Alan R. Millard, *La Statue de Tell Fekherye et son inscription bilingue assyro-araméenne* (Paris: ERC, 1982).
Abusch, Tzvi, "Ghost and God: Some Observations on a Babylonian Understanding of Human Nature," in A. I. Baumgarten, Jan Assmann, and G. G. Stroumsa, eds., *Self, Soul and Body in Religious Experience* (SHR 78: Leiden: Brill, 1998) 363–83.
Aelian, *Historical Miscellany* (ed. N. G. Wilson; LCL 486; Cambridge: Harvard University Press, 1997).
Ahl, Frederick M., "The Rider and the Horse: Politics and Power in Roman Poetry from Horace to Statius," *ANRW* II.32.1 (1984) 40–110.
Ahlström, Gösta, *The History of Ancient Palestine from the Palaeolithic Period to Alexander's Conquest* (ed. Diana Edelman; JSOTSS 146: Sheffield: Sheffield Academic Press, 1993).
——, *Psalm 89: Eine Liturgie aus dem Ritual des leidenden Königs* (Lund: Gleerup, 1959).
——, *Royal Administration and National Religion in Ancient Palestine* (Leiden: Brill, 1982).
Akurgal, Ekrem, *Spaethethitische Bildkunst* (Ankara: Archaeologisches Institut der Universitaet Ankara, 1949).
Albertz, Rainer, *A History of Israelite Religion in the Old Testament Period* (2 vols.; Louisville: Westminster/John Knox, 1994).
Albrektson, Bertil, *History and the Gods: An Essay on the Idea of Historical Events as Divine Manifestations in the Ancient Near East and in Israel* (Lund: Gleerup, 1967).
Albright, William F., "The Oracles of Balaam," *JBL* 63 (1944) 207–33.
——, "The Phoenician Inscriptions of the Tenth Century B.C.," *JAOS* 67 (1947) 153–62.
Allen, Leslie C., *Psalms 101–150* (WBC 21; Waco, TX: Word, 1983).
Alt, Albrecht, "Das Königtum in den Reichen Israel und Juda," in idem, *Kleine Schriften zur Geschichte des Volkes Israel* (2 vols.; Munich: Beck, 1953) 2. 116–34.
——, "Das System der assyrischen Provinzen auf dem Boden des Reiches Israel," *ZDPV* 52 (1929) 220–42.
Althann, Robert, *Studies in Northwest Semitic* (BibOr 45; Rome: Pontifical Biblical Institute, 1997).
Anderson, A. A., *2 Samuel* (WBC 11; Dallas: Word, 1989).
Anderson, Gary, *A Time to Mourn, a Time to Dance: The Expression of Grief and Joy in Israelite Religion* (University Park, PA: Pennsylvania State University Press, 1991).
Antonaccio, Carla M., *An Archaeology of Ancestors: Tomb Cult and Hero Cult in Early Greece* (Lanham, MD: Rowman & Littlefield, 1995).
Ap-Thomas, D. R., "Saul's Uncle," *VT* 11 (1961) 241–45.
Arneth, Martin, *"Sonne der Gerechtigkeit": Studien zur Solarisierung der Jahwe-Religion im Lichte von Psalm 72* (BZAR 1; Wiesbaden: Harrassowitz, 2000).
Artzi, Pinhas, "Rationality in the Ancient Near Eastern International Relations in the 'Extended Age of the Amarna Archive,' ca. 1460–1200 BCE: The Force of ṭēmu 'Mind'," in Chaim Cohen, Avi Hurvitz, and Shalom Paul, eds., *Sefer Moshe: The Moshe Weinfeld Jubilee Volume* (Winona Lake, IN: Eisenbrauns, 2004) 339–50.
Asad, Talal, "Remarks on the Anthropology of the Body," in Sarah Coakley, ed., *Religion and the Body* (Cambridge: Cambridge University Press, 1997) 42–52.
Assmann, Jan, *Ägyptische Hymnen und Gebete* (Zurich: Artemis, 1975).

———, *Der König als Sonnenpriester* (ADAIK 7; Glückstadt: Augustin, 1970).
———, *Ma'at: Gerechtigkeit und Unsterblichkeit im Alten Ägypten* (Munich: Beck, 1990).
———, "Die Macht der Bilder: Rahmenbedingungen ikonischen Handelns im alten Ägypten," *Visible Religion* 7 (1990) 1–20.
———, "State and Religion in the New Kingdom," in James P. Allen, et al., eds., *Religion and Philosophy in Ancient Egypt* (New Haven: Yale Egyptological Seminar, 1989) 55–88.
Aubet, Maria, *The Phoenicians and the West* (Cambridge: Cambridge University Press, 2001).
Austin, J. L., *How To Do Things with Words* (2d ed.; Cambridge: Harvard University Press, 1975).
Avalos, Hector, "Daniel 9:24–25 and Mesopotamian Temple Rededications," *JBL* 117 (1998) 507–11.
———, *Illness and Health Care in the Ancient Near East: The Role of the Temple in Greece, Mesopotamia, and Israel* (HSM 54; Atlanta: Scholars, 1995).
Avigad, Nahman and Benjamin Sass, *Corpus of West Semitic Stamp Seals* (Jerusalem: Israel Academy of Sciences and Humanities, 1997).
Avishur, Yitzhaq, *Studies in Hebrew and Ugaritic Psalms* (Jerusalem: Magnes, 1994).
———, *Stylistic Studies of Word Pairs in Biblical and Ancient Literatures* (AOAT 210; Neukirchen-Vluyn: Neukirchener, 1984).
Bachelot, Luc, "La Fonction politique des Reliefs Neo-Assyriens," in D. Charpin and F. Joannes, eds., *Marchands, diplomates et Empereurs* (Paris: ERC, 1991) 109–28.
Baltzer, Klaus, *Deutero-Jesaja* (KAT 10/2; Gütersloh: Gütersloher Verlagshaus, 1999).
Bär, Jürgen, *Der assyrische Tribut und seine Darstellung* (AOAT 243: Neukirchen-Vluyn: Neukirchener, 1996).
Barkay, Gabriel and Amos Kloner, "Jerusalem Tombs from the Days of the First Temple," *BAR* 12 (1986) 22–39.
Barkay, Gabriel, Amihai Mazar, and Amos Kloner, "בית הקברות הצפוני של ירושלים בימי בית ראשון," *Qadmoniot* 8 (1975) 71–76.
Barr, James, "'Thou Art the Cherub': Ezekiel 28.14 and the Post-Ezekiel Understanding of Genesis 2–3," in Eugene Ulrich et al., *Priests, Prophets and Scribes* (JSOTSS 149; Sheffield: Sheffield Academic Press, 1992) 213–23.
Beal, Timothy K. and David M. Gunn, eds., *Reading Bibles, Writing Bodies: Identity and the Book* (London: Routledge, 1997).
Beckwith, Sarah, *Christ's Body: Identity, Culture and Society in Late Medieval Writings* (London: Routledge, 1993).
Begg, Christopher T., "The Death of Josiah in Chronicles: Another View," *VT* 37 (1987) 1–8.
Berquist, John, *Controlling Corporeality: The Body and the Household in Ancient Israel* (New Brunswick, NJ: Rutgers University Press, 2002).
Begrich, Joachim, *Der Psalm des Hiskia: Ein Beitrag zum Verständnis von Jesaja 38, 10–20* (FRLANT 25: Göttingen: Vandenhoeck & Ruprecht, 1926).
Beiner, G., *Shakespeare's Agonistic Comedy: Poetics, Analysis, Criticism* (Rutherford, NJ: Fairleigh Dickinson University Press, 1993).
Bell, Catherine, *Ritual: Perspectives and Dimensions* (New York: Oxford University Press, 1999).
———, *Ritual Theory, Ritual Practice* (Oxford: Oxford University Press, 1992).
Ben-Barak, Zafrira, "Succession to the Throne in Israel and in Assyria," *Orientalia Lovaniensia Periodica* 17 (1986) 85–100.
Benthall, Jonathan and Ted Polhemus, eds., *The Body as a Medium of Expression* (London: Lane, 1975).
Bentzen, Aage, *Messias, Moses redivivus, Menschensohn* (Zurich: Zwingli, 1948).
Berges, Ulrich, *Die Verwerfung Sauls: Eine thematische Untersuchung* (FB 61; Würzburg: Echter, 1989).
Berlinerblau, Jacques, "Preliminary Remarks for the Sociological Study of Israelite

'Official Religion'," in Robert Chazan, William W. Hallo, and Lawrence H. Schiffman, eds., *Kī Baruch Hu: Ancient Near Eastern, Biblical, and Judaic Studies in Honor of Baruch A. Levine* (Winona Lake, IN: Eisenbrauns, 1999) 153–70.

Bernhardt, Karl-Heinz, *Das Problem der altorientalischen Königs-Ideologie im Alten Testament* (VTSupp 8; Leiden: Brill, 1961).

Betz, Hans Dieter, ed., *The Greek Magical Papyri in Translation, including the Demotic Spells* (Chicago: University of Chicago Press, 1986).

Beuken, Willem A. M., *Isaiah, Part II*, vol. 2: *Isaiah Chapters 28–39* (Historical Commentary on the Old Testament; Leuven: Peeters, 2000) 382–86.

Bikai, Patricia and Pierre Bikai, "Tyre at the End of the Twentieth Century," *Ber* 35 (1987) 67–96.

Billows, Richard A., *Kings and Colonists: Aspects of Macedonian Imperialism* (Leiden: Brill, 1995).

Birch, Bruce, *The Rise of the Israelite Monarchy: The Growth and Development of 1 Samuel 7–15* (SBLDissS 27; Missoula, MT: Scholars, 1976).

Birkeland, Harris, *Die Feinde des Individuums in der israelitischen Psalmenliteratur* (Oslo: Gröndahl, 1933).

Blacking, John, "Toward an Anthropology of the Body," in idem, ed., *The Anthropology of the Body* (ASAM 15; London: Academic, 1977) 1–28.

Blenkinsopp, Joseph, *A History of Prophecy in Israel* (2d ed.; Louisville: Westminster/John Knox, 1996).

———, *Isaiah 1–39* (AB 19; New York: Doubleday, 2000).

Bloch, Marc, *The Royal Touch: Sacred Monarchy and Scrofula in England and France* (1923; London: Routledge & Kegan Paul, 1973).

Bloch-Smith, Elizabeth, *Judahite Burial Practices and Beliefs about the Dead* (JSOTSS 123; Sheffield: JSOT, 1992).

Boadt, Lawrence, *Ezekiel's Oracles against Egypt: A Literary and Philological Study of Ezekiel 29–32* (BibOr 37; Rome: Biblical Institute Press, 1980).

Bodendorfer, Gerhard, "Zur Historisierung des Psalters in der rabbinischen Literatur," in Erich Zenger, ed., *Der Psalter in Judentum und Christentum* (HBS 18; Freiburg: Herder, 1998) 215–34.

Bodi, Daniel, *The Book of Ezekiel and the Poem of Erra* (OBO 104; Gottingen: Vandenhoeck & Ruprecht, 1991).

Boling, Robert G., *Judges* (AB 6A; Garden City, NY: Doubleday, 1975).

Bonhême, Marie-Ange, "Kingship," *Oxford Encyclopedia of Ancient Egypt* (2001) 2. 238–45.

Börker-Klähn, Jutta, *Altvorderasiatische Bildstelen und vergleichbare Felsreliefs* (2 vols.; BF 4; Mainz: von Zabern, 1982).

Bowes, A. Wendell, "The Basilomorphic Conception of Deity in Israel and Mesopotamia," in K Lawson Younger, William W. Hallo, and Bernard F. Batto, eds., *The Biblical Canon in Comparative Perspective* (Scripture in Context 4; Lewiston: Mellen, 1991) 235–75.

Braulik, Georg, "Deuteronomy and the Commemorative Culture of Israel," in idem, *The Theology of Deuteronomy: Collected Essays of Georg Braulik, O.S.B.* (Berkeley: BIBAL, 1994).

Braun, Joachim, *Music in Ancient Israel/Palestine: Archaeological, Written, and Comparative Sources* (Grand Rapids: Eerdmans, 2002).

Braun, Roddy, "Solomon, the Chosen Temple Builder: the Significance of 1 Chronicles 22, 28, and 29 for the Theology of Chronicles," *JBL* 95 (1976) 581–90.

Brenner, Athalya, "On Feminist Criticism of the Song of Songs," in eadem, ed., *A Feminist Companion to the Song of Songs* (Sheffield: JSOT Press, 1993) 28–37.

Brettler, Marc Zvi, *The Creation of History in Ancient Israel* (London: Routledge, 1995).

———, *God is King: Understanding an Israelite Metaphor* (JSOTSS 76; Sheffield: Sheffield Academic Press, 1989).

———, "Images of YHWH the Warrior in Psalms," *Sem* 61 (1993) 135–65.

Brueggemann, Walter, *The Psalms and the Life of Faith* (ed. Patrick Miller; Minneapolis: Fortress, 1995).
Briggs, Charles A. and Emilie G. Briggs, *The Book of Psalms* (2 vols.; ICC; Edinburgh: T. & T. Clark, 1906).
Bright, John, *A History of Israel* (3d ed.; Philadelphia: Westminster, 1981).
Briquel-Chattonet, F., *Les Relations entre les Cités de la Côte Phénicienne et les Royaumes d'Israël et de Juda* (OLA 46; Leuven: Peeters, 1992).
Brodwin, Paul, "Symptoms and Social Performances: The Case of Diane Reden," Mary-Jo Delvecchio Good et al., eds., *Pain as Human Experience* (Berkeley: University of California Press, 1992).
Brown, Peter, *The Body and Society: Men, Women, and Sexual Renunciation in Early Christianity* (New York: Columbia University Press, 1987).
Brown, William P., *Seeing the Psalms: A Theology of Metaphor* (Louisville: Westminster/John Knox, 2002).
———, "A Royal Performance: Critical Notes on Psalm 11:3aγ-b," *JBL* 117 (1998) 93–96.
Burkert, Walter, *Greek Religion* (Cambridge: Harvard University Press, 1985).
Busink, Th. A., *Der Tempel von Jerusalem von Salomo bis Herodes*, vol. 1: *Der Tempel Salomos* (Leiden: Brill, 1970).
Butler, Judith, *Bodies That Matter: On the Discursive Limits of "Sex"* (New York and London: Routledge, 1993).
Bynum, Caroline, *The Resurrection of the Body in Western Christianity* (New York: Columbia University Press, 1995).
———, "Why All the Fuss about the Body? A Medievalist's Perspective," *Critical Inquiry* 22 (1995) 1–33.
Calame, Claude, *Choruses of Young Women in Ancient Greece: Their Morphology, Religious Role and Social Function* (Lanham: Rowman and Littlefield, 1997).
Campagno, Marcelo, "God-Kings and King-Gods in Ancient Egypt," in C. J. Eyre, ed., *Proceedings of the Seventh International Congress of Egyptologists* (OLA 82; Leuven: Peeters, 1998) 237–43.
Campbell, Antony F., *1 Samuel* (FOTL 7; Grand Rapids: Eerdmans, 2003).
Campbell, Antony F. and Mark A. O'Brien, *Unfolding the Deuteronomistic History: Origins, Upgrades, Present Text* (Minneapolis: Fortress, 2000).
Cancik-Kirschbaum, Eva, "Konzeption und Legitimation von Herrschaft in neuassyrischer Zeit," *WdO* 26 (1995) 5–20.
Caquot, Andre and Philippe de Robert, *Les Livres des Samuel* (Geneva: Labor et Fides, 1994).
Carlson, R. A., *David, The Chosen King: A Traditio-Historical Approach to the Second Book of Samuel* (Stockholm: Almqvist & Wiksell, 1964).
Carter, Jane B., "Ancestor Cult and the Occasion of Homeric Performance," in Jane B. Carter and Sarah P. Morris, eds., *The Ages of Homer: A Tribute to Emily Townsend Vermeule* (Austin: University of Texas Press, 1995) 285–312.
Cazelles, Henri, "פרעה," *TWAT* 6 (1989) 760–63.
Childs, Brevard, *Isaiah* (OTL; Louisville: Westminster/John Knox, 2001).
Christensen, Duane L., *Transformations of the War Oracle in Old Testament Prophecy* (HDR 3; Missoula: Scholars, 1975).
Cifola, Barbara, *Analysis of Variants in the Assyrian Royal Titulary from the Origins to Tiglath-Pileser III* (Naples: Istituto Universitario Orientale, 1995).
von Clausewitz, Carl, *On War* (New York: Penguin, 1968).
Coakley, Sarah, "Introduction: religion and the body," in eadem, ed., *Religion and the Body* (Cambridge: Cambridge University Press, 1997) 1–12.
Cogan, Mordechai, "A Lamashtu Plaque from the Judaean Shephelah," *IEJ* 45 (1995) 155–61.
Cogan, Mordechai and Hayim Tadmor, *II Kings* (AB 11; New York: Doubleday, 1988).

Cohen, Susan, *Canaanites, Chronologies, and Connections: the relationships of Middle Bronze IIA Canaan to Middle Kingdom Egypt* (Winona Lake, IN: Eisenbrauns, 2002).
Cole, Steven W., "The Destruction of Orchards in Assyrian Warfare," in Simo Parpola and R. M. Whiting, eds., *Assyria 1995* (Helsinki: Neo-Assyrian Text Corpus Project, 1997) 29–40.
Cole, Steven and Peter Machinist, *Letters from Priests to the Kings Esarhaddon and Assurbanipal* (SAAS 13; Helsinki: Helsinki University Press, 1999).
Collon, Dominique, "Banquets in the Art of the Ancient Near East," in R. Gyselen et al., eds., *Banquets d'Orient* (Bures: Groupe pour l'Étude de la Civilisation du Moyen-Orient, 1992) 23–30.
Coote, Robert B. and Keith W. Whitelam, "The Emergence of Israel: Social Transformation and State Formation Following the Decline in Late Bronze Age Trade," *Sem* 37 (1986) 107–47.
Corney, Richard W., "What Does 'Literal Meaning' Mean? Some Commentaries on the Song of Songs," *ATR* 80 (1998) 494–516.
Corral, Martin Alonso, *Ezekiel's Oracle Against Tyre: Historical Reality and Motivations* (BibOr 46; Rome: Pontifical Biblical Institute, 2002).
Craigie, Peter C., *Psalms 1–50* (WBC 19; Waco, TX: Word, 1983).
Croft, Steven J. L., *The Identity of the Individual in the Psalms* (JSOTSS 44; Sheffield: Sheffield Academic Press, 1987).
Cross, Frank Moore, *Canaanite Myth and Hebrew Epic* (Cambridge: Harvard University Press, 1973).
——, *From Epic to Canon: History and Literature in Ancient Israel* (Baltimore: Johns Hopkins University Press, 1998).
——, "The Stele Dedicated to Melcarth by Ben-Hadad of Damascus," *BASOR* 205 (1972) 36–42.
Crowfoot, J. W., Kathleen M. Kenyon, and E. L. Sukenik, *The Buildings at Samaria* (London: Palestine Exploration fund, 1942).
Crüsemann, Frank, *Der Widerstand gegen das Königtum* (WMANT 49; Neukirchen-Vluyn: Neukirchener, 1978).
Csordas, Thomas J., "Introduction: the body as representation and being-in-the-world," in idem, *Embodiment and Experience: The existential ground of culture and self* (Cambridge: Cambridge University Press, 1994) 1–24.
Culley, Robert C., *Oral Formulaic Language in the Biblical Psalms* (Toronto: University of Toronto Press, 1967).
Curtis, John, "Assyrian Furniture: The Archaeological Evidence," in Georgina Herrmann, ed., *The Furniture of Western Asia, Ancient and Traditional* (Mainz: von Zabern, 1996) 167–80.
Dahood, Mitchell, *Psalms 1–50* (AB 16; Garden City, NY: Doubleday, 1965).
——, *Psalms 51–100* (AB 17: Garden City, NY: Doubleday, 1968).
——, *Psalms 101–150* (AB 17A; Garden City, NY: Doubleday, 1970).
Davis, Ellen F., "Romance of the Land in the Song of Songs," *ATR* 80 (1998) 533–46.
Davis, Natalie Zemon and Arlette Farge, eds., *A History of Women: Renaissance and Enlightenment Paradoxes* (Cambridge: Harvard University Press, 1993).
Davis, Virginia Lee, "Remarks on Michael V. Fox's 'The Cairo Love Songs'," *JAOS* 100 (1980) 111–14.
Day, John, ed., *King and Messiah in Israel and the Ancient Near East: Proceedings of the Oxford Old Testament Seminar* (JSOTSS 270; Sheffield: Sheffield Academic Press, 1998).
——, *Yahweh and the Gods and Goddesses of Canaan* (JSOTSS 265; Sheffield: Sheffield Academic Press, 2000).
DeBoer. Martinus C., *Johannine Perspectives on the Death of Jesus: Contributions to Biblical Exegesis & Theology* (Kampen: Kok Pharos, 1996).

de Fraine, J., *L'Aspect Religieux de la Royauté Israélite* (Rome: Pontifical Biblical Institute, 1954).
de Moor, Johannes C and Wilfred G. E. Watson, *Verse in Ancient Near Eastern Prose* (AOAT 42; Neukirchen-Vluyn: Neukirchener, 1993).
de Vaux, Roland, *Ancient Israel: Its Life and Institutions* (1961; reprint ed.; Grand Rapids: Eerdmans, 1997).
Dever, William G., "Archaeology and the 'Age of Solomon': A Case-Study in Archaeology and Historiography," in Lowell K. Handy, ed., *The Age of Solomon: Scholarship at the Turn of the Millennium* (Leiden: Brill, 1997) 217–51.
———, *What Did the Biblical Writers Know & When Did They Know It?* (Grand Rapids: Eerdmans, 2001).
De Vries, Simon J., *1 Kings* (WBC 12; Waco, TX: Word, 1985).
———, *Prophet Against Prophet: The Role of the Micaiah Narrative (1 Kings 22) in the Development of Early Prophetic Tradition* (Grand Rapids: Eerdmans, 1978).
de Ward, Eileen, "Mourning Customs in 1, 2 Samuel," *JJS* 23 (1972) 20–21.
Dick, Michael B., ed., *Born in Heaven, Made on Earth: The Making of the Cult Image in the Ancient Near East* (Winona Lake, IN: Eisenbrauns, 1999).
Dion, P.-E., *Les Araméens à l'âge du Fer* (Paris: Gabalda, 1997).
Doré, J., "L'évocation de Melchisédech et le problèm de l'origine du *Psaume* 110," *Transeuphratène* 15 (1998) 19–53.
Douglas, Mary, *Implicit Meanings* (2d ed.; London: Routledge, 1999).
———, *Natural Symbols* (New York: Vintage, 1973).
———, *Thought Styles* (London: Sage, 1996).
Duden, Barbara, *Disembodying Women: Perspectives on Pregnancy and the Unborn* (Cambridge: Harvard University Press, 1993).
———, *The Women Beneath the Skin: A Doctor's Patients in Eighteenth-Century Germany* (Cambridge: Harvard University Press, 1991).
Duhm, Bernhard, *Die Psalmen* (2d ed.; KHKAT; Tübingen: Mohr/Siebeck, 1922).
Dutcher-Walls, Patricia, *Narrative Art, Political Rhetoric: The Case of Athaliah and Joash* (JSOTSS 209; Sheffield: Sheffield Academic Press, 1996).
Eagleton, Terry, *The Illusions of Postmodernism* (Oxford: Blackwell, 1996).
———, *Marxism and Literary Criticism* (Berkeley: University of California Press, 1976).
Eaton, John H., "Dancing in the Old Testament," *ExpTimes* 86 (1975) 136–40.
———, *Kingship and the Psalms* (2d ed.; Sheffield: JSOT Press, 1986).
Eco, Umberto, *Kant and the Platypus: Essays on Language and Cognition* (New York: Harcourt, 2000).
———, *The Limits of Interpretation* (Bloomington: Indiana University Press, 1990).
———, *The Role of the Reader: Explorations in the Semiotics of Texts* (Bloomington: Indiana University Press, 1979).
———, *A Theory of Semiotics* (Bloomington, IN: Indiana University Press, 1976).
Eco, Umberto, et al., *Interpretation and Overinterpretation* (Cambridge: Cambridge University Press, 1992).
Edelman, Diana Vikander, *King Saul in the Historiography of Judah* (JSOTSS 121; Sheffield: Sheffield Academic Press, 1991.
Eichrodt, Walther, *Ezekiel* (OTL; London: SCM, 1970).
Eilberg-Schwartz, Howard, "The Problem of the Body for the People of the Book," in Timothy K. Beal and David M. Gunn, eds., *Reading Bibles, Writing Bodies: Identity and the Book* (London: Routledge, 1997) 34–55.
Ellen, Roy F., "Anatomical Classification and the semiotics of the Body," in John Blacking, ed., *The Anthropology of the Body* (London: Academic Press, 1977).
Elshtain, Jean Bethke, *Women and War* (New York: Basic Books, 1987).
Eslinger, Lyle, *House of God or House of David: The Rhetoric of 2 Samuel 7* (JSOTSS 164; Sheffield: JSOT Press, 1994).
Exum, J. Cheryl, "A Literary and Structural Analysis of the Song of Songs," *ZAW* 85 (1973) 47–79.

———, "Seeing Solomon's Palanquin (Song of Songs 3:6-11)," *BibInt* 11 (2003) 301-16.
———, *Tragedy and Biblical Narrative: Arrows of the Almighty* (Cambridge: Cambridge University Press, 1992).
Ewald, Heinrich, *Geschichte des Volkes Israel* (3d ed.; 7 vols; Göttingen: Dieterisch, 1864-68).
Eynikel, Erik, *The Reform of King Josiah and the Composition of the Deuteronomistic History* (OTS 33; Leiden: Brill, 1996).
Fabry, Heinz-Josef, "לב," *TWAT* 4 (1984) cols. 413-51.
———, "רוח," *TWAT* 7 (1993) cols. 401-3.
Fales, F. M., ed., *Assyrian Royal Inscriptions: New Horizons* (Rome: CNR, 1981).
Falk, Marcia, *The Song of Songs* (San Francisco: Harper San Francisco, 1990).
———, "The *wasf*," in Athalya Brenner, ed., *A Feminist Companion to the Song of Songs* (Sheffield: JSOT Press, 1993) 225-33.
Farber, Walter, "Bīt rimki—ein assyrisches Ritual?" in Hartmut Waetzoldt and Harald Hauptmann, eds., *Assyrien im Wandel der Zeiten* (29th Rencontre Assyriologique Internationale, 1992; Heidelberg: Heidelberger Orientverlag, 1997) 41-46.
———, "Lamashtu," *RLA* 6 (1980-83) 439-42.
———, "Magic at the Cradle: Babylonian and Assyrian Lullabies," *Anthropos* 85 (1990) 139-48.
———, *Schlaf, Kindchen, Schlaf: Mesopotamische Baby-Beschwörungen und Rituale* (Winona Lake: Eisenbrauns, 1989).
Ferch, Arthur J., "A Review of Critical Studies of Old Testament References to Heshbon," in Lawrence T. Geraty and Leona G. Running, eds., *Hesban 3: Historical Foundations* (Berrien Springs, MI: Andrews University Press, 1989) 37-58.
Finkelstein, Israel, *Archaeology of the Israelite Settlement* (Jerusalem: Israel Exploration Society, 1988).
———, "Archaeology of the United Monarchy: an Alternative View," *Levant* 28 (1996) 177-87.
Fischer, Alexander Achilles, *Von Hebron nach Jerusalem: Eine redaktionsgeschichtliche Studie zur Erzählung von König David in II Sam 1-5* (BZAW 335; Berlin: de Gruyter, 2004).
Fitzmyer, Joseph, *The Aramaic Inscriptions of Sefire* (BibOr 19/A; Rome: Pontifical Biblical Institute, 1995).
———, "The Aramaic Letter of King Adon to the Egyptian Pharaoh," in idem, *A Wandering Aramean* (reprint ed.; Grand Rapids: Eerdmans, 1997) 231-42.
Flanagan, James W., *David's Social Drama: A Hologram of Israel's Early Iron Age* (Sheffield: Almond, 1988).
Flanagan, Owen, *The Problem of the Soul: Two Visions of Mind and How to Reconcile Them* (New York: Basic Books, 2002).
Fokkelman, J. P., *Narrative Art and Poetry in the Books of Samuel: A Full Interpretation Based on Stylistic and Structural Analyses*, vol. 2: *The Crossing Fates (I Sam. 13-31 and 2 Sam. 1)* (Assen: Van Gorcum, 1986).
Fokkelman, J. P., *Narrative Art and Poetry in the Books of Samuel*, vol. 3: *Throne and City (II Sam. 2-8 & 21-24)* (Assen: van Gorcum, 1990).
Foster, Benjamin, *Before the Muses: An Anthology of Akkadian Literature* (2 vols.; Bethesda: CDL, 1996).
Foucault, Michel, *Discipline and Punish* (New York: Pantheon, 1977).
———, *The History of Sexuality* (3 vols.; New York: Vintage, 1988-90).
———, *Power/Knowledge: Selected Interviews and Other Writings 1972-1977* (New York: Pantheon, 1980).
Fox, Michael, "The Cairo Love Songs," *JAOS* 100 (1980) 101-9.
———, *The Song of Songs and the Ancient Egyptian Love Songs* (Madison, WI: University of Wisconsin Press, 1985).
Foxhall, Lin, "Pandora Unbound: A Feminist Critique of Foucault's *History of Sexuality*," in David H. J. Larmour, Paul Allen Miller, and Charles Platter, eds.,

Rethinking Sexuality: Foucault and Classical Antiquity (Princeton: Princeton University Press, 1998) 122-37.

Freedman, David Noel, "Divine Names and Titles in Early Hebrew Poetry," in Frank Moore Cross et al., eds., *Magnalia Dei: The Mighty Acts of God* (New York: Doubleday, 1976) 55-102.

Fretheim, Terence, "Psalm 132: A Form-Critical Study," *JBL* 86 (1967) 289-300.

Friedman, Richard Elliott and William H. C. Propp, eds., *Le-David Maskil: A Birthday Tribute for David Noel Freedman* (Winona Lake, IN: Eisenbrauns, 2004).

Frontain, Raymond-Jean and Jan Wojcik, eds., *The David Myth in Western Literature* (West Lafayette, IN: Purdue University Press, 1980).

Gager, John G., "Body-Symbols and Social Reality: Resurrection, Incarnation and Asceticism in Early Christianity," *Rel* 12 (1982) 345-63.

Galil, Gershon, *The Chronology of the Kings of Israel and Judah* (Leiden: Brill, 1996).

Gallagher, Catherine and Thomas Laqueur, eds., *The Making of the Modern Body: Sexuality and Society in the Nineteenth Century* (Berkeley: University of California Press, 1987).

Garelli, Paul, "La Conception de la Royauté en Assyrie," in F. Mario Fales, ed., *Assyrian Royal Inscriptions: New Horizons in Literary, Ideological, and Historical Analysis* (Rome: Istituto per l'Oriente, 1981) 1-11.

———, "Les sujets du roi d'Assyrie," in H. Limet, ed., *La Voix de l'Opposition en Mésopotamie* (Brussels: Institut des Hautes Études de Belgique, 1975) 189-213.

Garr, W. Randall, *Dialect Geography of Syria-Palestine 1000-586 BCE* (Philadelphia: University of Pennsylvania Press, 1985).

Geertz, Clifford, *Negara: The Theatre State in Nineteenth-Century Bali* (Princeton: Princeton University Press, 1980).

Geller, Stephen A., "The God of the Covenant," in Barbara N. Porter, ed., *One God or Many? Concepts of Divinity in the Ancient World* (TCBAI 1; Casco Bay: Casco Bay Assyriological Institute, 2000) 273-319.

Gellner, Ernest, *Nations and Nationalism* (Ithaca, NY: Cornell University Press, 1983).

George, A. R., *Babylonian Topographical Texts* (OLA 40; Leuven: Peeters, 1992).

George, Mark K., "Assuming the Body of the Heir Apparent," in Timothy K. Beal and David M. Gunn, eds., *Reading Bibles, Writing Bodies* (London: Routledge, 1997) 164-74.

———, "Body Works: Power, the Construction of Identity, and Gender in the Discourse on Kingship" (Ph.D. diss., Princeton Theological Seminary, 1995).

———, "Constructing Identity in 1 Samuel 17," *BibInt* 7 (1999) 389-412.

———, "Yhwh's Own Heart," *CBQ* 64 (2002) 442-59.

Gerardi, Pamela, "Thus, He Spoke: Direct Speech in Esarhaddon's Royal Inscriptions," *ZA* 79 (1989) 245-60.

Gerstenberger, Erhard, *Psalms, Part 1 With an Introduction to Cultic Poetry* (FOTL 14; Grand Rapids: Eerdmans, 1988).

———, *Psalms, Part 2 and Lamentations* (FOTL 15; Grand Rapids: Eerdmans, 2001).

Gese, Hartmut, "Die Religionen Altsyriens," in Hartmut Gese, Maria Höfner, and Kurt Rudolph, *Die Religionen Altsyriens, Altarabiens und der Mandäer* (RdM 10.2; Stuttgart: Kohlhammer, 1970).

Gevirtz, Stanley, *Patterns in the Early Poetry of Israel* (Chicago: University of Chicago Press, 1963).

Gibson, J. C. L., *Canaanite Myths and Legends* (Edinburgh: Clark, 1978).

Gillingham, S. E., *The Poems and Psalms of the Hebrew Bible* (Oxford: Oxford University Press, 1994)

Gilman, Sander, *The Jew's Body* (New York: Routledge, 1991).

———, *Making the Body Beautiful: A Cultural History of Aesthetic Surgery* (Princeton: Princeton University Press, 1999).

Ginsberg, H. L., "Psalms and Inscriptions of Petition and Acknowledgement," in

Louis Ginzberg Jubilee Volume (New York: American Academy for Jewish Research, 1945) 159–71.
——, "Reflexes of Sargon in Isaiah after 715 BCE," *JAOS* 88 (1968) 47–53.
Girard, Rene, "Generative Scapegoating," in Robert G. Hamerton-Kelly, ed., *Violent Origins* (Stanford: Stanford University Press, 1987) 73–105.
——, *Violence and the Sacred* (Baltimore: Johns Hopkins University Press, 1977).
Gitin, Seymour, "The Neo-Assyrian Empire and its Western Periphery: The Levant, with a Focus on Philistine Ekron," in Simo Parpola and R. M. Whiting, eds., *Assyria 1995* (Helsinki: Neo-Assyrian Text Corpus Project, 1997) 77–103.
Gitin, S., T. Dothan, and J. Naveh, "A Royal Dedicatory Inscription from Ekron," *IEJ* 47 (1997) 1–16.
Giveon, Raphael, *The Impact of Egypt on Canaan* (OBO 20; Göttingen: Vandenhoeck & Ruprecht, 1978).
Goldberg, Ilana, "צור העיצוב האמנותי של הקינה על מלך," *Tarbiz* 58 (1989) 277–81.
Goldstein, Sidney, *Suicide in Rabbinic Literature* (Hoboken, NJ: KTAV, 1989).
Gordis, Robert, *The Song of Songs and Lamentations* (rev. ed.; New York: KTAV, 1974).
——, "A Wedding Song for Solomon," *JBL* 63 (1944) 263–70.
Görg, Manfred, *Gott-König-Reden in Israel und Ägypten* (BWANT 105; Stuttgart: Kohlhammer, 1975).
Gottwald, Norman K., "The Participation of Free Agrarians in the Introduction of Monarchy to Ancient Israel: An Application of H. A. Landsberger's Framework for the Analysis of Peasant Movements," *Sem* 37 (1986) 77–106.
——, *The Politics of Ancient Israel* (Louisville: Westminster John Knox, 2001).
Goulder, Michael, *The Psalms of the Return (Book V, Psalms 107–150)* (JSOTSS 258; Sheffield: Sheffield Academic Press, 1998).
Gnuse, Robert, *No Other Gods: Emergent Monotheism in Israel* (JSOTSS 241; Sheffield: Sheffield Academic Press, 1997).
Grätz, Sebastian, *Der strafende Wettergott: Erwägungen zur Traditionsgeschichte des Adad-Fluchs im Alten Orient und im alten Testament* (BBB 114; Bodenheim: PHILO, 1998).
Gray, John, *I & II Kings* (OTL; London: SCM, 1964).
Greenberg, Moshe, *Ezekiel 21–37* (AB 22A; New York: Doubleday, 1997).
Gressmann, Hugo, *Der Messias* (FRLANT 43; Göttingen: Vandenhoeck & Ruprecht, 1929).
Grønbæk, Jakob H., *Die Geschichte vom Aufstieg Davids (I. Sam. 15–2. Sam. 5): Tradition und Komposition* (Copenhagen: Munksgaard, 1971).
Gröndahl, F., *Die Personennamen der Texte aus Ugarit* (StPohl 1; Rome: Gregorian Pontifical University, 1967).
Grottanelli, Cristiano, "The Enemy King is a Monster," in idem, *Kings and Prophets: Monarchic Power, Inspired Leadership & Sacred Text in Biblical Narrative* (New York: Oxford University Press, 1999) 47–72.
Gruber, Mayer, *Aspects of Nonverbal Communication in the Ancient Near East* (StPohl 12/1–2; 2 vols.; Rome: Biblical Institute Press, 1980).
Gruen, Erich S., "Seleucid Royal Ideology," *SBL Seminar Papers* 38 (1999) 24–53
Grünbeck, Elisabeth, *Christologische Schriftargumentation und Bildersprache* (SVC 26; Leiden: Brill, 1994).
Gubel, Eric, "Cinq Bulles inédites des Archives tyriennes de l'époque Achéménide," *Semitica* 47 (1997) 58–62.
——, "The Iconography of Inscribed Phoenician Glyptic," in Benjamin Sass and Christoph Uehlinger, eds., *Studies in the Iconography of Northwest Semitic Inscribed Seals* (OBO 125; Göttingen: Vandenhoeck & Ruprecht, 1993) 101–29.
——, "The Influence of Egypt on Western Asiatic Furniture and Evidence from Phoenicia," in Georgina Herrmann, ed., *The Furniture of Western Asia Ancient and Modern* (Mainz: von Zabern, 1996) 139–51.
——, *Phoenician Furniture* (StPh 7; Leuven: Peeters, 1987).

Gunkel, Hermann, *Einleitung in die Psalmen* (1933; ed. Joachim Begrich; 2d ed.; Göttingen: Vandenhoeck & Ruprecht, 1966).
——, "Die Königspsalmen," *Preussische Jahrbücher* 158 (October-December 1914) 42–68.
——, *Die Psalmen* (Göttingen: Vandenhoeck & Ruprecht, 1929).
Gunn, David, *The Fate of King Saul: An Interpretation of a Biblical Story* (JSOTSS 14; Sheffield: Sheffield Academic Press, 1980).
Haas, Volkert, *Geschichte der hethitischen Religion* (Leiden: Brill, 1994).
Habermas, Jürgen, "Some Questions Concerning the Theory of Power: Foucault Again," in Michael Kelly, ed., *Critique and Power: Recasting the Foucault/Habermas Debate* (Cambridge: MIT Press, 1994) 79–107.
Hackett, Jo Ann, *The Balaam Text from Deir ʿAllā* (HSM 31; Chico: Scholars, 1984).
——, "Can a Sexist Model Liberate Us? Ancient Near Eastern 'Fertility' Goddesses," *JFSR* 5 (1989) 65–76.
——, "In the Days of Jael," in Clarissa Atkinson, Constance Buchanan, and Margaret Miles, eds., *Immaculate and Powerful* (Boston: Beacon, 1985) 15–38.
——, "Religious Traditions in Israelite Transjordan," in Patrick Miller, Paul Hanson, and S. Dean McBride, eds., *Ancient Israelite Religion* (Cross Festschrift; Philadelphia: Fortress, 1987) 125–36.
——, "Some Observations on the Balaam Tradition at Deir ʿAllā," *BA* 49 (1986) 216–22.
Hacking, Ian, *The Social Construction of What?* (Cambridge: Harvard University Press, 1999).
Haller, Max, *Die Fünf Megilloth: Ruth, Hoheslied, Klagelieder, Esther* (HAT 18; Tübingen: Mohr/Siebeck, 1940).
Hallo, William W., "The Death of Kings: Traditional Historiography in Contextual Perspective," in Mordechai Cogan and Israel Ephal, eds., *Ah, Assyria . . .: Studies in Assyrian History and Ancient Near Eastern Historiography Presented to Hayim Tadmor* (Jerusalem: Magnes, 1991) 148–65.
——, "The Royal Correspondence of Larsa: I. A Sumerian Prototype for the Prayer of Hezekiah?" in Barry L. Eichler et al., eds., *Kramer Anniversary Volume* (AOAT 25; Neukirchen-Vluyn: Neukirchener, 1976) 209–24.
Halpern, Baruch, *The Constitution of the Monarchy in Israel* (HSM 25; Chico, CA: Scholars, 1981).
——, *David's Secret Demons: Messiah, Murderer, Traitor, King* (Grand Rapids: Eerdmans, 2001).
——, *The First Historians: The Hebrew Bible and History* (San Francisco: Harper & Row, 1988).
Halpern, Baruch and Deborah Hobson, *Law and Ideology in Ancient Israel* (JSOTSS 124; Sheffield: JSOT Press, 1991).
Halpern, Baruch and David Vanderhooft, "The Editions of Kings in the 7th–6th Centuries BCE," *HUCA* 62 (1991) 170–244.
Hamilton, Jeffries M., "Caught in the Nets of Prophecy? The Death of King Ahab and the Character of God," *CBQ* 56 (1994) 649–63.
Hamilton, Mark W., "The Past as Destiny: Historical Visions in Samʾal and Judah under Assyrian Hegemony," *HTR* 91 (1998) 215–50.
Handy, Lowell K., "Speaking of Babies in the Temple," *Eastern Great Lakes and Midwest Biblical Societies Proceedings* 8 (1988) 155–65.
Hanson, Paul D., "The Song of Heshbon and David's *Nîr*," *HTR* 61 (1968) 297–320.
Hasel, Gerhard, "נָגִיד nāgîd," TDOT 9 (1998) 187–202.
Hasel, Michael G., *Domination and Resistance: Egyptian Military Activity in the Southern Levant, ca. 1300–1185 BC* (Probleme der Ägyptologie 11; Leiden: Brill, 1998).
Hauge, M. R., "Sigmund Mowinckel and the Psalms—a Query into His Concern," *SJOT* 2 (1988) 56–71.
Hendel, Ronald S., "Aniconism and Anthropomorphism in Ancient Israel," in van der Toorn, *Image and the Book*, 205–28.

Hermisson, Hans-Jürgen, "Die 'Königsspruch' Sammlung im Jeremiabuch: Von der Anfangs- zur Endgestalt," in idem, *Studien zu Prophetie und Weisheit* (FAT 23; Tübingen: Mohr/Siebeck, 1998) 37–58.
Herzfeld, Michael, *Anthropology through the looking-glass: Critical ethnography in the margins of Europe* (Cambridge: Cambridge University Press, 1987).
——, *Cultural Intimacy: Social Poetics of the Nation-State* (New York/London: Routledge, 1997).
——, "On Some Rhetorical Uses of Iconicity in Cultural Ideologies," in Paul Bouissac, Michael Herzfeld, and Roland Posner, eds., *Iconicity: Essays on the Nature of Culture* (Tübingen: Stauffenberg, 1986) 401–19.
——, "The Poeticity of the Commonplace," in Michael Herzfeld and Lucio Melazzo, eds., *Semiotic Theory and Practice* (2 vols.; Berlin and New York: Mouton/de Gruyter, 1988) 1. 383–91.
——, *The Poetics of Manhood: Contest and Identity in a Cretan Mountain Village* (Princeton: Princeton University Press, 1985).
——, *The Social Production of Indifference* (New York: Berg, 1992).
Hevia, James L., "Sovereignty and Subject: Constituting Relations of Power in Qing Guest Ritual," in Angela Zito and Tani E. Barlow, eds., *Body, Subject & Power in China* (Chicago: University of Chicago Press, 1994) 181–200.
Hill, John, *Friend or Foe? The Figure of Babylon in the Book of Jeremiah MT* (BIS 40; Leiden: Brill, 1999).
Hillers, Delbert, "Dust: Some Aspects of Old Testament Imagery," in John H. Marks and Robert M. Good, eds. *Love & Death in the Ancient Near East* (Guilford, CT: Four Quarters, 1987) 105–9.
——, "Ritual Procession of the Ark and Psalm 132," *CBQ* 30 (1968) 48–55.
Hobbs, T. R., *2 Kings* (WBC 13; Waco, TX: Word, 1985).
Hoffmeier, James K., "The Arm of God Versus the Arm of Pharaoh in the Exodus Narratives,"*Bib* 67 (1986) 378–87.
Holladay, William L., *Jeremiah* (Hermeneia; 2 vols.; Minneapolis: Fortress, 1989).
Hossfeld, Frank-Lothar and Erich Zenger, *Die Psalmen I* (Würzburg: Echter, 1993).
Hrouda, B., "Die Assyrische Streitwagen," *Iraq* 25 (1963) 155–58.
Hubert, Henri and Marcel Mauss, *Sacrifice: Its Nature and Functions* (Chicago: University of Chicago Press, 1964).
Hurowitz, Victor (Avigdor), *I Have Built You an Exalted House: Temple Building in the Bible in Light of Mesopotamian and Northwest Semitic Writings* (JSOTSS 115; Sheffield: Sheffield Academic Press, 1992).
Huwyler, Beat, *Jeremia und die Völker: Untersuchungen zu den Völkersprüchen in Jeremia 46–49* (FAT 20; Tübingen: Mohr/Siebeck, 1997).
Ishida, Tomoo, *History and Historical Writing in Ancient Israel* (Leiden: Brill, 1999).
——, *The Royal Dynasties in Ancient Israel* (BZAW 142; Berlin: de Gruyter, 1977).
Jaggar, Alison, *Feminist Politics and Human Nature* (Sussex: Harvester, 1983).
Japhet, Sara, *I & II Chronicles* (OTL; Louisville: Westminster/John Knox, 1993).
Eadem, "Some Biblical Concepts of Sacred Space," in Benjamin Z. Kedar and R. J. Zwi Werblowsky, eds., *Sacred Space: Shrine, City, Land* (New York: New York University Press, 1998) 55–72.
Jeffers, Ann, *Magic and Divination in Ancient Palestine and Syria* (Leiden: Brill, 1996).
Johnson, Aubrey, *The Cultic Prophet and Israel's Psalmody* (Cardiff: University of Wales Press, 1979).
——, "Hebrew Conceptions of Kingship," in S. H. Hooke, ed., *Myth, Ritual, and Kingship* (Oxford: Clarendon, 1958) 204–35.
——, *Sacral Kingship in Ancient Israel* (Cardiff: University of Wales Press, 1955).
Kaiser, Otto, "David und Jonathan: Tradition, Redaktion und Geschichte in I Sam 16–20, Ein Versuch," *EthL* 66 (1990) 281–96.
——, *Isaiah 1–12* (OTL; 2d ed.; London: SCM, 1981).
——, *Isaiah 13–29* (OTL; London: SCM, 1974).

———, "Some Observations on the Succession Narrative," *OTWSA* 27/28 (1986) 130–47.
Kantorowicz, Ernst H., *The King's Two Bodies: A Study in Mediaeval Political Theology* (Princeton: Princeton University Press, 1957).
Katzenstein, H. Jacob, *The History of Tyre: From the Beginning of the Second Millennium B.C.E. until the Fall of the Neo-Babylonian Empire in 538 BCE* (Jerusalem: Schocken Institute, 1973).
Keegan, John, *A History of Warfare* (New York: Vintage, 1993).
Keel, Othmar, *Deine Blicke sind Tauben* (SBS 114/115; Stuttgart: Katholisches Bibelwerk, 1984).
———, *Das Hohelied* (ZB; Zurich: Theologischer Verlag, 1986).
———, *The Song of Songs* (Minneapolis: Fortress, 1994).
Kelkar, Ashok R., "Prolegomena to an understanding of semiotics and culture," in Robin P. Fawcett et al., eds., *The Semiotics of Culture and Language*, vol. 2: *Language and other Semiotic Systems of Culture* (London: Pinter, 1984) 101–34.
King, L. W., *Bronze Reliefs from the Gates of Shalmaneser King of Assyria B.C. 860–825* (London: British Museum, 1915).
King, Philip J., *A Study of Psalm 45 (44)* (Rome: Lateran Pontifical University, 1959).
Kittel, Rudolf, *Geschichte des Volkes Israel*, vol. 2: *Das Volk in Kanaan: Quellenkunde und Geschichte der Zeit bis zum babylonischen Exil* (3d ed.; Gotha: Perthe, 1917).
Klein, Ernest, *A Comprehensive Etymological Dictionary of the Hebrew Language for Readers of English* (Jerusalem: Carta/University of Haifa, 1987).
Klein, Jacob, "The Coronation and Consecration of Šulgi in the Ekur (Šulgi G)," in *Ah, Assyria.... Studies in Assyrian History and Ancient Near Eastern Historiography Presented to Hayim Tadmor* (ed. Mordechai Cogan and Israel Eph'al; Jerusalem: Magnes, 1991) 292–313.
Klein, Ralph W., *1 Samuel* (WBC 10; Waco: Word, 1983).
Klingbeil, Martin, *Yahweh Fighting from Heaven: God as Warrior and as God of Heaven in the Hebrew Psalter and Ancient Near Eastern Iconography* (OBO 169; Göttingen: Vandenhoeck & Ruprecht, 1999).
Knoppers, Gary N., *Two Nations Under God: The Deuteronomistic History of Solomon and the Dual Monarchies*, vol. 1: *The Reign of Solomon and the Rise of Jeroboam* (HSM 52; Atlanta: Scholars, 1993).
———, *Two Nations Under God: The Deuteronomistic History of Solomon and the Dual Monarchies*, vol. 2: *The Reign of Jeroboam, the Fall of Israel, and the Reign of Josiah* (HSM 53; Atlanta: Scholars, 1994).
Koch, Klaus, *Geschichte der ägyptischen Religion: Von den Pyramiden bis zu den Mysterien der Isis* Stuttgart: Kohlhammer, 1993).
Kottsieper, Ingo, "Anmerkungen zu Pap. Amherst 63," *ZAW* 100 (1988) 117–44.
Kraus, Hans-Joachim, *Psalmen* (BKAT; Neukirchen-Vluyn: Neukirchener, 1960).
Kselman, John, "Psalm 72: Some Observations on Structure," *BASOR* 220 (1975) 77–81.
———, "Psalm 101: Royal Confession and Divine Oracle," *JSOT* 33 (1985) 45–62.
Kuriyama, Shigehisa, *The Expressiveness of the Body and the Divergence of Greek and Chinese Medicine* (New York: Zone, 1999).
Kutscher, Raphael, *O Angry Sea (a-ab-ba hu-luh-ha): The History of a Sumerian Congregational Lament* (New Haven: Yale University Press, 1975).
Laato, Antti, *History and Ideology in the Old Testament Prophetic Literature: A Semiotic Approach to the Reconstruction of the Proclamation of the Historical Prophets* (CBOTS 41; Stockholm: Almqvist & Wiksell, 1996).
Lackenbacher, Sylvie, *Le Roi Bâtisseur: Les recits de construction assyriens des origines Teglatphalasar III* (Paris: ERC, 1982).
LaCocque, André, *Romance She Wrote: A Hermeneutical Essay on Song of Songs* (Harrisburg, PA: TPI, 1998).

Laessøe, Jørgen, *Studies on the Assyrian Ritual and Series* bīt rimki (Copenhagen: Munksgaard, 1955).
Lambert, W. G., ed., *Babylonian Wisdom Literature* (Winona Lake, IN: Eisenbrauns, 1996).
Landsberger, Benno, "Das 'gute Wort'," in *Altorientalische Studien* (Bruno Meissner Festschrift; MAOG 4; Leipzig: Harrassowitz, 1928–29) 294–321.
Langlamet, François, "De 'David, fils de Jessé' au 'Livre de Jonathan'," *RB* 100 (1993) 321–57.
———, "'David-Jonathan-Saül' ou le 'Livre de Jonathan': 1 Sam 16,14–2 Sam 1,27," *RB* 101 (1994) 326–54.
Lasine, Stuart, *Knowing Kings: Knowledge, Power, and Narcissism in the Hebrew Bible* (Atlanta: Scholars, 2001).
Launderville, Dale, "Ezekiel's Cherub: A Promising Symbol or a Dangerous Idol?" *CBQ* 65 (2003) 165–83.
———, *Piety and Politics: The Dynamics of Royal Authority in Homeric Greece, Biblical Israel, and Old Babylonian Mesopotamia* (Grand Rapids: Eerdmans, 2003).
Lehmküller, Karsten, *Kultus und Theologie: Dogmatik und Exegese in der religions-geschichtliche Schule* (FSöT; Göttingen: Vandenhoeck & Ruprecht, 1996).
Lemaire, André, "Déesses et Dieux de Syrie-Palestine d'apres les inscriptions (c. 1000–500 av. N.E.)," in Walter Dietrich and Martin Klopfenstein, eds., *Ein Gott allein? JHWH-Verehrung und biblischer Monotheismus im Kontext der israelitischen und altorientalischen Religionsgeschichte* (OBO 139; Göttingen: Vandenhoeck & Ruprecht, 1994) 127–58.
———, *Les Inscriptions araméennes de Sfiré et l'Assyrie de Shamshi-ilu* (Geneva: Droz, 1984).
———, "Les Inscriptions sur Plâtre de Deir 'Allā et leur Signification Historique et Culturelle," in Jacob Hoftijzer and G. van der Kooij, eds., *The Balaam Text from Deir 'Allā Re-evaluated* (Leiden: Brill, 1991) 33–57.
———, "Oracles, propagande et littérature dans le royaumes araméens et transjordaniens," in Jean-Georges Heintz, ed., *Oracles et Prophéties dans l'antiquité* (Paris: de Boccard, 1997) 171–93.
Lemche, Niels Peter, *Prelude to Israel's Past: Backgrounds and Beginnings of Israelite History and Identity* (Peabody: Hendrickson, 1998).
Lesses, Rebecca, *Ritual Practices to Gain Power: Angels, Incantations, and Revelation in Early Jewish Mysticism* (Harrisburg, PA: TPI, 1998).
Levenson, Jon, "From Temple to Synagogue: 1 Kings 8," in Baruch Halpern and Jon Levenson, eds., *Traditions in Transformation: Turning Points in Biblical Faith* (Winona Lake: Eisenbrauns, 1981) 143–66.
Levine, Baruch, *Leviticus* (JPSTC 3; Philadelphia: JPS, 1989).
Levy-Bruhl, Lucien, *How Natives Think* (London: Allen & Unwin, 1926).
Lewis, Theodore, *Cults of the Dead in Ancient Israel and Ugarit* (HSM 39: Atlanta: Scholars, 1989).
Lipinski, Eduard, *Le Poème royal du Psaume LXXXIX 1–5, 20–38* (Paris: Gabalda, 1967).
Littauer, Mary A. and J. H. Crouwel, *Chariots and Related Equipment from the Tomb of Tut'ankhamen* (Oxford: Griffith, 1985).
Liverani, Mario, "The Ideology of the Assyrian Empire," in Mogens T. Larsen, ed., *Power and Propaganda* (Copenhagen: Akademisk, 1979) 297–317.
Livingstone, Alasdair, ed., *Court Poetry and Literary Miscellanea* (Helsinki: Helsinki University Press, 1989).
Lohfink, Norbert, "Was There a Deuteronomistic Movement?" in Linda Schearing and Steven McKenzie, eds., *Those Elusive Deuteronomists: the Phenomenon of Pan-Deuteronomism* (JSOTSS 268; Sheffield: Sheffield Academic Press, 1999) 36–66.
Long, Burke O., *2 Kings* (FOTL 10; Grand Rapids: Eerdmans, 1991).
Long, V. Philips, "How Did Saul Become King? Literary Reading and Historical

Reconstruction," in A. R. Millard, James K. Hoffmeier, and David W. Baker, eds., *Faith, Tradition, and History* (Winona Lake, IN: Eisenbrauns, 1994) 271–84.

———, *The Reign and Rejection of King Saul: A Case for Literary and Theological Coherence* (SBLDissS 118; Atlanta: Scholars, 1989).

Lord, Albert, *The Singer of Tales* (New York: Atheneum, 1968).

Loretz, Oswald, *Götter – Ahnen – Könige als gerechte Richter: Der "Rechtsfall" des Menschen vor Gott nach altorientalischen und biblischen Texten* (AOAT 290; Münster: Ugarit, 2003).

———, *Die Königspsalmen: die altorientalisch-kanaanäische Königstradition in jüdischer Sicht* (UBL 6; Münster: Ugarit-Verlag, 1988).

———, *Studien zur althebräischen Poesie 1: Das althebräische Liebeslied* (AOAT; Neukirchen-Vluyn: Neukirchener, 1971).

Lyke, Larry, *King David with the Wise Woman of Tekoa: The Resonance of Tradition in Parabolic Narrative* (JSOTSS 255; Sheffield: Sheffield Academic Press, 1997).

Machinist, Peter, "Assyria and Its Image in the First Isaiah," *JAOS* 103 (1983) 719–37.

———, "Assyrians on Assyria in the First Millennium BC," in Kurt Raaflaub, ed., *Anfänge politischen Denkens in der Antike* (Munich: Oldenbourg, 1993) 77–104.

———, "Kingship and Divinity in Ancient Assyria" (unpublished paper).

———, "The Transfer of Kingship: A Divine Turning," in Astrid B. Beck, et al., *Fortunate the Eyes That See* (Grand Rapids: Eerdmans, 1995) 105–20.

MacRae, Donald G., "The Body and Social Metaphor," in Jonathan Benthall and Ted Polhemus, eds., *The Body as a Medium of Expression* (London: Lane, 1975) 59–73.

Maderna-Sieben, Claudia, "Der König als Kriegsherr und oberster Heerführer in den Eulogien der frühen Ramessidenzeit," in Rolf Gundlach and Christine Raedler, eds., *Selbstverständnis und Realität* (Wiesbaden: Harrassowitz, 1997) 49–79.

Madhloom, T. A., *The Chronology of Neo-Assyrian Art* (London: Athlone, 1970).

Magen, Ursula, *Assyrische Königsdarstellungen: Aspekte der Herrschaft* (Mainz: von Zabern, 1986).

Malamat, Abraham, "The Aramaeans," in D. J. Wiseman, ed., *Peoples of Old Testament Times* (Oxford: Clarendon, 1973) 134–55.

———, "Is There a Word for the Royal Harem in the Bible? The Inside Story," in David P. Wright, David Noel Freedman, and Avi Hurvitz, eds., *Pomegranates and Golden Bells: Studies in Biblical, Jewish, and Near Eastern Ritual, Law, and Literature in Honor of Jacob Milgrom* (Winona Lake: Eisenbrauns, 1995) 785–87.

Marcus, Michelle, "Geography as Visual Ideology: Landscape, Knowledge, and Power in Neo-Assyrian Art," in Mario Liverani, ed., *Neo-Assyrian Geography* (Rome: CNR, 1995) 193–208.

Margueron, Jean-Claude, "Palace," *Oxford Encyclopedia of Archaeology in the Near East* 4 (1997) 197–200.

Mariaselvam, Abraham, *The Song of Songs and Ancient Tamil Love Poems: Poetry and Symbolism* (Rome: Pontifical Biblical Institute 1988).

Martínez Borobio, Emiliano, *Targum Jonatan de los Profetas Primeros en Tradicion Babilonica*, vol. 2: *I-II Samuel* (Madrid: Instituto de Filología, Departamento de Filología bíblica y de Oriente Antiguo, 1987).

Matthews Grieco, Sara F., "The Body, Appearance, and Sexuality," in Natalie Zemon Davis and Arlette Farge, eds., *A History of Women: Renaissance and Enlightenment Paradoxes* (Cambridge: Harvard University Press, 1993) 46–84.

Matthiae, Paolo, "The Painted Sherd at Ramat Rahel," in Yohanan Aharoni, ed., *Excavations at Ramat Rahel: Seasons 1961 and 1962* (Rome: Centro di Studi Semitici, 1964) 85–94.

Mattingly, Gerald, "Moabite Religion and the Mesha Inscription," in Andrew Dearman, ed., *Studies in the Mesha Inscription and Moab* (Atlanta: Scholars, 1989) 211–38.

Mauss, Marcel, "Body Techniques," in idem, *Sociology and Psychology: Essays* (1934; trans. Ben Brewster; London: Routledge & Kegan Paul, 1979) 97–123.
McCarter, P. Kyle, *I Samuel* (AB 8; Garden City, NY: Doubleday, 1980).
———, *II Samuel* (AB 9; Garden City, NY: Doubleday, 1984).
McCarthy, Dennis J., *Treaty and Covenant* (AnBib 21A; 2d ed.; Rome: Biblical Institute Press, 1978).
———, "The Inauguration of Monarchy in Israel: A Form-Critical Study of I Samuel 8–12," *Int* 27 (1973) 401–12.
McGinnis, John, "A Neo-Assyrian Text Describing a Royal Funeral," *SAAB* 1/1 (1987) 1–13.
McKenzie, Steven, "Cette Royauté qui fait Problème," in Albert de Pury, Thomas Römer, and Jean-Daniel Macchi, eds., *Israël construit son histoire* (Geneva: Labor et Fides, 1996) 267–95.
———, *King David: A Biography* (Oxford: Oxford University Press, 2000).
———, "The So-Called Succession Narrative in the Deuteronomistic History," in Albert de Pury and Thomas Römer, eds., *Die sogennante Thronfolgegeschichte Davids* (OBO 176; Göttingen: Vandenhoeck & Ruprecht, 2000) 123–35.
———, *The Trouble With Kings: The Composition of the Book of Kings in the Deuteronomistic History* (VTSupp 42; Leiden: Brill, 1991).
McNay, Lois, *Foucault: A Critical Introduction* (Cambridge: Polity, 1994).
Meier, Samuel A., "Shahar," *ABD* 5 (1992) 1150–51.
Menzel, Brigitte, *Assyrische Tempel* (Studia Pohl Series Maior 10; 2 vols.; Rome: Biblical Institute Press, 1981).
Mettinger, Tryggve, N. D., "Israelite Aniconism: Developments and Origins," in van der Toorn, *Image and the Book*, 173–204.
———, *King and Messiah: The Civil and Sacral Legitimation of the Israelite Kings* (CBOTS 8; Lund: Gleerup, 1976).
Metzger, Martin, *Königsthron und Gottesthron* (AOAT 15/2; Neukirchen-Vluyn: Neukirchener, 1985)
Meyer, Eduard, *Geschichte des Altertums*, vol. 2: *Der Orient vom zwölften bis zur Mitte des achten Jahrhunderts* (2d ed.; Stuttgart: Cotta, 1931)
Meyer, Jan-Waalke, "Tempel und Palastbauten im eisenzeitlichen Palästina und ihre bronzezeitlichen Vorbilder," in Bernd Janowski, Klaus Koch, and Gernot Wilhelm, eds., *Religionsgeschichtliche Beziehungen zwischen Kleinasien, Nordsyrien und dem Alten Testament* (OBO 129; Göttingen: Vandenhoeck & Ruprecht, 1993) 319–28.
Meyers, Carol, "Gender Imagery in the Song of Songs," in Athalya Brenner, ed., *The Feminist Companion to the Bible 1* (Sheffield: JSOT Press, 1993) 197–212.
Meyers, Eric M., *Jewish Ossuaries: Reburial and Rebirth* (BibOr 24; Rome: Biblical Institute Press, 1971).
Midgley, Mary, "The soul's successors: philosophy and the 'body'," in Sarah Coakley, ed., *Religion and the Body* (Cambridge: Cambridge University Press, 1997) 53–68.
Milgrom, Jacob, *Leviticus 1–16* (AB 3; New York: Doubleday, 1991).
———, *Numbers* (JPSTC; Philadelphia: Jewish Publication Society, 1990).
Millard, A. R., "King Og's Bed and Other Ancient Ironmongery," in Lyle Eslinger and G. Taylor, eds., *Ascribe to the Lord: Biblical and Other Studies in Memory of Peter C. Craigie* (Sheffield: JSOT Press, 1988) 481–92.
Miller, James E., "The mælæk of Tyre (Ezekiel 28,11–19)," *ZAW* 105 (1993) 497–501.
Miller, J. Maxwell, "Israelite History," in Douglas A. Knight and Gene M. Tucker, eds., *The Hebrew Bible and Its Modern Interpreters* (Chico, CA: Scholars, 1985) 1–30.
———, "Moab and the Moabites," in Andrew Dearman, ed., *Studies in the Mesha Inscription and Moab* (Atlanta: Scholars, 1989) 1–40.
Miller, J. Maxwell and John H. Hayes, *A History of Ancient Israel and Judah* (Philadelphia: Westminster, 1986).

Miller, Patrick, "Israelite Religion," in Douglas A. Knight and Gene M. Tucker, eds., *The Hebrew Bible and Its Interpreters* (Chico: Scholars, 1985) 201–37.

———, "Psalms and Inscriptions," in J. A. Emerton, ed., *Congress Volume: Vienna 1980* (VTSupp 32; Leiden: Brill, 1981) 311–32.

Mitchell, T. C., "Furniture in the West Semitic Texts," in Georgina Herrmann, ed., *The Furniture of Western Asia, Ancient and Traditional* (Mainz: von Zabern, 1996) 49–60.

Moenickes, Ansgar, *Die grundsätzliche Ablehnung des Königtums in der Hebräischen Bibel* (BBB 99; Beltz: Athenäum, 1995).

Monod, Paul Kléber, *The Power of Kings: Monarchy and Religion in Europe, 1589–1715* (New Haven: Yale University Press, 1999).

Montgomery, James A. and Henry S. Gehman, *The Book of Kings* (ICC; Edinburgh: Clark, 1951).

Morenz, Siegfried, "Ägyptische und davidische Königstitulatur," in idem, *Religion und Geschichte des Alten Ägyptens* (Cologne: Böhlau, 1975) 401–3.

Morgenstern, Julian, "The King god among the Western Semites and the Meaning of Epiphanes," *VT* 10 (1960) 138–97.

Mowinckel, Sigmund, *He That Cometh* (Nashville: Abingdon, 1955).

———, *Psalmenstudien I: Āwän und die individuellen Klagepsalmen* (Kristiania: Dybwad, 1921).

———, *Psalmenstudien 2: Das Thronbesteigungsfest Jahwäs und der Ursprung der Eschatologie* (Kristiania: Dybwad, 1922).

———, *The Psalms in Israel's Worship* (2 vols.; Oxford: Blackwell, 1962).

———, "Der Ursprung der Bilʿāmsage," *ZAW* 48 (1930) 233–71.

Mulder, Johannes S. M., *Studies on Psalm 45* (Nijmegen: Witsiers, 1972).

Mulzer, Martin, *Jehu schlägt Joram* (St. Ottilien: EOS, 1992).

Munro, Jill M., *Spikenard and Saffron: A Study in the Poetic Language of the Song of Songs* (JSOTSS 203; Sheffield: Sheffield Academic Press, 1995).

Murphy, Roland E., *The Song of Songs* (Hermeneia; Minneapolis: Fortress, 1990).

Murray, Donald F., *Divine Prerogative and Royal Pretension: Pragmatics, Poetics and Polemics in a Narrative Sequence about David (2 Samuel 5.17–7.29)* (JSOTSS 264; Sheffield: Sheffield Academic Press, 1998).

Nagel, Wolfram, *Der mesopotamische Streitwagen und seine Entwicklung im ostmediterranen Bereich* (Berliner Beiträge zur Vor- und Frühgeschichte 10; Berlin: Hessling, 1966).

Nagy, Gregory, *The Best of the Achaeans: Concepts of the Hero in Archaic Greek Poetry* (2d ed.; Baltimore: Johns Hopkins University Press, 1999).

———, *Poetry as Performance: Homer and Beyond* (Cambridge: Cambridge University Press, 1996).

Neely, Mark E., *The Last Best Hope on Earth: Abraham Lincoln and the Promise of America* (Cambridge: Harvard University Press, 1993).

Negbi, Ora, *Canaanite Gods in Metal: An Archaeological Study of Ancient Syro-Palestinian Figurines* (Tel Aviv: Tel Aviv University Institute of Archaeology, 1976).

Nelson, Janet L., "The Lord's anointed and the people's choice: Carolingian royal ritual," in David Cannadine and Simon Price, eds., *Rituals of Royalty: Power and Ceremonial in Traditional Societies* (Cambridge: Cambridge University Press, 1987) 137–80.

Newsom, Carol A., "A Maker of Metaphors: Ezekiel's Program of Restoration," in James Luther Mays and Paul Achtemeier, eds., *Interpreting the Prophets* (Philadelphia: Fortress, 1987) 188–99.

———, "Woman and the Discourse of Patriarchal Wisdom," in Timothy K. Beal and David M. Gunn, eds., *Reading Bibles, Writing Bodies* (London: Routledge, 1997) 116–31.

Niccacci, Alviero, "The Stele of Mesha and the Bible: Verbal System and Narrativity," *Or* 63 (1994) 226–48.

Niditch, Susan, *Oral World and Written Word* (Louisville: Westminster/John Knox, 1996).
Niehr, Herbert, "In Search of YHWH's Cult Statue in the First Temple," in Karel van der Toorn, ed., *The Image and the Book: Iconic Cults, Aniconism, and the Rise of Book Religion in Israel and the Ancient Near East* (Leuven: Peeters, 1997) 73–95.
Niemann, Hermann Michael, *Herrschaft, Königtum und Staat: Skizzen zur soziokulturellen Entwicklung im monarchischen Israel* (FAT 6; Tübingen: Mohr/Siebeck, 1993).
Nihan, Christoph, "'Is Saul also Among the Prophets?' 1 Samuel 10.10–12 and the Reworking of Saul's Story in the Postexilic Era" (paper presented at the annual meeting of the SBL, Nashville, Tenn., 19 November 2000).
Nims, Charles F. and Richard Steiner, "A Paganized Version of Psalm 20:2–6 from the Aramaic Text in Demotic Script," *JAOS* 103 (1983) 261–74.
Nissinen, Martti, "Akkadian Rituals and Poetry of Divine Love," in R. M. Whiting, ed., *Mythology and Mythologies* (Melammu Symposium 2; Helsinki: Neo-Assyrian Text Corpus Project, 2001) 93–136.
——, "Love Lyrics of Nabû and Tašmetu: An Assyrian Song of Songs?" in Manfried Dietrich and Ingo Kottsieper, eds., *"Und Mose schrieb dieses Lied auf"* (Loretz Festschrift; AOAT 250; Münster: Ugarit, 1998) 585–634.
Noll, K. L., *The Faces of David* (JSOTSS 242; Sheffield: Sheffield Academic Press, 1997) 160.
Noort, Ed, "Gan-Eden in the Context of the Mythology of the Hebrew Bible," in Gerard P. Luttikhuizen, ed., *Paradise Interpreted: Representations of Biblical Paradise in Judaism and Christianity* (Leiden: Brill, 1999) 21–36.
von Nordheim, Eckhard, *Die Selbstbehauptung Israels in der Welt des Alten Orients* (OBO 115; Göttingen: Vandenhoeck & Ruprecht, 1992).
Noth, Martin, *The History of Israel* (London: Black, 1958).
——, *A History of the Pentateuchal Traditions* (trans. Bernhard W. Anderson; Atlanta: Scholars, 1981).
Ochs, Peter, *Peirce, pragmatism and the logic of scripture* (Cambridge: Cambridge University Press, 1998).
Oded, Bustenay, *War, Peace and Empire: Justifications for War in Assyrian Royal Inscriptions* (Wiesbaden: Reichert, 1992).
Ohly, Friedrich, *Hohelied-Studien: Grundzüge einer Geschichte der Hoheliedauslegung des Abendlandes bis um 1200* (Wiesbaden: Steiner, 1958).
Olivier, J. P. J., "The Scepter of Justice and Ps. 45:7b," *JNWSL* 7 (1979) 45–54.
del Olmo Lete, Gregorio, *Canaanite Religion According to the Liturgical Texts of Ugarit* (Bethesda, MD: CDL, 1999).
——, "Royal Aspects of the Ugaritic Cult," in J. Quaegebeur, ed., *Ritual and Sacrifice in the Ancient Near East* (Leuven: Peeters, 1993) 51–66.
Olyan, Saul, *Rites and Rank* (Princeton: Princeton University Press, 2000).
Orthmann, Winfried, *Untersuchungen zur späthethitischen Kunst* (Bonn: Habelt, 1971).
Otto, Eckart, "Psalm 2 in neuassyrischer Zeit: Assyrische Motive in der judäischen Königsideologie," in *Textarbeit: Studien zu Texten und ihrer Rezeption aus dem Alten Testament und der Umwelt Israels* (eds. Klaus Kiesow and Thomas Meurer; FS Peter Weimar; AOAT 294; Münster: Ugarit-Verlag, 2003).
Otzen, B., "שלל," *TDOT* 5 (1986) 323–30.
Pardee, Dennis, *Ritual and Cult at Ugarit* (Atlanta: Society of Biblical Literature, 2002).
Park, Heon-Wook, *Die Kirche als 'Leib Christi' bei Paulus* (Giessen: Brunnen, 1992).
Parker, Simon B., "Possession Trance and Prophecy in Pre-exilic Israel," *VT* 28 (1978) 271–85.
——, *Stories in Scripture and Inscriptions: Comparative Studies on Narratives in Northwest Semitic Inscriptions and the Hebrew Bible* (Oxford: Oxford University Press, 1997).
Parmentier, Richard J., *Signs in Society: Studies in Semiotic Anthropology* (Bloomington: Indiana University Press, 1994).

Parpola, Simo, *Letters from Assyrian Scholars to the Kings Esarhaddon and Assurbanipal*, vol. 1: *Texts* AOAT 5/1; Neukirchen-Vluyn: Neukirchener, 1970).
———, *Letters from Assyrian Scholars to the Kings Esarhaddon and Assurbanipal*, vol. 2: *Commentary and Appendices* (AOAT 5/2; Neukirchen-Vluyn: Neukirchener, 1983).
Parry, Donald W., "The Aftermath of Abner's Murder," *Textus* 20 (2000) 83–96.
Patro, Subhasito S., "Royal Psalms in Modern Scholarship" (Ph.D. diss., University of Kiel, 1976).
Paul, Shalom M., "The 'Plural of Ecstasy' in Mesopotamian and Biblical Love Poetry," in Ziony Zevit, Seymour Gitin, and Michael Sokoloff, eds., *Solving Riddles and Untying Knots: Biblical, Epigraphic, and Semitic Studies in Honor of Jonas C. Greenfield* (Winona Lake: Eisenbrauns, 1995) 585–97.
———, "Psalm 72:5—A Traditional Blessing for the Long Life of the King," *JNES* 31 (1972) 351–54.
Pedersen, Johannes, *Israel: Its Life and Culture* (2 vols.; Oxford: Oxford University Press, 1940).
Peirce, Charles Sanders, *Collected Papers of Charles Sanders Peirce* (ed. Charles Hartshorne, Paul Weiss, and Arthur W. Burks; 8 vols.; Cambridge: Harvard University Press, 1931–58).
———, "Logic as Semiotic: The Theory of Signs," in Marcel Danesi and Donato Santeramo, eds., *Introducing Semiotics: An Anthology of Readings* (Toronto: Canadian Scholars' Press, 1992) 11–28.
Pelletier, Anne-Marie, *Lectures du Cantique des Cantiques* (Rome: Pontifical Biblical Institute, 1989).
Perlitt, Lothar, "Riesen im Alten Testament: Ein literarisches Motiv im Wirkungsfeld des Deuteronomismus," in idem, *Deuteronomium-Studien* (FAT 8; Tübingen: Mohr/Siebeck, 1994) 205–46.
Peterson, Gregory, *Minding God: Theology and the Cognitive Sciences* (Minneapolis: Fortress, 2003).
Pisano, Stephen, "2 Samuel 5–8 et le deutéronomiste: critique textuelle ou critique litteraire?" in Albert de Pury, Thomas Römer, and Jean-Daniel Macchi, eds., *Israël construit son histoire* (Geneva: Labor et Fides, 1996) 237–63.
Pitard, Wayne T., *Ancient Damascus: A Historical Study of the Syrian City-State from Earliest Times until Its Fall to the Assyrians in 732 BCE* (Winona Lake, IN: Eisenbrauns, 1987).
———, "The Arameans," in Alfred Hoerth, Gerald Mattingly, and Edwin Yamauchi, eds., *Peoples of the Old Testament World* (Grand Rapids: Baker, 1994) 207–30.
———, "The Ugaritic Funerary Text RS 34.126," *BASOR* 232 (1979) 65–75.
Podella, Thomas, *Das Lichtkleid JHWHs: Untersuchungen zur Gestalthaftigkeit Gottes im Alten Testament und seiner altorientalischen Umwelt* (FAT 15; Tübingen: Mohr/Siebeck, 1996).
Pongratz-Leisten, Beate, *Ina Šulmi Īrub: Die kulttopographische und ideologische Programmatik der Akītu-Prozession in Babylonien und Assyrien im 1. Jahrtausend v. Chr.* (BF 16; Mainz: von Zabern, 1994).
Pope, Marvin, *El in the Ugaritic Texts* (Leiden: Brill, 1955).
———, *Song of Songs* (AB 7C; Garden City, NY: Doubleday, 1977).
Porada, Edith, "Notes on the Sarcophagus of Ahiram," in *The Gaster Festschrift* (*JANES* 5 [1973]) 355–72.
Porter, James I., ed., *Constructions of the Classical Body* (Ann Arbor: University of Michigan Press, 2002).
Provan, Iain, "The Terrors of the Night: Love, Sex, and Power in Song of Songs 3," in J. I. Packer and Sven K. Soderlund, eds., *The Way of Wisdom* (Waltke Festschrift; Grand Rapids: Zondervan, 2000) 150–67.
Quintens, Werner, "La vie du roi dans le Psaume 21," *Bib* 59 (1978) 516–41.
von Rad, Gerhard, "The Royal Ritual in Judah," in idem, *The Problem of the Hexateuch and Other Essays* (New York: McGraw-Hill, 1966) 222–31.

———, "There Still Remains a Rest for the People of God: An Investigation of a Biblical Conception," in idem, *The Problem of the Hexateuch and Other Essays* (New York: McGraw-Hill, 1966) 94–102.

Rappoport, Roy, *Ritual and Religion in the Making of Humanity* (Cambridge: Cambridge University Press, 1999).

Reade, J. E., "The Neo-Assyrian Court and Army: Evidence from the Sculptures," *Iraq* 34 (1972) 87–112.

Redford, Donald B., *Egypt, Canaan, and Israel in Ancient Times* (Princeton: Princeton University Press, 1992).

Rehm, Martin, *Der königliche Messias im Licht der Immanuel-Weissagungen des Buches Jesaja* (Kevelaer: Butzon & Bercker, 1968).

Reich, Ronny, "Palaces and Residencies in the Iron Age," in Aharon Kempinski and Ronny Reich, eds., *The Architecture of Ancient Israel: From the Prehistoric to the Persian Periods* (Jerusalem: Israel Exploration Society, 1992) 202–22.

Reiner, Erica and Miguel Civil, "The Babylonian Fürstenspiegel in Practice," in *Societies and Languages of the Ancient Near East* (Diakonoff Festschrift; Warminster: Aris & Phillips, 1982) 320–26.

Reinhartz, Adele, "Anonymity and Character in the Books of Samuel," *Sem* 63 (1993) 117–41.

Renaud, Bernard, "Un oracle prophétique (2 S 7) invalidé? Une approche du Psaume 89," in Jean-Georges Heintz, ed., *Oracles et Prophéties dans l'antiquité* (Paris: Boccard, 1997) 215–29.

Rendsburg, Gary, *Linguistic Evidence for the Northern Origin of Selected Psalms* (SBLMS 43; Atlanta: Scholars, 1990).

Ribar, J. W., "Death Cult Practices in Ancient Palestine" (Ph.D. diss., University of Michigan, 1973).

Richlin, Amy, "Foucault's *History of Sexuality*: A Useful Theory for Women?" in David H. J. Larmour, Paul Allen Miller, and Charles Platter, eds., *Rethinking Sexuality: Foucault and Classical Antiquity* (Princeton: Princeton University Press, 1998) 138–70.

Riley, William, *King and Cultus in Chronicles* (JSOTSS 160; Sheffield: JSOT Press, 1993).

Ringgren, Helmer and Otto Kaiser, *Das Hohe Lied-Klagelieder-Das Buch Esther* (ATD 16.2; Göttingen: Vandenhoeck & Ruprecht, 1981).

Ritchie, Ian D., "The Nose Knows: Bodily Knowing in Isaiah 11:3," *JSOT* 87 (2000) 59–73.

Robert, A. and R. Tournay, *Le Cantique des Cantiques* (Paris: Gabalda, 1963).

Roberts, J. J. M., "The Davidic Origin of the Zion Tradition," *JBL* 92 (1973) 329–44.

———, "In Defense of the Monarchy: The Contributions of Israelite Kingship to Biblical Theology," in Patrick Miller, Paul Hanson, and S. Dean McBride, eds., *Ancient Israelite Religion* (Philadelphia: Fortress, 1987) 377–96.

———, "The Enthronement of Yhwh and David: The Abiding Theological Significance of the Kingship Language of the Psalms," *CBQ* 64 (2002) 675–86.

———, "Whose Child Is This? Reflections on the Speaking Voice in Isaiah 9:5," *HTR* 90 (1997) 115–30.

———, "Zion in the Theology of the Davidic-Solomonic Empire," in Tomoo Ishida, ed., *Studies in the Period of David and Solomon and Other Essays* (Winona Lake, IN: Eisenbrauns, 1982) 93–108.

de Romanis, Federico, *Cassia Cinnamomo Ossidiana: Uomini e merci tra Oceano Indiano e Mediterraneo* (Rome: Bretschneider, 1996).

Römer, Thomas and Albert de Pury, "L'historiographie deutéronomiste (HD): Histoire de la recherche et enjeux du debat," in Albert de Pury, Thomas Römer, and Jean-Daniel Macchi, eds., *Israël construit son histoire* (Geneva: Labor et Fides, 1996) 9–120.

Rosner, Fred, "Suicide in Jewish Law," in Kalman J. Kaplan and Matthew Schwartz, eds., *Jewish Approaches to Suicide, Martyrdom, and Euthanasia* (Northvale, NJ: Aronson, 1998) 61–77.
Rost, Leonhard, *Die Überlieferung von der Thronnachfolge Davids* (Stuttgart: Kohlhammer, 1926).
Rouillard, Hedwige and Josef Tropper, "*trpym*, rituals de guérison et culte des ancêtres d'apres 1 Samuel 19:11–17 et les texts parallèles d'Assur et de Nuzi," *VT* 37 (1987) 340–61.
Routledge, Bruce, "Learning to Love the King: Urbanism and the State in Iron Age Moab," in Walter Aufrecht, Neil A. Mirau, and Steven W. Gauley, eds., *Urbanism in Antiquity* (JSOTSS 244; Sheffield: Sheffield Academic Press, 1997) 130–44.
Rudolph, Wilhelm, *Das Buch Ruth-Das Hohe Lied-Das Klagelieder* (KAT 17.1–3; Gütersloh: Mohn, 1962).
Rupp, David W., "The 'Royal Tombs' at Salamis (Cyprus): Ideological Messages of Power and Authority," *Journal of Mediterranean Archaeology* 1 (1988) 111–39.
Russell, John Malcolm, *Sennacherib's Palace Without Rival at Nineveh* (Chicago: University of Chicago Press, 1991).
———, *The Writing on the Wall: Studies in the Architectural Context of Late Assyrian Palace Inscriptions* (Winona Lake, IN: Eisenbrauns, 1999).
Rüterswörden, Udo, "Der Bogen in Genesis 9: Militärhistorische und traditionsgeschichtliche Erwägungen zu einem biblischen Symbol," *UF* 20 (1988) 249–63.
Sader, Helen, "Phoenician Stelae from Tyre," *Ber* 39 (1991) 101–26.
Sader, Hélène S., *Les États Araméens de Syrie: Depuis leur fondation jusqu'à leur transformation en provinces assyriennes* (BTS 36; Wiesbaden: Steiner, 1987).
Saebø, Magne, "Vom Grossreich zum Weltreich: Erwägungen zu Pss. lxxii 8, lxxxix 26, Sach. ix 10b," *VT* 28 (1978) 83–91.
Said, Edward, *Orientalism* (New York: Pantheon, 1978).
Salameé-Sarkis, Hassān, "La Nécropole de Tyr: a propos de publications récentes," *Ber* 34 (1986) 193–205.
Salvesen, Alison, "The Trappings of Royalty in Ancient Hebrew," in Day, *King and Messiah*, 119–41.
Schade-Busch, Mechthild, *Zur Königsideologie Amenophis' III.: Analyse der Phraseologie historischer Texte der Voramarnazeit* (HÄB; Hildesheim: Gerstenberg, 1992).
Schäfer-Lichtenberger, Christa, *Josua und Salomo: Eine Studie zu Autorität und Legitimität des Nachfolgers im Alten Testament* (VTSup 58; Leiden: Brill, 1995).
Scheffler, Eben, "Saving Saul from the Deuteronomist," in Johannes de Moor and Harry van Rooy, eds., *Past, Present, and Future: The Deuteronomistic History and the Prophets* (OTS 44; Leiden: Brill, 2000) 263–71.
Scheper-Hughes, Nancy and Margaret Lock, "The Mindful Body: A Prolegomenon to Future Work in Medical Anthropology," *MAQ* 1 (1987) 6–41.
Schipper, Bernd Ulrich, *Israel und Ägypten in der Königszeit: Die kulturellen Kontakte von Solomo bis zum Fall Jerusalems* (OBO 170; Göttingen: Vandenhoeck & Ruprecht, 1999).
Schlumberger, "La Coiffure du Grand Roi," *Syria* 48 (1971) 375–83.
Schmidt, Hans, *Die Thronfahrt Jahves* (SGV 122; Tübingen: Mohr/Siebeck, 1927)
Schmidt, W. H., "דבר dābhar," *TDOT* 3 (1978) 84–125.
Schmitt, Hans-Christoph, "Das Hesbonlied Num. 21,27abb–30 und die Geschichte der Stadt Hesbon," *ZDPV* 104 (1988) 26–43.
Schmitt, Rüdiger, *Bildhafte Herrschaftsrepräsentation im eisenzeitlichen Israel* (AOAT 283; Münster: Ugarit-Verlag, 2001).
Schniedewind, William M., *How the Bible Became a Book* (Cambridge: Cambridge University Press, 2004).
———, *Society and the Promise to David: The Reception History of 2 Samuel 7:1–17* (New York: Oxford University Press, 1999).

Schrader, Eberhard, *Die Keilinschriften und das Alte Testament* (Giessen: Ricker, 1872; 3d ed.; Berlin: Reuther, 1903).
Schroer, Silvia and Thomas Staubli, *Body Symbolism in the Bible* (Collegeville, MN: Liturgical Press, 2001).
Schuttermayr, G., *Psalm 18 und 2 Samuel 22: Studien zu einem Doppeltext: Probleme der Textkritik und Übersetzung und das Psalterium Pianum* (Munich: Kösel, 1971).
Sebeok, Thomas A., *Semiotics in the United States* (Bloomington, IN: Indiana University Press, 1991).
Seebass, Horst, "Einige vertrauenswürdige Nachrichten zu Israels Anfängen: Zu den Söhnen Hobabs, Sichon und Bileam im Buch Numeri," *JBL* 113 (1994) 577–85.
———, "בוש," *TDOT* 2 (1975) 50–60.
Seiler, Stefan, *Die Geschichte von der Thronfolge Davids (2 Sam 9–20; 1 Kön 1–2): Untersuchungen zur Literarkritik und Tendenz* (Berlin: de Gruyter, 1998).
Seitz, Christopher, *Zion's Final Destiny: The Development of the Book of Isaiah, A Reassessment of Isaiah 36–39* (Minneapolis: Fortress, 1991).
Seow, C. L., *Myth, Drama, and the Politics of David's Dance* (HSM 44; Atlanta: Scholars, 1989).
Seux, M.-J., *Épithètes Royales Akkadiennes et Sumériennes* (Paris: Letouzey et Ané, 1967).
Seybold, Klaus, *Die Wallfahrtspsalmen: Studien zur Entstehungsgeschichte von Psalm 120–134* (Biblisch-theologische Studien 3; Neukirchen-Vluyn: Neukirchener Verlag, 1978).
———, *Die Psalmen* (HAT 1.15; Tübingen: Mohr/Siebeck, 1996).
Shenkel, James Donald, *Chronology and Recensional Development in the Greek Text of Kings* (Cambridge: Harvard University Press, 1968).
Shiloh, Yigal, *Excavations at the City of David: 1978–1982* (Qedem 19; Jerusalem: Hebrew University Institute of Archaeology, 1984).
Shipp, R. Mark, *Of Dead Kings and Dirges: Myth and Meaning in Isaiah 14:4b–21* (Academia Biblica 11; Atlanta: Society of Biblical Literature, 2002).
Simonse, Simon, *Kings of Disaster: Dualism, Centralism and the Scapegoat King in Southeastern Sudan* (Leiden: Brill, 1992).
Sissa, Giulia, "Sexual Bodybuilding: Aeschines against Timarchus," in *Constructions of the Classical Body* (ed. James I. Porter; Ann Arbor: University of Michigan Press, 2002) 147–68.
Sivan, Daniel, *A Grammar of the Ugaritic Language* (HO 28; Leiden: Brill, 1997).
Smelik, Klaas A. D., "Distortion of Old Testament Prophecy: The Purpose of Isaiah xxxvi and xxxvii," *OTS* 24 (1986) 70–93.
———, "King Mesha's Inscription," in idem, *Converting the Past: Studies in Ancient Israelite and Moabite Historiography* (Leiden: Brill, 1992) 59–92.
———, "The Origin of Psalm 20," *JSOT* 31 (1985) 75–81.
Smith, Henry Preserved, *The Books of Samuel* (ICC; Edinburgh: Clark, 1899).
Smith, Jonathan Z., "A Pearl of Great Price and a Cargo of Yams: A Study in Situational Incongruity," in idem, *Imagining Religion: From Babylon to Jonestown* (Chicago: University of Chicago Press, 1982) 90–101.
Smith, Mark S., "The Heart and Innards in Israelite Emotional Expressions: Notes from Anthropology and Psychobiology," *JBL* 117 (1998) 427–36.
van der Spek, R. J., "A Comparative Study of War and Empire in Assyria, Athens, and Rome," in Mark E. Cohen, Daniel C. Snell, and David Weisberg, eds., *The Tablet and the Scroll* (Bethesda, MD: CDL, 1993) 262–70.
Sperling, S. David, *The Original Torah: The Political Intent of the Bible's Writers* (New York: NYU Press, 1998).
Stade, Bernhard, *Geschichte des Volkes Israel* (2 vols.; Berlin: Grote'sche Verlagsbuchhandlung, 1887).
Stadelmann, Luis I. J., *The Hebrew Conception of the World* (AnBib 39; Rome: Biblical Institute Press, 1970).
———, *Love and Politics: A New Commentary on the Song of Songs* (New York: Paulist, 1992).

Stager, Lawrence, "The Archaeology of the Family in Ancient Israel," *BASOR* 260 (1985) 1–35.
——, "Jerusalem and the Garden of Eden," *EI* 26 (1999) 183*–94*.
Starbuck, Scott R. A., *Court Oracles in the Psalms: The So-Called Royal Psalms in their Ancient Near Eastern Context* (SBLDissS 172; Atlanta: Society of Biblical Literature, 1999).
Stemberger, Günter, "Psalmen in Liturgie und Predigt der rabbinischen Zeit," in Erich Zenger, ed., *Der Psalter in Judentum und Christentum*, (HB 18; Freiburg: Herder, 1998) 199–213.
Stern, Ephraim, *Archaeology of the Land of the Bible*, vol. 2: *The Assyrian, Babylonian, and Persian Periods 732–332 BCE* (ABRL; New York: Doubleday, 2001).
Sternberg, Meir, *Hebrews Between Cultures: Group Portraits and National Literature* (Bloomington, IN: Indiana University Press, 1998).
Steymans, Ulrich, *Deuteronomium 28 und die adê zur Thronfolgeregelung Asarhaddons: Segen und Fluch im Alten Orient und in Israel* (OBO 145; Göttingen: Vandenhoeck & Ruprecht, 1995).
Stordalen, T., *Echoes of Eden: Genesis 2–3 and Symbolism of the Eden Garden in Biblical Hebrew Literature* (Leuven: Peeters, 2000).
Sullivan, Lawrence E., "Body Works: Knowledge of the Body in the Study of Religion," *HistRel* 30 (1990) 86–99.
Sweeney, Marvin, *Isaiah 1–39 With an Introduction to Prophetic Literature* (FOTL 16; Grand Rapids: Eerdmans, 1996).
——, *King Josiah of Judah: The Lost Messiah of Israel* (Oxford: Oxford University Press, 2001).
——, *Zephaniah* (Hermeneia; ed. Paul Hanson; Minneapolis: Fortress, 2003).
Tadmor, Hayim, "Autobiographical Apology in the Royal Assyrian Literature," in Hayim Tadmor and Moshe Weinfeld, *History, Historiography, and Interpretation: Studies in biblical and cuneiform literatures* (Jerusalem: Magnes, 1983) 36–57.
——, "History and Ideology in the Assyrian Royal Inscriptions," in F. Mario Fales, ed., *Assyrian Royal Inscriptions: New Horizons in Literary, Ideological, and Historical Analysis* (Rome: Istituto per l'oriente, 1981) 13–33.
——, "Monarchy and the Elite in Assyria and Babylonia: The Question of Royal Accountability," in S. N. Eisenstadt, ed., *The Origins and Diersity of Axial Age Civilizations* (Albany: SUNY Press, 1986) 203–24, 518–21.
——, "The Sin of Sargon," *EI* 5 (1958) 150–62 [Hebrew].
Tadmor, Hayim, Benno Landsberger, and Simo Parpola, "The Sin of Sargon and Sennacherib's Last Will," *SAAB* 3/1 (1989) 3–51.
Tambiah, Stanley, *Culture, Thought, and Social Action: An Anthropological Perspective* (Cambridge: Harvard University Press, 1985)
——, "A Performative Approach to Ritual," *Proceedings of the British Academy* 45 (1979) 113–69.
Tappy, Ron E., *The Archaeology of Israelite Samaria*, vol. 1: *Early Iron Age through the Ninth Century BCE* (Atlanta: Scholars, 1992).
Teeter, Emily, *The Presentation of Maat: Ritual and Legitimacy in Ancient Egypt* (SAOC 57; Chicago: Oriental Institute, 1997).
Terrien, Samuel, *The Psalms: Strophic Structure and Theological Commentary* (Eerdmans Critical Commentary; Grand Rapids: Eerdmans, 2003).
Thornton, T. C. G., "Charismatic Kingship in Israel and Judah," *JTS* 14 (1963) 1–11.
Throntveit, Mark A., *When Kings Speak: Royal Speech and Royal Prayer in Chronicles* (SBLDissS 98; Atlanta: Scholars, 1987).
Thureau-Dangin, F., *Rituels Accadiens* (reprint ed.; Osnabruck: Zeller, 1975).
Timm, Stefan, *Die Dynastie Omri* (FRLANT 124; Göttingen: Vandenhoeck & Ruprecht, 1982).
van der Toorn, Karel, *Family Religion in the Babylonia, Syria and Israel: Continuity and Change in Forms of Religious Life* (Leiden: Brill, 1996).

——, ed., *The Image and the Book: Iconic Cults, Aniconism, and the Rise of Book Religion in Israel and the Ancient Near East* (Leuven: Peeters, 1997).
Tosato, Angelo, "The Literary Structure of the First Two Poems of Balaam (Num. xxiii 7–10, 18–24)," *VT* 29 (1979) 98–106.
Tropper, Josef, *Die Inschriften von Zincirli* (ALASP 6; Münster: Ugarit, 1993).
Tsukimoto, Akio, *Untersuchungen zur Totenpflege* (kispum) *im alten Mesopotamien* (AOAT 216; Neukirchen-Vluyn: Neukirchener, 1985).
Tsumura, David Toshio, "The Interpretation of the Ugaritic Funerary Text KTU 1.161," in Eiko Matsushima, ed., *Official Cult and Popular Religion in the Ancient Near East* (Heidelberg: Winter, 1993) 40–55.
Turner, Bryan S., The body in Western society: social theory and its perspectives," in Sarah Coakley, ed., *Religion and the Body* (Cambridge: Cambridge University Press, 1997) 15–41.
Uehlinger, Christoph, "Anthropomorphic Cult Statuary in Iron Age Palestine and the Search for Yahweh's Cult Images," in van der Toorn, *Image and the Book*, 97–155.
——, "Northwest Semitic Inscribed Seals, Iconography and Syro-Palestinian Religions of Iron Age II: Some Afterthoughts and Conclusions," in Benjamin Sass and Christoph Uehlinger, eds., *Studies in the Iconography of Northwest Semitic Inscribed Seals* (OBO 125; Göttingen: Vandenhoeck & Ruprecht, 1993) 257–88.
Ussishkin, David, *The Conquest of Lachish by Sennacherib* (Tel Aviv: Tel Aviv University, Institute of Archaeology, 1982).
——, "The Necropolis from the Time of the Kingdom of Judah at Silwan," *BA* 33 (1970) 34–46.
——, *The Village of Silwan: The Necropolis from the Period of the Judean Kingdom* (Jerusalem: Israel Exploration Society, 1993).
Vanderhooft, David, *The Neo-Babylonian Empire and Babylon in the Latter Prophets* (HSM 59; Atlanta: Scholars, 1999).
Vanderkam, James, "Davidic Complicity in the deaths of Abner and Eshball: A Rhetorical and Redactional Study," in idem, *From Revelation to Canon: Studies in the Hebrew Bible and Second Temple Literature* (JSTSup 62: Leiden: Brill, 2000) 31–52.
Van Dijk, H. J., *Ezekiel's Prophecy on Tyre (Ez. 26,1–28,19): A New Approach* (BibOr 20; Rome: Pontifical Biblical Institute, 1968).
Van Seters, John, "The Creation of Man and the Creation of the King," *ZAW* 101 (1989) 333–342.
——, *In Search of History: Historioraphy in the Ancient World and the Origins of Biblical History* (reprint ed.; Winona Lake, IN: Eisenbrauns, 1997).
——, *The Life of Moses: The Yahwist as Historian in Exodus-Numbers* (Louisville: Westminster/John Knox, 1994).
Vaughn, Andrew G., *Theology, History and Archaeology in the Chronicler's Account of Hezekiah* (Atlanta: Scholars, 1999).
Veijola, Timo, *Die Ewige Dynastie: David und die Entstehung seiner Dynastie nach der deuteronomistischen Darstellung* (Helsinki: Tiedeakatemia, 1975).
——, *Das Königtum in der Beurteilung der deuteronomistischen Historiographie* (Helsinki: Suomalainen Tiedeakatemia, 1977).
——, *Verheissung in der Krise: Studien zur Literatur und Theologie der Exilszeit anhand des 89. Psalms* (Helsinki: Suomalainen Tiedeakatemia, 1982).
Vollmer, Jochen, *Geschichtliche Rückblicke und Motive in der Prophetie des Amos, Hosea und Jesaja* (BZAW 119; Berlin: de Gruyter, 1971).
Wälchli, Stefan, *Der weise König Salomo: Eine Studie zu den Erzählungen von der Weisheit Salomos in ihrem alttestamentlichen und altorientalischen Kontext* (BWANT 141; Stuttgart: Kohlhammer, 1999).
Warren, Robert Penn, *The Collected Poems of Robert Penn Warren* (ed. John Burt; foreword by Harold Bloom; Baton Rouge: LSU Press, 1998).
Watanabe, Kazuko, *Die adê Vereidigung anlässlich der Thronfolgeregelung Asarhaddons* (Baghdader Mitteilungen 3; Berlin: Mann, 1987).

Weber, Max, *Economy and Society: An Outline of Interpretive Sociology* (1920; ed. Guenther Roth and Claus Wittich; 2 vols.; Berkeley: University of California Press, 1978).
Wegner, Paul D., *An Examination of Kingship and Messianic Expectation in Isaiah 1–35* (Lewiston, NY: Mellen, 1992).
Weinfeld, Moshe, "'Rider of the Clouds' and "Gatherer of the Clouds'," *JANES* 5 (1973) 421–26.
Weippert, Helga, *Palästina in vorhellenistischer Zeit* (Munich: Beck, 1988).
Weiser, Artur, *Die Psalmen* (ATD; Göttingen: Vandenhoeck & Ruprecht, 1955).
Weissert, Elnathan, "Royal Hunt and Royal Triumph in a Prism Fragment of Ashurbanipal (82-5-22,2)," in Simo Parpola and R. M. Whiting, eds., *Assyria 1995* (Helsinki: Neo-Assyrian Text Corpus Project, 1997) 339–58.
Weitzman, Steven, "David's Lament and the Poetics of Grief in 2 Samuel," *JQR* 85 (1995) 341–61.
———, *Song and Story in Biblical Narrative: The History of a Literary Convention in Ancient Israel* (Bloomington: Indiana University Press, 1997).
Wellhausen, Julius, *Israelitische und jüdische Geschichte* (2d ed.; Berlin: Reimer, 1895).
———, *Der Text der Bücher Samuelis untersucht* (Göttingen: Vandenhoeck & Ruprecht, 1871).
———, *Prolegomena zur Geschichte Israels* (1989; 6th ed.; Berlin: de Gruyter, 1926).
Wénin, André, *Samuel et l'instauration de la monarchie (1 S 1–12): Une recherche littéraire sur le personnage* (Frankfurt: Peter Lang, 1987).
Westenholz, Joan Goodnick, *Legends of the Kings of Akkade* (Winona Lake, IN: Eisenbrauns, 1997).
———, "Love Lyrics from the Ancient Near East," *CANE* 4 (1995) 2471–84.
Westermann, Claus, *Praise and Lament in the Psalms* (Louisville: John Knox, 1981).
White, Marsha, "'The History of Saul's Rise': Saulide State Propaganda in 1 Samuel 1–14," in Saul Olyan and Robert Culley, eds., *"A Wise and Discerning Mind"* (Long Festschrift; BJS 325; Providence: Brown Judaic Studies, 2000) 271–92.
Whitley, C. F., "Textual and Exegetical Observations on Ps. 45, 4–7," *ZAW* 98 (1986).
Whybray, R. N., *The Succession Narrative: A Study of II Sam. 9–20 and 1 Kings 1 and 2* (SBT 9; Naperville, IL: Allenson, 1968).
Wildberger, Hans, *Isaiah 28–39* (Continental Commentary; Minneapolis: Fortress, 2002).
———, *Jesaja* (BKAT 10/1–3; 3 vols.; Neukirchen-Vluyn: Neukirchener, 1972–82).
Williamson, H. G. M., "The Death of Josiah and the continuing Development of the Deuteronomistic History," *VT* 32 (1982) 242–47.
———, "Reliving the Death of Josiah: A Reply to C. T. Begg," *VT* 37 (1987) 9–15.
Willis, John T., "A Cry of Defiance—Psalm 2," *JSOT* 47 (1990) 33–50.
———, "The Function of Comprehensive Anticipatory Redactional Joints in 1 Samuel 16–18," *ZAW* 85 (1973) 294–314.
Wilson, E. Jan, *"Holiness" and "Purity" in Mesopotamia* (AOAT 237; Neukirchen-Vluyn: Neukirchener, 1994).
Wilson, Robert R., "The Death of the King of Tyre: The Editorial History of Ezekiel 28," in John H. Marks and Robert M. Good, eds., *Love & Death in the Ancient Near East: Essays in Honor of Marvin H. Pope* (Guilford, CT: Four Quarters, 1987) 211–18.
———, "Prophecy and Ecstasy: A Reexamination," *JBL* 98 (1979) 321–37.
Winter, Irene J., "Art *in* Empire: The Royal Image and the Visual Dimensions of Assyrian Ideology," in Simo Parpola and R. M. Whiting, eds., *Assyria 1995* (Helsinki: Neo-Assyrian Text Corpus Project, 1997) 359–81.
———, "The Body of the Able Ruler: Toward an Understanding of the Statues of Gudea," in Hermann Behrens, Darlene Loding, and Martha T. Roth, eds., *DUMU-E₂-DUB-BA-A: Studies in Honor of Åke Sjöberg* (Philadelphia: Kramer Fund, 1989) 573–83.

——, "Idols of the King: Royal Images as Recipients of Ritual Action in Ancient Mesopotamia," *JRS* 6 (1992) 13–42.

——, "Sex, Rhetoric, and the Public Monument: The Alluring Body of Naram-Sin of Agade," in *Sexuality in Ancient Art: Near East, Egypt, Greece, and Italy* (ed. Natalie Boymel Kampen; Cambridge: Cambridge University Press, 1996).

Wiseman, D. J., "Murder in Mesopotamia," *Iraq* 36 (1974) 249–60.

——, *Nebuchadnezzar and Babylon* (Oxford: Oxford University Press, 1985).

Wolff, Hans Walter, *Hosea* (Hermeneia; Philadelphia: Fortress, 1974).

Wreszinski, Walter, *Löwenjagd im alten Ägypten* (Leipzig: Hinrichs, 1932).

Wright, David P., *The Disposal of Impurity: Elimination Rites in the Bible and in Hittite and Mesopotamian Literature* (SBLDissS 101; Atlanta: Scholars, 1987).

——, *Ritual in Narrative: The Dynamics of Feasting, Mourning, and Retaliation Rites in the Ugaritic Tale of Aqhat* (Winona Lake: Eisenbrauns, 2001).

Würthwein, Ernst, *Die Erzählung von der Thronfolge Davids* (Zurich: Theologischer Verlag, 1974).

——, *Ruth, Das Hohelied, Esther* (in *Die Fünf Megillot*; HAT 18; Tübingen: Mohr/Siebeck, 1969).

——, "Zur Komposition von 1 Reg 22,1–38," in F. Maass, ed., *Das ferne und nahe Wort* (BZAW 105; Berlin: de Gruyter, 1967) 245–54.

Xella, Paolo, *I Testi Rituali di Ugarit*, vol. 1: *Testi* (Rome: CNDR, 1981).

Yadin, Azzan, "Goliath's Armor and Israelite Collective Memory," *VT* 54 (2004) 373–95.

Zadok, Ran, *The Pre-Hellenistic Israelite Anthroponymy and Prosopography* (OLA 28; Leuven: Peeters, 1988).

Zakovitch,Yair, "David's Birth and Childhood in the Bible and in the Midrashim on Psalms," in Erich Zenger, ed., *Der Psalter in Judentum und Christentum* (HBS 18; Freiburg: Herder, 1998) 185–98.

Zevit, Ziony, *The Religions of Ancient Israel* (London/New York: Continuum, 2001).

Zibelius-Chen, Karola, "Theorie und Realität im Königtum der 25. Dynastie," in Rolf Gundlach and Christine Raedler, eds., *Selbstverständnis und Realität* (ÄAT 36.1; Wiesbaden: Harrassowitz, 1997) 81–95.

Zimmerli, Walther, *Ezekiel* (Hermeneia; 2 vols.; Philadelphia: Fortress, 1983).

INDEX OF MODERN AUTHORS

Abitz, F. 146, 249
Abusch, T. 165, 173
Aelian 85, 230
Ahl, F. 15, 36, 72, 130
Ahlström, G. 88–89, 91–92, 115, 185, 190
Akurgal, E. 162
Albertz, R. 120, 275
Albright, W. 154, 243
Allen, L. 65, 74, 13, 248
Alt, A. 23
Althann, R. 71
Anderson, A. 130, 208
Anderson, G. 101
Antonaccio, C. 166
Ap-Thomas, D. 122
Arneth, M. 75, 77, 79, 134
Artzi, P. 191
Asad, T. 12
Assmann, J. 112, 165, 248, 275
Aubet, M. 229
Austin, J. 19, 48, 63, 106–107, 112, 143, 166
Avalos, H. 86, 99
Avigad, N. 108
Avishur, Y. 95

Bachelot, L. 162
Baltzer, K. 186
Bär, J. 255
Barkay, G. 147, 175
Barr, J. 232
Beal, T. 3–4
Begg, C. 178
Berquist, J. 3–5, 13
Begrich, J. 23, 34, 99
Bell, C. 32, 83, 138, 143, 276
Ben-Barak, Z. 76
Benthall, J. 13
Bentzen, A. 61
Berges, U. 157, 164, 203
Berlinerblau, J. 41
Bernhardt, K.-H. 21, 24
Beuken, W. 98
Birch, B. 120, 126
Birkeland, H. 36
Blenkinsopp, J. 98, 109, 214, 262

Bloch, M. 240
Bloch-Smith, E. 148–149, 166
Boadt, L. 249–250, 252
Bodendorfer, G. 33
Boling, R. 246
Bonhême, M.-A. 248
Bowes, A. 47
Braulik, G. 122
Braun, J. 139
Braun, R. 219
Brenner, A. 13
Brettler, M. 30, 91, 245–246
Brueggemann, W. 102
Briggs, C. 33, 38, 61
Briquel-Chattonet, F. 228
Brodwin, P. 100
Brown, P. 11
Brown, W. 49, 68, 224, 230
Burkert, W. 160
Butler, J. 10
Bynum, C. 11, 267

Calame, C. 186
Campagno, M. 249
Campbell, A. 119, 128, 153, 168, 186, 188–189, 197, 200, 203–204, 216
Cancik-Kirschbaum, E. 47, 255
Caquot, A. 125, 131, 152, 168, 189, 194, 198, 200–201, 207, 217
Carlson, R. 208, 212
Carter, J. 166
Cazelles, H. 255
Childs, B. 98
Christensen, D. 253
Cifola, B. 72, 93, 185, 190
von Clausewitz, C. 35, 184
Coakley, S. 1, 12
Cogan, M. 46, 79, 136, 147, 170, 177, 214, 239, 256
Cohen, S. 249
Cole, S. 213
Collon, D. 121
Coote, R. 25–26, 62
Corral, M. 228–229
Craigie, P. 38, 40, 43, 51, 61, 64, 102, 106–107, 226

Croft, S. 36–37
Cross, F. 50, 84, 102, 118–119, 133, 178, 227, 239, 243, 248
Crüsemann, F. 120
Csordas, T. 142
Culley, R. 119, 151
Curtis, J. 67

Dahood, M. 38, 41, 49, 51, 61, 62–63, 65, 69, 74–76, 79–80, 89–90, 93–94, 97, 102, 104, 106–107
Davis, N. 13
Davis, V. 55
Day, J. 25, 27, 91
DeBoer, M. 267
de Fraine, J. 24
de Moor, J. 187, 190
de Vaux, R. 25, 177–178
Dever, W. 218, 225
De Vries, S. 170
de Ward, E. 216
Dick, M. 59, 74
Dion, P.-E. 237
Doré, J. 65–66
Douglas, M. 10, 12, 35, 142, 225
Duden, B. 6, 127
Duhm, B. 33
Dutcher-Walls, P. 137

Eagleton, T. 1, 19, 118, 265
Eaton, J. 35–37, 95, 191
Eco, U. 7, 16–18, 47, 111, 113–114, 182, 187, 207, 233
Edelman, D. 120, 152, 157, 163–164, 194, 200, 203
Eilberg-Schwartz, H. 4
Elshtain, J. 184
Eslinger, L. 219, 226
Exum, J. 55
Ewald, H. 21

Fabry, H.-J. 126–127
Fales, F. 91, 93, 185, 255
Farber, W. 46, 87, 202
Finkelstein, I. 225
Fischer, A. 130, 216
Fitzmyer, J. 254
Flanagan, J. 21
Flanagan, O. 6
Fokkelman, J. 152–153, 158, 161, 165, 168, 188, 201–203, 217
Foster, B. 57
Foucault, M. 4–5, 13–14, 15, 81

Fox, M. 55
Foxhall, L. 13
Freedman, D. 54, 102, 235
Fretheim, T. 85
Friedman, R. 119
Frontain, R. 21

Galil, G. 132, 177
Gallagher, C. 13
Garelli, P. 93, 123, 185
Garr, W. 85
Geller, S. 115
Gellner, E. 270
George, M. 4, 128, 186, 196
Gerardi, P. 257
Gerstenberger, E. 33, 35, 48, 61, 65, 80, 84, 88–89, 95, 102
Gese, H. 70
Gevirtz, S. 187
Gibson, J. 199
Gilman, S. 6
Ginsberg, H. 42, 73, 150, 262
Girard, R. 154
Gitin, S. 73, 77
Giveon, R. 249
Goldberg, I. 228
Goldstein, S. 161
Gottwald, N. 23, 25–27, 62
Goulder, M. 33, 84–85, 95
Gray, J. 136, 176
Greenberg, M. 140, 230, 232, 235–237, 250, 252–253
Gressmann, H. 23–24, 34, 61, 65, 67, 157, 272
Grottanelli, C. 226
Gruber, M. 44, 75, 216
Gubel, E. 233
Gunkel, H. 23, 33–38, 65, 79, 94
Gunn, D. 3–4, 164, 204, 206

Haas, V. 166
Habermas, J. 14
Hackett, J. 13, 243
Hacking, I. 2, 13
Hallo, W. 41, 47, 99, 146–147
Halpern, B. 3, 27, 65, 90–91, 118, 120, 130, 132, 149, 152, 158, 186, 189, 190–192, 208–209, 218, 245
Handy, L. 137, 199, 218
Hanson, P. 72, 226, 242–243
Hasel, G. 25, 126
Hauge, M. 37
Hendel, R. 141

Herzfeld, M. 19–20, 48, 62, 112, 139, 180, 194, 209, 264, 270
Hevia, J. 12, 44
Hill, J. 220
Hillers, D. 78, 84–85
Hobbs, T. 175
Hoffmeier, J. 120, 254
Holladay, W. 167, 254
Hossfeld, F. 61, 102, 106
Hrouda, B. 137, 160
Hurowitz, V. 85, 218
Huwyler, B. 253–254

Ishida, T. 25, 33, 126, 135, 195, 207

Jaggar, A. 13
Japhet, S. 41, 72, 131, 138, 171, 178, 219
Jeffers, A. 235
Johnson, A. 24, 34, 65, 115

Kaiser, O. 57, 98–99, 109, 146, 186, 207, 244, 258–259, 262
Kantorowicz, E. 2, 9–10, 28, 30, 74, 109, 134, 142, 165, 266
Katzenstein, H. 228, 235, 237
Keegan, J. 183
King, L. 235
Kittel, R. 22
Klein, E. 55
Klein, J. 79
Klein, R. 200
Klingbeil, M. 49, 224, 227
Knoppers, G. 178
Koch, K. 67, 218, 248, 251
Kottsieper, I. 57, 106
Kraus, H.-J. 38, 40, 43, 94
Kselman, J. 75, 77, 79–80

Laato, A. 17, 136
Lackenbacher, S. 84–85, 218
LaCocque, A. 58
Lambert, W. 80
Landsberger, B. 40, 147, 150
Langlamet, F. 185
Lasine, S. 28, 100, 186, 199, 236, 238
Launderville, D. 28, 48, 87, 157, 199, 212, 215, 233, 240, 245
Lehmküller, K. 35
Lemaire, A. 243
Lesses, R. 235
Levenson, J. 218
Levine, B. 41, 165

Lewis, T. 146
Lipinski, E. 88, 91
Littauer, M. 160
Liverani, M. 78, 255
Livingstone, A. 58
Lohfink, N. 119
Long, B. 137–138, 213, 238–239
Long, V. 120
Lord, A. 95
Loretz, O. 28, 57, 80
Lyke, L. 210

Machinist, P. 57, 86, 213, 247, 255–256, 258, 260
MacRae, D. 13
Maderna-Sieben, C. 255
Madhloom, T. 48, 104, 114
Magen, U. 8, 93, 104, 137, 141, 162, 256, 260
Malamat, A. 54, 237
Marcus, M. 78
Margueron, J.-C. 214
Mariaselvam, A. 58
Martínez Borobio, E. 162
Matthews Grieco, S. 13
Matthiae, P. 256
Mattingly, G. 227, 237
Mauss, M. 11–12, 97
McCarter, P. K. 122, 128, 130–131, 133, 147, 152–153, 155, 158, 166, 168–169, 189, 191, 196, 201, 204–205, 211, 217
McCarthy, D. 120, 124
McGinnis, J. 156
McKenzie, S. 3, 27, 119–120, 122, 124, 129, 146, 170, 189, 192, 195, 208
McNay, L. 14
Meier, S. 70
Menzel, B. 219
Mettinger, T. 25, 84, 120, 126, 138, 141, 197
Metzger, M. 233
Meyer, E. 22
Meyer, J.-W. 218
Meyers, E. 147, 214
Midgley, M. 1
Milgrom, J. 54, 125, 167, 226, 246
Millard, A. 120, 226
Miller, J. M. 225, 241–242
Miller, P. 13, 35, 42, 72, 102, 243
Mitchell, T. 38, 226
Monod, P. 9
Montgomery, J. 171, 214

Morenz, S. 51
Morgenstern, J. 228
Mowinckel, S. 24, 34–37, 61, 65–66, 80, 84–86, 91, 94, 99, 102, 107, 115, 243
Mulder, J. 38, 47–48
Mulzer, M. 174–175
Murphy, R. 55–57

Nagel, W. 160
Nagy, G. 95, 166
Neely, M. 211
Negbi, O. 57, 74, 90, 199
Nelson, J. 9
Newsom, C. 3–4, 13, 228, 231
Niccacci, A. 242
Niditch, S. 95
Niehr, H. 59, 67
Niemann, H. 190
Nihan, C. 126
Nims, C. 106
Nissinen, M. 57
Noll, K. 134, 158
Noort, E. 231
von Nordheim, E. 89
Noth, M. 24, 226

Ochs, P. 7
Oded, B. 259
Olivier, J. 51
del Olmo Lete, G. 70, 93, 146
Olyan, S. 119, 129, 151, 155
Orthmann, W. 114, 121
Otto, E. 33
Otzen, B. 70

Pardee, D. 70
Park, H.-W. 267
Parker, S. 42, 192
Parpola, S. 74, 77, 147, 150, 164, 173, 184, 202–203, 213, 244, 255, 261, 272
Parry, D. 217
Patro, S. 23
Paul, S. 76, 191
Pedersen, J. 24
Peirce, C. 7–8, 17–18, 113
Perlitt, L. 226
Peterson, G. 6
Pisano, S. 219
Pitard, W. 146, 237, 239
Podella, T. 33, 49, 59, 96, 263, 271, 273
Pongratz-Leisten, B. 35

Pope, M. 55–57, 59, 228, 231
Porada, E. 92, 166
Porter, J. 1, 10, 13, 115
Provan, I. 55

Quintens, W. 106

von Rad, G. 220
Reade, J. 160
Redford, D. 160
Rehm, M. 108
Reich, R. 81
Reiner, E. 80
Reinhartz, A. 188
Renaud, B. 88–89, 219
Rendsburg, G. 85
Ribar, J. 148
Richlin, A. 13
Riley, W. 220
Ringgren, H. 57
Ritchie, I. 109
Roberts, J. J. M. 33, 51, 61, 70, 72, 119, 269
de Romanis, F. 54
Römer, T. 120, 145, 186, 219
Rosner, F. 161
Rost, L. 145, 207
Rouillard, H. 200
Routledge, B. 241–242
Rudolph, W. 70
Rupp, D. 175
Russell, J. 8, 218
Rüterswörden, U. 103

Sader, H. 237, 239
Saebø, M. 77
Salvesen, A. 27
Schade-Busch, M. 51
Schäfer-Lichtenberger, C. 122
Scheper-Hughes, N. 142
Schipper, B. 249
Schlumberger 114, 193
Schmidt, H. 24
Schmidt, W. 40
Schmitt, H.-C. 226
Schmitt, R. 67, 96, 193, 244, 252, 256
Schniedewind, W. 119, 224
Schrader, E. 22
Schroer, S. 3, 96
Schuttermayr, G. 102
Sebeok, T. 7–8, 17, 194
Seebass, H. 226
Seitz, C. 98

Seow, C. 17, 191
Seux, M.-J. 72, 127, 133
Seybold, K. 38, 61, 84
Shenkel, J. 170
Shiloh, Y. 74
Shipp, R. 70, 262
Simonse, S. 123-124, 154
Sissa, G. 13
Sivan, D. 129
Smelik, K. 98, 106, 242
Smith, H. 200-201, 211
Smith, J. 123
Smith, M. 110
van der Spek, R. 185
Sperling, S. 73, 133
Stade, B. 21, 22
Stadelmann, L. 70
Stager, L. 59, 148, 233, 235
Starbuck, S. 21, 36, 60, 67, 84
Stemberger, G. 35
Sternberg, M. 198
Steymans, U. 94
Stordalen, T. 232, 233
Sullivan, L. 6, 10
Sweeney, M. 3, 27, 109, 178, 242

Tadmor, H. 91, 123, 136, 147, 150, 158, 177, 184, 214, 239, 256
Tambiah, S. 19, 20, 38-39, 43-45, 66, 83, 100, 136
Teeter, E. 248
Terrien, S. 38, 95
Thornton, T. 23
Throntveit, M. 219
Thureau-Dangin, F. 69
Timm, S. 170, 174
van der Toorn, K. 59, 67, 141, 146, 199
Tosato, A. 243
Tropper, J. 200
Tsukimoto, A. 146
Tsumura, D. 146

Uehlinger, C. 199, 233-235
Ussishkin, D. 147, 150, 175

Vanderhooft, D. 118, 132, 149, 247, 261-262

Vanderkam, J. 216
Van Dijk, H. 234, 236
Van Seters, J. 47, 118, 207, 225, 248, 255
Vaughn, A. 132
Veijola, T. 88, 120-121, 168
Vollmer, J. 108

Warren, R. 145, 156
Watanabe, K. 94, 150, 156
Weber, M. 10
Wegner, P. 109
Weinfeld, M. 50, 158
Weiser, A. 38, 40, 43, 51, 61, 65, 79, 95, 102, 106-107
Weissert, E. 244
Weitzman, S. 153, 187
Wellhausen, J. 22, 197
Wénin, A. 120
Westenholz, J. 150, 153, 274
Westermann, C. 102
White, M. 119, 151
Whitelam, K. 25-26, 62
Whitley, C. 49
Whybray, R. 210
Wildberger, H. 98-100, 108-109, 111, 244, 259, 260, 262
Williamson, H. 178
Willis, J. 61, 197
Wilson, E. 93
Wilson, R. 192, 228, 235, 237
Winter, I. 8, 74, 86, 261
Wiseman, D. 147, 261
Wolff, H. 139, 193
Wreszinski, W. 244
Wright, D. 54, 168
Würthwein, E. 170, 208

Xella, P. 70, 74, 146

Yadin, A. 128

Zadok, R. 72
Zakovitch,Y. 33
Zevit, Z. 266
Zibelius-Chen, K. 248
Zimmerli, W. 229, 234-235, 249-250, 252

TOPICAL INDEX

Abiner 130, 204, 204 n. 72, 205, 216, 217, 217 n. 108, 236
Absalom 128 n. 32, 184, 207–9, 210 n. 87, 211–13, 270–73
Aelian 230
Ahab 147 n. 9, 148, 170, 170 n. 76, 174–75, 181, 190
Akish 153, 190, 192–95
Amalekite 152–53, 155, 159–61, 170, 202
Amaziah 149 n. 14, 176–77, 177 n. 94, 179, 240
Anointing 10, 24, 89–90, 92, 111, 122, 125–26, 128, 128 n. 29, 130, 132–33, 135–37, 141–43, 191, 202, 208
Antimonarchic party 123–24
Aramaic 63 n. 103, 106, 232
Ark 65–66, 67 n. 121, 68, 85, 85 n. 8, 85 n. 10, 85 n. 11, 112
Assurbanipal 79, 147, 164, 173 n. 85, 203 n. 66
Athaliah 135, 137–40, 149 n. 14, 175

Baal-zebul 214
Beard 114, 183, 191, 191 n. 31, 193, 206, 260
Ben-Hadad 238–39
Bethshean 164
Biological determinism 2, 5, 11, 13, 141–42
Bir-rakib 76, 92 n. 38, 103, 151–52, 157
bīt rimki 36 n. 19, 87, 87 n. 18, 184 n. 3, 202
Black Obelisk 108
Builder, king as 218–20
Burial 76, 123 n. 14, 130, 147–49, 165–66, 168–69, 173, 175–76, 253, 262–63, 267
Byblos 45 n. 44, 71 n. 158, 95, 103, 154

Canaanite(s) 22, 27, 34, 72, 104, 119, 146, 166, 231 n. 30
Carchemish 162

Chariot 48, 57, 96, 106 n. 91, 137, 142–43, 160, 160 n. 46, 162, 172–73, 175, 175 n. 90, 176, 178–79, 209, 213, 273
Charismatic kingship 23, 24 n. 66, 193
Cherub 232
Child bearing rituals 46
Coup d'etat 123, 147, 174, 176 n. 93, 180, 189, 189 n. 20
Cremation 166, 166 n. 66
Crown prince 116
Cuthean Legend 274

Danilu 237
Davidides 34, 62, 110, 133, 152, 159, 174
Death 145–82
Deir 'Alla 243
Deuteronomistic History (DH) 2, 23, 28–29, 65, 84 n. 6, 86, 89, 118, 120, 122, 144, 146, 148, 153, 178–79, 216 n. 103, 240, 270
Dibon 241–42
Disguises 171–73, 178–79, 199
Divine Warrior 227, 227 n. 16, 234, 269
Dream 69
Dynastic kingship 23

Ears 109
Eden 232, 235, 235 n. 46, 237
Edom 132 n. 43, 177, 227 n. 18
Egypt 27, 51 n. 65, 124 n. 19, 132 n. 43, 161, 225, 243–44, 247–49, 249 n. 95, 251–55, 272
Elohim 30, 50, 51–54, 92, 174, 229
Endor 152, 155
Enemies 2, 20, 32, 37, 40, 44, 59, 63–64, 66–67, 77, 87, 89–90, 93, 96, 106, 138–41, 150, 156, 162, 164 n. 58, 165, 188, 192–93, 195–98, 201–12, 215, 219, 224, 227, 236, 257, 264, 268
Epithalamium 37–38, 106
Esarhaddon 86, 156 n. 34, 163, 213
Eulogist, king as 216–18

Euthanasia 239
Eyes 2, 56, 81, 128, 189, 191, 196–97, 202, 208, 257, 259, 261, 263, 274

Fasting 216–18
Foot 67, 96, 103–4, 117, 151, 208, 258, 261, 263, 274
Funeral 145–82

Galilee 132
Garden 58–59, 232, 234–36
Gender 2, 10 n. 23, 13–14, 16, 19, 65, 116, 163, 221, 269, 273
Genitalia 10, 58 n. 85, 105, 163, 198, 206, 236
Gibeonites 168–69
Glyptic 8, 96, 233, 233 n. 56, 234, 236, 251–52, 255
Goliath 4, 128, 135, 164, 186 n. 9

Hair 56, 58, 105, 202, 208, 263
Hand 58, 61, 91, 117, 139, 140 n. 66, 207, 254
Hands, striking of 139–40
Harem 54, 268
Hazael 238–41, 247
Head 56, 58–59, 74–75, 104–5, 108, 117, 135–36, 145, 156, 165, 171, 204–6, 208
Heart 1, 6, 40, 81, 107–10, 126–29, 150, 177, 179, 203 n. 68, 208, 211, 229–30, 249–50, 254–55, 259, 262, 266, 274
Helel ben Shahar 262
Hezekiah 86, 126 n. 22, 184, 213–15, 240, 256–57, 259, 261
History of David's Rise 185–86
Hofstil 23, 34, 182, 272
Hophra 253–54
Hunting 112, 162 n. 52, 201, 244, 256

Icon/iconicity 121, 127, 130, 139 n. 65, 148, 175, 183, 193, 207, 233–37
Ideology 19 n. 50, 28, 45, 118, 132, 134, 147, 185 n. 5, 221, 265
Ish-baal 130–33, 149 n. 14

Jabesh Gilead 165, 167–68
Jehoiada 135
Jehoshaphat 171–72, 174, 242
Jehu 8, 38, 108, 122, 174–75

Jerusalem 32, 37, 56, 62, 65, 67, 72–73, 81, 84–88, 116, 131–32, 135, 148, 156, 175–76, 178, 216, 218, 256, 258, 263, 269
Jezebel 174
Joash 86, 135–43, 149, 159, 175–77, 181
Joram 174–75

Kemosh 227, 241
Kilamuwa 64, 95, 108
Kirta 50, 69, 213
kispu 146

Lion hunting 101, 162 n. 52, 201, 244–45
Lulubo 123–24

maat 248
Marduk-apla-iddinna 261
Marriage, royal 33, 38, 51, 52–55, 60, 82–83, 112–14, 198, 200, 267
Medicine 53, 127
Mediterranean economy 229 n. 24, 237
Mesha 24–42
Micaiah 174
Michal 17, 197–200
Moab 226–27, 241–42, 244–46, 257
Mouth 109–10, 117, 150, 216, 257–58, 260–61, 263

Naaman 240
Nabal 200
Naboth 175
Nabunaid 261
Naram-Sin 272
Nebuchadrezzar 167, 250–51, 254, 261–62
Necho 178, 253–54, 258

Og 225–26

Palace 21, 42, 45, 68, 81–82, 87, 148, 176–77, 214, 218, 235, 235 n. 45, 238, 267
Panammu 151–52
Pectorale/breastplate 235
Penis 58, 162, 208, 236
Pharaoh 51 n. 65, 161, 231, 248–55, 262, 271
Phoenicians 230, 236
Phrygian cap 108
Plowden 9, 30

Power 2, 13–15, 19, 21, 24, 26, 31, 44, 53–54, 67, 78–79, 81–82, 93–94, 97, 99, 110, 113, 122, 130, 137, 142–43, 171, 173, 177, 179, 184, 189, 193–94, 196, 198, 203, 207, 209, 217, 225–26, 229, 233–34, 236, 240–41, 247, 251–52, 254, 257, 259–60, 262
Prayer 5, 37 n. 25, 47, 75, 106, 146, 218 n. 112, 256–57
Prophet/prophecy 40, 41, 63, 66–68, 89, 98, 107 n. 93, 122 n. 13, 125, 128, 136 n. 53, 192–93, 214
Purification rites 69, 71, 73–74, 93, 115, 138, 154, 256

Rain 134, 150, 156–57
Ramat Rahel 67
Ramoth-Gilead 170
Regicide 158, 175–78, 238–39, 245–46
Reproduction 93

Sabbath 135, 138
Samal 76, 103, 151
Samaria 32, 43 n. 41, 132, 147–48, 172–73
Saul 1, 90, 119–30, 133–37, 139, 141, 149, 151–171, 178–79, 181, 184–85, 187–93, 195–222, 226, 236, 250, 258, 266, 270
Sculpture 8, 114
Sefire 94, 150, 168
Sennacherib 257, 258
Sex 11, 53, 58 n. 85, 93, 114, 127, 172, 179, 198, 208, 212
Shalmaneser III 8, 91 n. 33, 224, 235, 239, 260
Sheol 115, 252, 271
Sickness 87, 89, 98–101, 115, 150, 183, 213–15, 241, 267, 271, 273
Sihon 225–27
Singing 95–96
Sobek 250
Solomon 22, 55, 71, 75, 109, 139 n. 64, 145, 190 n. 25, 218 n. 112, 219–20, 249 n. 95

Song of Heshbon 226–27
Sphinx thrones 233
Spices 53–54, 56, 167
Striding god(s) 112 n. 109
Substitute king 173
Sudan 123–4

Tactics in battle 172, 241
Temple 21, 33–35, 37, 50, 59, 67–72, 75, 81, 84–87, 92, 112, 124–25, 135–42, 167–68, 177 n. 94, 180, 209, 215, 218–20, 235 n. 45, 256, 267, 273
Teraphim 199–200
Third Intermediate Period 254 n. 110, 255
Tiglath-pileser III 72, 117, 132, 151
Transjordan 132, 225
Twenty-fifth Dynasty 248
Twenty-sixth Dynasty 248
Tyre 43 n. 41, 224, 227–37, 247, 263

Ugarit 70–71, 73, 93 n. 40
Ultimate sacred postulates 30
United Monarchy 22

Vassal treaties 94 n. 44, 99, 150, 156, 168 n. 73
Victim, king as 124, 154, 162, 199, 202–3, 205–6, 213
Violence 80, 104, 112, 116, 151, 154, 180, 196, 269

Weapons 91, 92, 97, 106 n. 91, 135–37, 140, 143, 183, 253, 268, 274
Women as singers 154–55, 157, 165, 179, 186–89, 191, 199, 221, 250, 258, 273

Yashar, Book of 156

Zakkur 239
Zençirli 45 n. 44, 63 n. 104, 151, 154, 272

INDEX OF ANCIENT NEAR EASTERN TEXTS

DT		1.41	64 n. 108, 69 n. 129, 70 n. 132
1	80	1.46	64 n. 108, 69 n. 129, 70 n. 132
KAI			
1	45 n. 44, 76 n. 159, 95, 130	1.87	69 n. 129, 70 n. 132
		1.103	47 n. 47
4	85 n. 12, 103	1.105	64 n. 108, 70 n. 139
9	101 n. 72, 117	1.106	70 n. 132, 74 n. 147
10	103	1.109	64 n. 108, 70 n. 139
11	71 n. 158, 117	1.112	64 n. 108, 69 n. 129
13	232 n. 33	1.113	146
14	232 n. 33	1.119	64 n. 108, 69 n. 129
24	64, 73, 77–78, 79 n. 170, 95, 117, 224 n. 3	1.124	64 n. 108
		1.127	64 n. 108
26	74 n. 147, 79 n. 169, 117	1.132	69 n. 127, 69 n. 129
35	45 n. 44	1.161	76 n. 159, 146 n. 5, 146
43	112	5–6	157
46	95		
181	241	*RIMA*	
202	85 n. 12, 239 n. 60	0.102	91 n. 35, 105 n. 88, 224 n. 2, 260 n. 125
214	45 n. 44, 117		
215	76 n. 159, 89 n. 22, 110 n. 103, 117, 151, 157	9.102	239 n. 61
216	89 n. 22, 103, 110	*RIMB*	
219	89 n. 22	6.32.6	86 n. 55
222	117		
223	117	*SAA*	
224	45 n. 44, 117	3.11	66 n. 117, 79
233	191 n. 30	3.14	57 n. 82
266	109	3.37	58 n. 83
		3.38	58
KTU		*TIM*	
1.3	90	9	57 n. 83
1.5	50 n. 61		
1.6	50 n. 61	*VAT*	
1.14	50 n. 61, 69, 129 n. 33	13831	66 n. 117
1.23	58 n. 84, 70 n. 132		

INDEX OF BIBLICAL TEXTS

Genesis
1:2 229
2–3 231
14 73
14:18–20 72–73
24:60 187
26:1 227
31:30–35 199
38:14 93
38:24 165
39:6 128
49:8 104
50:10 165
50:25 101

Exodus
1–14 254
3 121
3:9 124
3:15 74
4:16 92
7:19 255
8:15 255
10:2 161
13:19 101
15 96, 252
15:1–18 186
15:21 154
18:25 104

Leviticus
21:9 165–66

Numbers
1:16 104
10:3 139
10:4 139
10:7 139
10:8 139
10:36 187
11:15 232
20:14 227
21 226
21:21–30 225
21:27–30 226
22–24 242–43
23:24 244

24:8 49
31:6 139

Deuteronomy
1:4 225
2:24–3:11 225
3:11 226
5:24 232
17 122, 136
17:14–20 77, 106, 119, 122, 125, 136
17:18 125
22:6–7 260
29:6 225
31:4 225
32:30 187
33:17 187

Joshua
2:10 225
7:15 166
9:10 225
10 225
10:13 155
12 225
12:2 225
12:4 226
13:13 227
21:45 40
23:14–15 40
24:32 101

Judges
3 201, 242
3:9 172
3:10 238
3:12–30 245
3:15 172
3:20 245
5 186, 252
5:7 95
6 121
9:8–15 176
9:9 176
10:18 104
10:10 172
11:8–11 104

INDEX OF BIBLICAL TEXTS

11:17	227	17:51	164
14:3	198	17:53–54	159
14:6	201	18	196–97
15:8	198	18:7	154, 187–88
16	208	18:7–8	187
16:6	172	18:9–30	196–97
19:25	161–62	18:10	159
20:10	187	18:11	159
		18:30	198
1 Samuel		19	199
1:19–27	130	19:9	159
3	121	19:10	159
6:6	161	19:11–17	199
7:8–9	172	19:20–24	193
8	122–24	19:24	191, 193
8–10	23	20:30	198
8:5	181–82	20:33	159
8:10–18	122	21	193
8:18	172	21:9	159
8–12	122, 124–25, 143, 270	21:12	187, 190
		24	163, 200–1, 204, 209
9–11	122		
9–12	120	24:10–23	202
9:1–10:16	120	24:15	210
9:16	124	26	163, 200, 203, 209
9:20	122	26:11	159
10	129, 193	26:12	159
10:1	126	26:15–16	205
10:9	1, 126, 230	26:16	159
10:11	193	26:22	159
10:17–27	124–25	28:8	171
10:18	124	28:14	93
10:19	124	29:5	154, 187, 194
10:23	208	29:6–11	192
10:25	125, 136–37	29:7	187
10:26	122	30	159
10:27	122, 127	31	152–53, 155, 159–61, 164, 168, 170, 204–5
11	128		
12:8	172		
12:10	172	31:4	162, 198
12:17–18	156	31:12–13	165
14:6	198		
15	159–60	2 Samuel	
15:11	172	1	151–53, 156, 159, 161, 163, 168, 185
15:23	200		
15:33	246	1:1–16	159
15:35	171	1:1–17	152, 155
16	128–30, 207	1:17–27	186, 236
16:12	208	1:18–27	152, 154, 156–58, 169
16:20	210		
17	128	1:10	136, 152
17:26	198	1:20	191, 198
17:36	198	1:24	188
17:42	128	2	130–131

2–3	130	1:44–47	52
2:8–11	130	2:1–5	190
2:9	131	3	48, 109
3	216	3:1	249
3:3	227	5–9	218
3:13–14	227	7:2	176
3:31–33	236	8	47, 71, 219
3:31–39	216–17	8:56	40
4:7	149	9:16	249
5:1–3	133	10:29	238
6	85	11:18	249
6:20–23	16	11:40	249
7	89, 215, 219	12:7	40
8	184–85, 237, 239	14:13	40
8:9	237	14:25	249
8:18	71	14:30	147
9	168	15	238
10:4	193	15:8	147
10:16	237	15:24	147
14:25	128, 208	15:28	149
15–19	207	16:10	149
15–20	207	16:18	149
15:1–6	209	16:22	149
15:13–16:23	209	16:28	147
16	210	17:1	156
16:8	207	18	238
16:9	210	18:1	156
16:21–22	208	20:1	238
17:4	208	20:20	238
17:8–10	210, 211	20:22	238
17:14	210	20:23	238
18:9	208	22	170–74
18:14	208	22:3	238
18:14–15	211	22:29–38	172
18:21–28	44	22:31	238
19:4	212	22:37	149, 173
19:6–8	212	22:39	170
21	246	22:40	147–48
21:1–14	168	28:23	223
21:12–13	101		
22	37, 102, 157	2 Kings	
22:3	90	1	238–40
22:15	49	1:2–17	213–14
22:24	103	1:17	238
22:26	103	2:51	147
23:1–7	133–34	3	224, 242
23:5	134	3:9	227
		3:12	227
1 Kings		3:19	242
1–2	43, 142	3:26	227
1:31	74, 231	5	238
1:38	74	5:1	238
1:40	139	5:5	238
1:44–46	51	5:6	240

5:17	240	16:20	147
6:8	238	17:4	249
6:11	238	17:7	249
6:24	238	18–20	100
6:24–33	184	18	214
8:7	238	18:13	214
8:9	238	18:21	249, 251
8:7–15	238	19	264
8:12	239	19:1	257
8:24	147	19:1–19	256
8:28	238	19:13	237
8:29	238	19:16	257
8:53	155	19:21–28	256–57
9	122	19:21	258
9–10	174	19:22	258
9:8	174	19:28	258
9:11	192	20	98, 222
9:14–15	238	20:1–11	214
9:15	170	20:21	147
9:24	149	21:23	149
9:26–29	175	21:26	147
9:28	178	21:18	147
11	135, 137, 141, 159	22:20	178
11:9	138	23	86
11:10	135, 159	23:3	140
11:11	137	23:26–27	178
11:12	135–36, 159	23:29	149
11:16	149	23:29–30	178–79
12	86	23:30	148
12:18	238	24–25	261
12:19	238		
12:20	149	1 Chronicles	
12:21–22	175–76	2:23	227
12:22	147	3:2	227
13:3	238	10:4	198
13:4	238	10:12	166
13:7	238	13:8	139
13:22	238	15:28	139
13:24	238	16:6	139
14	176	16:27	49
14:16	147	16:42	139
14:17–20	176	18	237
14:19	149	19:16	237
14:29	147	22:8	209
15:5	50, 72, 213	28	219
15:7	147	28:2	67
15:10	149	28:3	219
15:14	149		
15:25	149	2 Chronicles	
15:30	149	1:14–17	220
15:37	238	10:7	40
15:38	147	12:12	40–41
16:5–7	238	15:14	139
16:10–20	71	16:2	238

314 INDEX OF BIBLICAL TEXTS

16:7	238	20:5	127
18:30	238	20:8	106
20:9	172	21	107–8, 231
20:28	139	21:2–7	106
22:5	238	21:3	127
22:6	238	21:4	105
23:1	159	21:5	74, 79, 231
26:16	72	21:6	49
26:19–21	213	21:8	106
28:5	238	21:9–14	106
29	86	21:9–13	106
29:26	139	22	36
29:27	139	22:2	36
29:28	139	22:6	172
30	131	26	37
32:20	172	29:2	69
33:14	75	29:7	227
35	178	33:6	109
35:20–25	178	34:1	191
35:22	171	45	33, 37–38, 40–41, 47, 51–52, 60, 63, 100, 103, 106, 108, 112, 116, 134, 136, 146, 216, 231, 240, 268–69
Ezra			
3:10	139		
Nehemiah			
2:3	74	45:2	41
9:4	172	45:4	48
12:35	139	45:7	74, 79, 230
		45:8	90
Job		45:9	53
6:4	49	59:13	47
6:6	191	67:4	132
30:10	191	67:6	132
38:23	96	72	33, 61, 75–79, 116, 134, 156
Psalms		72:5–6	134
2	33, 60, 61–65, 68, 138, 145, 174, 223, 244, 257, 260, 262–64	72:6	156
		72:8	134
		72:19	74
		77:7	126
2:1	100, 265	82:6	174
2:8	108	82:7	231
2:9	109	83:15	227
3:4	75	89	88–94, 115, 170, 212, 215, 221, 269, 271–72
8	33		
17:1	47		
18	37, 93, 102–5, 112	89:5	79
18:3	90	89:28	92, 246
18:9	110, 227	89:35	47
18:13	227	89:37	79
18:14	227	89:53	74
18:44	104–5	91:7	187
18:51	79, 102	97:13	227
20	106–7, 115, 252, 272	98:6	139

INDEX OF BIBLICAL TEXTS

99:5	67	7:20	78
101	61, 75–82, 95, 129, 268, 272	8:19	100
		9	70, 146
101:2	127, 232	9:6	139, 268
101:3	189	10:5–10	259, 264
101:6	232	10:10–11	88
107:13	172	10:13–14	256, 260–61
107:14	63	11	37
107:19	172	11:1–9	108, 111
110	60, 64–75, 112, 138, 263	11:3–5	116
		11:4	47, 110
110:1	64	14	70
110:3	69, 137	14:12	70
110:4	71, 79	14:18	132
110:8	75	14:4b–21	150, 262
119:65	40	15:9	244
126	84	19:11	248
129	84	29:4	100
132	37, 84–87, 112, 269	30:19	172
132:5	85	37	264
132:7	67	37:1–20	256
132:9	90	37:22–29	256, 257
135:13	74	37:13	237
136	243	38	37, 115, 214, 240, 271
142:6	172		
144	94–97, 103, 160, 211, 227, 239, 263	38:9–20	97–98
		50:6	191
144:1	219	57:8–10	58
144:1–2	252	61:10	93
144:2	97	63:1–6	90
144:10–11	224, 257	66:1	67
144:11	172		
		Jeremiah	
Proverbs		1	121
7:17	53	2:20	63
12:25	40	5:5	63
22:11	47	11:11	172
25:2	209	13:18	108
26:16	191	25:22	228
30:19	229	27:3	227–28
		29:10	40
Song of Songs		29:26	192
3:6–11	56	30:8	63
3:9	55	31:7	104
4:1–5:9	56	33:14	40
5:10–16	37, 55–60	34:5	167
6:2	59	39:5	237
		40–44	261
Isaiah		46	247, 253, 261
5:17	50	46:17	258
5:27	87	49:19	244
6	121	49:28	261
7:1	238	49:30	261
7:14	109	50:44	244

51:31	261	Hosea	
51:34	261	5:8	139
52:9	237	7:14	172
52:27	237	8:2	172
		9:7	192
Lamentations			
2:1	67	Amos	
		1:4	238
Ezekiel		2:1	166, 227
1	113	6:2	237
5:16	49	6:10	101, 123
11:15	132		
20:40	132	Jonah	
21:18–23	261	1:14	172
21:19	140		
21:22	140	Micah	
21:26	200	2:12	50
22:13	140	3:4	172
23:12	132	3:7	93
28	228, 230	6:5	243
28:1–19	234–35		
28:18	235	Nahum	
29–32	249–50, 252	1:13	63
29:2	132		
29:3	251	Habaqquq	
29:6–7	251	1:2	172
30	254	3	96
32	262	3:4	90
32:9–10	150	3:8	91
35:15	132		
36:10	132	Zephaniah	
43:9	167	2:8	242
		2:10	242
Daniel			
4:19–36	213	Zechariah	
9:24	86	1:13	40
		9:2	237
		9:14	49

www.ingramcontent.com/pod-product-compliance
Lightning Source LLC
Chambersburg PA
CBHW021819300426
44114CB00009BA/233